The University Handbook

The University Handbook

SECOND EDITION

Harris W. Wilson
University of Illinois

Louis G. Locke
Madison College

Holt, Rinehart and Winston, Inc.
New York, Chicago, San Francisco, Toronto, London

Preface

The University Handbook, Second Edition is designed as a practical classroom instrument. It is meant to be an aid to the student in the complex process of learning to write respectably and well. The examples and exercises are copious; we have tried to make them consistently relevant to the material at hand and, at the same time, mature and interesting.

The book has been organized for ready and easy reference. Inside the front cover is a comprehensive theme correction chart, which lists in detail the most frequent errors in student writing and keys them directly to appropriate pages in the text. Inside the back cover the theme correction chart is continued and includes the conventional correction symbols with page references for each symbol. Also within the back cover is a list of standard proofreading symbols, with an explanation for each. A glossary of grammatical terms and a glossary of usage immediately precede the index.

We have taken what we believe to be a realistic view of our subject. When the student leaves the composition course, most of his writing will be for readers who are traditional and conservative in their attitudes toward the conventions of language. We feel, consequently, that a handbook for the basic composition course in the American college and university should furnish the student with a clear guide, not confusing alternatives, in the crucial areas of conventional form in which he is most likely to falter. Chapter 3, "Basic Grammatical Errors," for instance, covers in some detail the major errors encountered most frequently in the early part of the course. The early isolation of these flagrant lapses should impress the student with the necessity of eliminating them from his writing as soon as possible and should save the instructor the wearisome experience of seeing them persist throughout the quarter or semester. Chapter 4, "The Parts of Speech and Related Problems," is an intensive review of grammatical conventions and is designed for both classroom work and reference.

In our treatment of other elements of composition—diction, sentence, paragraph, theme—we have presented those rhetorical principles we have found most effective in our own classes. Our aim has been to instruct the student, not intimidate him. Illustrative material is drawn largely from student writing, although we have not hesitated to use selections from established writers when we felt the need. The student writing in *The Green Caldron*, a magazine of freshman writing at the University of Illinois, has been a major resource. Our thanks go to the following students whose themes we have used in this book: Sheila Bittman, Margaret Boswell, Milford Casteel, Alex Chambers, David Comings, Jack W. Ehret, Arlie Fender, Dan A. Godeke, Arthur Goldstein, Ralph L. Goodman, Edwin E. Kerr, Virginia Nell McManus, Nancy L. Mullenix, Gerald M. Peterson, Judith Sensibar, Robert Snetsinger, George L. Warner, and Quendred Wutzke.

The authors would like to express a great indebtedness to Professor Charles W. Roberts of the University of Illinois. Although he made no direct contribution to the book, we can only hope it reflects the wisdom and common sense that have marked a most distinguished career in teaching and administering the composition course. Professor Richard S. Beal of Boston University deserves our warm thanks for friendly, yet incisive criticism of the manuscript in its various stages. These men have made substantial contributions to the strengths of the book; whatever weaknesses it may have are our own responsibility.

Urbana, Illinois   **Harris W. Wilson**
Harrisonburg, Virginia   **Louis G. Locke**
March 1966

Contents

The University Handbook

1.

The English Language

"In the beginning," according to St. John, "was the Word"; and he was right, even in a secular sense. Not much happened until man learned to speak; not much really happened until he began to write. Although the beginnings of speaking and writing are shrouded in mystery, it is important that before you proceed to the detailed study of the techniques involved in an effective English prose style you know something of the history of the language that you have been speaking and writing for nearly two decades—how it has happened that you speak and write the way you do. The tracing of the development of English as we know it today is a tremendously complex process and falls within the province of philological scholars; but every university student, regardless of his specialization, should have at least a general knowledge of the history of his language.

Old English: The Beginning

English became a linguistic possibility when, according to the Venerable Bede in his *Ecclesiastical History* (A.D. 730), a Germanic tribe called the Jutes, whose native home

1

was in the upper part of the Danish peninsula, landed in southeast England in A.D. 449. The Jutes were followed by two other Germanic tribes, the Saxons and Angles. From the Angles, England derived its name (Engla-land). These Germanic tribes settled in the new country and eventually pushed the resistant, native Celts into the general areas now known as Cornwall and Wales. From the dialects of the Angles, Saxons, and Jutes and the addition of massive borrowings from the Scandinavian, Latin, and French languages, to name only the most important, the English language as we know it today evolved through a complicated and gradual process.

Two important foreign influences on Old English should be mentioned at this point. Before they invaded England, the Angles, Saxons, and Jutes had some contact with Rome, mainly through Roman merchants. Consequently, the invading Germanic tribes had some Latin borrowings in their vocabularies when they arrived—about fifty words, it is estimated. Also, long before the Germanic invasion, England came under Roman rule in A.D. 43 and remained under it until A.D. 410. But the Roman domination was strictly a military one, and the influence of Latin (transmitted through the native Celts) on English was limited to about five borrowings. The most important influence of Latin on Old English came with the Christianization of England that began in A.D. 597. Before the end of the Old English period, according to surviving records, some 350 Latin words had been added to the language.

The major influence on Old English, however, came from another Germanic people, the Danes, or Vikings, who were to have an even greater influence later in the Middle English period. In the latter part of the eighth century the Vikings, devoted simply to plundering, began a series of raids on the island; about A.D. 850 they started to establish settlements. The Vikings' conquest of England reached its culmination when Svein, king of Denmark, established himself as king of England; with the succession of his son Cnut, England was under Viking rule from 1014 to 1035.

The assimilation of the Danes in England was greatly facilitated in that they and the Angles and Saxons were fellow Scandinavians; and, consequently, the effect of the Danish language on Old English was proportionately greater. As far as scholars can determine, the Danish additions to the Old English vocabulary number about 900. Perhaps more important, however, was the effect of the amalgamation of the two languages on Old English grammar and syntax. There is strong evidence that this blending of similar words with different grammatical forms was an initial factor in the process of the simplification of grammatical structure— one of the most striking features in the development of English to its present state.

The conventional dates bounding the Old English period are A.D. 450, the approximate date of the first invasions of the Germanic tribes, to 1066, the date of the Norman Conquest of England. Old English was an inflected language, which means that word forms and endings were highly important in determining the function of words in sentences as compared to the relative unimportance of these forms and endings in Modern English. Consider, for instance, the phrase "the good man." In Modern English the phrase is unchanged, regardless of its function in the sentence—subject, indirect or direct object, object of a preposition—except in two instances, and then only in the noun: the plural number (the good *men*) and the possessive case (the good *man's* or *men's*). Compare these relatively simple changes with the Old English declension of the same phrase:

	Singular	Plural
Nominative Case	sē gōda mann	ðā gōdan menn
Possessive Case	ðaes gōdan mannes	ðāra gōdena manna
Dative Case	ðāēm gōdan manne	ðāēm gōdum mannum
Objective Case	ðone gōdan mann	ðā gōdan mannas

If the phrase was used as the subject of the sentence, it would take the nominative form indicated; if it was used as an indirect or direct object, it would take the dative and objective forms, respectively. Hence the phrase functioned in the sentence according to its form, not according to its position as is largely true in Modern English. Only the personal pronoun in Modern English compares with Old English in its variation of inflection according to function.

This loss of inflections from Old English to Modern English was not entirely to the advantage of the language. Inflected languages such as Old English, Latin, Greek, and German are, according to some linguists, capable of nuances that cannot be attained in Modern English with its comparatively rigid word order (see pages 167–169). But the simplification of the inflections in English over the centuries has constituted one of its major strengths and makes it the leading candidate for adoption as a world language. At least the comparative grammatical simplicity of Modern English should, if you have difficulty with English grammar, make you thankful that you were not born an Englishman between A.D. 450 and 1066.

If the loss of inflection in English is not, in the view of some linguists, an unmixed blessing, the loss of arbitrary grammatical gender is an absolute one. Nouns in Old English were placed into three inherited categories, according to gender, that were sometimes quite illogical but with which all modifiers had to agree in their varying forms. "Horse," for instance, was neuter; "wife" was neuter; "maiden" was neuter; "day" was masculine, "night," feminine. Modern English, to its great advantage, has cast off this cumbersome and illogical grammatical convention and adopted what might be called a "natural" gender in which a man is "he," a woman is "she," and a tree is "it."

Old English can be illustrated by the West Saxon version of the Lord's Prayer:

Faeder ūre
þū þe eart on heofonum
sī þīn nama gehālgod
Tōbecume þīn rīce.
Gewurþe ðīn willa on earð an swā swā on heofonum
Ūrne gedaeghwāmlīcan hlāf syle ūs tō daeg
And forgyf ūs ūre gyltas, swā swā wē forgyfað ūrum gyltendum.

And ne gelǣd þū ūs on costnunge,
ac ālȳs ūs of yfele. Sōþlīce.

This passage appears to be written in a completely foreign language, not the language from which our own developed. But if examined carefully, similarities in words are quite easy to discern, keeping in mind that the symbols þ and ð would appear in Modern English as *th*. The nouns "Faeder," "nama," "willa," "eorðan," "hlaf," "daeg," can be easily recognized as ancestors of our own "Father," "name," "will," "earth," "loaf," and "day." "þu" has become our "Thou" and "þin" has become our "Thine"; the verbs "eart" and "forgyf" become "art" and "forgive" respectively. Many of the differences, consequently, are more apparent than real.

This is not to say that there are not great differences between the two languages. After the French conquest of England, the grammar changed radically and a great number of French words were added to the vocabulary. This has led some scholars to maintain that French and Latin are actually more our parent languages than is Old English. The fact remains, however, that even though Old English words are outnumbered in our vocabulary by borrowings from French and other languages, in terms of frequency of occurrence Old English words still predominate heavily, as can be verified by looking up the etymology of each word in a passage of Modern English prose. And any English-speaking person acquainted with Old English and its literature can be proud of his linguistic heritage.

Middle English: The Ordeal

The most momentous historical occurrence in terms of the eventual development of the English language was the Norman Conquest of England in 1066, the last successful invasion of that beleagured island. England's old enemies, the Vikings, in the ninth and tenth centuries, had conquered and established themselves in the southwest of France, much as they had in the north and east of England. The "Northmen" quickly adapted themselves to French culture and especially to the French language. By the time of the invasion of England, the original Vikings in Normandy were essentially French in both culture and language.

William the Conqueror, duke of Normandy, disappointed in his expectations of falling heir to the English crown after the death of Edward the Confessor, his second cousin, invaded England from the south. At the battle of Hastings, he defeated the English forces under Harold, the son of an influential English nobleman and appointed successor to Edward. William, within four years, had subjugated all of England; and the subjugation was virtually complete. By the last decade of the eleventh century the majority of English nobility and the clergy were, with few exceptions, Frenchmen speaking French. In this situation, the language of prestige in England became French. As Robert of Gloucester, in 1300, put it:

> For but a man know French men count of him little
> But low men hold to English and to their own speech yet.

English, then, became for a considerable period, the main language of the lower classes and consequently more of a spoken language than written. The tendency toward simplification of grammatical structure that had already begun, as we have noted, before the Norman Conquest was greatly accelerated during the early part of the Middle English period. The reasons for changes in linguistic structure are mysterious. Some prominent contemporary philologists maintain that the conjunction of the Norman Conquest and the radical simplification of the grammatical structure of English were coincidental. But, some linguists feel that such grammatical simplification will take place more rapidly in any language freed from the restrictions of official sanction and the conventions imposed by a written standard. If a foreign occupation of our own country occurred on the same scale as the Norman occupation of England, our present language might well lose many of the relatively few grammatical irregularities it still contains. For instance, the terminal *s* of the third person present indicative of regular verbs (I walk, you walk, *he walks*) could well disappear. Language tends, without artificial restraints, to discard through the principle of analogy useless and inconsistent elements.

We can only speculate what the English language would have been in our own time if William the Norman had never conquered England and, with his followers, superimposed French as the language of upper-class English people. Almost certainly it would have been a more highly inflected language grammatically than it is now, much closer to, say, modern German. If, as most linguists believe, the simplification of English grammatical structure is a strength of our language today, the Norman Conquest must be looked upon as a stroke of linguistic luck.

If the situation in England under the Normans had remained as it was during the twelfth century, French might well have remained in permanent use. But in 1214, King John of England lost his rule of Normandy. National rivalries began to build up between England and France; the upper class in England, although initially many of them still held continental possessions, started to think of themselves as English rather than French. The French language held sway among the English upper class for many years, mainly because of the cultural prestige of France in Europe in the thirteenth century; but by 1400 English was used throughout England, and by 1500 the French language had practically disappeared.

Fifteenth century English was very different, however, from Old English. It had taken into its vocabulary almost countless French words. Its grammatical structure had become for the most part the grammatical structure of Modern English. The elaborate Old English declension illustrated on page 3 had been simplified to essentially the same forms we use now. The process can be very briefly illustrated by two Middle English passages, one a version of the Lord's Prayer written in the Kentish dialect in 1340 and the other by William Caxton in 1490:

Vader oure þet art ine hevenes,
y-halȝed by þi name,
cominde þi riche, y-worþe þi will ase ine hevene: and ine erþe.
bread oure echedayes: yef ous today.
and vorlet ous oure yeldinges: ase and we vorleteþ oure yelderes.
and ne ous led naȝt: in-to vondinge.
ac vri ous vram queade. zuo by hit.

DAN MICHEL, *Ayenbite of Inwyt*

And certaynly our langage now used varyeth ferre from that
whiche was used and spoken whan I was borne. For we englysshe
men ben borne under the domynacyon of the mone, whiche is
never stedfaste, but ever waverynge, wexynge one season, and
waneth & dyscreaseth another season. And that comyn englysshe
that is spoken in one shyre varyeth from a nother.

WILLIAM CAXTON, *Eneydos*.

The Middle English version of the Lord's Prayer is still
somewhat removed from Modern English, but it gives the
impression (if we consider the symbol þ as *th*) of a less
completely foreign language than the Old English version
of pages 4–5. The Caxton passage illustrates the fact that by
1500 in major respects English had become, except for a
lack of standard spellings, the language that is used today.

Modern English: The Maturity

The most important process in the development of Modern
English is the establishment of a linguistic discipline. The
question of how much discipline to be imposed has been
the source of sometimes very bitter argument from the beginning of the period to our own time. The passage just
quoted from Caxton clearly illustrates the need for the
English of 1490 to have some kind of standardization of
spelling. An additional complication was the number of
dialects (the subject of Caxton's remarks) that had grown
up in England during the Middle English period and, in
some cases, prevented one Englishman from communicating
with another. Latin was at hand and was used widely among

the educated classes; but the growing national pride among Englishmen demanded a language of England's own. Modern English was eventually established, largely through the Englishmen's spirit of compromise.

There were several historical factors that contributed to the establishment of a standardized English. A major one was Caxton's introduction into England of the printing press with movable type in 1476. Caxton and his successors used London English in their books—as was entirely natural, since London was the capital of England and its cultural center—and consequently set a practically irresistible example. Reinforcing this influence was the spread of literacy through increased facilities for education among the people. Because of these and other less important influences, London English was generally established, in spite of Caxton's complaint in the quoted passage, as standard English by the beginning of the Modern Period.

But even given a generally accepted standard English dialect, there were still many difficulties. Spelling was chaotic and varied from person to person. Although in major respects the grammar of 1500 was our own grammar, in many instances there were various constructions from which the speaker or writer had to choose. There were still extensive borrowings, especially from the Romance languages, almost at will by scholars and churchmen, that presented obvious problems to the native reader. The flexibility of the language during the sixteenth and seventeenth centuries is not a condition to be regretted; without it we might never have had a Spenser, Shakespeare, or Milton. But as the language became more and more the tool for logical discourse and practical communication, the stronger many influential literary men felt the need for its regularization.

The first concerted attempt to subject the language to rule was a movement to set up an academy that would act as a kind of supreme court in linguistic matters. Such a group would have the power to prescribe grammatical rules and "to cleanse and purify" English vocabulary. Early supporters of the proposal of an academy were such important literary

9

philologist has remarked that linguists are capable of explaining what has happened to the English language, but in most important instances, they are unable to tell why it happened. Language is, in its own way, the most mysterious and miraculous of man's accomplishments.

2.

Writing the Theme

As a college student you are entering upon a very important period in your life. You undoubtedly have been advised of that fact frequently by this time, but repetition does not make it any less true. You have committed yourself to becoming an educated person, and as such a person you must take upon yourself not only the privileges involved but also definite responsibilities. One of the most important of these responsibilities, regardless of the field you plan to enter, is to attain a reasonable amount of competence in the use of English prose.

The principal means by which you will attain this competence will be the *theme*, written regularly throughout the composition course, graded carefully by your instructor and, in turn, revised carefully by you. A theme can be many things, but in the composition course it is a relatively short piece of writing concerned with a single idea or *theme*. All other elements discussed in the basic course—grammar, spelling, words, paragraphing—are means toward the end of increasing your skill in producing a good theme. The theme itself, of course, is a means toward competence in any writing assignment that may be required of you in your college or professional life. And even though the theme is a special-ized instrument of instruction in the basic writing course, the principles involved in writing a good theme hold true for writing of any sort. The student who masters writing the theme, consequently, can meet with confidence any future demands upon his writing skill.

Approach to Writing

Many college students come to their basic writing courses with wrong attitudes. If you are one of them, perhaps you have been led to believe that you have no talent for English —that writers are born, not made, and if writing does not come easily for you, your entire case is hopeless. Or perhaps grammar and spelling loom as obstacles that seem impos-sible for you to overcome.

You should discard at this point any preconceptions you may have concerning written expression. If you are reason-ably intelligent, if you can observe the people and things around you and are capable of reacting to them, you are capable of good writing. Most students do not realize that writing well is just as much a matter of application as of inspiration. No one would expect to sit down at a piano for the first time and play a Beethoven sonata, or to go into a football game without previous experience and perform adequately the duties of a T-formation quarterback. Any person of normal intelligence is capable of competent writ-ing, but like any other skill, it demands application and practice. Your attitude toward writing, consequently, should be one of respect, but at the same time you should look upon writing competence as a goal which, with reasonable effort, you can certainly achieve.

The Writing Process

At the very beginning we should admit that the process of turning out a good piece of writing is an arduous one. Nothing is more erroneous than the belief that a writer simply sits down and dashes off page after page of lucid prose. And there is no greater cause for an inadequate performance in composition courses than the all too common practice among students of writing one draft of a theme and turning it in as the finished copy. A good theme, like any other good piece of work, is almost always the result of an orderly and quite businesslike process. The next few paragraphs describe briefly a procedure that most student writers have found successful; these paragraphs are followed by a case study showing how one student used this procedure in the actual writing of a theme.

1. Selecting a Topic   There are two major requirements for a satisfactory topic. First, it should hold interest for you. The second requirement usually, though not always, follows necessarily on the first: You should have enough information on the subject to develop it in adequate detail. Instructors in college composition typically will provide a list of topics from which you will select one relevant to your interests and background. Your first thought may sometimes be that no topic appears in the assigned list on which you have anything to say. If you examine your own store of information and experience, however, you will very probably find a subject in the list that begins to suggest possibilities. Although the instructor may include some topics of specialized interest that he knows will appeal to certain members of the class, he will also include topics of general interest that are bound to elicit some sort of reaction or opinion from any student. Later in this chapter are listed typical theme topics for the various types of writing.

2. The Incubation Period   At this stage, frequently the most pleasant and exciting part of the process, you will mull over your subject. During this period, you will limit the topic to a specific and manageable area and decide upon an original and interesting approach to the subject (sometimes called the central idea). You may formulate a title (although this frequently comes at the very end of the process) and may visualize major divisions of the topic. This period of mental formulation should not be too extended, however; many potentially excellent compositions never progress past this most dangerous stage. Indeed, most experienced writers do not consider themselves really into the act of composition until they put pencil to paper.

3. The Rough Outline   The next step consists of a preliminary outline. Jot down your ideas under the major divisions without much regard for coherence and order. The important thing is that you record *all* ideas that would seem to have any pertinence to your treatment of the subject. Then revise this rough outline and carefully select and rearrange your ideas until you achieve an orderly and coherent presentation.

4. The First Draft   You will write your first draft from the revised outline. Write this preliminary draft fairly rapidly, with little or no regard for grammatical or mechanical correctness. Your principal aim here is content—getting your ideas down as spontaneously and as naturally as possible. If you write from the beginning cramped by fear of grammatical or mechanical lapses, your final copy will probably have little spontaneity or flow.

5. The Revision   After you complete the first draft, the next step is the very important one of revision. Subject the first draft to a thorough scrutiny for faulty sentence constructions, improper or ineffective punctuation, misspellings, and other mechanical faults. Revision in phrasing and organization takes place at this stage, and you should be ruthless in rejecting irrelevant, inappropriate, or awkward material that inevitably creeps into the first draft. Most writers do not enoy this revisionary process, but the good writer never slights it. He knows that it is just as important as the creative or inspirational aspect of writing, in that even the best ideas will lose most of their effect if expressed in slipshod prose. Inadequate attention to this extremely important step is the main fault of most beginning writers.

6. The Final Copy After you feel that through your revisions the theme has become as effective as you can possibly make it within the limits of your time and ability, write the final copy. Some revision will probably take place in this step, but your attention should be directed, for the most part, toward an accurate and neat transcription. You should not underestimate the importance of the physical appearance of your paper. A discussion of the conventional manuscript form of themes is provided in section P-26. Also your instructor will give you detailed directions concerning the external form of your themes, and you should follow his instructions exactly. One mark of the competent writer is his ability to follow prescribed manuscript form.

7. Proofreading The inexperienced writer tends to slight this relatively simple but very important step in the writing process. Many a theme grade has been lowered at least one point because the student failed to correct typographical or careless errors. The trick in proofreading is to make certain that you do not, through familiarity with your own material, skip individual words and, consequently, errors. Any device which will force your eyes to look at each particular word will be of service, such as the point of a pencil held above the page and run slowly along each line, or a ruler moved down the page revealing only one line at a time.

These basic steps in the writing process, of course, vary in emphasis with the individual concerned and the task at hand. We will see later that the research paper, for instance, involves a much more complicated procedure. But if you follow conscientiously the process outlined, you will have taken a long step toward the mastery of the theme.

A Case Study in Writing the Theme

As a concrete example of the writing process at work, let us take the actual case of a student in a college composition course, a student whom we shall call Richard Roe, faced with the problem of composing a six- to eight-hundred-word theme. Keep in mind that Richard's solution of his problem is not presented as an ideal one; it is simply an example of how a conscientious student, setting about his task in a workmanlike manner, completed his assignment to the satisfaction of both his instructor and himself.

Selecting a Topic In a Monday morning class, Richard's instructor in composition gave a list of topics and asked that themes on these topics be completed and turned in by the following Friday. The topics given were fairly broad, and the students were told to treat some specific aspect of each topic. One of the topics was "Mass Entertainment in America."

As it happened, Richard had recently been confined to bed for a few days with a bad cold. During his confinement, he listened to the radio and watched television a great deal. The topic, "Mass Entertainment in America," therefore, interested him immediately. But within that topic, what could he write on? To treat "Mass Entertainment in America" adequately would require a book-length composition. Should he discuss "Musical Programs on Radio"? "Drama on Television"? Or "Radio and Television Comedians"?

While Richard had been ill, his attention was particularly caught by the melodramas so popular in daytime radio and television schedules. He was amazed by the lugubrious content of these serial programs. As he listened, he wondered how, considering the harrowing nature of the events related, such programs retained their apparent appeal. He had a firsthand knowledge, from the listener's point of view, of one form of mass entertainment, the "soap opera," and consequently could speak with some authority on the subject.

The Incubation Period Richard spent the remainder of Monday and a part of Tuesday turning over in his mind, in his spare moments, the subject and suitable approaches to it. At first he considered doing a straightforward criticism of the overly sentimental and distorted picture of life presented by the programs. Then he considered a satire, in which he would hold the programs and the people who listened to them up for ridicule. But he was still not satisfied. He knew that the very term "soap opera" was an indication of a generally derogatory attitude toward the programs and that a negative approach could offer little in terms of originality. Finally he decided that the best approach to the subject would be an analysis of why these programs which concentrate upon all sorts of domestic tragedies should have such an enduring appeal to their obvious audience, the American housewife.

That analysis became the *purpose* for his theme, the aim he wanted to accomplish. Then, because a writer should be able to state in one sentence the *central idea* of his theme, Richard decided that his central idea was this: The continued popularity of radio and television "soap operas" is a result of the fact that they meet a legitimate psychological need of the average American housewife.

The Outline Having his approach to the subject clearly in mind, Richard could now proceed to the preliminary outline of his theme. Tuesday night he sat down with paper and pencil to rough out his organization. His first jottings looked like this:

SOAP OPERAS

1. Description
2. Background
3. Listeners
4. Popularity—why?
5. Result
   a. Good
   b. Bad

Richard could see the points he had to cover to establish his central idea. He could also see that he must sharpen these points so that he could determine *what* to say *about* them. Note how he refined the title. By turning it into a question, he knew better what he should try to say under each point. Also, by going now to a standard outline form, he made room for subpoints to stand for specific details.

WHY SOAP OPERAS?

I. What is "soap opera"?

   A. Name comes from fact that ordinarily programs are sponsored by soap manufacturers

   B. Aimed at housewife, since she obviously uses most soap

II. What is its background?

   A. Who started it, and when?

   B. What has been the most successful program, or programs?

III. Who listens to it?

   A. Must be people who are free to listen to radio and watch television during normal working hours

   B. Nature of subjects would appeal largely to feminine audience

   C. Housewives, therefore, constitute large part of audience

IV. What are reasons for popularity?

   A. Familiar characters

   B. Escape (romance)

   C. Vicarious thrill of extramarital activities

   D. Need to minimize own troubles by comparison with worse ones

V. Ultimate effects

   A. Good

      1. Provide diversion from monotony of housework
      2. Instill sound moral principles
      3. Afford emotional release

   B. Bad

      1. Present distorted picture of life
      2. Increase dissatisfaction with own status
      3. Ruin taste for good drama

In looking over his still-rough outline, Richard saw immediately that he could not cover in a relatively short theme with any effectiveness the material set forth; his main job in revising, consequently, would be one of compression and deletion. After twenty minutes' work, he had achieved an outline that seemed to him good enough to serve as the basis for his first draft:

WHY SOAP OPERAS?

I. Definition
    A. Thirty-minute radio and television serials portraying domestic tragedies
    B. Sponsors' insistence, in spite of events portrayed, that life is worth living

II. Analysis of appeal
    A. Audience
        1. Restricted to daytime audience having time and opportunity to listen
        2. Limited largely, therefore, to housewives
    B. Cast
        1. Leading figure usually a housewife
        2. Heroine, unlike ordinary housewife, involved in all sorts of melodramatic adventures

III. Reasons for popularity
    A. Make housewife realize her own troubles aren't so bad
    B. Create illusion that her own life can also be exciting

IV. Effect of soap operas
    A. Actually do not harmfully mislead housewife
    B. Provide positive psychological relief from routine

Note that in his revision Richard eliminated entirely Section II, the historical background of his subject. He decided, rightly, that even though such material would be of interest, it would not allow him to develop his main idea sufficiently in a theme of less than one thousand words. Also, instead of dealing in the concluding section with both the good and bad aspects of soap operas, he decided in the interest of economy and effect to restrict himself only to the good. Other deletions and compressions were based on the same considerations.

You will find further recommendations for outlining in Chapter 7 of this book.

The First Draft and Revision Having completed his outline, Richard proceeded immediately to his first draft and revision as follows:

Why Soap Operas?

The ~~setting of a~~ typical soap opera ~~deals~~ *is* mainly ~~with~~ *a* hospital~~s~~ or courtroom~~s~~. It's characters are mothers undergoing serious operations, wives being bullied by wastrel husbands, fathers being tried for perj*u*ry, bigamy, or drunken driving. Yet after thirty minutes of traged*y* and heart*ache* between some doleful organ music, an announcer will break in feelingly and say that life is worth living.

Considering all this misfortune portrayed, why do people continue to listen to soap operas?

It would be best to examine first the people who listen to soap operas. ~~Soap operas~~ These programs are on the air from *eight* ~~8~~ to *five* ~~5~~ each day. As it happens, this is the time when nearly everyone *who works* is at work. It is also the time when most children are at school. The only large group with both time and opportunity to listen *to soap opera* is composed of housewives. *The housewife* ~~She~~ feels that her job is dull routine, usually appreciated by no one. She

22

~~feels~~ *fears* that life is passing her by while she lives in the shadow of cleaning and cooking. She ~~wants~~ *is eager for a* dramatic experience~~s~~ ~~of any kind~~, even if it is merely vicarious.

Secondly, we must take into account the cast of the typical soap opera. The leading figure in this cast will be an attractive woman in her late thirties and she will usually be *more or less,* a housewife. She will have all kinds of adventures, both romantic and dramatic, *all starting* ~~and~~ *from a point within the circle of her life as a housewife.* ~~starting from the home.~~ Around this central housewife-heroine will be several lesser figures, one of ~~which~~ *these* is her husband. He is cast as a kind, strong, well-meaning man who seems to be just a little simple. Or perhaps he is smart enough, but emotionally unable to face life without his wife's support. The other characters in the cast are incidental and serve only as ~~the~~ source*s* of complication, ~~for trouble, adventure and drama.~~

From a consideration of the audience and the cast, it becomes apparent that daytime serials are really stories for housewives about housewives. The fact that the housewives in the stories seem to live somewhat more dramatic lives than do the housewives who listen is no disadvantage. Listening to some-one else's trouble on the radio *or television* makes the housewife realize that her own troubles are really not so bad. When she hears ~~of a husband who commits~~ *that Ma Jones's husband is committing* adultery almost daily, she will forgive her own husband for forgetting

an anniversary. When ~~another woman's~~ *Ma Jones's* son is expelled
from school for peddling dope, she is happy that her
own son has only low grades. When ~~another woman~~ *Ma Jones* is in
the hospital for three whole episodes, the housewife
is glad that she has only sore feet.

Soap opera gives the houswife the feeling that
romance is waiting just around the corner, if she
should choose to look for it. When ~~the heroine~~ *young Widow Smith* is
pursued by a long succession of ~~eager~~ *debonair* and eligible
suitors, each housewife is convinced that she ~~would~~ *too*
might be so pursued if she were not now
~~have a chance to be in the same situation except for her~~
happily married.
~~present marriage status.~~ One program now on the air
p~~e~~rports to prove that a woman can find romance even
after ~~35~~ *thirty-five.* Such programs give the housewife the happy
feeling that it is not too late for her to b~~e~~ *gay,* glamorous,
and romantic.

~~The nice part about all this is that the housewife~~
is not really dec~~i~~eved. Her troubles are not really
so bad, and it is probably not too late for her to be ~~romantic~~
and
glamorous if she wishes to be. The soap opera entertains her by *reassuring and* encouraging her. It may be that soap
opera is like a huge psychoanalytic couch. Upon it,
the housewife can ~~lie, figuratively, and arise from it~~ *daily lay her routine-dampened spirit,*
and from it that spirit arises
with a renewed sense of ~~her~~ *its* own well-being.

It is impossible to show here the full process of revision to
which Richard subjected his first draft—the struggle, usually

by trial and error, for the right phrase; the checking of words in the dictionary for spelling and meaning; the shifting of sentences and sometimes whole paragraphs for increased emphasis.

A few improvements are especially worth noticing. In the first sentence, *is* seems more direct than *deals mainly with.* Besides, the revised sentence is more accurate than the original one. Soap operas are not necessarily about a hospital or a courtroom, but scenes often take place in them. In paragraph three, Richard was wise to replace *She* in line seven with *The housewife* because the only possible antecedent for *she* was housewives in the previous sentence—a plural noun. *Fears* in line nine is stronger than *feels* and also avoids repeating *feels* of the sentence before.

In paragraph four, *trouble, adventure, and drama* are complications and do not need listing here. Note the specificity (and heightened reader interest) of the introduction of Ma Jones instead of the general *a husband* and *another woman.* In the final sentence of the theme, the idea of a routine-dampened spirit is more vivid than *housewife . . . figuratively.*

With his first draft and revision completed, Richard left off his actual composition until Wednesday night. But he took away with him a dissatisfaction with the introduction as it stood in his original draft. Consequently, when he set to work again Wednesday night, he reshaped the entire first part of his theme and eventually came up with the following:

Turn on the radio or television set almost any time during the day and you stand a good chance of hearing or viewing a string of thirty-minute melodramas called daytime serials. Each of these thirty-minute episodes, often called "soap operas," is a small body of distress entirely surrounded by organ music.

The typical soap opera may open with a hospital scene, in which faithful old Ma Jones is being operated on for appendicitis, cancer, and indigestion. Then the scene will shift across town to a courtroom, where her husband is being tried for perjury, bigamy, and drunken driving. Just before the close of the program, the scene will shift again to a dingy rented room, where her daughter is shielding an illegitimate child from the blows of a ruffian who may be either its father or the meter reader. At the end of all this the announcer will tell you that this is the program which proves that life can be beautiful.

With all this misfortune, this prevalent air of disaster, why do soap operas entertain? Perhaps it would be better to ask, in what way do soap operas entertain?

The main improvement Richard has made in revamping his introduction is that of making his definition of soap opera more concrete and vivid by the early introduction of Ma Jones, and describing a typical program in terms of her predicament. This device came to him, you will note, through the revision of that part of his first draft dealing with the comfort the housewife derives from the troubles of her counterpart in soap opera. Thus what might appear as pure inspiration in the finished copy actually came from the workaday business of revisions.

The Final Copy and Proofreading Thursday evening Richard transcribed his revised draft neatly on regulation theme paper, proofread it carefully, and turned it in to his composition instructor the following morning. Richard's finished product was as follows:

LIFE CAN BE BEAUTIFUL?

Turn on the radio or television almost any time during the day and you stand a good chance of hearing or viewing a string of thirty-minute melodramas called daytime serials. Each of these thirty-minute episodes, often called "soap operas," is a small body of distress entirely surrounded by organ music.

The typical soap opera may open with a hospital scene in which faithful old Ma Jones is being operated on for appendicitis, cancer, and indigestion. Then the scene will shift across town to a courtroom, where her husband is being tried for perjury, bigamy, and drunken driving. Just before the close of the program, the scene will shift again to a dingy rented room, where her daughter is shielding an illegitimate child from the blows of a ruffian who may be either its father or the meter reader. And at the end of all this the announcer will tell you that this is the program which proves that life can be beautiful.

With all this misfortune, this prevalent air of disaster, why do soap operas entertain? Perhaps it would be better to ask, in what way do soap operas entertain?

It would be best to examine first the people who
listen to soap operas. These programs are on the air
between eight to five each day. As it happens, this
is the time when nearly everyone who works is at work.
It is also the time when most children are at school.
The only large group with both time and opportunity to
listen to soap opera is composed of housewives. The
housewife feels that her job is dull routine, usually
appreciated by no one. She fears that life is passing
her by while she lives in the shadow of cleaning and
cooking. She is eager for dramatic experience, even
if it is merely vicarious.

Secondly, we must take into account the cast of
the typical soap opera. The leading figure in this cast
will be an attractive woman in her late thirties, and
she will usually be more or less a housewife. She will
have all kinds of adventures, both romantic and dramatic, all starting from a point within the circle of
her life as a housewife. Around this central housewife-
heroine will be several lesser figures. One of these
is her husband. He is cast as a kind, strong, well-
meaning man who seems to be just a little simple. Or
perhaps he is smart enough, but emotionally unable
to face life without his wife's support. The other
characters in the cast are incidental and serve only
as sources of complication.

From a consideration of the audience and the cast,

it becomes apparent that daytime serials are really stories for housewives about housewives. The fact that the housewives in the stories seem to live some-what more dramatic lives than do the housewives who listen is no disadvantage.

Listening to someone else's troubles on the radio makes the housewife realize that her own troubles are really not so bad. When she hears that Ma Jones's hus-band is committing adultery almost daily, she will forgive her own husband for forgetting an anniversary. When Ma Jones's son is expelled from school for ped-dling dope, she is happy that her own son only has low grades. When Ma Jones is in the hospital for three whole episodes, the housewife is glad that she only has sore feet.

Soap opera gives the housewife the feeling that romance is waiting just around the corner, if she should choose to look for it. When young Widow Smith is pursued by a long succession of debonair and eligible suitors, each housewife is convinced that she too might be so pursued if she were not now happily mar-ried. One program now on the air purports to prove that a woman can find romance even after thirty-five. Such programs give the housewife the happy feeling that it is not too late for her to be gay, glamorous, and romantic.

The nice part about all this is that the housewife

is not really deceived. Her troubles are really not so bad, and it is probably not too late for her to be gay and glamorous if she wishes to be. The soap opera entertains her by reassuring and encouraging her. It may be that soap opera is like a huge psychoanalytic couch. Upon it the housewife can daily lay her routine-dampened spirit, and from it that spirit arises with a renewed sense of its own well-being.

Notice here, also, Richard's new and improved title. By taking a line from a well-known soap opera, he reminded his readers of the soap opera programs. By adding the question mark, he sets a tone of satire and prepares his readers for a critical analysis.

As we indicated in the beginning, Richard's case is not meant to be an ideal one. "Life Can Be Beautiful?" is by no means perfect; you and your instructor can quite probably find many faults with it; but by any standards, it is a good theme. And you can find dramatic proof of the value of careful revision by comparing Richard's first draft before revision with his final copy.

The Impromptu Theme

Your instructor will require you periodically to write impromptu or in-class themes. You will have approximately fifty minutes in which to formulate, write, and revise a composition based upon topics given to you at the beginning of the class hour. The impromptu theme is admittedly unrealistic in terms of the ordinary writing experience. Seldom after you leave college, unless you are in journalism, will you have to attempt a finished composition in so short a time. As a college student, however, you will profit in at least two ways from writing impromptu themes.

In the first place, the impromptu theme gives you valuable practice in writing the essay examination, which you will face frequently in the course of your college career. No matter what the subject, the requirements for formulating a good answer to an examination question demanding a fairly extensive statement are the same as those for writing a good impromptu theme. In the second place, the impromptu theme will usually reveal your weaknesses in composition much more clearly than will themes written outside class. Careful and thorough revision of outside themes, including judicious rephrasing to avoid points of grammar or sentence construction of which you are uncertain, will successfully conceal your writing weaknesses; but for the purpose of instruction, it is well that these uncertainties be brought to the surface by the time pressure of the impromptu theme. The in-class theme, consequently, is a valuable instructional aid both to you and to your instructor.

The procedure for writing the impromptu theme is the same as that for writing any composition, except that the whole process is, of course, highly compressed in time. You must arrive at your subject comparatively quickly; and in the usual fifty-minute class period, you should spend no more—but certainly no less—than five minutes in working out your preliminary outline. The composition itself should be approximately three hundred words long, depending upon the individual writer, but the length should be such as to allow you at least five minutes at the end of the class period for revising and proofreading. Unless the instructor specifically forbids it, you should write impromptu compositions in pencil so that you can use an eraser for corrections and revisions.

The chief student complaint concerning the impromptu theme is the difficulty of choosing a subject on such short notice. Actually, this misgiving is probably due more to a reluctance to get down to the act of writing than to a lack of interesting subjects. Your instructor will include in his list of topics subjects to which you as a human being are bound to react. In fact, the theme topic is rare which will leave you nothing to say.

You should accept the impromptu theme as a necessary means of increasing your writing skill. In addition, it offers a good opportunity for you to display your resourcefulness and achieve, on occasion, personal triumphs of spontaneous expression.

Theme Analysis

One of the best ways to increase your skill in writing is to analyze the writing of others. If you can detect the merits and faults of another person's composition, you will be much more competent to recognize the merits and faults of your own. The products of the professional writer—those found in a collection of readings designed for writing courses, for instance—will provide valuable ground for this kind of exercise. Since, however, your immediate concern is writing the theme, it is especially important that you realize what constitutes a successful theme. Your instructor will probably give you a chance to evaluate and discuss the themes of your classmates. Throughout the rest of this chapter you will find a series of student themes for your consideration. The following suggestions are meant to give you a systematic approach to the analysis of the themes of others and, of course, to enable you to evaluate more accurately your own.

8. The Central Idea We have noted before that the theme is usually a short composition. It is important, consequently, that you limit your subject (narrow it down to one specific facet of the subject), determine your purpose (the result you wish to accomplish—to inform, to explain, or to persuade by means of analysis, reconstruction, or recall), and to decide on the one central idea. The idea may have several divisions, but the idea itself must be single. The first question to ask, therefore, in evaluating a theme is, Does it concern itself with a clearly established central idea?

Suppose, for instance, that you should decide to write a theme on modern architecture. If you restricted your topic no further, you would soon find you had set yourself an impossible task. Even if you limited your topic to modern residential architecture, you would still find yourself in considerable difficulty. Only when you decided upon a particular, comparatively restricted approach to your subject, such as "The Principal Improvements of Modern over Traditional Residential Architecture," or "The Chief Trends in Modern Residential Architecture," would you have established a workable central idea.

The theme without a clear-cut central idea, however well written, will give a total impression of incompleteness and inconclusiveness. The organization is likely to be inadequate, since good organization requires a central point on which to focus. On the other hand, a well thought out central idea will help give a theme directness, purpose, and force, or what is called "unity." In such themes, the central idea may always be expressed in a single phrase or sentence, as illustrated in the preceding paragraph.

9. The Introduction   The introduction, consisting in most themes of one paragraph, is usually the part of the theme most difficult for students. At the same time, it is a very important part of the theme because most readers are swayed by first impressions and are inclined to allow the introduction to color their opinion of the entire composition.

The good introduction provides a keynote to the content of the theme. Elaborate flourishes at the beginning of a composition serve only to distract the reader. Some writers recommend writing out the entire first draft of a theme, then eliminating the introductory paragraph altogether and allowing the original second paragraph to stand as the introduction. This practice will undoubtedly in many instances plunge the reader immediately into the theme without his having to suffer through the opening artificialities to which so many writers are addicted. But in general, a plain, workaday preparation for your central idea will provide an entirely satisfactory introduction:

For many years I have thought the most important single thing in life to be financial success. But since I was fortunate enough to take a course in comparative religions under Dr. Paul Brown, I have realized that even though material things are necessary to life, the spiritual provides the basic motivation for all mankind's endeavors.

"Democracy" is a difficult term to define, even though most of us, as Americans, feel that we have a very good idea of what it is. England and France, among others, are countries whose governments would fall within the meaning of the word "democracy." What, then, are the main features which distinguish American democracy from the democracies in other parts of the world?

A concrete example used to illustrate or anticipate the central idea is one very reliable device. A student writing on segregation in public schools began his theme as follows: "In school the children of America are taught that 'all men are created equal.' They are expected to believe this. . . ." Another student dealing with television wrestling wrote, "The screen bursts into brilliance. The hum of sound becomes translatable into the atavistic grunts of heavily fleshed behemoths locked in mock-mortal combat. . . ." Both of these introductions plunge the reader immediately and concretely into the subject matter at hand.

There are many kinds of effective introductions. One very good device is the use of a pertinent quotation. This method is especially effective in book reviews, but is useful in any kind of theme, as long as the quotation is apt. The writer of the following introduction made very telling use of a quotation, in this case combining the quotation with a startling opening sentence:

INVOLVED, BUT NOT DIMINISHED

Any man's death diminishes me, because I am involved in mankind, and therefore never send to know for whom the bell tolls; it tolls for thee.—JOHN DONNE.

Personally, whenever I hear the bell tolling, I do not feel diminished in the least (that's assuming, of course, that I don't know the individual cashing in his chips). . . .

Another effective introduction, especially in narrative themes, is the use of a climactic event: "Before I knew it, I was in the air, floating down rather gently. The parachute billowed overhead like a huge mushroom. It was beautiful. It really had opened." Humorous introductions can also be good, although humor is generally a very difficult thing for the inexperienced writer to handle successfully: "I have just returned from Epidermia, which, as you well know, is the country where nudism is the national custom. So impressed was I with the mode of life there that, since my return, I have become this country's foremost advocate of nudism. . . ."

A good introduction, then, will, first, convey the reader directly into the subject. Second, it will arouse his interest to the extent that he will wish to read the rest of what the writer has to say. When you find these two requirements met, either in your own or another's writing, you can be satisfied, but certainly with no less. A good introduction, more than any other part, gives the theme the important quality of originality.

10. Transitions The writer of an effective theme must make the direction and organization of his theme absolutely clear to the reader by erecting signposts, as it were, which will lead the reader naturally and effortlessly along the way the writer wishes him to take. These verbal signposts are called *transitions,* and the skillful use of them is essential for effective prose.

One of the most simple transitional devices is the use of the words *first, second* (or variations such as *in the first place, in the second place*) to mark successive divisions of the theme. Many writers prefer the simple *first, second* and *third* to the more cumbersome *firstly, secondly, thirdly*—a series that becomes unwieldy with *fourthly, fifthly, sixthly.* To connect divisions that contrast in thought or treatment, common transitional words and phrases are *however, nevertheless, yet, still, but, on the other hand, on the contrary, in spite of.* Supplementary or added material may be indicated by *in addition, moreover, furthermore, next, again.* Transitional devices to mark exact stages in the organization are

to begin with, so far, we now turn, finally, in conclusion.
Correlative conjunctions, such as *either . . . or, neither
. . . nor, not only . . . but also,* help to move an exposition
along by suggesting comparison and contrast. So do such
words and phrases as *rather, instead, in comparison to, in
comparison with, in contrast with,* and *otherwise.* On occasion a complete sentence or paragraph may be needed to
provide a transition between major divisions of the theme:

Having examined the causes of these consecutive low-pressure
areas, we can proceed to the consideration of the torrential rains
that result.

The external facts concerning this small Midwestern town are
now before us. We know the population, the area, the total production, the number of schools, and the number of churches. But
what of the individual citizen in Prairieville? It is to this extremely
important figure that we must now direct our attention.

This discussion of transitional devices should not close,
however, without a word of warning. In addition to the explicit transitions that we have discussed, there are other
transitions which might be called "implicit." Pronouns, the
coordinating and subordinating conjunctions—any word or
phrase which recalls, anticipates, or connects is actually a
transition even though it is an integral part of its sentence.
In the logical, clearly developed theme, these implicit transitions will carry most of the burden of transition. Important
as explicit transitional words and phrases are to the well-
organized theme, they should not be overused. Artificial,
elaborate connectives have no place in modern prose. Explicit transitional devices should be used, consequently, only
when there is a definite need to mark a shift, a beginning, or
a termination in the thought of the theme. Note the skillful,
yet at the same time unobtrusive, use of transitional elements
in the following paragraphs taken from a student theme. The
transitional words are in italics.

America is a country committed to the belief *that* all men are
created equal. *When* the early leaders of *America* set the stand-

ards of the *country's* government, *they* did *so* believing *that equal* economic, political, cultural, *and* religious opportunities could be furnished to *all men* only by a society *which* was based on free enterprise *and* political democracy. *These men* realized *that* perfection was well-nigh impossible. *They* knew there would be discrimination, inequality, exploitation of *man* by *man, and*, in general, *elements which* would prevent the complete liberty of *all men* in *America. However, they* had faith in the sovereignty of the individual, *and they* believed *that* the common *man* with all of *his* shortcomings would, given time, condemn *and thus* eliminate *these imperfections.*

Russia, *like America,* is *also committed to the belief that all men are created equal. As it was in America, this commitment* was made at the end of a revolution *which* was fought by the people *because* of despotism on the part of *their* rulers. In the case of Russia the *revolution* was against Tsarism. Out of *this revolution* came much confusion and political interplay. *However,* the details of how *Russian* Communism was evolved from the philosophies of Marx, Engels, *and* Lenin are relatively unimportant. *What is important* is that the original *Communism* had as *its* end the *same* moral achievements for *which such men* as Washington, Franklin, Jefferson, *and* Lincoln fought so earnestly. The *difference* came in the means by *which* the *Russian leaders* hoped to improve the lot of the *common man*—dictatorship and collectivism. *Like the early American leaders,* the organizers of Communism knew *that imperfections* were inevitable. *However, their* theory was *that* the whole of a *country's population* should undergo the suffering of conflict and the coercion of a dictatorship. *These rigors* would be terminated when the *masses* had been educated to the purposes of *Communism.* After the periods of *revolution,* education, and adjustment, the agents of state oppression would relax and fade away, leaving the *perfection* of a cooperative and classless *society.*

11. The Conclusion   The conclusion of the theme, usually consisting of a single paragraph, is the last impression made upon the reader. Too many beginning writers fail to exploit this last opportunity to leave a precise and relatively permanent idea of the main content of the theme in the reader's mind. Some themes simply stop; they do not "conclude."

The concluding paragraph may take the form of a brief,

succinct summary of the principal ideas set forth in the composition, an apt anecdote which illustrates the points you have established, a plea for action, or a restatement of your central idea.

The following conclusion of a theme concerned with the definition of culture summarizes the ideas already presented:

This is culture—the artifacts, the language, the social customs, the moral laws, the religion—everything that has its established basis in society and is passed from generation to generation until it becomes the guide to correct living for its particular society.

A theme with persuasive or emotional intent might well end on a strong emotional note, as in this conclusion of a piece comparing the founding of the state of Israel to the birth of the United States:

Israel and the United States are melting pots, and the flame which blends the ingredients is the flame of freedom and democracy. And it will be the people who shall cause the deserts and fields to "bloom as the Rose of Sharon."

Probably the most common conclusion, however, is one that simply restates forcibly the central idea of the theme, as does this one concerning the sales devices of unscrupulous merchants:

These are just a few of the tricks used in everyday business. There are many more. The important idea behind these illustrations is that when you go into a store, look out. There is no telling what new tricks merchants will think up next to swindle the unsuspecting customer. So remember, anytime the word "sale" appears, think twice before running down to the store, because the customer is going to be the loser and certainly not the merchant, who will always be one step ahead.

Or this one, arguing the beneficial effects of television:

Television has been called the opiate of the masses. But must the connotation of the word *opiate* always be that of a harmful potion, a veritable witch's brew which destroys the mind and stifles ambition? A doctor would certainly disagree with that interpretation; as long as drugs do not become habit-forming, they may be taken safely to relieve pain or to calm nerves. Why shouldn't television, then, be used for the same purposes, as a carefully self-administered drug, useful for temporarily relieving tension, useful for permitting a man to relax for a few hours, enveloped in a pleasant opium dream?

Like good introductions, good conclusions spring from the mind of the individual writer. In common, however, they are marked by an absence of the trite, the forced, and the superfluous. The essence of the effective conclusion is that it reinforces in the mind of the reader the central idea or ideas that the writer has presented.

12. The Whole Theme The whole theme is, of course, much more than any of its parts. The introduction and conclusion are significant only in relation to the body of the theme. We turn now to the types of themes commonly assigned in the writing course. Here we shall consider basic problems of organization and those other qualities of the whole theme that mark effective writing.

Personal Reaction and Experience. The early themes in your basic composition course are likely to concern your own ideas and experience. There are several reasons for such assignments. In the first place, the great majority of human beings are very much interested in themselves. Consequently, when the instructor assigns a theme based upon your own experience, he can be reasonably certain that your interest in your subject will be high. In the second place, the instructor can take for granted a thorough acquaintance with the subject. You need no outside sources for knowledge of your own lives and thoughts.

The key to the interesting autobiographical theme is the selection of an incident, a person, an environment or a philosophical stance that has influenced your life. In order to make an impact on your readers, you must be willing to sacrifice a chronological narrative from birth to date. You must omit all nonessential facts that, though true, have no bearing on your selected central idea. You must, with strict self-discipline, eliminate all descriptive details that will detract from the single reaction—based on one event, one person, one situation, or one point of view—you have chosen to discuss.

Themes based on personal reactions and experience should possess, above all, candor and sincerity. The student who tries to impress his instructor or classmates with high-sounding sentiments and borrowed ideas will quite probably not succeed. The basic composition class affords one of the few opportunities a student has to express in writing his convictions to a sympathetic audience. It is only common sense to take advantage of this opportunity, as the writers of the following themes have done.

HONEST? OF COURSE I AM

Last summer when I was being interviewed for a scholarship, the interviewer asked me if I considered myself to be an honest person. I replied, "Yes," and thought a little indignantly, of course I am. Does he suppose that I'm going to use the scholarship money for something besides college?

I was correct in saying that I was honest in respect to the scholarship money. I would have considered misusing it a crime. My definition of dishonesty included, among other things, any form of stealing. Actually, though, if I or one of my friends had taken a package of chewing gum or some other small insignificant item from the corner grocery, I probably would have made a joke of it.

It appears that I wouldn't have applied my standard of dishonesty to myself or to my friends. This would have been especially true if the dishonest act was committed on a dare or without thinking. That is, I wouldn't have applied it before I was caught in dishonesty myself.

I was employed last summer by a dairy company at the state fair. The employees where I worked received their lunches free by merely going through the kitchen and behind the counter to get the food. I had been eating in back of the kitchen with a friend who was working at another part of the fairgrounds. With the original intention of paying for it, I got his lunch at the same time I got mine, so that he wouldn't have to wait in the long lines. However when I couldn't get to the cashier, I didn't pay. The third time this incident occurred the manager called me aside, stated that he had seen me, and then fired me.

Of course my friends told me that everyone "stole" a milkshake now and then, and that I just happened to get caught. Probably it seems ridiculous to suffer a guilty conscience over a couple of pilfered milkshakes, but then most people haven't been caught stealing. They haven't had their inflated opinions of their honesty pricked, as I have.

When asked if they are honest, I wonder if these people can reply, "Honest? Of course I am." I couldn't.

MATURITY HAS ITS DRAWBACKS

They were long summers. The creek moved sluggishly past my feet when, as a child, I sat on its bank in the tall weeds and cast leaves upon it to watch them make their way slowly down to the bend, where finally they would reach the rapids and be swept under by the current, or left high and dry on a stone. They were long winters. The old study hall clock in our grade school had an eternity between every tick-tock. There were *so many years*—so many years to pass until I could myself be wearing ladies' dresses ordered from the Sears Roebuck catalog, and high heels and nylons and lipstick—until I could cut off my braids—until I could be an adult.

Adults don't have to go to school, you know. They don't have to go to bed at bedtime, either, and they do such glamorous things as falling in love and getting married and having careers. Adults have all the advantages, it's easy to see. Kids can't vote or attend any of those mysterious club meetings, and movies that are labeled "for adults only." They have all the excitement while kids have all the drab preliminaries—oh, to be grown up!

Last summer was an extremely short one. One week of it was spent at the Illinois 4-H State Junior Leadership Conference, where we discussed maturity and its absolute necessity for leadership. One of the outstanding points made at the conference was this: "A leader is one who wants to do what he knows he ought to do, whether he wants to do it or not." We began to realize that leadership is a product of maturity—sociological maturity—and that this maturity has more drawbacks than physical maturity (when men hate their razors and women their foundations). This maturity brings with it not only the privileges of an adult, but the duties of an adult, and, with a mature state of mind, the obligation to carry out these duties willingly.

I now see myself as one of my cast leaves suddenly arriving at the bend of the creek and being taken up in the rapids from which there is no turning back. The rapids are tiring. The never-ending routine of lipstick, pincurls, and pressing date dresses is itself as nothing compared to the never-ending routine of work—of becoming in every way a useful adult.

The autobiographical incident is another common introductory theme topic. Few lives are so dull that they contain no significant event. Even very placid existences include incidents that, though not striking or sensational in themselves, have a deep significance for the person who experiences them. In fact, the theme is usually more effective which avoids such hackneyed subjects as "My Vacation" or "My First Date" and concentrates on an event of more lasting importance in the writer's life.

The theme based on an autobiographical incident is organized chronologically though it may begin in the present and use the flashback technique of development. The principal requirements are proper restriction of the subject matter and the effective selection and use of concrete detail. In the following themes the writers deal with events that cover only a few hours in time and make their experiences vivid to the reader through the use of detail.

HOLIDAY ON THE CAMPUS

My landlady made a fine Thanksgiving dinner, but I left, almost impolitely, after I had finished. Her family was there, and I felt uneasy. I was really a stranger, and Thanksgiving should be a family gathering.

The library seemed like a good place to spend the afternoon. I would feel comfortable there, and I couldn't study with all the company in the house. I slipped on my jacket and opened the back door. The sun shone brightly, but a north wind blew very hard. As I closed the door it chilled me through.

I walked down the alley, dodging the muddy puddles that had frozen over the night before. Turning onto the sidewalk, I was hurried along by a gust of wind which sent the dead leaves racing along the curb.

Few people were on the street. Occasionally I would pass a house with several cars parked in front. Glancing into the window, I would see a family laughing and talking and enjoying the holiday. I guessed that these must be reunions.

As I neared the library, I passed an Oriental standing by a scraggly hedge. I wondered why he was standing in the open as he was. It was much too cold merely to be taking a walk. He didn't seem to notice me when I passed him, but after I had gone a few steps farther, I looked around and he was watching me. I don't know why people do that. They always seem to be watching you when you turn around. Maybe they wonder too.

I hurried up the library steps, but I could see the steel lock in the crack between the tall doors. Odd, I thought; surely everyone doesn't go home for the holidays. I turned and walked slowly down the steps, then towards the quadrangle.

The brick buildings seemed colder and more unfriendly than they had the day before. There was no one on the broadwalk. The stiff wind rattled the dead limbs in the tops of the elms and pushed a weathervane back and forth, its rusted shaft squeaking as it moved. A rope on an empty flagpole slapped against the steel spire, beating metallic notes from its core.

My ears were stinging. I blew into my hands and cupped the palms over my ears, but it didn't help. I pulled my collar up. It was too short. I shoved my hands back into my pockets and leaned into the icy wind.

It was much more comfortable as I stepped into the hall of the Union. I saw no one but the boy in the check room. From the lounge, though, I heard a piano. Upon walking into the lounge I found it empty except for a lone figure hunched over the keyboard. He was completely engrossed in his pleasure and failed to notice me at first. He played until he sensed my presence, then stopped suddenly and turned to me. He got up and began to leave, but I asked him to continue. He said he didn't often play for an audience. I assured him that I was enjoying the music. I asked him to play "Clair de Lune." He began to play, timidly at first, but soon his timidity was forgotten. He played many things for me. There seemed to be nothing with which he was not

43

familiar. When he was through I thanked him and told him that I envied his talent. As I left he thanked me also. This seemed strange at first.

I stepped outside. It was warmer than before.

PLACES OF PLEASURE

One night, because we had nothing better to do, my roommate and another girl and I hopped in the car and set off for a grand tour of the campus "joints." On my journey I found neither dens of iniquity nor glimpses of a promised land, but merely the mildly amusing sequence of scenes I had expected. I say amusing, for nothing is more a point of gentle laughter than a child; no one can help smiling when he sees a youngster mimicking the ludicrous actions of his elders in all seriousness; and at every place I went I saw children playing at being adults.

I saw children smoking in every way they had ever seen: in a nervous, endless chain; languidly as Cleopatra; in the fashion of underworld characters; or with a pseudo-sophisticated flick of the wrist.

I saw children talking in every tone imaginable: boisterously, pretentiously in earnest, in the manner of men and women of the world, or with an air of boredom.

I saw children drinking beer: they drank it from bottles, from glasses, from pitchers; they sipped it, they gulped it, they studied it; they adored it.

And all the time I felt I was in a land of Lilliputians with everything built to size: there were small rooms, cozy seats, tiny bottles, pint-sized ash trays, baby-faced proprietors, and little boy waiters. What could be more charming! And yet after a few moments of amusement I found myself becoming absolutely bored.

Not once did I see any one of these imitation cosmopolitans smoking for the sheer pleasure of it, talking because he had something to say, or drinking because he liked beer. Rather, they all gave me the impression that they had come, had sat, had smoked, had talked, had drunk, and were waiting for the enchanted words to be spoken and the magic dust sprinkled on their curly little heads and the wonderful miracle of "having a good time" to occur. I could see it running through their minds: "Adults can do what they want; this is what they do, so it must be fun."

My feeling of boredom melted to pity and I felt moved to cry out in a ringing voice with dramatic pauses—"Unhappy generation! You are right in your unhappiness. Your pleasures are not dictated to you. There is more joy to living than this. Rise up! Go forth!"—when suddenly it occurred to me that perhaps I was the odd personality, unable to enjoy standard entertainment. Maybe they were really having a good time.

In a cloud of uncertainty I followed my friends back to the dorm and got into the shower, the only place where my powers of reasoning function properly, and began to talk to myself.

"Jane," I said, "you have smoked L & M, Lucky Strike, Viceroy, Marlboro, Winston, Kentucky Brand, Camel, Chesterfield, and homemade cigarettes. You have talked to priests, psychiatrists, businessmen, teachers, teenagers, Chinese, Czechoslovakians, Japanese, Hawaiians, Germans, Hungarians, Swedish, English, and Americans about life, death, philosophy, sex, politics, morals, religion, and the future of America. You have drunk whiskey, vodka, rum, gin, vermouth, champagne, and your father's wine in bedrooms, barrooms, bathrooms, bowling alleys, basements, cocktail lounges, cars, and swimming pools. Have or have not all these things been fun?"

"Yes," I sighed, remembering.

"And have you or have you not enjoyed, along with smoking, jabbering, and drinking, the pleasures of reading, listening to music, watching plays, and praying on your knees to a hidden God?"

"I have," I replied beginning to see the light.

"Then what right have you to laugh at, sneer at, pity, or judge the people you saw in the places you went to tonight?"

"No right at all," I whispered, scrubbing my ears.

But as I turned on the cold water all my confidence and defiance came back to me and "There was something sad and wrong in those places!" I cried to my departing self.

SUGGESTED TOPICS FOR THEMES

Personal Reactions and Experiences

My first fight
My first encounter with the law
My first encounter with racial discrimination

My first job
My first spanking (On being punished for the first time)

The longest minute I ever spent

The wisest thing I ever did

Prize memory of the year (Regrets of the year)

A Christmas thrill (Christmas this year)

Thoughts on New Year's Eve

How I learned to drive a car

How I learned to dance

An unforgettable experience

The fun of being sick

Moving into a strange town

Learning to like vegetables

One of life's comedies (or tragedies) in which I played a star part

Things I have lost

Why I dislike my name

Why _____ is my favorite sport

Why I like a small town

Why I go to church

Why I came to college

Why _____ is my favorite picture

Why I do (not) play cards

Why I smoke

Why I believe in immortality

Why I do not believe in divorce

Why I want to be a _____

Why I prefer jazz to classical music (or vice versa)

Why I joined the _____

Why I don't like comic strips

My idea of hard work

My idea of a good dinner

My idea of a good course

My idea of a gentleman (or a lady)

My idea of a dull evening

My idea of the perfect school

My first dollar

My first formal dance

My most important decision and why I made it

My most embarrassing moment

The most stupid thing I ever did

My most serious accident

My narrowest escape

I was scared

A trip to the fair (church, theater, zoo)

A sports event I will never forget

An initiation I will always remember

An obstacle I overcame (or must overcome)

A hunting (fishing) trip

The little red schoolhouse (Sunday school or kindergarten as I remember it)

An incident of childhood which has affected my personality

What animal I should like to be for a day

What I got out of my summer job

What I get out of music

What religion means to me

What's wrong with my home town

What I think about science laboratories, student participation in extracurricular activities, air travel, campus hangouts

What I'd do to prevent World War III

What I want in a wife
What I have gained from bull
  sessions

What I think about athletics
Where am I going?
What I really enjoy doing

The Character Sketch. Since most of us have small inclination to become hermits, other people hold a good deal of interest for us. Our happiness and success in life will depend largely upon our reactions to them and theirs to us. Because of the inherent interest of the subject, theme assignments in the basic composition course, especially in the early part, will probably include a character sketch.

The most successful character sketches are usually concerned with some salient and interesting aspect or aspects of the person described. This doesn't necessarily mean that the subject of the sketch must be an eccentric. The most normal individual will have a predominant trait upon which the writer can seize; if no such trait exists, then the very colorlessness would make an excellent point of departure. The thing to remember is that the good character sketch is not a monotonous detailing of clothes and appearance, although these qualities may well be included. The writer should attempt to penetrate to that uniqueness which most people possess and evoke that uniqueness with concrete, illustrative detail. Librarians, for instance, are not noted for their glamour. But consider the following account of one.

PORTRAIT OF A LIBRARIAN

She worked in the library. She sat at a little table behind the huge main desk. I happened to watch her closely one day when she waited on a young man who wanted a pamphlet from some obscure file.

"Well, now, let me check this in the catalogue, and I'll be right with you," she said, smiling. ". . . Ah, here we are." She approached the desk again. "Now this pamphlet should be in the business room. I'll show you."

They set out together. He, with his erect, graceful figure, confident and relaxed gait, struck a conspicuous contrast to her, with her tall body, erect enough, but with long legs, knees hardly bending, alternating in a connecting rod fashion, cranking her way across the floor. And oh, those arms, straight and bony, even under two layers of material, elbows taut like brakes on a railroad car, hinges at the shoulders, crackling occasionally, arms pendulating to and fro, perhaps keeping her upright with their gyroscopic effect. Her hands flipped intermittently. She carried a pencil in one, a card in the other. Head and eyes straight ahead, onward she went, steering around posts and people, past famous paintings and mosaic walls, vases, busts of Shakespeare, Longfellow, Lincoln, Andrew Carnegie; past rows of tables, chairs, people poring over books, pencils wiggling furiously and heads being scratched; under indoor sunshine at noon on bald pates set between tiny, long, parallel gold bars; past shelves and past cases, past "Reserved" and "Do Not Open"; man looking at the woman over there bending over, door slamming upstairs, sneeze exploding, jingle-tinkle of sinner's penance on burnished mahogany; musty, mellow, archaic odor of yellow pages and moldy covers and wet glue and cord and wrapping paper and wooden shelves and varnish and tons of old newspapers, of oily floors and waxed woodwork and sweeping compound. Shuffle, scuffle, scrape, on hard polished parquet she went, never heeding distraught glances, caring less for criticism, shifting now, lurching to the leeward, pumping and rocking, down the stairs she went.

They arrived at the shelves. She reached up for the pamphlet and the lace cuff of her white satin blouse moved out from the sleeve. She always wore a trim gray or brown suit, with little pleats on the coat sometimes, and occasionally a tidy little hanky in her left breast pocket. No, I couldn't say she was affected, for her gait and stance were just that way; it seemed, just natural, one might say. But besides, it showed in her face. To get up close and talk to her, to look into those deep, lustrous eyes with almost transparent irises of blue, to get a close view of the thousands of fine lines, horizontal on her forehead, convex around her cheeks, concave under her chin, vertical along her neck, leading in smooth semicircles up from the corners of a thin-lipped mouth, was to behold her countenance—or at least it seemed that way to me—as a subtle picture of frankness, integrity, and broad-mindedness.

She handed the pamphlet to him, saying, "Well, young man, here is the paper you want." How those thin lips would curve into a warm, sincere, personable smile, not aristocratic nor cultured nor sophisticated! And how her deep-red tongue clucked and zawwed and hammered softly against platinum cheeks when she spoke, curving or flattening on each vowel, ticking off each consonant like a grandfather clock, helping her precise lips to produce correct syllables. Her voice had a cooing, purring, melodious tone, not like a chicken or bird or cat, but like the singing of an old hen just going to roost late on a summer afternoon—soft, guttural, but not rasping, cheerful, contented, but not smug. It had a ring to it, too, like a medium-sized desk bell, or like the bell on the door of an old-fashioned grocery store; it seemed to indicate vitality and self-confidence and humbleness and fairness, industriousness and cheerfulness; just a touch of sadness, perhaps loneliness too, and sometimes it seemed to reveal tiredness; only occasionally had a tint of happiness. Something else, too—irresoluteness, no; or, a feeling of being out of place—that's it, I guess—in a voice!—I don't know why.

Her hair, hand-tooled silver, swept back from a high, rather narrow forehead, over antique temples, past lightly tanned, fragile ears, thin like oriental tissue, veined like damask webbing well-formed like pansies, and gathered at the very back under the command of a strong, daintly jeweled, sterling-silver barette.

They returned by the same route to the main desk, and she stamped the card. As the young man turned to leave, she smiled again. To me she seemed really sweet. Not cute. Somehow, again I can't say why, I liked her. She seemed, oh, so much kinder than the other librarians. Maybe she came from a farm or from some poor family or from some remote district, and had to earn her own way, adapt herself to "polished" life. I don't know. But I liked her, have always kept thoughts of her tucked away in my mind;—and I suppose I'll never lose them—not that I want to.

As opposed to the character sketch of an individual, the sketch of a type of person concentrates upon characteristics universal to the type and not particular to the individual. If you characterize a type be careful to select as a subject a type that possesses convincing and recognizable common characteristics. These group characteristics show up among people within a common occupation—teachers, lawyers, pilots, for instance. Geographical localities may provide the unifying characteristics, i.e., New Yorkers, Southerners, Yankees. A dominating personality trait may cut across all these lines, as in such subjects as the athlete, the bookworm, or the yokel. The danger of the type sketch is superficiality; people are individual, and it is in a certain sense unfair to present them as indistinguishable parts of a group. For this reason, perhaps, most type sketches are at least partly derogatory in purpose. Nevertheless, the type sketch developed with convincing, carefully selected detail can be an illuminating and entertaining piece of work.

COLLEGE FRESHMAN

The college freshman is a human being. This is probably the one fact that is universally agreed upon about one of the world's most controversial figures. He is also that miserable creature who, in spite of the many conflicting opinions about him, lives a hectic, nerve-racking existence. He lives suspended between two conceptions, endeavoring simultaneously to live down what is presumed about him and to live up to what is expected of him.

To his instructors the freshman is that crew-cutted, pink-sweatered, suede-shoed Einstein-Brando combination that bounds abruptly from mother's lap to fraternity house and immediately becomes the imagined center of gravity for the entire university. Having groped his way through the catacombs of high school years, trying constantly to impress everyone within earshot with his importance, he has emerged a profound egotist, having convinced only himself. Since he already possesses infinite knowledge of the universe, he cannot be advised; he can only be prodded, commanded, or ignored.

A freshman is a blob of protoplasm which exists only for the convenience of the upperclassman. He can be molded to fit any purpose—an extra for blind dates, a drinking partner (when nothing better is available), or a cash register that can be tapped at the end of an expensive week. He exists as a room number, a pair of cuff links, or an alibi for a broken date.

To his kid sister, the college freshman is the unpublished name behind all scandalous headlines and newspaper articles. He leads panty raids, spends all his leisure time drinking beer and playing pool, and his week ends are one wild party after another. He attends classes only occasionally and gets his homework from a fraternity file.

Outwardly, there is nothing to suggest that beneath this multi-personality lies a bewildered, disgusted, discouraged individual who has discarded all aspirations to become a doctor, an engineer, or a lawyer and would be content as a fisherman, janitor, jockey, or anything not pertaining to college. Map in hand, he has stumbled through twenty miles of registration and groped his way through a maze of buildings and classrooms, his lofty ambitions crumbling with every weary step. He has slaved for hours on a single algebra problem only to discover it was the wrong one. He has survived for days on hot dogs alone after searching hopefully through the mail each morning for the check that is invariably late. Ultimately, he walks about in a daze, caring for nothing but the end of the semester. His only encouragement is "Where there's life, there's hope."

SUGGESTED TOPICS FOR THEMES

The Character Sketch
(Individuals)

A person I have almost forgotten

My friend _____ (someone of a different race or nationality)

A person I can't bear

My distinguished ancestor

My best friend

A person who has influenced my life

What I learned from Dad (In defense of Dad) (My Dad)

The most prominent citizen in my home town

The most disreputable person I ever saw

A person I will never forget

A brief sketch of myself (any age, any mood)

Meet the Doc

Meet the family

My roommate

My landlady

My favorite teacher (relative, commentator)

The most wonderful person I know

A first-rate teacher

My most interesting friend

The person I admire most

Grandfather

The most abused public servant

The man who never had a chance

An historical character

An interesting public personality

A character from fiction I should like to meet

My favorite hero/heroine

Brothers under the skin

Eyes of blue

From the other side of the tracks

(Types)

Day dreamer	Soldier on leave
Juke box addict	The movie detective
Chicago taxi-driver	Do-gooder
The practical joker	A stag at a mixer dance
The proud parent	Straw boss
The "successful" man or woman	That tired waitress
Master of ceremonies	Bleacher athlete
The American woman	The football idol
An interesting TV personality	The local policeman
The drunkard	Teachers who bore me
The student	Little old lady
Baby sitter	TV announcer
Preacher's son (or daughter)	A personal appearance
Student waiter	Meet John Doe (the average American)
Mrs. Doakes, landlady	
Camp counselor	The alum
Betty Coed	The great lover
Joe College	The traveling salesman

Description. Closely allied to the character sketch are descriptions of structures, landscapes, and phenomena. Your descriptions will usually order the parts of descriptions according to arrangement in space—what we call *spatial order*. In describing the interior of a house, for instance, you might start with the hall, proceed to the living room, the dining room, the kitchen, and so on. Spatial arrangement also involves the problem of a consistent point of view. In writing a theme organized according to the position of the parts in space, you must be careful to establish the point of view and maintain it with consistency and logic. If you are describing, for instance, the view from the window of your room, you must establish that point of view at the very beginning of the theme and restrict your theme only to those things perceptible from your window. Or, if you wish to extend your description, you must make the change in your point of view clear and specific at the time the change occurs.

The theme which follows involves the description of a physical landscape, in this instance a city street. The writer maintains a consistent physical point of view; in fact, a part of the theme's effect is due to the restriction of the point of view to the street itself.

THE HIDING PEOPLE

After you leave Crescent Street and before you go very far on Fulton, you come to a section of Brooklyn known as Brownsville. The streets, during the day, are usually very crowded, but at night a strange quiet settles over them. The pushcarts are gone, the hawkers retired to no one knows where. The automobiles which choked the street during the day now line the curbs, resting quietly like sleeping beasts.

The houses are all connected one to the other, and their long dim grimness seems to form a wall against intruders. The soot and dirt of the city have turned the brownstone façade into a grimy, blackened grimace. Streaked here and there by the rain, spotted by the birds, and crumbling with neglect, the buildings seem, somehow, forbidding—yet pathetic. The staring windows, the gaping doorways seem to carry the stamp of idiocy, of senility; and like things that were once proud and have fallen in disgrace, the buildings convey an inevitable feeling of isolation.

The people in the buildings, the ones that make these lonely things their home, seem to be the same as the buildings themselves. Each person seems to be, somehow, something less than he must have been once. Each person, somehow, seems to be streaked by the soot and lined by the weather. And each person, too, seems to be afraid of showing what is inside himself.

The silence of the now deserted streets is punctuated by the sound of footsteps—hurrying, hurrying. You can feel the urgency, the need to be off the streets, the need to be locked in the tomb, away from the world and other men. If the glances of two of these silent hurriers ever meet, there is a quick turning away, a feeling almost of panic. The words are never spoken, but they are heard as clearly as if they were shouted in a frenzy of fear—"Leave me alone! Don't look at me!" And the footsteps quicken, to regain their solitude the faster.

As each building is passed, a sound can be heard, very faintly—more of an undertone than a definite sound, but it's there. It carries through the sound of radios playing too high, and people laughing too hard, and voices talking too loud. It carries through all the falseness the people wear outside. It comes and is inside you before you know you have heard it, and it clutches at your soul. It is the sound of weeping. It is the great, pain-choked sobs of weariness—the tears of loneliness. . . .

Down the street the cold wind blows, and the houses seem to shiver and cringe, and the wind seems lonely too.

Sometimes you may wish to adopt the "omniscient" point of view. You will not assume a specific physical point of view, but will allow yourself the liberty of surveying a scene without reference to any single point in space. The writer of "Dawn at Dake's Landing" uses this method. Notice the importance of selective detail in descriptive writing.

DAWN AT DAKE'S LANDING

Through the mist a gull cries. The wind whines in reply. A red lantern on the Missouri side of the river nods in cadence with the ripples. On the towhead the willows shiver as a sharp gust strips them of their yellow leaves. Every gust launches fleets of *Salix* ships bent on an invasion of Louisiana. Overhead grimy clouds besmear the moon with shadows.

Two dim beams of light cut their way up from Sainte Genevieve. A weak-eyed truck snorts to a stop. The door panels bear the label "GUS CRAIG, TRUCKER, GREER SPRINGS, MISSOURI." Three blasts of a 1939 "Chevy" horn, one bleat by a small Guernsey calf, and the passage of five minutes bring the hacking, the sputtering, the wheezing, and finally the catching of a ferryboat motor. Chugging with only slight enthusiasm, the ferry tacks upstream to the Missouri side. The engine misfires twice and the ferry scrapes to a stop. White smoke fumes out of the mouths of the driver and the ferryman as they load the grunting truck aboard. The grumpy ferry recrosses the Mississippi River and dispatches its cargo. As a small red light disappears in the direction of Modoc, the ferry sinks into a sullen stillness.

Coughing up from Chester looms a gray oiler with consumption in its metal chest. It is headed for the Standard Oil Refinery at Alton. Now a wisp of smoke hangs over the Dake farmhouse. In the cooling shed the banging of milk cans covers hints of morning. Over Prairie du Rocher a cold glow issues. The wind falls. A golden spider pokes first his antennae, then his forelegs, and finally, with great effort, scrambles upon the prairie north of Peter's Creek.

A crow caws, circles twice, and glides to a dead carp upstream on the Missouri side. A fox squirrel chatters nervously for no apparent reason. Overhead a turkey buzzard wheels. A small red pickup truck speeds up the prairie from Novac. The driver races the engine impatiently as he waits for the ramp to be put in place. The wind brushes aside the web of golden haze and the sun spins high above the horizon. From a tree behind the Dake homestead a tardy rooster proclaims morning.

Description can be, of course, factual and still vivid. Note this description of the early military bases built in sixteenth century Spanish America:

. . . Each had four pointed bastions so that all flanks could be covered in the event of an attack; connecting the bastions were steep curtain walls topped with gunholes along an elevated platform. The bastions and stone curtains formed an open square, a central patio, which gave access to compartments with vaulted ceilings, and a ramp led to an elevated platform. The entire fortress was surrounded by a moat, and there was a drawbridge, approached through the barbican, the small outside fortification that guarded the bridge.

GUILLERMO DE ZÉNDEGUI, "The Oldest City in the United States," *Américas*, 16 (May, 1964), 12.

SUGGESTED TOPICS FOR THEMES

Description

The most beautiful spot I know
Colors in everyday life
Snowfall
Spring in the country
An impressive sight
Rural England (France, Belgium, etc.) as I saw it
Winter in _____
Across the United States by rail
A local building (interior or exterior)

A scene for a photographer
Night shift
What my study table looks like
The most horrible sight I ever saw
The main street of my home town (describing stores, people, landmarks, etc.)
A meal at a quick-lunch counter
Classroom atmosphere

A typical railway station

Getting a meal in a crowded restaurant

Sunday dinner (Family dinner)

Waiting for the 4:15

My room

The auto of the future

The ideal home, room

Our home

Current costumes

A mysterious sound

My mathematics class

Bargain day

Seven o'clock Saturday night at the Ice Rink (or Roller Rink)

Night on the streets of _____

Dancers

Home of a famous person

An old shop

My favorite haunt

A plan for a recreation room

An efficient kitchen

The state (county) fair

A favorite restaurant

An unusual custom in _____

Saturday night in _____

The Windy City

Sounds at night

Farm sale

In a strange land (real or imaginary)

A night in a Pullman berth

A great engineering (or other) project

Chicago night spots (any other city)

With pen and brush

A street scene

Interior of a business house (shoe repair shop, barbershop, music store)

Strolling down Michigan Boulevard (Maxwell Street, Fifth Avenue, Wilshire Boulevard, Main Street)

Setting of a novel or a play

The home town drugstore

A lonesome road

The well-dressed man or woman

Description of a foreign city

The most disreputable building I ever saw

My ideal date

The _____ music festival

An interesting holiday in _____

Cats

Thanksgiving kitchen (or table)

An athlete's view of the opposing team

Bus passengers at night

Beauty in solid geometry

Cheering section

Definition. Themes of definition are useful as explanations of abstract ideas or technical terms. Six methods of definition are available to you in writing such themes: (1) classification, (2) derivation, (3) synonym, (4) illustration, (5) elimination, (6) context.

Definition by classification is the basic method used by lexicographers. A formal definition consists of a term to be defined, the *genus*, or class, to which the term belongs, and the *differentia*, or characteristics peculiar to the term which distinguish it from other members of its class.

Term	Genus	Differentia
A definition	is a statement or explanation	of what a thing is or of what a word or phrase means
A triangle	is a geometrical plane figure	formed by three straight lines which meet two by two in three points, thus forming three angles
Photosynthesis	is a process of green plants	by which carbohydrates are formed from the carbon dioxide and water of the air under the influence of light

Definition by derivation uses the word history, or etymology of the word, to explain its meaning. For instance, "definition" is based on the word "define" that comes from the Latin infinitive-*definere*, formed from the prefix DE, meaning *from*, plus FINERE, *to set a limit to, bound,* from FINIS, meaning *boundary*. "Triangle" comes from the Latin and Greek TRI based on the Greek TRIES, meaning *three*, plus the Latin ANGULUS, meaning a *corner*, based on the Greek ANKYLOS, meaning *crooked* or *bent*. "Photosynthesis" comes from the Greek PHOTOS, meaning *light*, plus the Greek SYN, meaning *together*, and ITHENAI, meaning *to place*. The derivation of a word often throws more light on its meaning than classification alone can.

The method of definition by synonym defines a word by naming another word with the same meaning. The method can be simple to use, but you should remember its pitfalls. First, not all synonyms are exact substitutes for each other.

"Definition" and "explanation" or "definition" and "description" are inexact replacements. They substitute for each other but inexactly or inadequately. Second, not all terms or concepts have single word synonyms. "Triangle" and "photosynthesis," which have been defined here, at least in nontechnical English, have no synonyms. Third, you must carefully watch for tone or attitude in defining by synonym. Consider the examples which follow.

"Firm," "headstrong," and "bull-headed" are synonyms of the word "stubborn." But note the difference when you say, "I am firm; you are headstrong; he is bull-headed." The *denotation*, or direct meaning, of all three is "stubborn"; but the *connotation*, or associated or suggested meaning, of each is quite different. You will create entirely different impressions in the minds of your readers if you define a "diligent" student as a "painstaking" student or a "tedious" one.

A variation of definition by synonym is the method of definition by metaphor. The definitions of happiness in a well-known book for children were all metaphors. Definition by metaphor heightens the vividness of the explanation. Notice, first, the informative sentence:

Haiti is the second smallest of the American republics.

and then the metaphor:

Haiti is a giant pair of tongs between the Atlantic Ocean and the Caribbean Sea.

You will want to use definition by metaphor but only as a supplement to other methods. Its exclusive use has more place in creative than in expository writing.

Throughout this discussion of methods of definition, you have been seeing also the use of definition by illustration. As each method was defined, an example was included to help you understand the method.

Definition by elimination uses the simple technique of telling what a thing or idea is not before telling what it is.

This last device is known as definition by context, putting a new personality or idea in terms of familiar personalities or ideas. Hermann Hagedorn, early in this century, found himself trying to explain the unique quality of Theodore Roosevelt:

. . . He was not a second Washington. He was not a second Lincoln. He was not a second Andrew Jackson. He was not a second anybody. He was Theodore Roosevelt, himself, unique. There has never been anybody like him in the past. . . .

> HERMANN HAGEDORN, *The Boy's Life of Theodore Roosevelt.*

Hagedorn continued a bit later:

For he had something of the Prophet Ezekiel in him and something of Natty Bumppo, something of Hildebrand the warrior, something of Olaf the sea-king, something of Cromwell, something of Charlemagne. He belongs to the Heroic Line. . . .

A speech professor, trying to define what a good speech is, began by telling what a speech is not:

A speech is not an essay; a speech is not a summary; a speech is not a mere report; a speech is not a recitation; a good speech is not necessarily a successful speech; good speaking is not self-exploitation.

> WAYLAND MAXFIELD PARRISH, *Speaking in Public.*

Terms like "triangle" and "photosynthesis" can be precisely defined in a short space, since they belong to the exact sciences. Terms like "democracy," "courage," and "honor," however, are quite another matter. The informal definition of such words provides a test not only of your powers of logic but also of your sensitivity to nuances of meaning. The informal definition has as its basis the formal definition, which is usually placed at the beginning of the theme. The writer then proceeds with his definition, not in the coldly logical terms of the formal definition, but in terms that will appeal to and interest his reader.

A DEFINITION OF TOLERANCE

Since tolerance is an abstract term, it seems almost indefinable. Semantics cannot classify it as a physical act, a state of mind, or a way of living. There are probably as many definitions for the word as there are people who use it. Most people would agree with the dictionary's definition of tolerance as "bearing with a person or putting up with views differing from one's own." This definition is cold and unfeeling, but perhaps very descriptive of the common man's conception of tolerance. To most people, tolerance means merely to "tolerate," and not, as it should, to learn to love as well.

Currently, "tolerance" is in vogue in America. That is, it is discussed by the women's groups and bandied about in the businessmen's conversation. Some people are proud of the fact that they are tolerant; others are just as proud that they are not. But by far the greatest majority are the indifferent ones who think they are tolerant because, having heard a lecture on the subject, they seldom condemn a particular race or religion in public. These are the people who make the fight against intolerance an uphill struggle, because they are certain that as long as they are not actually intolerant, they are on the right track and need not be moved to serious thought about the problem. They do not understand that true tolerance is based on love and not on indifference.

The roots of tolerance go deeper than the realm of conscious thinking; they lie at the depths of feeling rather than reasoning. Tolerance is more than a movement to allow Negroes to be served in white barber shops; it is more than allowing little Johnny to play with the neighbor's children whose parents came from Poland; it is more than remembering to serve fish on Friday if the guests are Catholic. These are outward signs which come from conscious thought. True tolerance is the unaffected feeling of brotherhood which comes from the heart, that does not question the fact that the man is more important than his customs and his way of life.

Someone has said that in understanding there is no need for forgiveness. The meaning of understanding, in this case, could also apply to tolerance, for understanding is the basis for love and love of fellow man is the basis for true tolerance. If we understand why a man believes as he does and if we really love him, not for what he does, but for what he is, then we are tolerant.

60

A very effective means of definition is the use of comparison and contrast, as the writer does in the following theme defining and discriminating between wit and humor.

WIT AND HUMOR

The dictionary tells us that wit is derived from the Anglo-Saxon word of the same spelling. In its obsolete and archaic forms wit was used in the general sense to mean "activity of mind or intellectual power." Even if it is virtually out of use today this definition provides the base from which the word has expanded. When we say a person has lost his wits, we mean he has lost his power of mind, his reasoning, and his sense. A person in a sane condition is sometimes spoken of as having wits, meaning that he has a certain state of balance and soundness.

Another definition tells us that wit may mean practical good judgment and wisdom. Wit and wisdom are not related enough to merit wide acceptance of this definition. Wisdom is calm, composed, and sober; wit is quick, sharp, and laughable. Wisdom is the serene sea; wit is the gurgling mountain stream, plunging over a jagged waterfall.

The most popular definition of wit is "mental alertness, especially the capacity for humorous expression." This expression often takes the form of association between words and ideas distantly related so as to produce a comical effect. An unexpected turn is often the course of wit. Wit is helpless without ingenuity on the part of the receptor. Wit must be received swiftly without deep thought. Thought kills wit.

Finally, as a noun referring to the animate, the word means "anyone who is apt in the expression of felicitous ideas." The growth of wit has been by specialization from any intellectual power to a certain ability to arouse humor by the use of clever, sharp, and often bitter expressions.

The word "humor" is an exact duplication of the Latin noun *humor*, meaning a moisture or fluid. In old physiology, humor was a "fluid or juice, especially one of the four fluids—blood, lymph, yellow and black bile—conceived as determining a person's health and temperament." Therefore, to ancient eyes, humor was one's disposition, state of mind, or mood. Since the mind is in a state of constant flux and uncertainty, the word came to mean a "whim or fancy." To many men fancy suggests the absurd and ridiculous. A fanciful person has one root on earth and the other dangling in space; hence he may seem humorous to the realist. Humor may signify a certain instability that is to be pitied. A fanciful person often can be intolerable. The most popular definition of humor today is "a quality that appeals to the sense of the ludicrous or absurdly incongruous." In other words, humor is laughable and amusing, but often ridiculous.

Wit and humor have several common usages. Both are expressions of a mental faculty. Both arouse sharp interest. Both provoke amusement. At this point the connotations tend to differ. There are suggestions in the pronunciations of the words. The pronunciation of wit is sharp and unhesitant like the thrust of a dagger. The pronunciation of humor is more prolonged and drawn out like the effects of sweet wine.

Wit suggests swiftness; humor suggests a laughable steadiness. Wit is the flight of the swallow, humor that of a crow. Wit is the language of the jester while humor is the expression of the clown. Wit runs; humor walks.

Humor implies human kindness and sympathy. Wit has the suggestion of bitterness and disregard for the feelings. Wit is a purely mental product, free from love, generosity, and warmth. Wit is a sudden flash; humor, a steady glow. Love is the only thing that separates wit from humor. Without love, wit and humor would be indistinguishable.

SUGGESTED TOPICS FOR THEMES

Definition

What is a man of integrity?	Blasphemy
The real meaning of democracy	The common man
Free enterprise	Sincerity
Russian communism	The American way
Loyalty	Sophistication
Charity	College and university
Heresy as a virtue	Education and literacy
The maternal instinct	Friend and acquaintance
Neurosis	Conservative
Patriotism	Reactionary
Socialism	Liberal
Grace	Radical
Brotherhood	Entertainment and recreation
Love and infatuation	

Expository Process. The simplest form of expository writing is the process theme. Such a theme tells how something is made or how something works. The arrangement of the parts of the theme is of necessity chronological. In order to be clear, the writer must indicate the individual steps of the process in their proper time sequence.

This is not to say that the process theme is easy to write. Anyone who has tried to follow a faulty set of directions in constructing a toy or operating a machine will realize the importance of careful planning and regard for clarity in writing of this kind. The following theme, explaining a rather complicated process, is clear enough to form a basis for a diagram.

THE FRASCH PROCESS

Throughout the nineteenth century the United States was forced to import a large quantity of sulfur. Ample deposits existed in the southern part of this country, but they were deep under the earth's surface, many of them underlying quicksand and swamps. In 1890 Herman Frasch, an American inventor, secured a patent on a process to obtain sulfur from these previously inaccessible deposits. This process, known by its inventor's name, has been considered a great step toward economic independence for our country.

To institute the Frasch process, a hole, eight to ten inches in diameter, is drilled down to a layer of solid rock directly above and within a foot or two of the sulfur deposits. (These deposits are usually 500 to 2,000 feet below the earth's surface.) A steel pipe with a diameter slightly less than the diameter of the hole is fitted with an insulation jacket. It is then inserted to the depth of the hole and secured in place. A drill bit, smaller in diameter than the pipe just installed, is used to extend the depth of the hole through the rock and into the sulfur deposit. Two concentric pipes are placed in this large pipe and extended down into the sulfur bed. When these three concentric pipes are secured in place, the surface ends of the pipes are connected to the proper sources and outlets. These outlets are equipped with checks and valves to regulate properly the flow of materials.

The smallest of the three pipes is connected to a supply of compressed air. The largest pipe is connected to a supply of water that has been heated under pressure to 165° centigrade temperature. The medium-sized pipe is vented into large open vats on the earth's surface.

The super-heated water traveling down the large pipe melts the sulfur. The compressed air from the small pipe forces the liquid sulfur through the vented medium-sized pipe into the open vats. The liquid sulfur cools in these vats to solid sulfur which is 99.5 to 99.9% pure.

The Frasch process has proven to be most successful in the past fifty years. Owing to its efficiency the United States produces not only a sufficient supply of sulfur for her own needs, but also 90% of the total world supply.

The process theme is not limited to technical subjects, as the following theme will illustrate.

HOW TO HUNT SQUIRRELS

Squirrel hunting is a sport long enjoyed by the American public. In the early days of our country, the squirrel was an important food commodity, but, due to the decrease in numbers, it is today only a small game animal. Some sportsmen shun this little "tree rat" because, as the saying goes, "Anybody can hit a squirrel." However, squirrel hunting is different from most sports in that the thrill is not in the shooting, but in the hunting. Although I am not an authority on the subject, I will try to present some of the aspects of a typical squirrel hunt.

The first steps taken toward any hunt are those of preparation. Because most squirrel hunting is done during the early hours of morning, all preparation must be taken care of in the evening. A good hunter travels light, but he must have two things: a proper outfit and a good gun. These articles should be laid out during the evening so that the morning will go like clockwork.

A squirrel hunting outfit consists of four parts: the suit, the shoes, the hat, and the coat or vest. The suit should be either green or brown. A mixture of the two is even better. It is better if the colors are dull, because dull colors seem to melt into the underbrush. A fine outfit can be made from an army fatigue uniform, the older the better. The shoes should have thin, rubber soles. An old pair of tennis shoes will do the trick. Many good hunters use no shoes at all, however. Wearing a hat is optional.

However, if a person has very light or very dark hair, it is to his advantage to wear a hat. A coat or vest, containing a game pocket, a knife, matches, and extra shells round out the personal equipment, leaving only the gun to be selected.

The gun varies according to personal likes and dislikes. However, most successful hunters use either a 12-gauge shotgun with a heavy load, or a .22 cal. repeating rifle. The reason for this is that a squirrel, high in a tree, can absorb a large amount of shot and still remain in the tree. The 12-gauge has enough penetration to kill the squirrel instantly if the shot is well placed. The better shots use a rifle because a ball between the eyes draws little comment from the squirrel and, at the same time, leaves the meat intact. Now that the gun and outfit have been laid out, the hunter is ready to go. He sets the alarm for 4:30 and goes to bed.

At 4:30 A.M. the hunter awakens with a start. He goes to the window and peers out. It's a perfect day! Not a breath of air is stirring. The hunter's natural impulse is to dress quickly, grab his gun, and hurry to the hunting woods. But, one of the most important preparations for a hunt is a good breakfast. The hunter who skips breakfast is often annoyed by upset stomach and stomach cramps during the excitement of the hunt.

When the breakfast is finished the hunter makes a final check of equipment and then climbs into his car, unless he is fortunate enough to have a woods nearby. By the time the hunter reaches the woods it is about 5:00 o'clock. As soon as he enters the woods, he is all ears. The most common way to locate a squirrel is by the sound of the nut hulls hitting the ground while a squirrel is feeding, or, as it is commonly termed, "cutting." When a hunter hears a squirrel cutting, he must then determine what type it is. There are only two types of game squirrels, and the cuttings of the two are distinctly different. The "fox" or "red" squirrel's cuttings are rather large, and are dropped in evenly spaced intervals, while a "gray" squirrel's cuttings are pin-point small and fall with great rapidity, sounding much like the light patter of rain. It is imperative that the hunter determine the variety, because the two are hunted in entirely different ways.

After a hunter has classified a squirrel, his next step is to locate it. This is rather easily accomplished on a still morning, because a squirrel generally makes quite a commotion while feeding, and the shaking trees can be seen for some distance. However, it is at this point that the inexperienced hunter loses his squirrel. Although he marks the top of the tree well, he fails to follow it down to the trunk. When he moves off a few steps, the squirrel stops feeding, and all the tree tops look the same. It is then almost impossible to relocate the squirrel.

Now that the squirrel has been typed and located, the actual stalking begins. If the animal is a "gray," the process is painstaking. The hunter must take his eyes off the squirrel and concentrate on making absolutely no noise at all. Should the "gray" hear an unusual sound, he will react in one of two ways, both of which are very effective. He may scamper up the tree to a large branch and "sit it out," or he may try running through the tree tops. Few indeed are the hunters who have "outsat" a "gray," and fewer still are those who have won the race to the den tree. However, if the hunter is very careful, he can get within twenty-five yards of a feeding "gray" without being seen or heard. This done, the game is over. When dealing with fox squirrels, however, it is a different matter.

To begin with, the fox squirrel has been named thus because of his color, not because of his brains. As a matter of fact, he seems to be somewhat dull. This trait makes him an easier animal to hunt than the "gray." When a "fox" has been typed and located, he must be stalked much like a "gray" up to a certain point. Then the change is great. The hunter sneaks to within thirty-five yards of the squirrel. Then, exposing himself completely, the hunter runs the next twenty yards as fast as he can. For some reason this action seems to frustrate the "fox," and he generally freezes, thus making the shot a simple one. However, if the "fox" should decide to sit it out, it is a good idea to sit with him, because, unlike the "gray," the "fox" will show himself after about ten minutes of quietness.

Each time a shot is fired the above steps are re-enacted until the limit of five squirrels is reached. But I must add in closing that squirrels are unpredictable and often the conventional method will not work. A true understanding of squirrel hunting may not be gained by reading alone. It is not often that an inexperienced person can tack five tails to the barn door after a morning in the woods.

SUGGESTED TOPICS FOR THEMES

Processes

How to care for a cat (or any animal)

How to train a dog in obedience

How to track a wild animal
How to develop self-control
How to prepare my favorite dish
How to cure a cold
How to take good snapshots
How to use make-up
How to prepare for an examination
How to take notes
How to get a job
How to enjoy exam week
How to plan a meal
How to criticize music
How to avoid air tragedies
How to make an ice cream soda
How to cure insomnia
How to keep friends
How to buy a used car
How I read a newspaper
How I balance my budget
How our club is financed
How to get along with a brother (or sister)
How to develop film
How to water ski
How to make coffee
How to spend your time profitably while standing in line
How a camera takes pictures
How to stock shelves in a grocery store
How to clean a rifle
How to be nonchalant when embarrassed
How to hunt with a camera
How to study systematically
How to overhaul an engine

How seeds scatter
How to show cattle
How to enjoy music
How to loaf intelligently
How a band moves into a formation
How to plan a garden
How to leave a party
How to dress a baby
How to paper a room
How to operate a switchboard
How to grow tomatoes (or any vegetable, grain, or flower)
How to administer artificial respiration
How to make tea
How (not) to prepare for a journey
How to caddy
How to make cheese
How to prepare ground for planting
The serve in tennis
How to make a Japanese flower arrangement
In case of fire _____
The best scheme I ever heard of to make money
Making something out of nothing
Making a hobby profitable
Making social organizations successful
Miracles nature never thought of
Planning a small farm
A good floor plan

Expository Analysis. Expository themes of a more complex nature—those concerned with ideas, opinion, organizations, and massive detail—demand a different kind of treatment from that of the process. The verb "analyze" means to separate the parts of a whole so as to reveal their relation to it and to one another. Thus a writer taking as his subject professional baseball in the United States would probably make a preliminary distinction between the major and minor leagues, discuss the subordinate divisions within each of the two major divisions, and show the relationships of all these divisions to each other. Or a theme having to do with a novel, such as a book review, might discuss the plot, the characterization, and the style, and show how these combine for a good or bad effect.

The methods of expository analysis are numerous and varied, but the principle of all these methods is a logical division and classification of subject matter. In the following theme, the writer has taken the general subject "caves" and has used as the basis for his logical divisions the causes of caves.

ESCAPE FROM REALITY

One of the most beautiful sights in the world is the reflection of light in a subterranean cavern. The crystalline minerals are prismatic and reflect ordinary light rays as a myriad of colors—tints and shades of red, white, blue, yellow, and all their tones. The awesome play of light in a cave is accompanied by the rhythmic sound of dripping water as it sculptures and creates weird mineral formations. The echoes of this endless sound create an eerie harmony that, despite its weirdness, pervades the soul with an inexplicable peacefulness. One frequently finds, after visiting a cave, that he asks himself, "Just what is a cave? What has caused such strange beauty and harmony?"

The tremendous force exerted by such natural agencies as air, water, and volcanic action has carved interesting chambers in the earth's crust. These chambers are called caves; they can be divided into several groups according to their method of formation—those formed by the action of water, those formed by the action of air, and those formed by the action of volcanoes or similar subterranean forces.

The solvent action of water has created the greatest number of caves. The continual friction of water in underground streams has resulted in the formation of huge, subterranean grottos in the solid rock. Caves often occur in limestone, since, of the more common rocks, limestone is most easily dissolved in ground water containing carbon dioxide. The Mammoth Cave of Kentucky, the Luray Caverns of Virginia, and the Matlock Grotto of Derbyshire are famous examples of this type of cave. Lining the walls of these caverns is a calcareous incrustation which reflects light in such a manner as to give the caves a strange, lustrous beauty. Apparently supporting the vaulted ceiling are pillars of stone called stalactites and stalagmites, peculiar growths of minerals which are deposited by water as it seeps through the top of the cave.

Oceans play a great part in the erosion of stone and the formation of caves. One can find numerous sea caves on almost any rocky coast line. These tunnels into the earth slant upward and are the result of the undermining of the cliffs by the grinding action of ocean water with its load of grit and sand. As huge ocean waves smash into the mouths of sea caves, air is compressed and driven into every fissure and crack in the cavern. Upon the sudden withdrawal of the pressure as the water runs out, the air expands, aiding the growth of the cave by ripping loose showers of fragments. Many sea caves continue to increase in depth until they emerge at the surface, forming "blow-holes" or "spouting horns" which send up white puffs of spray with every incoming wave during a storm.

In inland cliffs which are composed of alternate layers of hard and soft stone, the softer layers of stone are more easily eroded by the wind and by changes in temperature than are the harder layers. Eventually the wearing down of the softer layers results in the formation of shallow caves.

Large lava caves are to be found in Iceland and in the Hawaiian Islands. These caves, characteristic of volcanic regions, are formed as a result of the escape of molten stone from the lava flows, after the formation of a hard crust. Huge vacant areas beneath the earth's surface are formed when the upheaval caused by a volcano disrupts the strata there.

In the dawn of civilization, primitive man found shelter from the inclement world by inhabiting caves. He must have been awed by the strange beauty whch the light of his fires enabled him to see. With the aid of a good light, man can still escape the trials and frustrations of life (if only briefly) by stepping into a cave and letting his natural curiosity and appreciation of beauty inspire his thoughts.

The following is a historical analysis of the human tendency toward idealization as it manifests itself in hero worship.

AN ANALYSIS OF HERO WORSHIP:
ANCIENT TIMES AND TODAY

Hero worship is as old as man himself. This ancient trait of man developed along the same lines as did mythology and the primitive religions. Early man had little knowledge of the world and its forces, and what he did not understand he attributed to a supernatural being. At first these supernatural beings were spirits of nature, such as the "sun god" or the "god of rain." But man soon transferred his superstitions to forms which were more familiar and easier to understand. These new gods fashioned by the primitive mind of man were in the likeness of his own race, with characteristic appearances and habits. This worship of humanized gods is known as anthropomorphism. The anthropomorphic gods of early civilizations, the Greeks, the Romans, the Germans, the Vikings, and the Chinese, all had human characters and personalities along with their inhuman powers. They also had human frailties, such as vanity, greed, lust, and debauchery. Since man was now dealing with a force that was at least part human, he felt more secure. Also his life was made more interesting and colorful than ever before. Man's knowledge, however, was still insufficient to satisfy his curiosity, and his imagination created myths and fables that suited the personalities and powers of the gods.

These myths grew as they were passed on from generation to generation. And to satisfy his own vanity, man humanized the spirits he worshiped to an even greater extent until he found himself not only worshiping gods, but also men. Many of the hero-myths which existed were allegorical or merely fictitious, but for the most part the myths and tales of the deeds and activities of the ancient heroes could be traced back to a living man or woman of another age or era, who for some reason acquired sufficient public interest to be remembered and talked about.

As the stories concerning these so-called "heroes" were passed on from parent to child, they were enlarged and exaggerated until in some cases the hero was worshiped in the same manner as were the gods of that period. An illustration of this development of hero-myths and hero worship is the fable of the Greek hero, Heracles. Historians have proved that there was a Heracles who was king of the province of Tyrus before the time of the great King Agamemnon of Greece. He was a petty king of an extremely small state, but he did much good, performed miraculous deeds in the face of overwhelming difficulties, and thus made a name for himself. The story of the deeds of this minor king was not forgotten. It was told again and again, each time with an added touch to make it more exciting, more adventurous, more courageous, until finally the myths included the story of his being invited by Zeus and gods to Mount Olympus to reign with them as one of the gods. This hero, then, was literally worshiped thereafter, and made immortal in the minds of men. When Alexander the Great of Macedonia and the Romans took over the control of the known world, they adopted Heracles and the other Greek gods and heroes and spread the Greek culture, religion, and art throughout their empires in the process of Hellenizing the world. Heracles, or the Roman Hercules, has been illustrated in art and sculpture more than any other classical subject.

Although we may not worship our heroes and gods to the extent that the ancients did, how different are the deeds of the typical Greek god Perseus, who chopped off the head of the Medusa with his magic sword, from those of King Arthur "of the round table," who drove off dragons with his famous Excalibur? Today, as in ancient times, we worship our generals and combat heroes for their deeds of valor because most of us lack the character of courage ourselves. To believe in such myths or to worship the heroes of our own day is a normal psychological pattern of visualizing oneself in the place of the hero concerned. Although this unconscious mental process of escape or transference may not be very realistic or practical, it can be a satisfying and enjoyable emotional outlet; and from it has come some of our best and most famous works of art and literature.

SUGGESTED TOPICS FOR THEMES

Expository Analysis

A foreign custom we should borrow

The speed of twentieth century travel

Outmoded traffic laws

The best sport to watch

Advice to incoming freshmen

Roadside advertising

TV commercials

Local recreational facilities

71

A current reform in education
The case for early marriage
Comic books
Collegiate athletics
Professional football
Homesickness
Conversation
The South in fiction
Causes of racial prejudice
Varieties of patriotism
The honor system
Values of a college education
Sport spectacles
Loan agencies
Bull sessions
Three types of conversation
Science and war
The role of minority groups in America
Student politics
Holidays
College social customs
Sports for women
Mass entertainment media
Rural schools
Types of English
Levels of English usage
Bad habits and how to enjoy them
Cocktail parties
Urban living
Examinations
The intellectual elite
The beat generation
Electronic music
Recent fashions in clothes
Youthful lawlessness
The space age and the college generation
Grading systems
I would (wouldn't) worry

As you select your topic, notice that the wording is of just that—a topic, not a title. Remember to narrow the topic to your own capacity for the subject, and let the title reflect your singular emphasis.

Themes for Analysis

The following themes represent types commonly written in basic composition courses. Read them carefully and be prepared to discuss them in terms of what you have learned in the preceding chapter concerning the writing of themes. Questions are provided with each theme to aid you in your analyses.

Exercise 1

THE BULLFIGHT

(1) The arena is filled to capacity by the tumultuous crowd. Upon a given signal, however, the band strikes a chord, and si-

lence descends over the multitude. The bullfight is about to begin. Once more the drama of life versus death is to be enacted before an avid audience.

(2) Two massive doors at the edge of the arena open, and the parade procession appears. The constable of the event, mounted on a prancing steed, leads this procession; while directly behind him, on foot, follow the matadors, picadors, and banderillos that comprise the cast in this barbaric drama. Attired in costumes of heavy metallic brocades and brilliant silks, they walk slowly across the sand, an excellent illustration of the pomp and pageantry that is identified with bullfighting. Soft kid slippers, similar to those of a ballet dancer, serve as shoes and thus aid the toreros to attain the gracefulness and agility that are so important in the arena. The small black cap cocked on the torero's head gives a jaunty air to this man who goes forth to meet Death's emissary.

(3) The procession advances to the box of the president of the bullfight, the constable secures permission to begin the event, and the procession disappears once more behind the doors, accompanied by the strains of the primitive music. The silence is ominous.

(4) Then the bull, Death's champion, charges into the arena. He is a fierce beast of magnificent stature, and his eager horns and savage hoofs match his anger.

(5) The picador, the bull's first opponent, rides into the arena, mounted on a heavily padded horse and bearing a long lance. He attempts to maneuver the bull into such a position as to use his lance to lacerate its neck. His task accomplished, he retires from the arena, frequently minus his mount.

(6) The maddened bull is then faced by another opponent— the banderillo, who is on foot. This man's sole protection consists of the two long, barbed darts he holds in either hand, which he must plunge into the bull's neck. The banderillo's survival depends entirely upon his agility. As the angered bull charges him, the banderillo jumps aside at the last possible moment and thrusts the barbs deep into the bull as it thunders by. He performs this daring feat twice.

(7) The matador himself is next on the scene. Immaculately attired, he carries a pink cape with which to torment the bull. The bull charges viciously at the cape and the man, only to be confronted by empty space as the man steps gracefully aside. The matador displays his perfected turns and *veronicas* to the

applause of the crowd, the ovation increasing to match his daring. This contest nears its climax as the matador exchanges his pink cape for one the color of blood, thus signaling the audience of his intention to kill the bull. He carries a sword beneath the cape and proceeds to entice the bull into charging him. As the bull races past, the matador thrusts his sword to the hilt into the bull's neck, attempting to strike the heart. If his thrust is perfect, the sword will pierce the bull's heart and kill him instantly. If not, the matador must try again.

(8) The matador is not always the victor, but death is seldom cheated as man and beast vie for superiority.

(9) The bullfight, with its primitive savagery, pomp and splendor, background color, and dangerous atmosphere, repels some, fascinates many more. But it is never met with indifference.

Points for Discussion

1. What is the basis of organization in the above theme on "The Bullfight"? If you were outlining the theme, how many major divisions would your outline contain?
2. How would you judge the introduction? Does it give the central idea for the entire theme? Explain.
3. List five transitional words or phrases that serve as connectives between the major divisions of the theme.
4. You will note that paragraphs 4, 8, and 9 are very short. Should these paragraphs be more fully developed? Explain.
5. "The Bullfight" is a process theme, a type usually assigned early in the composition course. The defect in many process themes is that they tend to be dull and monotonous. Is this true of "The Bullfight"? Defend your answer.

Exercise 2

DIRTY BILL

(1) When I was a child we had a very wonderful man to tend our yard and furnace. His name was Bill Scooey, and he was the dirtiest man I've ever seen; he looked dirty and he talked dirty. Like most of the children in the neighborhood I was forbidden to "go within a mile of that dreadful man." Therefore, I spent most of my time with him, following him around the neighborhood as he did odd jobs at the various houses. I was not alone, for all the children followed Dirty Bill.

(2) One of the reasons for his excessive filth was that he had

no home; he owned an old car in which he kept his tools and personal belongings. In the winter he slept in the car; in the summer he slept next to the car. When he was drunk he would sleep on one of our porches, and there would be great excitement when two or three of the neighbor men came over to assist Bill back to his compact little home.

(3) As far as I was concerned, Dirty Bill led an ideal life. He ate what he pleased, said what he pleased to whom he pleased, had no obligations, inhibitions, or confinements, and he followed a minimum of rules. Furthermore he was a magnificent liar, which made his stories far more juicy than tame old fantasies. He did not believe in Santa Claus, but he was superstitious in the extreme and could describe in vivid detail less pleasant supernatural creatures and their activities. He constructed wonderfully obscene statements for us to make to our teachers and parents, and taught us great contempt for authority.

(4) Once, when our basement was flooding and Bill had been hastily summoned, he provoked the wrath of the gods and my family by childishly splashing around in the rising water and encouraging us to do the same before he fixed the leak. As he so aptly put it, this was the closest most of us would ever come to owning a private pool, and we should enjoy unexpected pleasures. But after the leakage was stopped and the surface drained, Bill was forgiven, for he was the only handy man in the neighborhood and therefore quite valuable.

(5) Through a period of perhaps twelve years, or until I was in my teens, Bill's tales, escapades, and battles with and against authority were interwoven with my life. The year that I entered high school we lost him. It was in the early fall, and Bill was in great demand for leaf-raking, fall bulb-planting, and storm-window repairing. It was unfortunate that he chose that time to go on a binge, but Bill was not a practical person, and he did not consider such things. For a week he reeled, lurched, and staggered about, ignoring the pleas and threats of the local homeowners. Toward the end of his week-long orgy he curled up on Doctor Allen's front porch for a nap, choosing, with his usual lack of consideration, the night of a party. The Allens apparently did not notice him until the first guests tripped over his sooty form, and there followed quite an uproar. Mrs. Allen insisted that she was disgraced, Dr. Allen was unable to arouse him, and in the confusion their better judgment was put aside, and they called the police to remove him.

(6) We have never been too sure what happened from then on. I do know that my father and Mr. Mills went down to the jail the next night, and Bill was released. Someone said they saw him when he climbed into his car and drove off. But his moving was as simple as his mode of living, and it all happened inside an hour. And we never heard of him again. Still, we children paid a fittting tribute to Bill. We wrote everything that he had taught us on the Allens' sidewalk, and in a way it was a memorial.

Points for Discussion

1. Criticize the introduction of the theme, "Dirty Bill." Does it attract the reader's attention? Does it give the keynote for the entire theme?
2. What is the basis of organization? Relate the organization to the central idea.
3. Point out the transitional devices used in the theme.
4. Is the conclusion effective? Give specific reasons for your answer.
5. "Dirty Bill" was written in response to a common assignment in the composition course—the character sketch. Most instructors would give the theme a grade of A or B. What is the principal reason for the theme's excellence?

Exercise 3

THE GAS TURBINE IN THE AUTOMOBILE

(1) Several months ago on a lonely stretch of highway near London a significant event took place which will do much to influence the evolution of the automobile. As the early morning fog began to lift, a group of engineers could be seen readying a small British automobile for its first test run. The general design of the car was entirely conventional.

(2) But as the machine was started and began to move down the highway, an unnatural silence prevailed. There was no roar of exhaust. Although the car was accelerating very rapidly, only a soft hissing sound could be heard. Even at high speeds the noise was barely noticeable.

(3) Upon reaching top speed, the driver signaled to the timer, who clocked the car's speed over a measured mile. After reading the instruments, the timer eagerly rushed to the engineers to give them the results. On this, the initial run of the world's first gas

turbine powered car, a speed of 152 miles per hour had been reached.

(4) To the reader who is acquainted with high performance automobiles, this speed would not seem out of the ordinary if it were not for the following facts: the fuel used was ordinary, cheap kerosene; the engine consisted of only two hundred parts. It contained no transmission or cooling system, and the complete power unit itself weighed just a little more than three hundred pounds. In contrast, a gasoline engine of comparable performance would weigh at least five times that much. It would need a transmission and cooling system and would incorporate about twelve hundred parts. If one compares the cost of assembling and operating these two types of power plants, he can easily see the many advantages that the gas turbine has over the gasoline engine.

(5) The gas turbine has solved two of the fundamental problems of efficient engine design. These problems—weight and reliability—have done much to limit the use of other types of engines. Weight is a natural disadvantage if the engine is to be used in transportation, since much of the engine's output is wasted in moving the engine itself. Reliability is a major problem because the greater the number of parts in an engine, the greater the chances of failure. Unlike other engines, the gas turbine has a minimum of parts, and its basic structure is made up of very light components.

(6) The development of the gas turbine is in its infancy. Still, considerable progress has been made, and the tremendous possibilities of this unit have been recognized by many industries. These industries are spending much money on research in the gas turbine engine and are confident that upon its perfection it will provide the solution to many power problems. There is little doubt that in time the gas turbine will completely replace the gasoline engine in the automobile and will find widespread use in many other types of transportation.

Points for Discussion

1. Divide this theme into three parts: introduction, body and conclusion. Is there a disproportion in the length of the parts? If so, is this disproportion a fault in the theme?
2. How does the introduction in this theme differ from that of "The Bullfight"? Can you explain the difference in terms of the different purposes of the two themes?

3. What is the basis of organization of "The Gas Turbine in the Automobile"? Why is this organization especially suited to this subject?
4. Point out at least five transitional devices in the theme.
5. What grade would you assign this theme? Would you take into consideration the nature of the subject in assigning the grade?

Exercise 4

THE WRITER AS A CRAFTSMAN

(1) The writer and the craftsman are fundamentally alike. They both must begin with a simple idea, perhaps a passing thought, a strong feeling, or sometimes an inspiration. They then develop this idea by analyzing it and proceed to work on their chosen project. This they "polish" until it is truly an expression of themselves. They have taken an idea and expressed it in terms of themselves; they have created.

(2) To do their work, both writer and craftsman must have an adequate background. The fine carpenter cannot begin aimlessly to build a desk; he must first have some idea of its size, design, and particular use. This idea will result from an awareness of structural design which the carpenter has developed by studying other examples of his craft, and often just nature itself. In a similar manner, the writer cannot begin aimlessly to write even a theme; he must first develop an idea. This idea can come only from an active mind which is constantly perceptive of the activities about it. Whether one is a carpenter, a composer, a writer, or a painter, all work is the result of thought.

(3) In addition to this adequate background, the writer and carpenter must have proper tools, and these tools must be kept in good condition. Just as the craftsman cares for his saw, hammer, and chisel, and views them with pride, so too must the writer establish and value his tools. He soon acquires a knowledge of grammar, punctuation, and spelling, and is constantly building up his vocabulary. With these, his basic tools, the writer can proceed to develop an individual style in which he can better express to others his own feelings. Faulty tools will always result in faulty craftsmanship.

(4) Once equipped with tools and an idea, the carpenter plans his project according to its purpose. The size and style of a

desk will be directly dependent upon whether it will be used in a doctor's office, the President's den, or a child's playroom. So too must the writer base his plan of development upon the purpose of his idea. Whether his writing is to be technically informative, as in a scientific report, or persuasive, as in a campaign speech, the writer must always keep his reader in mind. No matter how well a theme is written, it will have lost its purpose if it is not well suited for the person for whom it is intended, the reader.

(5) After the project has been planned and executed, there results a rough product, which must then be "polished." The carpenter must sand his desk until it is perfectly smooth, but he must also be careful not to sand his delicate design work too much lest its vividness be lost. In a similar manner the writer must revise his first draft and sometimes revise it again. Precaution must be taken against too much revising, however, or else the theme will no longer be lively and appealing but will be just accurate and dull. Perhaps a few "rough edges" would even be more interesting.

(6) Finally the writer and carpenter as craftsmen share the same feeling about their finished products. All people enjoy a feeling of satisfaction after a job well done, but craftsmen are doing more than just working—they are creating; theirs is a feeling of pride.

Points for Discussion

1. Point out the major divisions in this theme. Do they seem to you artificial or do they seem logical and natural?
2. What is the basis of organization? Could a theme of this nature be organized in any other way? Explain.
3. The author of this theme uses an "analogy" to make clearer the nature of writing—that is, she compares writing to carpentry. Is the analogy a good one? Does the author maintain it logically and consistently?
4. Point out at least five transitional devices.
5. Of the four themes presented here, which seems to you the best? Which one would you consider the most difficult to write?

3.

Basic
Grammatical Errors

Good writing is always a completely positive activity. As we indicated in Chapter 2, the main concern of the writer is to communicate his ideas to his reader. You should never think of your writing in the composition course as an exercise in avoiding grammatical errors. But the writer who violates the conventions of English grammar will at the very least distract the reader from the idea that the writer is attempting to communicate; in many instances grammatical errors will lead to confusion and misapprehension. Through experience college instructors have found that four grammatical errors most frequently and seriously mar the student's writing, especially in the beginning weeks of the course. These errors are:

1. the sentence fragment,
2. the comma splice and run-together sentences,
3. nonagreement of subject and verb, and
4. nonagreement of pronoun and antecedent.

Though a review of grammar will come in later sections of this book, this chapter is provided to enable you to avoid the serious grammatical errors you might make in the themes you will write immediately.

The Sentence Fragment

Instructors in English generally consider the unintentional sentence fragment the most serious of all grammatical errors, since the student who writes fragments as complete sentences indicates that he is unable to recognize a sentence, a basic unit of expression in our written language. In oral language, especially in conversation, people use partial or elliptical, sentences and are easily understood. For instance, most answers to questions are fragments: "Where are you going?" "Home." The inflection of the voice establishes a sense of completeness.

But written language demands complete sentences. A sentence is defined as a word or group of words that can stand alone in formal writing. The standard sentence in written English contains a subject, expressed or implied, and a verb:

subj.   v.
Men WILL TALK of this day forever.

v.
GIVE him his due.   (subject *you* implied)

v.
RUN!   (subject *you* implied)

Although fragmentary sentences occur in many forms in student writing, by far the most frequent are the dependent clause, the verbal phrase, and the terminal parenthetical element used as complete sentences.

1. Dependent Clause as a Sentence   The fact that a group of words contains a subject and verb does not necessarily mean that the construction is a complete sentence:

INCORRECT: The procedure is essentially correct. *Although I can't say I approve of the final result.*

81

INCORRECT: He asked my forgiveness. *Since he knew it was now in my power to retaliate*

The italicized constructions are dependent clauses (see page 173) used as complete sentences, and are therefore fragments. All that is needed to correct these fragments is a comma in place of the period and a small letter in place of the capital.

IMPROVED: The procedure is essentially correct, although I can't say I approve of the final result.

IMPROVED: He asked my forgiveness, since he knew it was now in my power to retaliate.

Note that each of these dependent clauses begins with a subordinating conjunction. You will find a list of the more commonly used of these conjunctions on page 157. No clause beginning with a subordinating conjunction can stand alone as a sentence.

2. Verbal Phrase as a Sentence   A verbal (see G-29–G-31) cannot be used as the verb of a sentence. A verbal phrase, therefore, cannot stand alone as a sentence.

INCORRECT: I was disappointed when the circus failed to arrive. *That being my only reason for coming to town.*

INCORRECT: My greatest desire has been a fairly simple one. *To live close to the sea within sound of the waves.*

INCORRECT: He attended to the injured civilian as soon as he could. *His blood running cold at the extent of the man's injuries.*

Again these fragments can be corrected in each case by simply integrating them with the preceding sentence:

IMPROVED: I was disappointed when the circus failed to arrive, that being my only reason for coming to town.

IMPROVED: My greatest desire has been a fairly simple one: to live close to the sea within sound of the waves.

IMPROVED: He attended to the injured civilian as soon as he could, his blood running cold at the extent of the man's injuries.

3. Terminal Parenthetical Element as a Sentence The inexperienced writer frequently breaks off terminal parenthetical phrases and clauses and punctuates them as sentences.

INCORRECT: This weapon might well save your life some day. *Especially if you learn to use it effectively.*

INCORRECT: He despised all things that most people consider of great value. *Such as ease, luxury, and social prestige.*

These constructions may be corrected as follows:

IMPROVED: This weapon might well save your life some day—especially if you learn to use it effectively.

IMPROVED: He despised all things that most people consider of great value, such as ease, luxury, and social prestige.

Although these three types of sentence fragments cover the great majority of such errors committed, you should check your themes with extreme care to see that they contain no fragmentary constructions of any type. It is true that the fragment or "broken" sentence is used frequently by some professional writers with good effect. Until you are certain of your competence and skill, however, it is better that you restrict yourself to the standard written sentence, which, if used properly, has a capacity for effect that can satisfy the most discriminating critic.

Exercise 1

Designate each construction as complete or as fragmentary. Be able to correct each fragmentary sentence and be prepared to explain the kind of sentence error represented.

1. All thinking men knew that this man was persecuted without cause.
2. I could scarcely believe my eyes. Being so sure that he would never return to this little village.
3. Although if one really exerted himself, he would be surprised at how much he could accomplish.
4. As he brushed his teeth, Arnold wondered if the day would hold romance. Or would it be like all the others?
5. We have often been told that courage is not a fixed star. That it varies from hour to hour and day to day.
6. Bouncing down the stairs, skidding through the hall, slamming out the door, energy personified, but without direction or coordination.
7. Let this be our creed. Never to underestimate our enemies, never to overestimate our friends.
8. Until he found out that persistence is the most important element in success and humiliation the least important element in failure.
9. History is filled with accounts of such people. Men who were able to rise above unfavorable beginnings to high success.
10. Good writing consists of imagination and discipline. The latter being fully as important as the former.
11. The jury's conviction broke the prisoner's heart. Because he thought the end of his world had come.
12. Haiti's export products are raised on small farms. Chiefly sugar, cacao, and coffee.
13. He continued to fall asleep in class. Probably because he had unloaded groceries during the night on his part-time job.
14. She finally enrolled as a sociology major. Which she had wanted to do all the time.
15. He registered at the university before the deadline. Though he had not received the scholarship he had applied for.

The Comma Splice and Run-Together Sentences

Another error that English instructors watch for carefully is inadequate punctuation between sentences. This error again indicates that the writer is lacking in what might be called "sentence sense"; consequently, the *comma splice* and *run-together sentences* are errors that you should be able to recognize and avoid.

4. The Comma Splice   The comma splice is the inadequate separation of two independent clauses by only a comma (see page 177 for classification of sentences). The independent clauses in such sentences may be separated in two ways:

1. By a comma *plus* a coordinating conjunction (*and, but, for, nor, or, so, yet*):

   The urge toward spirituality is strong in any *man, and* he who suppresses it does so at his own peril.

2. By a semicolon:

   The urge toward spirituality is strong in any *man; he* who suppresses it does so at his own peril.

If the coordinating conjunction is omitted, and the comma alone is used to separate the two independent clauses, a comma splice results:

com. spl.
The urge toward spirituality is strong in any *man, he* who suppresses it does so at his own peril.

com. spl.
He turned his face toward the *wall, I* was afraid to rouse him.

The comma splice occurs most frequently in connection with the *conjunctive adverb*:

com. spl.
He had spent twenty years perfecting the *process, therefore,* he savored his success to the full.

com. spl.
Mildred preferred popular music to *classical, nevertheless* she attended symphony concerts faithfully.

At the first class meeting, the instructor listed the names of

com. spl.
the required *texts, also* he advised those who were not serious students to drop the course.

Since the conjunctive adverb does not have the connective force of the coordinating conjunction, a semicolon is still required:

IMPROVED: He had spent twenty years perfecting the *process; therefore,* he savored his success to the full.

IMPROVED: Mildred preferred popular music to *classical; nevertheless,* she attended symphony concerts faithfully.

IMPROVED: At the first class meeting, the instructor listed the names of the required *texts; also,* he advised those who were not serious students to drop the course.

A list of the conjunctive adverbs is given on page 157. You should learn to distinguish between conjunctive adverbs and coordinating conjunctions, especially if you have difficulty with the comma splice or run-together sentences. The coordinating conjunctions separate independent clauses with the aid of the comma only; however, conjunctive adverbs require the aid of the semicolon.

5. Run-Together Sentences   Independent clauses run together without punctuation or coordinating conjunction result in the error called run-together sentences:

run-to. sent.
The temporary loss of a faith is sometimes *good it* may result in an eventual faith that is much deeper.

run-to. sent.
He found no solace in *company his* great desire was to be alone.

Run-together sentences are corrected by (1) making the clauses separate sentences, (2) inserting a semicolon between the clauses, (3) inserting a comma plus a coordinating conjunction between the clauses, or (4) making one of the independent clauses subordinate:

IMPROVED: He found no solace in company. His great desire was to be alone.

IMPROVED: The temporary loss of a faith is sometimes *good; it* may result in an eventual faith that is much deeper.

IMPROVED: He found no solace in *company, for* his great desire was to be alone.

IMPROVED: The temporary loss of a faith is sometimes *good, since* it may result in an eventual faith that is much deeper.

Exercise 2

Indicate those sentences that contain a comma splice, those that are run-together sentences, and those that are correct as they stand. Correct all faulty sentences.

1. He was unaware of her dislike, therefore her sudden anger took him by surprise.
2. Many men are capable of great devotion to a cause, in fact, they sometimes spend a lifetime in search of one.
3. The good student frequently goes beyond the textbook and the instructor, the bad student never does.
4. I was told that he was a reputable merchant I never dreamed he was such a scoundrel.
5. He was convinced of his own self-sufficiency, although he sometimes failed, he never blamed himself.
6. At last he found the reason for his consistent bad luck, he was the victim of a carefully planned conspiracy.
7. Harry ate a greasy pork chop and egg, from the juke box came music with a dying fall.
8. Blood brothers can seldom break the ties that bind them, however much they try.
9. Branson looked up in despair, the MIG was coming in steeply over his right wing.
10. The team's spirits were at a low ebb the harder they tried the less success they seemed to have.

11. He walked twenty miles before any traffic came along, then he was able to hitch a ride with a truck driver.
12. He bought old houses and remodeled them while his family lived in them for two or three years, thus they never felt as if they had a house of their own.
13. He promised to be at the next business meeting however he forgot.
14. She accepted the armful of roses graciously, then she began to sneeze.
15. I'll take the high road, you take the low road.

Nonagreement of Subject and Verb

A verb should agree in number with its subject, singular verb with singular subject, plural verb with plural subject. The problem of agreement in number between the subject and verb causes trouble in three situations particularly.

6. Singular Subject Separated from the Verb by Plural Element   Frequently the verb is separated from a singular subject by a subordinate construction containing a plural noun. The nearness of the plural noun leads the careless writer to use a plural verb:

> subj.
> The *remark* that he made with reference to the strikes at the
>
> v.
> Bellville factories IS (not ARE) both vicious and false.

> subj.   v.
> The *welcome* given to him by his comrades WAS (not WERE) heart-warming.

> subj.   v.
> *Maurice,* together with his friends, IS (not ARE) frequently seen at the concerts.

> subj.   v.
> The hardware *store,* as well as the two hotels, WAS (not WERE) destroyed in the fire.

When the phrase *together with* or *along with* is set off by commas, it is not considered part of the subject. One important reason for the occurrence of subject-verb nonagreement is inadequate proofreading and revision. A more serious reason, however, is the inability of the writer to distinguish the subject. If you feel at all uncertain of your ability to determine the subject of a sentence, study carefully the material on pages 164–172.

7. Mistaken Number in the Subject The indefinite pronoun (*everyone, each, either, neither,* and so on—see G-11) used as the subject takes a singular verb. It frequently causes difficulty in subject-verb agreement when it is followed by a prepositional phrase with a plural object:

subj.   v.
Each of the men is (not ARE) waiting his turn.

v.   subj.
DOES (not Do) *either* of you have a match?

subj.   v.
Neither of us HAS (not HAVE) one.

A compound subject connected by *and* requires a plural verb:

subj.   subj. v.
Steak and fresh *salad* ARE his favorite foods.

But a compound subject connected by the conjunctions *either . . . or, neither . . . nor* requires a verb that agrees with the subject *nearer* to the verb.

subj. (sing.) subj. (pl.) v. (pl.)
Neither *Julius* nor his *friends* ARE very much interested in music.

subj.(sing.) subj.(sing.) v.(sing.)
Either *Murphy* or *Schultz* is the person you want.

subj.(pl.)   subj.(sing.) v.(sing.)
Either the two *criminals* or your *brother* is lying.

89

8. Delayed Subject Of fairly frequent occurrence in English are the *there is* and *there are* constructions. The subject of sentences beginning with either of these constructions invariably falls after the verb.

> v. subj.
> There ARE two important *elements* which make up this compound.

> v. subj.
> There IS only one *explanation* for his refusing to go.

Note that in each of these two sentences, the number of the verb is determined, not by *there*, but by the subject which follows the verb.

You can avoid some of the problems caused by delayed subjects by avoiding when you can, the *there is* and *there are* beginnings of sentences. Such sentences become wordy and unemphatic. An improved version of the first sentence above is:

> Two important elements make up this compound.

Instead of:

> There is $135,000,000 of financial support from the United States Government for the Alliance for Progress.

Consider this improvement:

> The United States Government has granted $135,000,000 to support the Alliance for Progress.

Exercise 3

Select the proper form of the alternatives given. Be able to give the reason for your choice.

1. There (*are*) (*is*) a book, two pencils, and an eraser in the satchel.

2. Mary, as well as two of her fellow teachers, Joan and Margaret, (*is*) (*are*) going to attend the convention.
3. Either my mother or my sister (*is*) (*are*) coming for a visit during the Christmas holidays.
4. (*Is*) (*Are*) Bill or his friends planning to take a hiking trip this summer?
5. We discovered that each of us (*was*) (*were*) just as much at fault as the other.
6. John Turner, together with two men we didn't recognize, (*was*) (*were*) at the convention.
7. The opportunities for advancement (*is*) (*are*) great.
8. There (*is*) (*are*) many ways to build a home, but only a very few right ones.
9. The burden of protective tariffs (*falls*) (*fall*) mainly on the consumer.
10. A number of things (*was*) (*were*) wrong with your talk, but on the whole, it was a commendable effort.

Nonagreement of Pronoun and Antecedent

A pronoun is a word that takes the place of a noun or another pronoun. Consequently, the pronoun must have the same number and gender as its antecedent, the noun or pronoun it represents.

The girl took off *her* hat, and John saw that *she* was his cousin.

Since gender in English is natural, that is, nouns and pronouns are generally masculine, feminine, or neuter according to the objects which they represent, the problem of agreement in gender seldom arises. Complications frequently do arise, however, in connection with agreement in number between pronoun and antecedent (see G-9).

9. Pronoun with Collective Noun as Antecedent The collective noun (a word that names a collection of persons or things) may be either singular or plural, according to the writer's intention.

91

subj.   v.

By evening the *family* WERE all accounted for. (*family* considered as a group of individuals)

subj.   v.

His *family* WAS of great importance in shaping his character. (*family* considered as a single unit)

Pronouns having the collective noun as an antecedent must be consistent with the number of the collective noun as indicated in the number of the verb:

subj. v.   pron.

The *team* WAS finally able to complete *its* season. (We know that *team* must be considered singular because it is used with the singular verb *was*.)

subj.   v.   pron.

The *majority* of the congregation HAVE INDICATED *their* preference

10. Pronoun with Indefinite Pronoun as Antecedent A frequent error in student writing is the use of a plural pronoun to refer to such indefinite pronouns as *each, everyone, everybody, either, neither, nobody.* This error comes from a tendency in informal conversation to consider these pronouns as plural, even though they are singular in form and are so treated in writing.

ILLOGICAL: *Everybody* GIVES him *their* best wishes.

ILLOGICAL: *Neither* of the boys DOES as *they* are told.

Although the English language is far from logical in many respects, the careful writer and speaker will make certain that he does not distort logical grammatical relationships to the point of allowing a plural pronoun to stand for a singular antecedent.

Nobody admits that *he was* (not *they were*) present at the scene of the accident.

Either of the suspects might be perjuring *himself* (not *them-selves*).

Everyone tells me that he (not *they*) had a good time.

Exercise 4

Select the proper form of the alternatives given. Be able to give the reasons for your choice.

1. Each of the papers had (*its*) (*their*) own particular merit.
2. If anyone objects to this procedure, (*he*) (*they*) should make an official complaint.
3. Neither Tom nor his companions would admit that (*he was*) (*they were*) guilty of a misdemeanor.
4. The glee club was ushered into the wings and told that (*they*) (*it*) would sing next.
5. The crowd of people on the sidewalk were almost to much for Edward; he shuddered at (*their*) (*its*) plebeian touch.
6. Every member of a championship team must do (*his*) (*their*) part.
7. Either the soldier or the two sailors were guilty of perjury in (*his*) (*their*) testimony.
8. Everyone who would prefer special treatment will have to speak for (*himself*) (*themselves*).
9. One is often tempted toward unfairness, especially in judging (*his*) (*their*) teachers.
10. The board of directors has already handed down (*its*) (*their*) decision on the matter.

Exercise 5: Review

Detect the sentences which violate the grammatical principles set forth in this chapter. Be able to explain the reasons for all your decisions.

1. There are many men and women who seek any kind of publicity, but this couple sought passionately for privacy.
2. The two college seniors, along with a couple of naïve fresh-men, are the principal offenders in this matter.
3. Do either of the two emissaries have authority to speak for the prime minister?

4. Anyone who escaped sickness during the epidemic could consider themselves lucky.
5. Although if you understand my implications, you will realize my exact position in this controversy.
6. There was a child, its mother, and two other adults involved in the accident.
7. The coach having found good reason for putting Hugh off the football team.
8. None of those invited could come, therefore the party was postponed for two weeks.
9. Since the family was together for the first time in several years, they all enjoyed themselves immensely.
10. That he drank too much was the main reason for his defeat at the polls.
11. With head held high, George walked by the Zeta Phi sorority, did love stand tiptoe at some casement window?
12. Neither the premonition of danger nor the prospect of failure were reason enough to give up this important project.
13. Even though his scheme had been discovered; and I could clearly see his consternation.
14. She had known nothing but a luxurious and sheltered life, nevertheless, when the moment came she proved equal to the most arduous trials.
15. Everyone in the crowd at a given signal raised their voices in unison.
16. Some people—and Dan is one of them—cannot seem to find their happiness in the usual pursuits of life.
17. Whenever the right opportunity comes, be certain that you are able to recognize it.
18. He was soon to find, however, that many things he sneered at now would become very precious to him in the future.
19. Each and every one of you must bear your responsibility for the success of the show.
20. Nobody in their right mind could conceive of his being the thief.

4. The Parts of Speech and Related Problems

The mere mention of the parts of speech is frequently enough to make even the strongest student tremble. The study of grammar has too often become identified with the laborious and fruitless activity that prompted the following high school theme entitled, "Why I Hate Grammer."

It is a hot day (to hot for school). At the front of the room a voice drones as I sit sleeply and try to listen. Suddenly the voice swackes "Dean, sence you are so wide-awake, you may take apart the next sentence." A few laght as most have to much spring-fever to even listen. Stranulessly I decompose the sentence, at last the terrifying task is done. I relaxe again. "Dean you are intirely wrong. Now do it right," the voice growls. Wearly I try again and again and again. Oh woe! Again I'm wrong. Again I try. Oh how I wish I was dead. "Dean won't you ever learn anything. Come in after school till you learn your grammer" Fibbly I protest. But to no avail. Now you know why I can't stand grammer.

The mistake too many students make, including poor Dean, is to consider the study of grammar, or the parts of speech, an end in itself, and unfortunately their misconception has been strengthened in some cases by outmoded methods of teaching writing. Keep in mind, however, that simple proficiency in identifying the parts of speech looked upon as an isolated skill designed to please English teachers has very little, if any, value. But rightly considered as a method of classifying words so that you can talk about them intelligently, the ability to define and recognize the parts of speech with reasonable competence is useful to you as a student of writing. To talk about writing, you must be able to talk about words, and since there are more than a quarter of a million words in the English language, you must have some means of classification. This classification the eight parts of speech provide, a far from perfect classification it is true, but nevertheless quite adequate for use in the basic composition course.

This chapter presents an intensive review of the parts of speech and the principal errors associated with them. Much of the material you will already know, but here at the very beginning of your formal college training, you may find useful the opportunity to refresh your memory. As you "stranulessly decompose" the following exercises, keep firmly in mind that they are all designed, not to make you an expert grammarian, but to help you become a more efficient writer.

NOUNS

A noun is a word used to name a person, place, or thing.

McPherson ruled the *city* with an iron *hand*.

Note that the noun *hand* in this sentence means more than a concrete thing; it is used figuratively to mean a certain way of ruling. Consequently, a "thing" in our definition can include not only objects but also qualities, actions, and ideas or concepts.

QUALITY: The *sharpness* of the blow made him quail.

ACTION: *Murder* will out.

Other aids to the recognition of nouns are as follows:

1. The noun is the only word in the language which may form its plural by the addition of the letter *s*.
2. The noun is the only word that can be modified by the definite (the) and indefinite (a, an) articles.

Types of Nouns

There are five major types of nouns, classified according to the objects or qualities which they designate. *Proper nouns* name a particular person, place, or thing and begin with a capital letter (*McPherson, New York, February*). All other nouns are called *common nouns* and begin with a small letter (*man, city, hand*). Some proper and common nouns may be classified further as *collective nouns,* which are used to designate a group of persons or things (*Yankees, team, flock*). Two other classifications of nouns are convenient in discussing stylistic matters. *Abstract nouns* refer to intangibles, things that we cannot discern with any of our five senses (*kindness, sportsmanship, hate*); *concrete nouns* refer to tangibles, things that we can discern with our senses (*rose, house, dog*).

Aside from spelling and capitalization, which we shall deal with fully in later sections, the noun offers the college student very little difficulty. Certain areas of noun usage, however, do call for close attention.

Problems of Number in the Noun

1. Regular Plurals   The form of the noun usually varies to show whether it refers to one or a number of persons, places, or things. The plural of most nouns in the English language is formed as follows:

1. An *s* is added to the singular form of the noun: *girl, girls; Smith, Smiths.*
2. But *es* is added if the singular form of the noun ends in *s, sh, ch, x,* or *z: Jones, Joneses; grass, grasses; church, churches.*

2. Exceptional Plurals There are, however, exceptions to this general rule. Some of these exceptions are so familiar that we need only mention them.

1. In some nouns of Old English origin, the final *f* changes to *v* in the plural and *es* is added: *wife, wives; thief, thieves.*
2. A few nouns add an *en* to form the plural: *ox, oxen; child, children; brother, brethren* (restricted almost entirely to religious usage).
3. Some nouns form their plural by a change in the vowel: *foot, feet; man, men; woman, women; mouse, mice; louse, lice; goose, geese; tooth, teeth.*
4. Nouns ending in a *y* preceded by a consonant change the *y* to *i* and add *es: party, parties; battery, batteries.* Note, however, that this exception to the rule does *not* apply to proper names: *Murphy, Murphys; Gantry, Gantrys.*
5. Some nouns ending in *o* form their plural irregularly in *es.* The most common are *echo, echoes; hero, heroes; Negro, Negroes; potato, potatoes; tomato, tomatoes;* and *torpedo, torpedoes.*
6. Plurals of symbols, figures, letters, and words referred to as such are formed with an apostrophe and *s: i, i's; 8, 8's;* three *and's* in one sentence. (See P-15.)
7. Some nouns use the same form for both singular and plural: *deer, means, species, Japanese, hose, sheep, acoustics.*

3. Foreign Plurals More troublesome exceptions to the general rule are foreign nouns that for one reason or another have retained their distinctive plurals. The most common of these are as follows:

Singular	Plural	Singular	Plural
addendum	addenda	ellipsis	ellipses
alumna	alumnae	hypothesis	hypotheses
alumnus	alumni	larva	larvae
analysis	analyses	oasis	oases
antithesis	antitheses	parenthesis	parentheses
axis	axes	phenomenon	phenomena
basis	bases	stimulus	stimuli
crisis	crises	synopsis	synopses
criterion	criteria	thesis	theses
datum	data		

Most foreign nouns now show a strong tendency to form the plural by the regular *s* ending, although in many cases the foreign plural is still acceptable: *curriculum—curricula* or *curriculums; memorandum—memoranda* or *memorandums; medium—media,* or *mediums.* When in doubt, you should, of course, consult your dictionary.

4. Compound Nouns   Frequently a group of two or more words are used as a noun unit: *schoolhouse, brother-in-law, cupful.* The plural of these compound nouns is formed in the great majority of causes by adding the regular plural ending to the last word of the compound: *schoolhouses, cupfuls.* The following nouns are important exceptions to the general rule:

Singular	Plural
father-in-law (and all other *in-law* compounds)	fathers-in-law
court-martial	courts-martial
hanger-on	hangers-on
man-of-war	men-of-war
passer-by	passers-by

A special group of compound nouns used as adjectives are always in the singular: a *ten-foot* pole, a *two-acre* field, a *ten-dollar* bill. Note, however, in adverbial constructions these same nouns are regular: He vaulted *ten feet.* His garden covered *two acres.* He spent *ten dollars.* A somewhat similar distinction is made in nouns of quantity:

A crowd of forty *thousand* jammed the stadium.
   but
Thousands jammed the stadium.

5. Collective Nouns A collective noun names even in its singular form a group of persons or things. Some common examples are *team, jury, crowd, contents, couple, committee.* The collective noun causes difficulty only in connection with verb agreement and pronoun reference; these problems will be discussed in their appropriate sections. We might note here, however, that even though in theory the singular form of the collective noun can be considered as either singular or plural, in fact it is almost invariably considered singular or plural according to its form.

The crowd *has* dispersed.
The jury *is* now returning.

   but

The contents of the bag *were* surprising.
The Yankees *are* leading the American League.

Problems of Case in the Noun

The term "case" means the change in the form of a word, to indicate its relation to another word, or other words, in the sentence. The noun changes its form to indicate the *possessive case.* The possessive case of the noun does not, as the name might indicate, always indicate ownership. The varieties of relationships indicated by the form need not worry us, however, since the native speaker of English is seldom at a loss as to when the possessive form should be used. In written English especially, most of the difficulty centers on the form itself.

6. The "S" Possessive
1. The possessive singular of the noun is formed by adding an apostrophe and *s* to the singular form of the noun: *Mary's coat, the sun's rays.*

2. The possessive plural is formed by adding an apostrophe alone to the *s* plural form of the noun: *the Smiths' car, the boys' playground.*

Again, however, we must take into account exceptions to this general rule:

1. If the singular form of the noun ends in *s*, either the apostrophe and *s* or the apostrophe alone may be used to indicate singular possession: *Keats' poems* or *Keats's poems; Charles' father* or *Charles's father.* If the noun forming the possessive ends in *s*, contains two or more syllables, and modifies a noun beginning with *s*, the apostrophe alone is commonly used to indicate possession: *Dickens' sentences, the princess' slipper.* Note that these variations are based on difficulties of pronunciation —that is, the awkwardness of pronouncing two, especially three, *s* sounds together.
2. If the plural form of the noun does not end in *s*, the apostrophe and *s* are added to indicate plural possession: *the men's club, the children's laughter.*
3. A workable practice which encompasses the procedures just named in 1 and 2, is to take the word which will show possession, write it as it is spelled in an "of" possessive phrase (see page 103), add an apostrophe, and then add an *s* if you need it for sound. For example:

the coat of Mary
Mary
Mary's (*s* needed for sound)
Mary's coat

the car of the Smiths
Smiths
Smiths' (no extra *s* needed for sound)
the Smiths' car

the poems of Keats
Keats
Keats' (no extra *s* needed for sound)
Keats' poems

the laughter of children
children
children's (*s* needed for sound)
children's laughter

As a test for this procedure, you should be able to draw a line through the apostrophe of a possessive noun and find that to the left of the apostrophe is the word in question correctly spelled. Thus, you can avoid such illogical errors as these:

INCORRECT: Charle's father = father of Charle
CORRECT: Charles' father = father of Charles

INCORRECT: mens' club = club of the mens
CORRECT: men's club = club of the men

4. In compound nouns, the singular or plural possessive is always formed on the last element of the compound by an apostrophe plus *s: my brother-in-law's house, my brothers-in-law's houses.* This rule also applies to the so-called group possessive: *the King of England's decree, the chief of police's gun.* In compound possessives, the possessive is formed on the last word only if the words are thought of as a unit: *Rogers and Hammerstein's music, Wilson and Roe's law firm.* But if the words are thought of as separate, the sign of the possessive is used with each one: *John's and Mary's hats, Thackeray's and Trollope's novels.*

5. The only plurals (which are not also possessives) formed by the use of the apostrophe are plurals of figures, letters, and words referred to as words:

at 6's and 7's BUT at sixes and sevens
Mind your p's and q's.
Dot your i's and cross your t's.
. . . no if's and but's about it.

(Recently, though, printers have been printing *ifs* and *buts* without the apostrophes.)

7. The "Of" Possessive Theoretically we always have a choice between the apostrophe and *s* combination and an *of* phrase to indicate the possessive form of the noun: *the sun's rays, the rays of the sun; Keats' poetry, the poetry of Keats.* Our choice depends for the most part upon the degree of formality we wish to imply; for example, we would say in conversation "Keats' poetry," but we would entitle a term paper "The Poetry of Keats." Also, there is a tendency in Modern English to use the *s* possessive when speaking of animate things, the *of* possessive when speaking of inanimate things: *the man's shoulder, the shoulder of the road; the boy's hand, the hand of Fate.*

An interesting construction in the *of* possessive is the *double* possessive: a friend *of my brother's,* this book *of my teacher's.* These forms are well established in English, but it is probably best to avoid them in formal writing.

8. The Possessive with the Gerund A noun, without modifiers, directly preceding and modifying a gerund is generally in the possessive case.

ger.

They paid no attention to *John's leaving* early.

Since the gerund is a verb form used as a noun, an apostrophe *s* combination is used with a regular noun preceding it. In other words, the gerund *leaving* in the example given bears the same grammatical relation to the noun *John* as would the noun *hat* in *John's hat* or the noun *dog* in *John's dog.*

A noun modified by a participle, however, should be in the objective or regular form.

part.

We saw *Mary climbing* the stairs.

Note here that Mary is the direct object of *saw.* Mary is modified by the participle *climbing.* (For a discussion of the gerund and participle see G-29–G-30.)

Formal usage keeps the possessive case of a noun (or

pronoun) before a gerund although informal usage tends to forget it. In the sentences used as examples above, formal usage notes that it was not John whom "they" paid no attention to but his *leaving*, whereas "we" did see Mary in the act of climbing the stairs. Your observation of these formal usages in your writing will help to make your meaning precise.

Exercise 1

Some of the following sentences contain errors in noun usage; others are correct. Explain the rule of noun usage illustrated in each sentence and state whether or not the rule has been violated.

1. As he faced his troops, the commander in chief's countenance was flushed with rage.
2. The data shown in the preceding tables is of extreme importance for all men interested in this problem.
3. It would seem to me that he would be willing to do it for kindness's sake alone.
4. These memorandums are misleading.
5. The Thomases' cat quite often reflects the chief characteristics of its mistress.
6. Two weeks after he married, his sister-in-laws descended upon him like a plague.
7. Winston is a selfish, unscrupulous individual; my friend George is his exact antitheses.
8. The justice' of the peace office is about as exalted a one as he is capable of filling.
9. The impact had crushed the handle of the door flat against the body of the car.
10. Most men are capable of impulsive and disastrous action that a moments' reflection would have prevented.
11. The population of the United States is approximately 180 millions.
12. The haystack was at least twenty foot high.
13. Bruce and Philip's convertibles are the secrets of their popularity in college.
14. Mountains were made for climbing, and valleys were made for rest.

15. John Sears, the subject of this biography, had four brothers and two sisters, but he was the favorite of his father's.
16. The heroines of Henry James novels are great creations, but the heros tend to be somewhat insipid.
17. Most of his success was due to his father's-in-law influence.
18. The Boston Red Sox has always been his favorite team.
19. Two teaspoonsful of this medicine will relieve your pain.
20. Charles Dickens' life is the most interesting of all other Victorian novelists.

PRONOUNS

A pronoun is a word that substitutes for a noun or another pronoun.

The picture was a delightful study in folk humor, and *every-one who* looked at *it* was captivated.

The pronoun *it* is a substitute for the noun *picture* and enables us to avoid an awkward repetition. *Picture,* the noun replaced, is called the *antecedent* of the pronoun *it.* Most pronouns have antecedents, either expressed or implied. Note, however, that *everyone* has no antecedent, although it might be argued that its implied antecedent is unspecified individuals in a group. The antecedent of the pronoun *who* is another pronoun, *everyone.*

The pronoun changes its form according to its use in the sentence much more frequently than the noun. For instance, in the sentence "Bill loves Mary," the form of the nouns "Bill" and "Mary" would remain the same even if their positions were reversed: "Mary loves Bill." But if we substitute the appropriate pronouns, "*He* loves *her,*" in the original sentence, we cannot change the position of the pronouns without changing their form: "*She* loves *him.*"

There are seven major classifications of pronouns according to the way in which they designate the nouns for which they stand.

105

Types of Pronouns

Personal Pronouns   The personal pronouns designate the person speaking, the person spoken to, or the person or object spoken of. The forms of the personal pronoun are as follows:

	SINGULAR	PLURAL
First Person (Person Speaking)		
Nominative case	I	we
Possessive case	my, mine	our, ours
Objective case	me	us
Second Person (Person Spoken To)		
Nominative case	you	you
Possessive case	your, yours	your, yours
Objective case	you	you
Third Person (Person or Thing Spoken Of)		
Nominative case	he, she, it	they
Possessive case	his, her, hers, its	their, theirs
Objective case	him, her, it	them

Relative Pronouns   The relative pronouns provide a link between a subordinate clause and words on which it depends. For instance, the two sentences, "She is a student" and "She won the popularity prize," can be combined through the use of the relative pronoun into a single sentence: "She is the student *who* won the popularity prize." The relative pronouns are *who* (*whose, whom*), *which, that, whoever,* (*whomever*), *whichever, whatever* (*whosoever, whomsoever, whichsoever, whatsoever*). The relative pronoun *who* and its related forms are used to refer to persons, as illustrated in the sentence above. *Which* is used to refer to other living creatures and to things, while *that* is used to refer to either persons or things:

Here is the cow *which* gives so much milk.
Here is the cow *that* gives so much milk.

That was the straw *that* broke the camel's back.
He is a man *that* I admire.

Interrogative Pronouns   The interrogative pronouns are used in questions: "*Which* of the bicycle is yours?" "*Who* does he think he is?" The interrogative pronouns include *who, whose, whom, which,* and *what*.

Demonstrative Pronouns   The demonstrative pronouns point out precisely certain persons or things. "*This* is the end of the quest." "*Those* boys are incapable of anything but mischief." *This, these, that, those* are the principal demonstrative pronouns and also function as adjectives.

Indefinite Pronouns   The indefinite pronouns designate persons or things, but not specifically. "*Everyone* of any importance attended the reception." "*Each* of the books has its own particular merit." There are many indefinite pronouns in the English language, but a few of the more common are *everyone, anyone, someone, everybody, anybody, somebody, one, none, some,* and *all*. All the indefinite pronouns except *none* and *plenty* can function as adjectives as well as pronouns: *each boy, neither side, someone's book*.

Compound Personal Pronouns   The compound personal pronouns are combinations of the simple pronouns with the word *self* or *selves: myself, yourself, himself, herself, itself, oneself; ourselves, yourselves, themselves*. There are two uses of the compound personal pronouns:

As *reflexive pronouns*, which are objects of the verb or preposition and refer back to the subject of the sentence:

Walter hurt *himself* in the last game.

She seemed quite proud of *herself*.

As *intensive pronouns*, which serve as a means of emphasis, intensifying their antecedents: "And finally, the last of the disheartened group, came Bill *himself*."

107

Reflexive pronouns should not be used alone as subjects of sentences:

NOT: Bill and myself were going.
BUT: Bill and I were going.

Reciprocal Pronouns The reciprocal pronouns are actually compound indefinite pronouns used to indicate some mutual relationship between two or more persons or things. "The two teams had a good deal of respect for *each other*." "The three concepts complemented *one another*."

Along with the verb, the pronoun is the most highly inflected part of speech in the English language; that is, it changes its form frequently according to its use in the sentence. For the most part, however, the native-born speaker of English uses the various forms of the pronoun correctly. One would hardly say this side of infancy, "I gave it to he," or "Her gave it to he." There are, however, certain areas of pronoun usage that even college students are likely to be unsure of, and these need close attention.

Problems of Number in the Pronoun

9. Personal Pronouns A major function of a pronoun is to take the place of a noun. A personal pronoun, therefore, *must agree in number with the noun that it represents*:

The *men* had little choice as to who would be *their* masters.

The problem of agreement is sometimes complicated by the fact that a collective noun can be considered as either singular or plural in number:

The team is proud of *its* achievement.
The Chicago Cubs are my favorite team, even though *they* seldom win a pennant.

Note that the number of the collective noun in each of the sentences is indicated by the verb, and subsequent pronouns having the collective noun as an antecedent must reflect the same number.

When two or more antecedents are joined by *and*, the pronoun (with its verb) is plural:

Mark and Toby *are* leading *their* divisions.

When two or more *singular* antecedents are joined by *or* or *nor*, the pronoun (with its verb) is singular:

Either Mark or Toby *is* bound to lead *his* division.

When two or more *singular* and *plural* antecedents are joined by *or* or *nor*, the pronoun (with its verb) agrees with the nearer:

Neither Phyllis nor her sisters *show* the least interest in *their* caller.
Neither the older sisters nor Phyllis *shows* the least interest in *her* caller.

Except where unusual precision is necessary, the *he* or *she*, *his* or *her* construction can be reduced to simple *he* or *his*:

AWKWARD: This kind of person seldom seems to know *his or her* own mind.
IMPROVED: This kind of person seldom seems to know *his* own mind.

10. Relative Pronouns   Like personal pronouns, the relative pronouns assume the number of the noun or pronoun to which they refer, and take either a singular or plural verb accordingly:

There are many men *who are* afraid of their own thoughts.
Jones is one of those men *who are* always critical of others (*who* refers to *men*, not *one*).
He is a person *who* hates green salads (*who* refers to *person*).

109

11. Indefinite Pronouns The indefinite pronouns, which have no expressed antecedent, usually are unmistakably singular or plural according to their meaning:

Singular	Plural
everyone	some
everybody	few
somebody	both
anybody	all
each	several
none	plenty
one	any
either	
neither	

Consequently, pronouns having one of these indefinite pronouns as an antecedent should agree with it in number: "*Everybody* feels some concern for *his* own health." "*Each* of the girls in our troop took *her* punishment bravely." "*Some* of the men were reluctant to display *their* badges." "*Any* of the people involved will take *their* share of the responsibility." In informal usage of *everyone, everybody, either,* and *neither,* there is a temptation to make succeeding pronouns plural in reference: "*Everyone* took off their *hats.*" "Did *everybody* enjoy *themselves*?" You should resist this temptation in written English.

Exceptions. Some of the plural forms of the indefinite pronoun take the singular verb if they indicate a particular portion of a whole:

Some of the food *is* spoiled.
All of the fruit *was* stolen.

Conversely, the indefinite pronoun *none*, though singular in form, can be considered plural if the context demands it.

None of those things ever *happen* to me.

Exercise 2

Choose the correct form of the alternatives given. Be able to give the reasons for your choice.

1. Neither of these two famous men gave any promise of greatness in (*his*) (*their*) early manhood.
2. Each person must decide whether (*he*) (*they*) will concern (*himself*) (*themselves*) with people or with things.
3. He is one of those fortunate men who (*has*) (*have*) devoted (*himself*) (*themselves*) to a worthy and at the same time profitable cause.
4. Everyone seemed to feel that (*his*) (*their*) own troubles were quite enough for (*him*) (*them*) to bear.
5. Many a prominent man will concede that the main ingredient in (*his*) (*their*) success has been luck.
6. Both Leroy and Herbert took (*his*) (*their*) law degrees in the same year.
7. Neither Lawrence nor his contemporaries were able to understand the sterilities of (*his*) (*their*) own age.
8. Any of the contestants would have been able to improve (*his standing*) (*their standings*) by reading Markwell's book.
9. No progress is possible so long as everyone insists upon (*his*) (*their*) own individual rights.
10. Each person is entirely responsible for (*his*) (*his or her*) actions in this matter.

Problems of Case in the Pronoun

Case in the pronoun, as in the noun, simply means the change in the form of the pronoun according to its use in the sentence. *Personal, relative,* and *interrogative* pronouns all use distinctive forms to indicate the *nominative, possessive,* and *objective* cases. It is important for you to recognize these distinctions, since major problems of pronoun usage arise in connection with proper case forms.

12. Case Forms of Personal Pronouns When used as the *subject* of a verb or the *predicate nominative*, the personal pronoun takes the *nominative form* (see pages 164–167 for a discussion of the function of words in the sentence):

SUBJECT: *He* was told that *they* were unavail-
PREDICATE NOMINATIVE: able.
                            That is *she*.

When used as the *direct* or *indirect object* of the verb or verbal, or as the *object* of a preposition, the personal pronoun takes the *objective form*:

DIRECT OBJECT: The ball hit *him* on the leg.
INDIRECT OBJECT: Thomas gave *me* another chance.
OBJECT OF THE PREPOSITION: The girls went to *him* for advice.

The objective form of the personal pronoun is also used as the *subject of the infinitive* and as the *complement* of the *to be* infinitive. (For a discussion of the infinitive, see G-31.)

SUBJECT OF INFINITIVE: John asked *me* to go.
COMPLEMENT OF THE *to be* INFINITIVE: They considered the logical scapegoat to be *me*.

When used as the *possessive adjective*, the *possessive pronoun*, or the *modifier of a gerund*, the personal pronoun takes the *possessive form*:

MODIFIER OF A GERUND: I dislike *his* running away from un-
                           pleasantness. (This is the only in-
                           stance in which the   use of the
                           possessive form of the personal pro-
                           noun causes difficulty.)
POSSESSIVE ADJECTIVE: *Your* dog has hurt *its* leg.
POSSESSIVE PRONOUN: The card is *mine*.

13. Case Forms of Relative and Interrogative Pronouns

The nominative *who* and objective *whom* forms of the relative and interrogative pronouns follow the same case pattern as the personal pronouns:

NOMINATIVE FORMS

SUBJECT: I know *who* stole the car. *Who* did it?

PREDICATE NOMINATIVE: I don't know *who* you think you are. *Who* is the man at the door?

OBJECTIVE FORMS

DIRECT OBJECT: He is the one *whom* I selected. *Whom* did he choose?

INDIRECT OBJECT: *Whom* did you ask the question?

OBJECT OF THE PREPOSITION: He is a man to *whom* honor is life. For *whom* is the telegram meant?

SUBJECT OF INFINITIVE: He did not know *whom* to ask. *Whom* did he order to go?

COMPLEMENT OF *to be* INFINITIVE: *Whom* did you take him to be?

The distinction between the nominative and objective case forms of the relative and interrogative pronouns is frequently not made in conversation, but it is uniformly observed in formal speaking and writing.

POSSESSIVE FORMS

POSSESSIVE ADJECTIVE: He refused to reveal *whose* advice he had taken. *Whose* book are you reading?

POSSESSIVE PRONOUN: I shall take it, no matter *whose* it may be. *Whose* is this?

Exercise 3

Indicate the use of the italicized pronouns as a subject of the verb (sub.), the predicate nominative of a verb (p.n.), the direct object (d.o.) or indirect object (i.o.) of the verb or verbal (v.o.), the complement of the infinitive (o.in.), the object of a preposition (o.prep.), or the possessive adjective (p.a.)

1. He would never know *who* started the rumor about Jane and him.
2. Five of *us* boys turned the hose on *her* while she was sunbathing.
3. She did not consider *him* a very eligible suitor.
4. *Who* do *you* think could have done *it* better than Max?
5. *Nobody* is able to predict the future with any accuracy, especially *his* own.
6. *He* was unconcerned about *whom we* were going to see; he wanted to know *whom we* had seen.
7. If *everyone* would speak to *whoever* is concerned in this matter, the petition will be granted.
8. Do you think *I* would fight anyone who is bigger than *I*?
9. *This* is the time that *all* of *them* like to practice *their* singing.
10. If *I* were *she*, I would pay no attention to anyone except *you* and *me*.

14. The Nominative Case in the Personal Pronoun   *The nominative form of the personal pronoun should be used as the subject of a verb.* This rule is seldom violated except in the following construction:

> He is a better writer than *I*.

There is a strong tendency to use the objective form *me* in this construction, a tendency probably resulting from the similarity of "than I" to a prepositional phrase. The construction is best considered as being elliptical—"He is a better writer than I *am*"—which would call for the nominative form of the personal pronoun.

The nominative form of the personal pronoun should be used as a predicate nominative. When used as the complement of any form of the verb *to be*, except the infinitive, the pronoun should take the nominative form:

> It is *I*.
> If I were *he*, I would have been more careful.
> It is *they* whom we suspect.

Note that the pronoun in this construction occupies the position normally held by the direct or indirect object of the verb, both of which are always in the objective case. The force of habit is so strong that we frequently hear "It's me" or "It's them" in conversation, and there can be little question that these constructions have established themselves widely in informal usage. On a more formal level, however, the nominative forms should be used. The question is, after all, largely academic. The clipped forms "It's *I* (or *me*)" "It's *he* (or *him*)" are quite personal and intimate constructions and would seldom, if ever, appear on the formal level.

15. The Objective Case in the Personal Pronoun *The objective form of the personal pronoun should be used as the direct and indirect objects of the verb and verbal, the object of a preposition, and the subject of an infinitive.* This rule is sometimes violated because the primer school stress on the nominative form in such a construction as "John and *I* were absent" has left an impression that "John and me" in any context is incorrect. This error occurs mainly in compound indirect objects of the verb and compound objects of a preposition (especially compound objects of the preposition *between*).

INDIRECT OBJECT: Mary bought John and me (not *I*) some sandwiches.

OBJECT OF A PREPOSITION: This secret is strictly between you and me (not *I*).

The objective form of the pronoun should be used when linked with a noun in the objective case. Insistence in the student's early grammatical training on the use of the nominative form of the personal pronoun in such constructions as "We girls had a slumber party" leads sometimes to the use of the nominative form when the objective form is proper.

CORRECT: *We* boys loved to go swimming in Otter Creek.

INCORRECT: Several of *we* boys refused to enter the contest.

CORRECT: Several of *us* boys refused to enter the contest.

The objective form of the personal pronoun should be used as both the complement subject and of the TO BE infini-

tive. Unlike the forms of the verb *to be* (The culprit is *he*), the *to be* infinitive takes the objective form of the personal pronoun:

> They all thought the culprit to be *him.*
> They all thought *him* to be the culprit.

16. The Possessive Case in the Personal Pronoun *The possessive forms of the personal pronoun are self-contained and are not formed with the apostrophe.* Do not allow the contraction *it's* (for *it is*) nor the possessive form of most nouns (boy's, girl's) to lead you to the error of using the apostrophe with the possessive forms of the personal pronoun:

> He gave the team *its* (not *it's*) head.
> You keep *yours* (not *your's*) and we will keep *ours* (not *our's*).

The possessive form of the personal pronoun is used as the preceding modifier of a gerund. The gerund, even though its form is that of a verb, actually functions as a noun. A pronoun modifying a gerund, therefore, must be in the possessive form. Possessive adjective modifying a simple noun:

> poss.　　adj. n.
> He did not like *my hat.*

Possessive adjective modifying a gerund:

> poss. adj.　ger.
> He did not like *my running* away.

The objective form of the pronoun, however, should be used before the participle. The distinction between a participle and a gerund is usually quite clear.

> part.
> As we turned the corner, we saw *him limping* down the road.

(Here the pronoun *him* is used as the object of the verb *saw*. The pronoun *him* is modified by the participle *limping*.)

poss. adj. ger.

His limping was never very noticeable. (Here the verbal *limping* is clearly the subject of the sentence; therefore it is a gerund. The possessive pronoun *his* modifies the gerund *limping* as it would any other noun.)

17. The Possessive Case in the Indefinite Pronoun A number of the singular forms of the indefinite pronouns form the possessive case by the use of the apostrophe plus *s*:

COMPOUNDS WITH *any*: another's book, anybody's guess

COMPOUNDS WITH *every*: everybody's lawn, everyone's opinion

COMPOUNDS WITH *no* (except *none*): nobody's business

COMPOUNDS WITH *some*: somebody's hat, someone's wish

The indefinite pronoun *one* also forms its possessive by the apostrophe plus *s*:

one's book

Note carefully that the indefinite pronoun is the *only* pronoun that forms its possessive with the apostrophe.

INCORRECT: He gave the dog *it's* bone.

INCORRECT: *Who'se* book is this?

Exercise 4

Choose the correct form of the alternatives given. Be able to give the reason for your choice.

1. The order directed Bailey, Moake and (*I*) (*me*) to proceed immediately to the port of embarkation.
2. It was (*they*) (*them*) who would have to take responsibility.
3. His instructor was first amused, then annoyed by (*his*) (*him*) throwing spitballs at the girls.
4. If he persists in his efforts to disrupt the committee's plans,

117

    he will have two persons to contend with—Smith and (*I*) (*me*).

5. Mr. Jones was already quite familiar with the area and (*its*) (*it's*) history.

6. Marilyn insisted on giving Arthur and (*I*) (*me*) a share in the reward.

7. The president told the group that the matter was strictly between Brown and (*me*) (*I*).

8. You will have to admit that he has a more pleasant job than (*I*) (*me*).

9. Benson instructed the clerk to pay Wilson and (*I*) (*me*).

10. The main fault of (*us*) (*we*) editors is that we expect too much of our authors.

18. "Who" and "Whom" Forms of the Relative Pronoun

The most difficult problem in pronoun case is the distinction between the use of the nominative (*who*) and objective (*whom*) forms of the relative and interrogative pronouns. The difficulty can easily be cleared up, however, if you will keep three things in mind:

1. The case of the relative pronoun is determined by its use in its clause, *not by the case of its antecedent*:

    It was he *whom* we exposed.

The antecedent of the relative pronoun *whom* is *he*, a nominative form of the personal pronoun. The case of the relative pronoun, however, is determined by the fact that it is used as the direct object of the verb *exposed* in the subordinate clause. Hence the correct form is *whom*.

2. The use in the sentence of the subordinate clause containing the relative pronoun *has no effect upon the pronoun's case*:

    We could not discover *who* gave the conflicting order.

The entire subordinate clause, *who gave the conflicting order*, is used as the direct object of the verb *could discover*.

The relative pronoun, however, is used as the subject of the verb *gave* in the subordinate clause. Consequently the nominative form *who* must be used.

3. Parenthetical expressions like *I think, he thought* intervening between the nominative form of the relative pronoun and its verb *have no effect upon the pronoun's case*:

He listed all the people *who* he thought would attend.

The parenthetical expression *he thought* should not lead to the error of construing the relative pronoun as the direct object of the verb *thought*. It is the subject of the verb *would attend* and should take the nominative form *who*.

19. "Who" and "Whom" Forms of the Interrogative Pronoun The case forms of the interrogative pronoun are governed by exactly the same considerations as those governing the case forms of the relative pronoun, but the problem is complicated somewhat by the fact that the normal word order of the English sentence is distorted in most questions. The simplest method to determine the correct form of the interrogative pronoun is to change the question into a statement:

QUESTION: (*Who*) (*Whom*) did he consider the real villain of the play to be?

TRANSPOSED: He did consider the real villain of the play to be *whom*.

The interrogative pronoun serves as the complement of the infinitive *to be*, even though in the question the infinitive and its object are separated by the entire length of the sentence. The interrogative pronoun, consequently, takes the objective form *whom*.

Some grammarians and teachers today maintain that the *who, whom* distinction is valueless and is in the process of fading out of the language. The facts of present-day usage are as follows:

119

In the give-and-take of informal conversation, even the most discriminating speaker tends to use *who* rather than stop to analyze a complicated construction.

On the other hand, in formal speech and writing the correct distinction between *who* and *whom* is carefully maintained by the vast majority of educated speakers and writers.

Exercise 5

Choose the correct form of the alternatives given. Be able to give the reason for your choice.

1. He was one of the men (*whom*) (*who*) Roger particularly disliked.
2. (*Who*) (*Whom*) do you think will eventually attain the presidency?
3. Burt cast furtive glances at the man (*whom*) (*who*) he believed to be the source of all his woes.
4. The prize will be awarded to (*whoever*) (*whomever*) shows himself most deserving.
5. Do you know of a man (*who*) (*whom*) I could depend on in any emergency?
6. As he fell, Branson took one last shot at the Spaniard, (*who*) (*whom*) dodged, then leaped forward, his sword flashing in the sun.
7. (*Who*) (*Whom*) does Robinson consider the best-qualified man?
8. Will you please save dessert for (*whomever*) (*whoever*) comes in late?
9. The real villain is not any of the men (*who*) (*whom*) you have named.
10. Bob could not imagine for (*whom*) (*who*) the insult was intended.

Problems of Reference in the Pronoun

Most pronouns have antecedents, that is, nouns (or other pronouns) to which the pronouns refer, and these pronouns are meaningful only in relation to the nouns for which they stand. The writer must make the use of references precise and unambiguous; the noun or pronoun antecedent should be clear and logical.

Three cardinal principles of effective pronoun reference are (1) that the pronoun be reasonably close to its antecedent, (2) that no apparent antecedent intervene between the pronoun and its actual antecedent, and (3) that if the pronoun and its antecedent are not immediately conjoined, the antecedent be an important word in its constriction. The most common errors in pronoun reference can be classified as follows:

20. Vague Reference The careless writer frequently uses the pronouns *this* and *which* to refer to the idea of a preceding instruction instead of using a specific noun or pronoun in the construction.

> *a.* He accused me of misplacing his books and disturbing the contents of his desk drawer, *which* made me very angry.
>
> *b.* He was born in a hovel, but by early manhood owned two country estates; *this* explains his belief in free enterprise.

The relative pronoun *which* in sentence *a.* refers to the accusations described in the preceding clause. The reference would be much improved by the use of a specific noun to which the relative pronoun could refer.

> *a.* He accused me of misplacing his books and disturbing the contents of his desk drawer, *charges which* made me very angry.

The demonstrative pronoun *this* in sentence *b.* refers to a fact implied but not stated in the preceding clause. Again, a specific noun should be supplied to which the pronoun *this* could refer.

> *b.* He was born in a hovel, but by early manhood owned two country estates; *this independent achievement* explains his belief in free enterprise.

You may need to watch vague references for pronouns from one sentence to another or between paragraphs. Here is an example of what sometimes happens between sentences.

VAGUE: Some adults think that teenagers are corrupt and dishonest rather than honest and trustworthy. This is not true.

IMPROVED: Some adults think that teenagers are corrupt and dishonest. I have discovered them to be honest and trustworthy.

Notice these excerpts from two consecutive paragraphs:

VAGUE: The committee plans to establish one-year sponsorships for the organization. . . .
           Give this careful consideration and urge your fellow members to do the same.

IMPROVED: Give the idea of sponsorship your careful consideration. . . .

or

           Consider becoming a sponsor, and encourage your fellow members to volunteer also.

Professional writers quite often use the pronouns *this* and *which* with a generalized or implied antecedent, and if the reference is clear and unmistakable, there can be no objection. In the early stages of your training as a writer, however, you should examine such references in your own work very carefully, since this construction is one of the main reasons for inept and confusing sentences.

21. Indefinite Reference Immature writing is frequently characterized by the indiscriminate use of the pronouns *you* or *they* without specific references:

When you go into the service, you should realize that you have left all freedom behind you. They will not permit individual differences. You are expected to conform to their ideas of a soldier, and if you try to be anything else, you will find yourself in trouble.

Such pronoun usage is permissible only on the most informal and colloquial level, or for very special effects. Note the increased maturity of tone when the passage is revised:

When one goes into the service, he should realize that he has left all freedom behind him. The army will not permit individual differences. The recruit is expected to conform to his superiors' idea of a soldier, and if he tries to be anything else, he will find himself in trouble.

22. Split Reference There should be only one possible antecedent to which the pronoun may refer. If there are two, the sentence usually must be completely revised.

AMBIGUOUS: The natives were fond of the settler's children, and they spent a great deal of time with them.

CLEAR: *a.* The natives were fond of the settlers' children and spent a great deal of time with them.

or

CLEAR: *b.* The settlers' children were fond of the natives and spent a great deal of time with them.

or

AMBIGUOUS: Agnes told Mary that she should accept the invitation.

CLEAR: *a.* Agnes told Mary to accept the invitation.

or

CLEAR: *b.* Agnes told Mary, "You should accept the invitation."

Exercise 6

Examine each italicized pronoun in the following sentences and decide whether or not a principle of pronoun reference has been violated.

1. Ballowe tried to gain admittance to Harvard, but *they* turned him down.
2. One of the first lessons that a recruit learns is that *you* must obey orders unquestioningly.
3. Barzak told his son that *he* should not accept the bonus.
4. *It* has been raining for two days and shows no sign of stopping.

5. Watkins refused to allow his name to be entered in the race, *which*, was, we thought, a wise decision.
6. There is a lake surrounded by a dense forest *that* has seldom been seen by human eyes.
7. Political analysts have long been aware that *you* usually follow your father's party preference.
8. An appreciation of Henry James's later novels demands a good deal of literary sophistication. *This* is why many college undergraduates dislike them.
9. The prisoners fled toward the boat, *which* was hidden in a prearranged spot.
10. Mrs. Burns and Mrs. Kramer asked the girls if *they* were ready to adjourn the meeting.

Problems of Person in the Pronoun

Difficulties in the use of person in the pronoun are focused on consistency within the sentence.

23. Consistency of Person in the Pronoun   Take care to avoid needless shifts in person of the pronoun in consecutive clauses.

INCONSISTENT: When *one's* life is in danger, *you* don't think of anyone but yourself. (Shift from third person *one* to second person *you.*)

INCONSISTENT: I refuse to go to a show where you are not allowed to eat popcorn. (Shift from first person *I* to second person *you.*)

CONSISTENT: When *one's* life is in danger, *he* doesn't think of anyone but himself.

Just as one should avoid shift of person within a sentence, so should he remain consistent in person throughout a paragraph or theme.

Exercise 7

Correct inconsistencies in the person of pronouns.

1. The doctors say that a person's health depends to a great extent upon your state of mind.

2. If one's main desire is to win, make certain that the required preparation is carefully done.
3. A hospital convalescence can be a real pleasure for the patient if you will force yourself to relax and enjoy it.
4. When you wake up early in the morning after dancing half the night, a man sometimes wonders if it is worth it.
5. It is sincerely hoped that you will come next Thursday, and we will be expecting you.

Exercise 8: Review

Some of the following sentences contain errors in pronoun usage; other sentences are correct. Explain the rule of pronoun usage illustrated in each sentence and tell whether or not the rule has been violated.

1. Why would you choose to go with him rather than her?
2. Two of the girls in the class—Marilyn and me—planned to attend Swarthmore.
3. Tom stalked through the hall of the library, relishing its Gothic gloom.
4. The prize often goes to him who waits.
5. Markheim is one of those men who refuses to make even the slightest compromise.
6. Between the duchess and I has existed an understanding which death alone will destroy.
7. She will gladly give a high grade to whomever might earn it.
8. The Union patrol was on the hill before Branson saw it; he had run only a few steps when their bullets began to whistle around him.
9. Wilston formally invited Bunsen and I to his wedding reception.
10. Regnal told his son that he should have been more careful in his selection of friends.
11. Neither of the two prisoners had known that they were from the same division.
12. If I were she, I would refuse to appear in the benefit.
13. He could not decide whom to ask to help him.
14. I knew that one of the winners was bound to be he.
15. The rabbit doubled back and shot directly between Jim and I.
16. Maxwell wasn't certain that the raccoon was the thief until he saw it running away from the house.

17. If everyone were as smart as you and me, the world would be in much better shape.
18. Jackson hit a home run and two singles, which made the home crowd rejoice.
19. When one's work is well done, you can find real peace of mind.
20. Please forgive our not knowing whom you are.

VERBS

A verb is a word or group of words that states action, being, or state of being:

Rover *bit* the postman.
The lawn *is* full of weeds.
I *am betrayed* by what is false within.
He *will have been gone* three hours at five o'clock.

The verb is the most complicated part of speech. A complete analysis of its forms and shades of meanings would require a book in itself. The native speaker of English, however, can manage the verb for the most part with precision and accuracy. The following sections give special attention to those areas of verb usage that sometimes cause difficulty.

Kinds of Verbs

There are four kinds of verbs classified according to function:

Transitive Verbs Transitive verbs are those in which the action proceeds from the subject through the verb to an object which receives the action.

John *hit* the ball.

The subject, *John*, performs the action upon the object, *ball*.

126

I *put* the vase on the table.
The sturdy boat *fought* the waves.
The choir *sang* the hymn softly.

We can say, therefore, that a transitive verb always takes a direct object.

Intransitive Verbs Intransitive verbs are those which simply state an action or condition of being without any object or recipient of the action, as in the following examples:

I *am* very happy.
Archibald *sat* down to dinner.
The chairman *rose* to make a few remarks.
The truth *exists*.
Swift *lived* in the eighteenth century.

The intransitive verb never takes a direct object.

Linking Verbs Linking verbs are intransitive verbs which serve to link the subject to its complement. The most commonly used linking verb is *to be*. The other principal linking verbs are *seem, sit, taste, smell, appear, become, feel, get, go*. Note that all these verbs, and a few others like them, are incomplete in themselves, and require a following complement. We ordinarily refer to the complement more specifically as a predicate adjective or a predicate noun (or predicate nominative) if the complement is an adjective or noun, respectively. A predicate adjective modifies the subject but is not its equivalent. A predicate nominative is the equivalent of the subject and, grammatically at least, can be used interchangeably with it:

Dr. Thompson is a pediatrician.
The pediatrician is Dr. Thompson.

This beer *tastes* flat. (*Flat* is a predicate adjective modifying the subject *beer*.)
That story *seems* improbable. (*Improbable* is a predicate adjective modifying the subject *story*.)
George struck oil and *became* rich. (*Rich* is a predicate adjective describing the subject *George*.)

Eisenhower *became* President in 1953. (*President* is a predicate noun.)

Who *is* secretary of the club? (*Secretary* is a predicate noun.)

His face *appeared* red and puffy. (*Red* and *puffy* are predicate
adjectives modifying the subject *face*.)

Remember that adjectives, not adverbs, are used with linking verbs. (See G-39.)

Auxiliary Verbs The last word in a verb phrase is the
main verb; the others are *auxiliary*, or *helping*, verbs. They
are formed from *have, can, may, be, shall* and *will, ought,
must,* and *do*.

I *have been* told that story many times.

Warren *may* refuse the offer.

Junior *has* had too few spankings.

Grammatical Properties of Verbs

24. Voice: Active and Passive There are two voices,
active and *passive*. The active voice is used when the subject performs the action of the verb. The passive is used
when the action of the verb is performed upon the subject.
The passive voice is characterized by some form of the verb
to be followed by the past participle form of another verb,
as in the following:

The garden club *gave* Mrs. Jones a silver service. (active)

Mrs. Jones *was given* a silver service by the garden club.
(passive)

Oxford *locks* the college gates at 9:00 P.M. (active)

The college gates at Oxford *are locked* at 9:00 P.M. (passive)

You should note that passive verbs are always compound
in form. Though it is important to recognize passives when
you see them, it is more important to know that the excessive
use of passive verbs has a weakening effect upon your style.
Whoever desires to write well should always prefer the

active to the passive voice, whenever a choice is possible. There are, of course, many circumstances in which it is necessary to use a passive verb, but it is a good policy to use the active voice unless there is good reason to change. Strength in writing comes from verbs, not from adjectives or adverbs. Choose your verbs carefully. (See "Jargon," D-15.)

25. Mood: Indicative, Subjunctive, Imperative Mood expresses the attitude or thought of the speaker toward action of the verb. In English we have three moods: the *indicative,* the one we ordinarily use to make a simple statement of the fact; the *subjunctive,* by which we express a condition contrary to fact, a wish, a hope, or a plan; and the *imperative,* which we use for commands, orders, and so on.

I *was* in New York last month. (indicative)
I wish I *were* in New York right now. (subjunctive—a wish and a condition contrary to fact)
If I *were* in New York, I would see the plays. (subjunctive— condition contrary to fact)
Halt! (imperative—a command)

The subjunctive mood has largely disappeared from modern English usage and has been replaced by the indicative mood. The subjunctive does, however, survive—principally in the verb *to be*—in statements contrary to fact, in wishes, and in certain other "petrified" constructions.

Examples of Subjunctives in Current Usage

I wish I *were* a millionaire. (wish)
If I *were* you, I would improve my behavior. (condition contrary to fact)
I move that the meeting *be* adjourned. (parliamentary)
It is requested that any interested taxpayer *appear* before the Tax Adjustment Board.
Long live the Queen!
Heaven forbid!
Long may it wave!

Except for these constructions, indicative verb constructions are preferable to the subjunctive; indeed, if the subjunctive is maintained elsewhere than in these situations, the result is a stiff, archaic expression, quite unsuitable to a good contemporary style. For example:

> If the state *require* a driver's examination, a psychological test ought to be included.

Actually, contemporary style requires (both by usage and sense) the indicative verb in *if* clauses with a possibility of fulfillment:

> If the state *requires* [or is about to require] a driver's examination, a psychological test ought to be included.

26. Person and Number   The verb, except for *to be*, regularly indicates person and number only in the third person singular of the present tense.

	Singular	Plural
First person	I work	we work
Second person	you work	you work
Third person	he *works*	they work

The verb *to be*

	Singular	Plural
First person	I am	we are
Second person	you are	you are
Third person	he is	they are

27. Tense Defined   Tense is the means by which verbs indicate the time of their action. In English we commonly distinguish six tenses: present, past, future, present perfect, past perfect, and future perfect. These tenses may be illustrated schematically as follows:

Past Perfect	Past	Present Perfect	Present	Future Perfect	Future
I had worked	I worked	I have worked	I work	I shall have worked	I shall work

130

The so-called *progressive tense*, a form of the verb *to be* plus the present participle of the main verb, is actually a second conjugation (see page 135). The *emphatic tense*, formed by the auxiliaries *do* and *did*, is restricted to the simple present and past (see page 135).

Principal Parts of Verbs

The principal parts of the verb are those forms of the verb from which the complete conjugation may be derived. These parts are the present (*take*), the past (*took*), and the past participle (*taken*). In English most verbs may be classified as (1) *regular*, sometimes also called *weak*, or (2) *irregular*, sometimes called *strong*. Those verbs are regular which form their past tense and past particple by the addition of a *d* or *t* sound (e.g., *work, worked, worked*). The irregular verbs form their past and past participle by a change of vowel sound *within* the root itself (e.g., *sing, sang, sung*). Though there were seven separate classes of irregular verbs in Old English, there remain only about a hundred of these verbs in twentieth century use. Since regular verbs so vastly outnumber the irregular, there is a constant pull in the direction of the former. This linguistic pull causes some people, especially children, to treat *all* verbs as regular ones. Hence arise such constructions as "I drinked my milk"; "I knowed it"; "The corn growed a foot last week."

28. Difficulties with Irregular Verbs   Since the vast majority of English verbs are regular and form their pasts by adding *ed, d, t*, their principal parts offer students few, if any, difficulties (*ask, work, live, turn*). Instead, the difficulties lie in the correct use of the irregular verbs. Students should familiarize themselves with the following list of the most common irregular verbs, paying special attention to those marked with an asterisk.

**PRINCIPAL PARTS OF THE MOST FREQUENTLY USED
IRREGULAR VERBS**

Present	Past	Past Participle
arise	arose	arisen
awake	awoke	awoke
	(or awaked)	(or awaked)
be	was	been
bear (to bring forth)	bore	born
bear (to carry)	bore	borne
beat	beat	beaten (or beat)
begin	began	begun
bid	bade	bidden
bid (at cards or auction)	bid	bid
bind	bound	bound
bite	bit	bitten (or bit)
*blow	blew	blown
break	broke	broken
choose	chose	chosen
cling	clung	clung
come	came	come
dig	dug	dug
*do	did	done
draw	drew	drawn
*drink	drank	drunk
drive	drove	driven
*eat	ate	eaten
fall	fell	fallen
fight	fought	fought
find	found	found
flee	fled	fled
fly	flew	flown
forbid	forbade	forbidden
forget	forgot	forgotten
freeze	froze	frozen
get	got	got, gotten
give	gave	given
go	went	gone
grow	grew	grown
hang	hung	hung

Present	Past	Past Participle
hang (execute)	hanged	hanged
hide	hid	hidden
hold	held	held
know	knew	known
*lie	lay	lain
ride	rode	ridden
ring	rang	rung
*rise	rose	risen
see	saw	seen
shine	shone	shone
shoot	shot	shot
shrink	shrank (or shrunk)	shrunk
sing	sang	sung
sink	sank (or sunk)	sunk
*sit	sat	sat
*slay	slew	slain
slide	slid	slid
sling	slung	slung
speak	spoke	spoken
spin	spun	spun
spring	sprang (or sprung)	sprung
stand	stood	stood
steal	stole	stolen
stick	stuck	stuck
sting	stung	stung
stink	stank (or stunk)	stunk
stride	strode	stridden
strike	struck	struck
*strive	strove (or strived)	striven (or strived)
swear	swore	sworn
*swim	swam	swum
swing	swung	swung
*take	took	taken
tear	tore	torn
*throw	threw	thrown
wake	woke (or waked)	waked (woke or woken)
wear	wore	worn
weave	wove	woven
win	won	won
wring	wrung	wrung
*write	wrote	written

Conjugation of the Verb

All the aspects of the verb can be conveniently shown by the conjugation of the regular verb "work."

PRINCIPAL PARTS

Present	Past	Past Participle
work	worked	worked

INDICATIVE MOOD ACTIVE VOICE

Present Tense (Singular)

First person	I work
Second person	you work
Third person	he (she, it) works

Present Tense (Plural)

we work
you work
they work

Past Tense (Singular)

I worked
you worked
he worked

Past Tense (Plural)

we worked
you worked
they worked

Perfect (Singular)

I have worked
you have worked
he has worked

Perfect (Plural)

we have worked
you have worked
they have worked

Past Perfect (Singular)

I had worked
you had worked
he had worked

Past Perfect (Plural)

we had worked
you had worked
they had worked

Future Tense (Singular)

I shall work
you will work
he will work

Future Tense (Plural)

we shall work
you will work
they will work

Future Perfect Tense (Sing.)

I shall have worked
you will have worked
he will have worked

Future Perfect Tense (Plural)

we shall have worked
you will have worked
they will have worked

PASSIVE VOICE

Present Tense: I am worked, etc.
Past Tense: I was worked, etc.
Perfect Tense: I have been worked, etc.
Past Perfect Tense: I had been worked, etc.
Future Tense: I shall be worked, etc.
Future Perfect Tense: I shall have been worked, etc.

OTHER FORMS

Imperatives: work, be worked
Subjunctives: If I, you, he work; If I, you, he be worked
Infinitives: to work, to have worked, to be worked, to have been worked.
Gerunds: working, having worked, being worked, having been worked
Participles: working, worked, having worked, being worked, having been worked
Expanded forms: In addition to the simple verb forms there are also two expanded forms, namely,

The Progressive: I am working, I am being worked
The Emphatic: I do work

These expanded forms may be applied to the various tenses as follows:

PROGRESSIVE

Present progressive: I am working, etc.
Past progressive: I was working, etc.
Perfect progressive: I have been working, etc.
Past perfect progressive: I had been working, etc.
Future progressive: I shall be working, etc.
Future perfect progressive: I shall have been working, etc.

EMPHATIC

Pesent emphatic: I do work, etc.
Past emphatic: I did work, etc.

VERBALS

A simple and reasonably accurate definition of a verbal is that it is a form of the verb used as a noun or a modifier. The verbal appears either alone or in its own phrase as the examples in this section will show. One of the most significant things about verbals is that they cannot be used alone to form a sentence or a clause. No matter how long the verbal phrase may be, it still remains a phrase. A sentence or a clause may be as short as two words, like "birds sing" or "I go," either of which might constitute a clause or an entire sentence. On the other hand, "Men working their way through college by selling magazines in the summer and by firing furnaces and washing dishes in the sorority houses in winter" is not, in spite of its appearance, a sentence. Note, however, that by changing only one word, *working* to *work*, a true sentence may be formed.

There are three classes of verbals: participles, gerunds, and infinitives.

29. Participles   Participles are the present or past participle forms of the verb used as adjectives.

Working elephants are often seen in India.
He saw the two boys *running* from the barn.
An *exploded* shell is not a dud.
He exhibited a page *torn* from the diary.
The *burning* ship began to list.
The *dancing* girl tripped and fell.
Cynthia wore a hand-*blocked* linen dress and hand-*sewn* saddle oxfords.
Oddly enough, it was the absent-*minded* professor who found the *lost* colony.
Walking around the corner, he suddenly saw the fire.
Running to the window, George shouted lustily.
Having seen all the sights, the family was ready to go home.

136

30. Gerunds   Gerunds are the present participle forms of the verb used as nouns. (On rare occasions, the past participle form is used as a gerund.)

> *Swimming* has been my favorite sport since I was twelve. (subject)
> *Increasing* the wages of our employees will not be enough to satisfy them completely. (subject)
> Betty enjoys *dancing* more than I do. (object of verb)
> George's poorest sport has always been *skiing*, for invariably he falls down. (predicate nominative)
> *Being* a good sport is not always easy. (subject)
> The *defeated* in life are often the most interesting people to know. (subject)

31. Infinitives   Infinitives are the present forms of the verb, preceded by *to*, used as nouns, adjectives, or adverbs.

As noun:

> *To err* is human. (subject)
> *To dance* on Broadway was her highest ambition. (subject)
> She wanted *to dance* on Broadway. (object)
> Her ambition is *to dance* on Broadway. (subjective complement)

As adjective:

> This is the right plan *to follow*. (modifies *plan*)
> America has wheat *to export* to other countries. (modifies *wheat*)
> McGeorge Duffy is our candidate *to run* for sheriff. (modifies *candidate*)

As adverb:

> Mr. Duffy was not sufficiently interested *to listen* to my sales talk. (modifies *interested*)
> I am happy *to oblige* you with a loan of $500. (modifies *happy*)

Exercise 9

Classify each verbal in the following sentences.

1. Did you come here to see the Indian rope trick?
2. Last night Bárbara met a most fascinating man.
3. Swimming, riding, hiking, and camping are popular pastimes at the Bar X Ranch.
4. Don't blame him; he's just a poor, confused kid.
5. Orientals, it is said, always seem to be afraid of losing face.
6. To be or not to be, that is the question.
7. Thoreau advised his contemporaries to simplify their lives.
8. Emerson wanted Americans to be more self-reliant.
9. "Parting is such sweet sorrow," said Bill as we reached the door.
10. There is absolutely no way to justify his behavior at the Zeta dance.
11. Whatever the outcome may be, knowing you has been a pleasure.
12. To descend to the floor of the Grand Canyon is comparatively easy; but to return to the rim is arduous.
13. An inquiring mind, intellectual curiosity, and an ability to think are three great requisites for success in college.
14. America is fortunately still marked by an expanding economy as a result of a growing population.
15. Whatever your requirements may be, The Acme Machine Corporation is admirably prepared to meet them.
16. Diversifying is supposed to take some of the risk out of investment.
17. My family then hastily departed to try farming in the West.
18. Two of his cousins were charged with pushing a boy over a cliff.
19. Our tremendous use of pulpwood requires the constant planting of more pine trees.
20. To discover a new wonder drug like penicillin was his secret ambition.

Problems in Using Verbs and Verbals

32. Agreement of Subject and Verb (See BE-6) A basic rule is that the verb must agree with its subject in person and number. Ordinarily students have little difficulty with this rule when the simplest and most typical sentence form is followed, namely, subject—verb—object, although even here students sometimes fail to note the difference between the contractions *doesn't* (third person singular) and *don't* (first and second singular and all persons plural). Thus such expressions arise as "She don't go to college."

Failure to make the verb agree with the subject sometimes also results from an intervening phrase or clause between subject and verb:

Each of us *intends* to do his part.
A *plan* which will solve our traffic problems *was proposed* at the meeting last night.
Every day the *cat,* with all of her five kittens, safely *crosses* the Boston Post Road.

Still another cause for lack of agreement of subject and verb is the confusion arising from failure to recognize the expletive *there* for what it really is. The expletive *there* is used in idiomatic English to fill out a sentence, but it has no grammatical relationship to the other words of the sentence:

There are boys in this class who are potential delinquents.
There is a respiratory weakness in this patient.

In the first sentence, the subject is *boys*; therefore, the verb must be plural. In the second sentence, the singular subject *weakness* takes a singular verb. The expletive *there* has no effect on the number of the verb.

33. Problems with "Shall" and "Will"; "Should" and "Would" Distinction in the use of *shall* and *will* is still preserved in formal English only by the most careful writers; in conversation and informal writing the distinction is no longer always observed even by highly literate people. For example, even a well-educated person might now say "I will see my dentist tomorrow," with no thought whatever of making a promise or showing determination, but simply using the word *will* in the sense of simple futurity. But formal English still distinguishes between the simple future and another use of *shall* and *will* which indicates determination or promise. As an indication of simple future time, the following are the correct formal forms:

I shall return	We shall return
You will return	You will return
He will return	They will return

Note that the first person, both singular and plural, uses *shall* and that the second and third persons, both singular and plural, use *will*.

To express promise or determination this use of *shall* and *will* is reversed, with *will* being used in the first person and *shall* in the second and third persons:

I will	We will
You shall	You shall
He shall	They shall

General Douglas MacArthur's historically important promise, "I shall return," made upon the occasion of his leaving the Philippines during the Second World War, is, however, almost a classic example of the fact that the distinction between *shall* and *will* has largely broken down even in the usage of highly literate people. According to the strict rules of formal grammar, the General should have said, "I *will* return." Yet it is a safe assumption that most Americans accepted his use of *shall* in the sense of both promise and determination. MacArthur's statement is thus an illustration of the process of linguistic change by which the distinction maintained in the formal usage of the past has largely been invalidated.

The distinction between *should* and *would* is likewise fading out in conversation and in much writing. In the most conservative formal usage, *should* and *would* follow the same pattern as that established for the formal use of *shall* and *will,* namely, *should* in the first person and *would* in the second and third persons in expressing simple *future* expectation:

> I *should* like to have a copy of your new bulletin.
> You *would* like the beaches in Florida.

By reversing this order (using *would* for the first person, and *should* for the second and third persons) promise, determination, or command is expressed in formal usage:

> Only upon these terms *would* we be willing to enter the agreement with you. (promise)

34. Six Troublesome Verbs: "Sit," "Set"; "Lie," "Lay"; "Rise," "Raise" These six verbs, widely used in common speech, cause students more difficulties, perhaps, than other verbs, largely for two reasons: first, students seldom have studied these verbs enough to have the principal parts indelibly imprinted in their minds, and, second, students usually do not grasp the fact that these six verbs actually make three pairs, and that one member of each pair is a transitive verb (taking an object), whereas the other is intransitive (incapable of taking an object). Since mistakes in using these verbs are considered breaches of correct written and spoken English, you should study the following table until you master it. If you know the principal parts of each verb, then all you will have to do is decide whether you want the transitive or intransitive member, and proceed accordingly. In the following table, the first member of each pair is intransitive, and is labeled "I"; the second is transitive and labeled "T":

I—sit	sat	sat
T—set	set	set
I—lie	lay	lain

T—lay	laid	laid
I—rise	rose	risen
T—raise	raised	raised

Wilbur *sat* down on the porch to wait for Wilma, but after he *had sat* there forty minutes he became impatient. (intransitive)

Won't you *sit* down and rest? (intransitive)

We *set* traps for the muskrats in the entrances to their tunnels. (transitive—object, *traps*)

Mary *set* her table with Spode china and her best sterling. (transitive—object, *table*)

Charles *set* his watch at correct Eastern Standard Time. (transitive—object, *watch*)

The hoe still *lay* rusting in the yard where it *had lain* since last summer. (intransitive)

Please *lie* on that couch while I psychoanalyze you. (intransitive)

For heaven's sake, *lay* that pistol down. (transitive—object, *pistol*)

The conspirators *laid* a trap to catch the FBI agent. (transitive—object, *trap*)

My hens have never *laid* more eggs than during the month of March. (transitive—object, *eggs*)

Let us *raise* a standard to which the wise and brave can repair. (transitive—object, *standard*)

We must *rise* up and behave like men, not children. (intransitive)

As a result of the torrential spring rains, the river *rose* three feet last night. (intransitive)

During the Second World War, the price of wheat *rose* to $3.00 a bushel. (intransitive)

Lester *raised* chinchillas in his basement last year. (transitive—object, *chinchillas*)

Exercise 10

In the following sentences, select the correct form of the two italicized words.

1. The State Highway Commission (*sat*) (*set*) the speed limit at 60 mph.

2. I had hardly (*laid*) (*lain*) down to sleep before I heard someone trying to (*rise*) (*raise*) the window.

3. I (*rose*) (*raised*) my hand just as soon as the previous speaker had (*sat*) (*set*) down.

4. This lot (*lies*) (*lays*) on the crest of the hill.

5. Glamorous George (*laid*) (*lay*) very still after Ali Baba applied the Arabian Torture the third time.

6. Now that we have grown up, we have (*lain*) (*laid*) aside many of the beliefs we held as children.

7. We (*set*) (*sat*) down for one of those intimate man-to-man talks.

8. I will (*rise*) (*raise*) you three chips.

9. Prices have (*raised*) (*risen*) almost continuously since the end of the war.

10. Somehow or other Mr. Bilk (*raised*) (*rose*) the final payment on the mortgage.

11. At Appomattox the Confederate soldiers (*lay*) (*laid*) down their arms.

12. A new South has (*raised*) (*risen*) from the ashes of the old.

13. To ride a horse, you must (*sit*) (*set*) upright in the saddle and not fall off either side.

14. The lead mine (*lay*) (*laid*) forgotten for many decades until father came across the old geological survey.

15. Let us (*sit*) (*set*) a limit to the amount each member may spend on refreshments.

16. Here we (*set*) (*sit*) waiting for someone else to bring us help, without once trying to (*rise*) (*raise*) the quality of our product.

17. If your conscience is clear, you can (*lie*) (*lay*) down to pleasant slumbers, knowing that you did your best.

18. When Mr. Boggs admitted making $18,000 last year, the county assessor really (*sat*) (*set*) up and showed interest.

19. Here I have (*sat*) (*set*) down the fundamental principles of square dancing.

20. Don't you dare (*lie*) (*lay*) a finger on me.

35. Tense Sequence Verbs in the main and subordinate clauses of a sentence should indicate a logical relationship in time. Generally the tenses of the verbs correspond (see G-27).

Gerald *smiles* now whenever he *sees* me. (present)

Dr. Wilberforce *found* that the natives *were* completely hostile to white explorers. (past)

Poor Arbuthnot *had believed* that he *was* the life of the party. (past perfect—past)

He *wondered* whether he *had disgraced* himself. (past—past perfect)

The sequence is not observed, however, if the past tense in the main clause is followed by a statement of universal truth or a persisting condition.

Harvey *discovered* that the blood *circulates* through the body. (past—present)

For the first time he *realized* that he *is* no genius. (past—present)

A verb, infinitive, or participle in a subordinate clause must be made to agree logically with the verb in the main clause. The principal difficulties in correct sequence of tense arise in the use of infinitives and participles. Take care to see that the present infinitive is used to express action simultaneous with the action of the governing verb, or future to the action of the governing verb:

CORRECT: Bill was delighted *to locate* his old fraternity brother in his National Guard unit. (not *to have located*)
He immediately invited him *to come* to dinner next Friday. (future)

The perfect infinitive is used to indicate action prior to that expressed by the governing verb:

CORRECT: He considers it a privilege *to have talked* with the enigmatic Calvin Coolidge.

CORRECT: I should have expected Henry Ford *to have become* discouraged before attaining success.

In using participles, the present participle is used to express action simultaneous with the action of the governing verb, and the perfect participle for action prior to the action of the governing verb:

CORRECT: *Looking* up old college friends in New York, he was frequently surprised by their occupations.

CORRECT: *Having located* about fifteen of them, Grant decided to arrange a reunion banquet.

Exercise 11

Correct all errors in tense in the following sentences.

1. Other information had been collected that lead them to suspect her of being a communist.
2. If they continue their policy of filling our minds with their propaganda, one day we get up to find a communist flag flying over the capitol in Washington.
3. If we would really help other countries to become our allies, maybe Russia would respect us and our power instead of stepping on our toes every time we turned around.
4. Even though Egbert remained in Canada only one year, he was glad to have lived there.
5. Teen-agers aren't supposed to have any troubles, but to them their problems often are very big and real.
6. The first thing Evangeline ask him was, "Billy, are you rich?"
7. He swung at the ball as it flew past his ear.
8. I study every night until along came this character named Tommy Sullivan.
9. He would interrupt whatever I happened to be doing, and suggest that we go out to get a sandwich.
10. Every single time Bryan run he was defeated.
11. By flying we saw the West without having had to drive all those weary miles.
12. But there were many places we would have liked to have visited if we had only had a car.
13. When we returned to Illinois we felt disappointed in not having visited Glacier National Park.
14. Seniors were given the opportunity last June to have registered for the fall semester in advance.
15. We feel that registration proceeds more rapidly under this plan.

16. As Dr. Wilberforce finally succeeded in escaping from China, he thought of his family in Oregon and hoped to find them safe and well when he reaches home.

17. How she choose him for her life partner I can never understand.

36. Consistency in Tense Since tense is the grammatical expression of time, it is illogical and incorrect to shift from one tense to another without reason for changing. Thus in the same paragraph one would not change back and forth from present to past tense. One should remain consistent in tense throughout a theme also. Do not begin in the past and then shift to the present unless discussing historical or chronological sequence.

Frequently, however, grammatical tense does not conform to the actual time expressed, as, for instance, "If he is free I will talk to him tomorrow" or "If he will be free I will talk to him tomorrow."

INCORRECT: Bill *goes* over to the club, *walks* in, and *said*, "Hey, you guys, how about a little bet on the Series?" But nobody *took* him up, so then he *says*, "What's wrong with you fellows, anyway?"

Exercise 12

In the following passage, note all inconsistencies in tense.

The novel, *Room at the Top*, concerns a young Englishman who was determined to make a place for himself in the world of the rich. Attractive, aggressive and intelligent, he deliberately selected the daughter of the richest man in a provincial city. She proves willing, but the issue was complicated when he fell in love with a woman several years older than he is. He has been meeting the older woman during his courtship of the younger, but still planned to marry the rich girl when he could. The husband of the older woman found out about the affair and threatens him with exposure. What the young Englishman decides, and what was decided for him, forms the climax of the novel.

ADJECTIVES AND ADVERBS

Functions of Adjectives and Adverbs

Adjectives and adverbs are conveniently treated together since they are both *modifiers*. The adjective limits or describes a *noun* or *pronoun;* the adverb limits or describes a *verb*, an *adjective*, or another *adverb*.

Adjectives

Short journeys are *best*.

The adjective *short* modifies the meaning of the noun *journeys*. The adjective *best* also modifies the noun *journeys*, but since the linking verb *are* intervenes, we call the word *best* a predicate adjective. (*Short journeys are the best journeys*.)

The italicized words in the following examples are all adjectives. Note that the words *a, an*, and *the* function as adjectives, but these are commonly designated indefinite (*a, an*) and definite (*the*) articles.

The *red* barn loomed on the horizon.
Her *toothy* grin could hardly be called a smile.
The *inactive* club will never be revived.
He is an *old* settler.
The corn is *green*.
An avalanche is *irresistible*.

Adverbs

The ball bounced *sharply* against his head.
His wife is an *extremely* beautiful woman.
He walked *quite* jauntily to the car.

In the first sentence, *sharply* modifies the verb *bounced*. In the second sentence, *extremely* modifies the adjective *beautiful*. In the third sentence, *quite* modifies the adverb *jauntily*. *Sharply*, *extremely*, and *quite* are all adverbs.

Problems with Adjectives and Adverbs

The adjective and adverb do not change form according to their function in the sentence. Consequently, they cause the native speaker little difficulty. Only a few peculiarities of adjective and adverb usage need be pointed out.

37. Comparisons of Adjectives and Adverbs Most adjectives and adverbs have three forms, or degrees: positive, comparative, and superlative.

	Positive	Comparative	Superlative
ADJECTIVE:	brave	braver	bravest
ADVERB:	bravely	more bravely	most bravely

Some commonly used adjectives have irregular comparisons, but these seldom cause difficulty:

ADJECTIVE:	good	better	best
	bad	worse	worst
ADVERB:	well	better	best
	badly	worse	worst

When the adjective consists of more than two syllables, it is usually compared, like the adverb, by the use of *more* and *most: more beautiful* and *most beautiful*. Which form the speaker or writer chooses depends on the ease of pronunciation.

George is the *most reticent* young man I have ever dated.

One would not say *reticentest*. Some adjectives, however, may be compared either way.

His was the *handsomest* offer.
His was the *most handsome* offer.

The comparative degree of the adective or adverb is used in comparing two persons or things, the superlative in comparing three or more.

Adjective

COMPARATIVE: He is the *older* of their two sons.

SUPERLATIVE: Marbrook is the *brightest* of the three.

Adverb

COMPARATIVE: Gene Kelly dances *more beautifully* than Fred Astaire.

SUPERLATIVE: Ray Bolger dances *most comically* of them all.

Absolute Modifiers. Logically, adjectives like *perfect, unique, circular, straight* and adverbs like *perfectly* and *uniquely* name absolute qualities and cannot be compared. In formal writing and speaking it is probably best to avoid such comparisons.

ILLOGICAL: Bill Tilden's serve was the most perfect in tennis history.

LOGICAL: Perfect coordination of these elements is difficult to achieve.

ILLOGICAL: He has the most unique personality I have ever known.

LOGICAL: His personality is unique.

38. Confusion of Adjectives and Adverbs Since adjectives and adverbs are so closely related in function, the main difficulty in their correct usage arises from the problem of confusing the two parts of speech. Although many adverbs end in *ly,* this suffix, unfortunately, is not sufficient basis for identification, since many adjectives also end in *ly.* To add further complication, there are a number of words which may be either adjectives or adverbs, depending entirely on

149

their function in the sentence. Here follows a list of some of the more important of these, with examples of their use as adjectives and as adverbs:

	Adjective	Adverb
deep	He is a *deep* thinker.	*Deep* in the canyon Pick found uranium.
slow	Bill is a *slow* reader.	Drive *slow* after dark.
well	Mr. Roscoe is not a well man. (Used with reference to health)	You were *well* advised to make the deal.
	All is well.	
far	The prodigal son went into a *far* country.	How *far* is it to Gnawbone, Indiana?
late	The Capitol Limited is *late* tonight.	They came to the party three hours *late*.
early	President Truman is an *early* riser.	I'll see you *early* next week.
fast	The *fast* driver is not necessarily a bad one.	Hold *fast* until help comes!
just	A *just* judge is always impartial.	He had *just* arrived when he had to leave.
right	This is the *right* answer.	Fear God and do *right*.
hard	He gave him a *hard* blow on the chin.	Try *hard* to do your best.

Some adverbs have two parallel forms conveying exactly the same meaning. The adverb *slow*, for instance, has a parallel form *slowly*, which is generally used in formal speech and writing. This distinction will also hold true of such parallel adverbs as *deep–deeply* and *quick–quickly*. Other adverbs are parallel in form, but convey different meanings or shades of meaning.

late—lately	The train came *late*.	He has been ill *lately*.
hard—hardly	He was *hard* pressed.	I can *hardly* see.
just—justly	I have *just* eaten.	He decided the issue *justly*.
right—rightly	Come *right* in.	He was *rightly* criticized.

Where there are separate words for the adjective and adverb, the correct grammatical form should always be used, as in the following examples:

Adjective, Adverb	(Adjective example)	(Adverb example)
sure, surely	This is a *sure* thing.	*Surely* you can eat more.
different, differently	Bill is *different*.	How could you do *differently*?
real, really	Are you a *real* person?	I *really* don't know.
disgusting, disgustingly	Some of Swift's descriptions are *disgusting*.	How could he write so *disgustingly*?
beautiful, beautifully	She is a *beautiful* girl.	But she doesn't behave *beautifully*.
quiet, quietly	Be *quiet*, please.	The burglar *quietly* opened the window.
certain, certainly	Nothing in life is *certain*.	Caesar *certainly* was an extrovert.
good, well	A *good* man is hard to find.	She plays the piano *well*.

Only the use, or function, of the word in the sentence can determine whether the adjective or adverb is required.

39. Adjective with the Linking Verb Actually the greatest difficulty in the correct use of adjectives arises in connection with the so-called linking verbs, which always take predicate adjectives instead of adverbs. In addition to the verb *to be* in all its forms, the linking verbs are words such as *seem, appear, look, smell, taste,* and *feel.*

Examples

CORRECT: The pie tastes *good*.

INCORRECT: The pie tastes *well*.

CORRECT: Since my head aches, I feel *bad*.

151

INCORRECT: I feel *badly* today.

CORRECT: I feel *good* today.

CORRECT: I feel *well* today. (*Well* is here used as an adjective, not an adverb.)

CORRECT: Wilbur seems *happy* with his blind date.

CORRECT: The peasants danced *happily* on the village green.

CORRECT: These floribunda roses smell *sweet*.

CORRECT: She sang the old folk song *sweetly* and *sincerely*.

CORRECT: Betty Jane seems *sad*.

CORRECT: Their arguments appeared *right*.

Remember also that in formal usage, especially in writing, *real* and *sure* are adjectives and *really* and *surely* the adverbs. Keep the distinction clear in your own formal writing.

INCORRECT: That's *real* good.

CORRECT: That's *really* good.

INCORRECT: I *sure* like her.

CORRECT: I *surely* like her.

Exercise 13

In the following sentences select the correct form:

1. It (*sure*) (*surely*) is a pity that Coleridge didn't marry Dorothy Wordsworth.
2. That old dog never has had a bath in his life; it is little wonder that he smells (*bad*) (*badly*).
3. But he is a good hunting dog, and on the trail of game he smells (*good*) (*well*) enough.
4. I have a sinus headache this morning and bursitis in my left elbow, so I feel very (*badly*) (*bad*).
5. This pie tastes as (*good*) (*well*) as the ones that Mother used to make.
6. "Will you have·a Coke, Betty Sue?" "(*Sure*), (*Surely*), I'd just love one."
7. Letitia was one of her sister's bridesmaids, and sang "O Promise Me" (*beautiful*) (*beautifully*) in a clear soprano voice.

8. He seemed more (*eager*) (*eagerly*) to demonstrate his real or imagined ability when in the presence of company he respected.
9. His biographer, Professor James L. Clifford, says that Johnson always talked most (*brilliant*) (*brilliantly*) on the wrong side of an argument.
10. The common cat is able to see (*clear*) (*clearly*) in the darkest night.
11. The cat sees (*best*) (*better*) and the dog smells (*best*) (*better*) than any other animals known to man.
12. I wonder, thought the medical student as he sliced a cadaver, what race has the (*thicker*) (*thickest*) skin.
13. Dr. Johnson's marriage to Mrs. Porter, a widow twenty years his senior, appeared (*curious*) (*curiously*) to all his acquaintances.
14. (*Incredible*) (*Incredibly*) as it may seem, even Standard Oil of New Jersey is small in comparison.
15. Chance (*seldom*) (*seldomly*) favors the untrained mind.

PREPOSITIONS

Prepositions are words which connect an object and some other word in the sentence.

> He went *to* the dance.
> The child fell *under* the car.
> Dana spent two years *before* the mast.

A few of the more common prepositions are *at, by, for, from, in, on, with, about, along, above, below, beneath, during, except, without*. Most prepositions are short and nearly all are used with great skill and facility by the native speaker and writer to express a multitude of subtle meanings. Prepositions are probably the most difficult of the parts of speech for the foreign user of the language to master, but they pose no problem for the native user, with the possible exception of certain idioms (see "Idioms," D-10). Questions of usage of the preposition center largely on formal and informal style.

Problems in Usage of the Preposition

40. Double Prepositions Some compound prepositions like *at about, at around, off of, in (out) behind* are much more common in conversational than in written English. Though they may be permitted in the informality of conversation, they should be used very sparingly, if at all, in writing:

CONVERSATION:	We found the children smoking cigarettes *in (out) behind* the barn.
WRITING:	We found the children smoking cigarettes *behind* the barn.
CONVERSATION:	Is it true that the Queen of England eats *off of* golden plates every day?
WRITING:	Is it true that the Queen of England eats *off* golden plates every day?
CONVERSATION:	We plan to leave for the beach *at about* 7:00 A.M. tomorrow.
WRITING:	We plan to leave for the beach *about* 7:00 A.M. tomorrow.

41. Prepositions at the End of Sentences Contrary to the belief, and perhaps to the prior instruction, of many people, sentences may end in a preposition whenever it is natural for one to come at the end of the sentence.

Is this the town you come *from*?
Whom are you going *with*?
This is the pen I usually write *with*.

These expressions are surely more natural than the sentences one would have to make avoiding final prepositions:

Is this the town from which you come?
With whom are you going?
This is the pen with which I usually write.

In varying degrees these sentences sound unnatural and affected to many educated people. On the other hand, do not end sentences with prepositions awkwardly or superfluously:

Where shall we meet *at*?

The test of correctness is the naturalness of the expression, assuming always, of course, that the speaker is used to hearing Standard English. The test of naturalness cannot be universally applied; for those who have been brought up in an environment of substandard English, it is not a valid test. In some circles it may seem perfectly natural to say "Him and me done it." But assuming a fairly good Standard English in the speaker's background, the test of naturalness can be applied to the question of ending or not ending a sentence with a preposition.

Exercise 14

Choose the better alternative.

1. This is the place (*where we came in.*) (*in which we came.*)
2. Margaret, (*where did you come from?*) (*from where did you come?*)
3. Is it true that Mr. Reeves lives entirely (*off*) (*off of*) his relief check?
4. Let's meet at the Bellevue clock (*about*) (*at about*) 6:00 P.M.
5. Where shall we (*meet at?*) (*meet?*)
6. A double-barreled shotgun is not a toy (*to play with.*) (*with which to play.*)
7. Betsy, dear, (*about what are you thinking?*) (*what are you thinking about?*)
8. The wrecked automobile had been (*behind*) (*in behind*) the truck.
9. Holding his nose firmly, he jumped (*off*) (*off of*) the bridge.
10. Faith is (*that by which we live.*) (*what we live by.*)

CONJUNCTIONS

Types of Conjunctions

Conjunctions are words used to connect other words or groups of words. For convenience of discussion, we may divide conjunctions into four classes: coordinating conjunctions, subordinating conjunctions, conjunctive adverbs, and correlative conjunctions.

Coordinating Conjunctions. There are seven coordinating conjunctions.

and: Tom *and* I.
       Walter was absolutely wrong, *and* he must take the consequences.

but: Slow *but* sure.
       Mary was pretty, *but* Jean was even prettier.

for: We declined the invitation, *for* we knew the kind of party it would be.

A comma should always precede the conjunction *for* to distinguish it from the preposition *for*.

nor: They could not solve the mystery, *nor* were they ever able to.

or: Going *or* coming.
     Be careful in crossing the ice, *or* you will find yourself with a broken leg.

so: Walford failed three courses in his first semester, *so* he decided to go back to the farm.

yet: I knew he was dishonest, *yet* I never thought he would go this far.

The coordinating conjunction, with a comma before it, is one of the principal means by which we connect independent clauses (see page 173) in compound sentences, as the examples above indicate.

Subordinating Conjunctions. The most common subordinating conjunctions are as follows:

after	provided	until	why
although	since	when	as if
as	than	where	as though
because	that	whereas	except that
how	though	whether	in order that
if	unless	while	provided that

The subordinating conjunctions are used exclusively to connect a subordinate construction (a word, a phrase, or a dependent clause; see page 173) with the independent clause of a sentence or with a word within the independent clause.

We were told *that* he was willing to submit.
Paul was disappointed, *although* he knew his chances of winning were small.
He will report us *if* he sees us come in late.

Note carefully that a clause beginning with a subordinating conjunction can never stand alone as a complete sentence.

Conjunctive Adverbs. A special class of adverbs that not only modify verbs and clauses but also serve as connectives between two clauses are called *conjunctive adverbs.* The more frequently used conjunctive adverbs are as follows:

also	furthermore	likewise	nonetheless
accordingly	hence	meanwhile	otherwise
besides	however	moreover	still
consequently	indeed	nevertheless	then
			therefore

A number of word groups also serve as conjunctive adverbs:

in fact	on that account
in the first place	on the contrary
in the meantime	on the other hand

Marston knew his place; *nevertheless*, he seldom seemed satisfied with it.

In the lightest of her poems there is more than appears; *thus* a casual reading of her work is deceptive.

Johnson was impressed by the rows of beautifully bound books; *on the other hand*, he was practically certain that Murphy had read none of them.

You should mark very carefully the fact that the conjunctive adverb invariably has a semicolon before it when used between independent clauses.

Correlative Conjunctions. The principal correlative conjunctions are as follows:

> both . . . and
> not only . . . but also
> neither . . . nor
> either . . . or
> whether . . . or

The correlative conjunctions are used in place of the coordinating conjunction when a greater emphasis is desired:

The book is on the shelf *or* under the table.
The book is *either* on the shelf *or* under the table.
John *and* I refused to go.
Neither John *nor* I would go.

Problems with Conjunctions

Since conjunctions do not change their form to indicate number or case, they offer in themselves little trouble. Some general principles of the effective use of conjunctions should be noted, however.

42. Coordination through Conjunctions The coordinating conjunctions generally connect only those sentence elements of the same grammatical structure. (See S-1.)

INCORRECT: She was quite beautiful and of a very sunny disposition.

| CORRECT: | She was quite beautiful and possessed a very sunny disposition. |

INCORRECT: Men who wish to succeed in this business must be intelligent, personable, and have no vices.

CORRECT: Men who wish to succeed in this business must be intelligent, personable, and moral.

INCORRECT: Marie was the loveliest girl in the contest and who had the best personality.

CORRECT: Marie was the loveliest girl in the contest and she also had the best personality.

INCORRECT: The queen was not only a figurehead but also ruled.

CORRECT: The queen was not only a figurehead but also a ruler.

43. Misuse of the Preposition "Like" The word *like* has traditionally been either a preposition or a verb, not a conjunction. However, the conjunctive use of *like* (introducing a subordinate clause) is becoming more widespread, especially in conversation. Careful writers and speakers in formal language situations do not yet use *like* as a conjunction.

CORRECT: It looks *like* rain.

CORRECT: It looks *as though* it will rain.

INCORRECT: It looks *like* it will rain.

INCORRECT: Many things do not appear to us *like* they did to our grandparents.

CORRECT: Many things do not appear to us *as* they did to our grandparents.

44. Indiscriminate use of "While," and "Where," and "As" The subordinating conjunctions *while* and *where* have shown a tendency to supplant more exact conjunctions in informal usage.

INEXACT: Maurice is a Catholic, *while* Mary, his sister, is a Protestant.

EXACT: Maurice is a Catholic, *but* Mary, his sister, is a Protestant.

INEXACT: *While* money is very important, it is not everything.

EXACT: *Although* money is very important, it is not everything.

INEXACT: Gerald studied law, *while* Max studied medicine.

EXACT: Gerald studied law, *and* Max studied medicine.

WRONG: *Where* people used to object to a well-ventilated room, we now approve of it.

RIGHT: *Although* people used to object to a well-ventilated room, we now approve of it.

Let the subordinating conjunction *as* be used to indicate simultaneous action or example:

As I was walking down the street . . .

. . . *as* I should

INEXACT: *As* Milton did not come, we left.

RIGHT: *When* Milton did not come, we left.

        Because Milton did not come, we left.

45. Conjunctive Adverbs: Placement within Clause

Conjunctive adverbs generally have more connective force if buried within the clause rather than placed at the beginning. This placement is a matter of style and emphasis.

CORRECT: Tom made three attempts to enter the building; *however,* he was told each time that only members were allowed.

IMPROVED: Tom made three attempts to enter the building; he was told each time, *however,* that only members were allowed.

Exercise 15

Some of the following sentences contain errors in the use of conjunctions; others are correct. Explain the rule of conjunction usage illustrated and whether or not the rule has been violated.

1. Bruce knew that he would be unable to finish the assignment; however, he took consolation from his suspicion that few of his classmates would even attempt it.

2. Burt surveyed the campus from the library steps and thought cynically that things were not like they used to be.
3. As many students seldom read poetry, they have no conception of its strong appeal to the literate person.
4. The fielder catching a fly ball must do many things at once: he must judge exactly the arc of the ball, know the position of every base runner, and avoid collision with the other fielders.
5. Where the spirit is willing, the flesh will usually acquiesce.
6. The announcement was made that the prizes would be awarded purely on merit and not on the rank of the entrants.
7. It looks like it will be too rainy today for the ball game.
8. Football seems to call forth the largest crowds, whereas basketball seems to evoke the most enthusiasm.
9. He began to chatter away aimlessly like he always does.
10. My father refused either to punish me for an action I had denied or to even reprimand me.

Interjections

Interjections are exclamatory words which express an emotion, but have no grammatical relation to the rest of the sentence. Some of the common ones are *oh, well, ouch,* and *O.*

Oh, this is hire and salary, not revenge. . . .—SHAKESPEARE
Oh, what a noble mind is here o'erthrown!—SHAKESPEARE
Well, they will never catch him now.
Heavens, what a pest he is.

5.

The Sentence

A good writer must have a mastery of the written sentence. As a college student, you probably have already attained a high degree of skill in the spoken sentence, since you now have a good many years of practice behind you. But there are important differences between the spoken and the written sentence. In fact, most of the errors in sentence structure are a result of the attempt to carry over into the written sentence the structural flexibility of speech. A peculiarity of language is that the written sentence can be carried over into speech usually with good effect, but except for special purposes, the spoken sentence, with its ellipses, vague references, and fragmentations, seldom makes for good prose.

The written sentence, of course, lacks the gesture, pitch, stress, and other visual and vocal aids which naturally accompany the spoken sentence, though we are many times unconscious of them. Without these aids, the written sentence must depend upon certain well-defined structural rules for clear and effective communication.

In this chapter we shall consider, first, the grammatical structure of the sentence. The English sentence is, perhaps contrary to your previous conception, a carefully organized grammatical construction—or, at least, the well-written sentence is. The fact that the trained writer or speaker organizes his sentences for the most part without conscious effort or prior planning means only that he has become so expert that this quite complex procedure is to a large extent automatic. But even the most competent writer must often revise his sentences carefully in order to be certain that his intended meaning is clear and precise. It is in this revisionary process that a knowledge of the structural principles of the sentence is indispensable. Without this knowledge, the writer is vulnerable to the major structural errors discussed at some length in the central portion of this chapter.

A sentence may be impeccable in grammatical structure, however, and still be a very bad sentence. Sentences exist not only in themselves but also in relation to other sentences. Sentences must carry meaning, convey tone, establish emphasis, and accomplish various other rhetorical purposes. Consequently, the final section of this chapter will consider the means of achieving rhetorical effectiveness in the sentence, although you should always keep in mind that structure and effectiveness are interrelated and interdependent.

SENTENCE STRUCTURE

In Chapter 4 we discussed the words in the language according to a classification called the "parts of speech." This more or less absolute division of words into eight large groups is an extremely useful device for pointing out characteristic formations in each group—case in the pronoun, number in the noun, and so on. But words, after all, are used in sentences, and we can also classify words in terms of their use in sentences, or, to put it another way, according to their *function*. In addition, words, the basic unit of the sentence, are usually a grammatical part of larger internal units of the sentence called *phrases* or *clauses*, which in turn can be classified according to their use in the sentence. The principal internal units and their functions can be classified as follows.

The Function of Words

The Subject   The subject of the sentence, as the name implies, is a word that names the person, place, or thing with which the statement or sentence is chiefly concerned. Consequently, the subject must be either a noun or the nominative form of the pronoun (or a noun phrase or clause, which will be discussed in the appropriate section; see pages 170–174).

> The *water* slapped against the hull of the boat.
> *He* ventured too near the edge of the cliff.
> *Welford* swore off women for the hundredth time.

A pronoun used as the subject of an infinitive is regularly in the objective case.

> We found *him* to be an interesting person.

The Verb   The verb of a sentence indicates the action or state of the subject.

> Mr. Maynard always *walks* to or from his office.
> The road *is* slippery when wet.

The standard written sentence contains at the very least a subject, expressed or implied, and a verb.

> subj.   v.
> *Margaret fell.*
>
>   v.
> *Run!* (subject *you* implied).

The Direct and Indirect Objects   The direct and indirect objects, if present in the sentence, receive the action of the verb. The direct object answers the question *whom*? or *what*? with relation to the verb. The indirect object answers

164

to whom? or *to what?* and signifies to whom or to what the direct object is given. A sentence may have a direct object without an indirect object, but it cannot have an indirect object without a stated direct object.

Like the subject, the direct or indirect object must be a noun or one of its substitutes, but the pronoun is always in the objective case.

                         dir. obj.
Julie could never keep a *friend.*

            dir. obj.   dir. obj.
If you have *trouble,* call *me.*

          indir. obj. dir. obj.
John gave *Walt* an *aspirin.*

Direct and indirect objects of verbals are governed by the same rules that govern objects of verbs.

Giving *me* his *ticket,* he marched into the room.
To give *him* his *due,* he had courage.

Objects of Prepositions   The object of the preposition is a noun or a pronoun in the objective case whose relationship to some other part of the sentence is indicated by the preposition.

  obj. of prep.   obj. of prep.
Both of *us* were startled by his *appearance.*

          obj. of prep.   obj. of prep.
One of our *aircraft* is lost at *sea.*

The Predicate Nominative   The predicate nominative refers back to the subject. It occurs in the same position as the indirect or direct object, but *is used only with the intransitive* or *linking verb.* It is always a noun or one of its substitutes. If a pronoun, it must be in the nominative case.

William is my good *friend.*
The best student is *he* who budgets his time.

Modifiers   The modifiers, usually adjectives or adverbs, qualify or restrict the meaning of the subject, verb, object, predicate nominative, or other modifiers.

Adjectives modify subjects, objects, and predicate nominatives:

> *Gray* skies intensified *his gloomy* mood.
> Jean is *the prettiest* girl in town.

Adverbs modify verbs, adjectives, and other modifiers:

> Turner walked *slowly* to the water's edge.
> We were *very* glad to reach shelter.
> He *quite often* neglected to answer her letters.

Two of the verbals, the infinitive and the participle, may also serve as modifiers. The participle, in the great majority of constructions, serves as an adjective:

> The *swimming* exercises kept him in good shape.

The infinitive may serve as an adjective or adverbial modifier:

ADJECTIVE: An opportunity *to advance* came more quickly than he had expected.

ADVERB: We were ready *to go*.

The *predicate adjective* occurs in the same position as the predicate nominative and, also like the predicate nominative, is used only with the intransitive or linking verb.

> John is *handsome*.

Connectives   The connectives, *conjunctions* and *prepositions,* serve as links between the words of the sentence. Prepositions connect their objects with other words in the sentence. Conjunctions have no objects, but serve as connectives between any two or more words or groups of words in the sentence.

   prep. obj. of prep.   prep.

Tom was one *of* the *athletes* who ranked *among* the top ten

  obj. of preps.

percent of their *class.*

 conj.   conj.

Frank and *Hal* were *exhausted* but *elated* by their victory.

Interjections We may designate as interjections those words or groups of words that have no obvious grammatical connection with the rest of the sentence:

> *Oh,* how I wish I were there!
> *Why,* I didn't even know he was absent.
> *The boat having been repaired,* we continued our journey. (This construction is sometimes called a *nominative absolute.*)

The Order of Words

Major Sentence Elements The average speaker or writer of English is inclined to give little thought to the structure of his language. Throughout most of his life he has written or spoken with a reasonable assurance that he will be understood. If asked about the structural principles of his utterance, he would be hard put to find an answer. The fact of the matter is that most people consider the English sentence a haphazard conglomeration of words whose arrangement depends largely upon the whim or taste of the writer or the speaker. But consider the following example:

> Harold gave Mrs. Turner his examination paper.

Any change of position in the important elements of this sentence would result in either a radical change of meaning or nonsense:

> Mrs. Turner gave Harold his examination paper.
> His examination paper gave Harold Mrs. Turner.

The English sentence is actually governed by quite rigid rules, and all English sentences can be classified according

167

to a very few patterns. The vast majority of sentences begin with a subject and its modifiers followed by the verb and its modifiers. The most frequently used sentence consists of the subject-verb combination plus a direct object. Of less frequency is the subject-verb combination plus a predicate nominative or a predicate adjective. Only a comparatively few English sentences are spoken or written with this normal order reversed—that is, verb-subject—especially if we exclude questions.

>   subj.   v.
> The young *men worked* hard.

>   subj. v. dir. obj.
> The young *men ran* a *race*.

>   subj. v.   pred. nom.
> *William is* my best *friend*.

> subj. v. adj.
> *Susan is pretty*.

>   v.   subj.
> There *are* three *men* in the boat.

Modifiers Words used in the sentence to modify the meaning of other words also operate according to fairly definite structural principles. Consider the following sentence:

The young men worked gladly.

Note that the adjective *young* cannot be moved from its position without disrupting the sentence:

The men *young* worked gladly.
The men worked *young* gladly.

Consequently we may say that the adjective is bound rigidly to its place near the noun (this does not apply, of course, to the predicate adjective). The adverb *gladly*, on the other hand, can be used in several places in the sentence:

The young men *gladly* worked.
Gladly the young men worked.

168

Although most of us follow these patterns of the English sentence without thought, it is helpful to know the basic structural principles by which the language operates. In the last part of this chapter, you will also see how the manipulation of these patterns can improve in your prose style.

Exercise 1

Designate the function of each word in the following sentences according to this table:

S = subject	Op = object of preposition
V = verb	M = modifier
O = direct or indirect object	C = connective
PN = predicate nominative	

```
              M    M   S   V    V   M   O    C    M    M
EXAMPLE:     The three men were given five dollars for the day's
                  Op
             work.
```

1. About the middle of last winter I went to an opera at the theater in the Haymarket.
2. I saw two parties of very fine women, who had placed themselves upon the opposite sides of the theater and seemed drawn up in battle.
3. After a short survey of them, I found they were patched differently.
4. The faces of one party were spotted on the right side of the forehead and those of the other on the left.
5. I quickly perceived that they exchanged hostile glances.
6. Their patches were placed in different positions as party signals, distinguishing friend from foe.
7. The party on my left were Tories, and those on my right were Whigs.
8. In the middle of the theater were several ladies who were patched indifferently on both sides of their faces.
9. They seemed to sit there with the sole intention of seeing the play.
10. These last, however, as I afterwards found, diminished daily, and took their seats with one side or another.

—Adapted from *The Spectator*.

Phrases: Form and Function

The basic structural unit in the sentence is the phrase. Phrases may be classified into five kinds according to their principal elements and their functions in the sentence.

Prepositional Phrase   A prepositional phrase contains a preposition with its object and any accompanying modifiers. The prepositional phrase is used in the sentence as an *adverb* or an *adjective*:

> prep. phr.
> Max went *to town* (used as an adverb).

> prep. phr.
> Bennet Arkwright, who came *from a mining town* (adverb),
> prep. phr.
> could not readily accustom himself *to the distractions and*
> prep. phr.
> *luxuries* (adverb) *of a modern metropolis* (adjective).

Verb Phrase   A verb phrase contains a verb and its auxiliaries. The verb phrase is used in the sentence as a *verb*:

> v. phr.
> He *could* not *see* his way.

> v. phr.
> Wortham *will have worked* here twenty-five years next month.

Infinitive Phrase   An infinitive phrase contains an infinitive plus its object, if present, and any accompanying modifiers. The infinitive phrase is used in the sentence as a *noun*, an *adjective*, or an *adverb*:

> infinitive phrase
> infin. obj.
> *To know Mary* is a wonderful experience (used as a noun, the subject of the sentence).

170

infinitive phrase

infin. adv.　　prep. phr.

The ability *to adjust quickly to a new situation* is a sign of intelligence (used as an adjective modifying *ability*, the subject of the sentence).

infinitive phrase

infin.　obj.

Milton went *to visit his mother* once every year (used as an adverb, modifying the verb *went*).

Participial Phrase　A participial phrase contains a participle and its object, if present, and any accompanying modifiers. The participial phrase is used in the sentence as an *adjective*:

participial phrase

part.　　prep. phr.

Running toward the stricken man, Bruce shouted encouragement.

participial phrase

part.　obj.

The man *driving the car* is my uncle, John Roots.

Gerund Phrase　A gerund phrase contains a gerund and its object, if present, and any accompanying modifiers. The gerund phrase is used in the sentence as a *noun*.

gerund phrase

ger.　　obj.

Running a filling station is hard work.

gerund phrase

ger.　　obj.

His main effort was directed toward *creating an original poem.*

171

Exercise 2

In the following sentences underline each phrase (for a phrase within another phrase use a double line). Underneath each phrase designate its kind (preposition, verb, infinitive, participial, or gerund). Above each phrase designate its function in the sentence (adjective, adverb, noun, or verb).

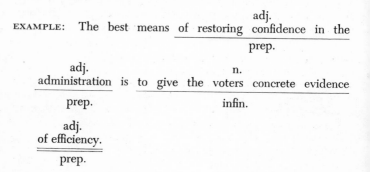

EXAMPLE: The best means _of restoring_ confidence in the
                      adj.
                      prep.

  adj.   n.
administration is _to give the voters_ concrete evidence
  prep.   infin.

  adj.
of efficiency.
  prep.

1. The turn of the last century saw many changes in the patterns of English culture.
2. At the beginning of the nineteenth century, social position was based largely on the ownership of land.
3. By the reign of Edward VII, this essentially feudal pattern had almost completely disappeared.
4. The landed aristocracy had merged into a landless plutocracy.
5. To make money, not earn it, became the sole aim of the vast majority of the upper class.
6. Released from their old responsibility toward the estate and tenant, the bulk of the English aristocracy had lost their historic mission.
7. Instead of running foxes, they wandered aimlessly from one Mayfair drawing room to another.
8. Forsaking their estates, they lent their prestige to limited liability companies.
9. Governing England was no longer their great preoccupation.
10. In 1923, with the advent of the Labor government, the last, sad remnants of a great class passed into virtual oblivion.

Clauses: Form and Function

The largest structural unit within the sentence is the clause. Clauses are classified as *independent* (or *main*) and *dependent* (or *subordinate*).

Form *The Independent Clause.* The independent clause differs from a complete sentence only in matters of capitalization and punctuation. In the following sentence, for instance, the independent clause can be made into a complete sentence simply by the addition of a period:

indep. cl.

He wanted to become a doctor because he had a deep desire to help other people.

He wanted to become a doctor. (complete sentence)

We can say, consequently, that an independent clause, like a sentence, must have a subject, expressed or implied, and a verb, and must express a complete thought. It naturally follows that a complete sentence must contain at least one independent clause.

The Dependent Clause. The dependent clause, like the independent clause, must contain a subject, expressed or implied, and a verb, but unlike the independent clause, it cannot stand alone:

dep. cl.

He wanted to become a doctor *because he had a deep desire to help other people.*

If we apply the same test to the dependent clause that we did to the independent clause, we see immediately the difference between the two: The dependent clause cannot stand alone as a sentence because it begins with a subordinating conjunction.

Because he had a deep desire to help other people. (sentence fragment)

173

The ability to distinguish accurately between independent and dependent clauses is of primary importance in effective sentence construction and punctuation.

Function Dependent clauses, like phrases, serve as functional units in the sentence.

The Noun Clause. A dependent clause may be used as a noun, and therefore may serve as the subject, direct or indirect object, predicate nominative, or object of a preposition.

n. cl.
What he knew went to the grave with him. (used as subject)

n. cl.
He said quite often *that he would refuse the grant.* (used as direct object)

n. cl.
Tell *whoever comes first* the good news. (used as indirect object)

n. cl.
Your luck is *what you make it.* (used as predicate nominative)

n. cl.
He gave the surplus to *whoever wanted it.* (used as object of preposition)

The Adjective or Relative Clause. A dependent clause may be used as the modifier of a noun or pronoun, thus as an adjective. The adjective clause usually begins with one of the relative pronouns, *who, whom, which, that, whoever,* and so on:

adj. cl.
Martha is the one *whom I saw.* (Modifies *one.*)

adj. cl.
Macaulay, *who showed great precocity as a child,* is remembered chiefly as a historian. (Modifies *Macaulay.*)

Frequently the relative pronoun, if it is not the subject of its clause, may be deleted:

Martha is the one I saw. (*whom* understood)
The man you told me about is here. (*whom* understood)

Occasionally an adjective clause is introduced by the relative adverbs, *where, when,* or *why*:

adj. cl.
This is a country *where everyone is happy.* (Modifies *country.*)

adj. cl.
Summer is the time *when this lake is most attractive.* (Modifies *time.*)

adj. cl.
I see no reason *why you should stay.* (Modifies *reason.*)

Adjective clauses may be classified as restrictive or non-restrictive. This classification assumes importance mainly in connection with comma punctuation and is discussed fully in P-4.

The Adverbial Clause. A dependent clause may be used as an adverb, and therefore may serve as the modifier of a verb, an adjective, or another adverb. These clauses are usually introduced by the subordinating conjunctions, *after, although, as if, because,* and so on. (See page 157 for a list of the more common subordinating conjunctions.)

adv. cl.
We arrived *while John was there.* (Modifies the verb *arrived.*)

adv. cl.
He spoke with such vehemence *that we were afraid to cross him.* (Modifies the adjective *such.*)

adv. cl.
Willow branches bend much more easily *than do oak branches.* (Modifies the adverb *more.*)

Adverbial clauses may be classified according to their relationship to the rest of the sentence. This relationship is indicated by the introductory subordinating conjunction.

CAUSE: (as, since, because, etc.) I ate *because I was hungry.*

175

TIME: (after, before, since, etc.) He rested *after he had eaten dinner.*

PLACE: (where, wherever, etc.) Bradford went *where he was invited.*

CONCESSION: (although, even though, etc.) *Although he seemed very happy,* he was exhausted.

MANNER: (as if, as though, etc.) She looked *as if she were going to cry.*

PURPOSE: (that, in order that, so that, etc.) He refused an attractive offer *in order that he might remain near his mother.*

RESULT: (that, such . . . that, etc.) He was so tired *that he fell asleep instantly.*

CONDITION: (if, unless, etc.) I am willing *if you are.*

COMPARISON: (as . . . as, than, etc.) She is taller *than you are.*

Exercise 3

In the following sentences distinguish between independent clauses and dependent clauses. Also indicate the function of the dependent clauses.

1. At one time the calendar of the Chaldeans consisted of twelve months of thirty days each.
2. In the convenience of having all months alike, they were actually better off than we are, after all these centuries of calendar reform.
3. Such a calendar, of course, makes a year of 360 days.
4. The Chaldeans discovered the ecliptic, the sun's annual path among the stars, along which eclipses occur.
5. They divided the ecliptic into 360 equal parts called steps or degrees, one for each day, and thus inaugurated the division of the circle into 360 degrees.
6. The first day when the Dog Star, Sirius, showed on the eastern horizon before sunrise marked the end of one year and the beginning of the next.
7. The interval between successive risings of Sirius was 365 days and a quarter.
8. There were different ways of taking up the slack of five days, which were called "extra days."

9. Some blotted the extra days from their memories by an orgy of wassail and feasting—chiefly wassail.
10. In some regions, the slack was taken up by giving every sixth year an extra month.

Classification of Sentences

Classification by Structure   Sentences are classified into four kinds according to their clausal structure:

Simple Sentence. The simple sentence contains a single independent clause:

Martindale is the chief character in the play.

Complex Sentence. The complex sentence contains one independent clause and one or more dependent clauses:

    indep.   dep.   dep.
He told me | that Walter was one of the men | who were responsible for the crime.

Compound Sentence. The compound sentence contains at least two independent clauses:

                  indep.
The professor turned toward the blackboard, | and at the
                  indep.
same time Ferrill rose from his seat and threw the book as hard as he could.

Compound-Complex Sentence. The compound-complex sentence contains at least two independent clauses and at least one dependent clause:

                indep.
                dep.
The terms | on which modern man is willing to accept life | bear small resemblance to those of his ancestors, | and there
      indep.   dep.
is little reason to believe | he will ever be content to return to the earlier standard.

Classification by Intention   Sentences may also be classified according to the writer's or speaker's intention.

Declarative Sentence. The declarative sentence makes a statement. A period is used as terminal punctuation.

The preacher came to our house for dinner.

Imperative Sentence. The imperative sentence expresses a command or entreaty and is characterized by a verb in the imperative mood. It is usually punctuated with a period, but if strong feeling is expressed, an exclamation point may be used.

Give me my pencil. (!)

Interrogatory Sentence. The interrogatory sentence asks a question and is normally characterized by a reversal of the usual order of the subject and verb. A question mark is used as terminal punctuation.

Have the members arrived yet?

Exclamatory Sentence. The exclamatory sentence conveys strong emotion. Its terminal punctuation is the exclamation point.

How I wish he would return!

Exercise 4

On a separate sheet of paper classify each of the following sentences according to this table:

S = simple
Cpd = compound
Cpx = complex
CC = compound-complex

1. The disparagers of culture make its motive curiosity; sometimes, indeed, they make its motive mere exclusiveness.

2. The culture which is supposed to plume itself on a smattering of Greek and Latin is a culture which is begotten by nothing so intellectual as curiosity.
3. It is valued either out of sheer vanity and ignorance, or else as an engine of social and class distinction, separating its holder, like a badge or title, from other people who have not got it.
4. No serious man would call this *culture,* or attach any value to it, as culture, at all.
5. To find the real ground for the very differing estimate which serious people will set upon culture, we must find some motive for culture in the terms of which may lie a real ambiguity; and such a motive the word "curiosity" gives us.
6. I have before now pointed out that we English do not, like the foreigners, use this word in a good sense as well as in a bad sense.
7. With us the word is always used in a somewhat disapproving sense.
8. A liberal and intelligent eagerness about the things of the mind may be meant by a foreigner when he speaks of curiosity, but with us the word always conveys a certain notion of frivolous and unedifying activity.
9. But as there is a curiosity about intellectual matters which is futile, and merely a disease, so there is certainly a curiosity which is, in an intelligent being, natural and laudable.
10. This is the true ground to assign for the genuine scientific passion, however manifested, and for culture, viewed simply as a fruit of this passion; and it is a worthy ground, even though we let the term "curiosity" stand for it.

Adapted from Matthew Arnold, *Sweetness and Light.*

Problems in Sentence Structure

The structural principles discussed in the preceding section not only give the writer an understanding of the framework of the basic English utterance, the sentence, but also enable him to avoid structural errors that the less informed writer frequently makes. Note carefully the following errors in sentence structure. Especially in revisions, check closely to be certain that the grammatical structure of your sentences is in concord with the meaning you intend to convey.

1. Faulty Parallelism Elements of the sentence equal in importance should be expressed by parallel grammatical constructions. (For a discussion of parallelism as a positive stylistic device, see S-17.)

RIGHT: She swam   swiftly and
                      gracefully.
        (Parallel adverbs)

RIGHT: He was told   to work,
                      to study.
                      to dream.
        (Parallel infinitive phrases)

RIGHT: He   closed the door,
             opened the windows, and
             threw himself on the couch.
        (Parallel verbs)

RIGHT: The   fortuneteller   predicted   that   he   would   inherit
                                          money,
                                          that   he   would   meet   a
                                          beautiful stranger,
                                          and
                                          that his first son would
                                          become President.

        (Parallel noun clauses)

Parallel ideas call for parallel grammatical structure:

FAULTY: The flowers were beautiful and of a great variety.

IMPROVED: The flowers were of great beauty and variety.

FAULTY: To succeed as a lawyer, one must be articulate, logical, and have great persistence.

IMPROVED: To succeed as a lawyer, one must be articulate, logical, and persistent.

A main clause and a subordinate clause should be connected by a subordinating, *not* a coordinating, conjunction:

WEAK: William is a person who likes prize fights and he has real sensitivity.

IMPROVED: William is a person of real sensitivity who also likes prize fights.

FAULTY: That young man you disparage is the class president and who is also an outstanding athlete.

IMPROVED: That young man you disparage is the class president and also an outstanding athlete.

The correlative conjunctions should introduce parallel grammatical constructions:

FAULTY: He was either sick or he was crazy.

IMPROVED: He was either sick or crazy.

FAULTY: I was not only wrong but I was very undiscerning.

IMPROVED: I was not only wrong but also very undiscerning.

For a discussion of parallelism in connection with the coordinating and correlative conjunctions, see G-42.

Exercise 5

Correct the errors in parallelism in the following sentences.

1. He was both ready and was even eager.
2. In the short story course, he learned the meaning of "protagonist," the importance of the single setting, and how to detect character change.
3. Milford did not suspect that his wife was unfaithful or her low opinion of her own husband.
4. His performance was neither impressive nor was it sensitive.
5. Jonathan, the third son, was shiftless, extravagant, and liked the bottle too much.
6. We must not only win, but we must also win fairly.
7. That young man of hers is the one who climbed the church steeple, and he also threw rocks at the congregation.
8. When the Jones family went on a picnic to the river, they would swim in the shallows, play baseball, or some other type of activity.

9. The principal not only told us that we would cut no more classes, but also that we would stay an hour after school each day for a week.

10. There are two major requirements for a winning football team: one, good conditioning, and two, there must be a real desire to win.

2. Misplaced Modifiers   Since the meaning of the English sentence depends to a large extent on the position of elements within the sentence, it is extremely important that the writer avoid the misplacement of modifiers. In general, modifiers should be placed as near as possible to the word or words which they modify.

CONFUSED: We were told that he was killed by telephone.

CLEAR: We were told by telephone that he was killed.

CONFUSED: I saw him jump from my window.

CLEAR: Looking out of my window, I saw him jump.

CONFUSED: Failing examinations usually is discouraging.

CLEAR: Failing examinations is usually discouraging.

CONFUSED: He almost ran two miles.

CLEAR: He ran almost two miles.

CONFUSED: He only lost two pounds in ten days.

CLEAR: He lost only two pounds in ten days.

Some grammarians defend the arbitrary placement of such words as *only, scarcely,* and *merely* on the grounds that through frequent use in conversation the construction has become idiomatic. But most discriminating readers and writers still prefer the placement of these words adjacent to the element that they modify.

Exercise 6

Correct the errors in modification in the following sentences:

1. He wore a cap on his head which was green.

2. My father came to Oklahoma with his grandfather when he was five.

3. She had a beautiful ring on her hand which John had bought for her.
4. Wilma only dates my brother when she has to.
5. He lent me books that I liked very frequently.
6. The small sapling was now a huge tree, which we had jumped over when we were children.
7. The drugstore only had one brand of liniment.
8. He told us about the accident which he had seen in full detail.
9. Benjy almost ate the whole plate before I could stop him.
10. We were sorry to see him leave for more reasons than one.

3. Dangling Modifiers A dangling modifier occurs when an element in the sentence—usually a participial phrase—has nothing to modify.

DANGLING: Walking around the corner, the Empire State Building came into view.

Obviously, the participial phrase, *Walking around the corner*, does not modify *Empire State Building* or any other element in the sentence. The sentence may be corrected in two ways:

1. By changing the verbal phrase to an adverbial clause which modifies the verb:

  As we walked around the corner, the Empire State Building came into view.

2. By providing a logical noun or pronoun for the participial phrase to modify:

  Walking around the corner, we saw the Empire State Building.

Other common types of dangling modifiers follow.

Dangling Infinitive

DANGLING: To enjoy football to the fullest extent, it is necessary to know the different formations.

183

CORRECTED: To enjoy football to the fullest extent, the spectator must know the different formations.

Dangling Prepositional Phrase with Gerund as Object

DANGLING: After walking for an hour, our packs became very heavy.

CORRECTED: After we had walked for an hour, our packs became very heavy.

Dangling Prepositional Phrase

DANGLING: At seventeen, my class graduated from high school.

CORRECTED: When I was seventeen, my class graduated from high school.

Dangling modifiers are not a heinous crime. In fact, their presence usually indicates that the writer is attempting to gain variation in his sentence patterns. But in your revisions of the first drafts of themes, you should be very careful to note and correct modifiers that have no clear word or words to modify in the sentence.

Exercise 7

Correct the errors in modification in the following sentences:

1. Eating only with their knives, the huge meal disappeared rapidly into their mouths.
2. To understand the meaning of the code, an elaborate key must be used.
3. Driving at fifty miles an hour, the motor scooter crashed into the wall.
4. At twenty-five, my whole world collapsed.
5. Being a very expensive fishing rod, I was eager to try it.
6. When hit by flack and out of formation, the navigator is one of the most important members of the crew.
7. When waving out the window, his car ran into a culvert.
8. Early in the summer, after graduating from college, my father put me to work in his garage.
9. His hair was burned while trying to put out the fire.

10. Watching the girls in the stands out of the corner of his eye, a long pass was thrown by the quarterback.

4. Mixed Constructions   Mixed constructions are almost invariably the result of carelessness, haste, or both of these together, and have no place in respectable writing. Mixed constructions occur when the writer begins a sentence with one grammatical plan and then midway shifts to another. Careful revision will eliminate mixed constructions from your themes.

MIXED: By making me late for bedcheck was his revenge. (A prepositional phrase with a gerund as its object is used as the subject of the sentence.)

REVISED: Making me late for bedcheck was his revenge. (The prepositional phrase is changed to a gerund phrase.)

or

By making me late for bedcheck, he gained his revenge. (The prepositional phrase is changed to a modifier of *he.*)

MIXED: Because he was tired is the reason he refused to work. (An adverbial clause is used as the subject of the sentence.)

REVISED: Because he was tired, he refused to work. (The adverbial clause is changed to a modifier of the verb *refused.*)

MIXED: A sonnet is when a poem has fourteen lines. (An adverbial clause is used as a predicate nominative.)

REVISED: A sonnet is a poem with fourteen lines.

A mixed construction that has gained some acceptance recently is "the reason is because" construction, but cautious writers will avoid it. A careful look at the construction will show you that the following sentences use linking verbs, which must be followed by predicate nominatives. A noun clause can be a predicate nominative, but an adverbial clause cannot. The word *that* can be used as an introductory word for a noun clause. The word *because* is a subordinate con-

185

junction which introduces an adverbial clause, a construction which is not used as a predicate nominative.

MIXED: The reason I left college was because I wanted to marry.

REVISED: The reason I left college was that I wanted to marry.

5. Mixed Figures of Speech Although not strictly an error in sentence construction, the mixed figure of speech should be mentioned here. Mixed figures occur when the imaginative student, attempting to make his writing vivid and evocative, goes over the line of logic into the illogical, and frequently into the ludicrous. Figures of speech are explicit (the simile) and implicit (the metaphor) imaginative comparisons. These comparisons, however, should be logical and appropriate:

METAPHOR: A democratic society should not train its members to be automatons on an assembly line, to be human screwdrivers.

SIMILE: Wit is like the flight of a swallow, humor that of a crow.

The intention of the students who used the following metaphors must be applauded, but the result is to be deplored:

The bitter taste of last year's sport scandals put a dent in the minds of all participants, coaches, faculty members, and students. (*taste* making a *dent*?)

My classes in college are just a steppingstone in setting off the fuses which will make me think. (*fuse* with a *steppingstone*?)

This little plant, the bacterium, has left a big footstep on the face of time. (*footsteps* on a *face*?)

Exercise 8

Correct the mixed constructions in the following sentences:

1. If the White Sox continue to play such good ball, the Cubs will have to take a hind seat in the fan's eye.

2. A "rumble" is when two gangs decide to have a war.
3. By causing the teacher to think you are interested is a good way to get an A in the course.
4. The reason I went is, purely and simply, because I wanted to see the movie.
5. Though Maypole College is not yet out of the woods, yet with a firm hand at the helm she can be brought safely into port.
6. At the corner of the fence, we found a small hole, which upon making it larger, we were able to observe the dog's movements.
7. He was scared was the reason he didn't come.
8. About midnight is when he goes to bed.
9. Just because she married him is no reason for her to lead the life of a dog.
10. It was a windfall which he had difficulty to explain.

6. Incomplete and Illogical Comparisons

The written sentence is more demanding in terms of logic and completeness of comparisons than the spoken. The writer should make certain that his comparisons are free of the illogicality and ellipsis that would go for the most part unnoticed in speech:

ILLOGICAL:	He is a better scholar than any man in his class. (Can he be better than himself?)
LOGICAL:	He is a better scholar than any other man in his class.
INCOMPLETE:	I like John better than Henry.
COMPLETE:	I like John better than I like Henry. *or* I like John better than Henry does.
INCOMPLETE:	In the American way of life, the small town is as important, if not more important than, the city. (As important *than* the city?)
COMPLETE:	In the American way of life, the small town is as important as, if not more important than, the city.
IMPROVED:	In the American way of life, the small town is as important as the city, or perhaps even more so.

Exercise 9

Correct incomplete and illogical comparisons in the following sentences.

1. Geraldine sees him more than Martha.
2. John Miller is as logical a candidate, if not more logical, than Warren Hiles.
3. Percy is a better fielder than any man on the team.
4. The longevity of an educator is more extended than most professions.
5. Coeds in large universities usually do poorer work.
6. Mildred is the better cook of the five sisters.
7. A teacher's salary is sometimes lower than a janitor.
8. Making good grades is at least as difficult, and probably a great deal more difficult, than making an athletic team.
9. Lowell was more impressed and interested in the display than I was.
10. Alton is closer to St. Louis than Belleville.

7. Split Infinitives Since the infinitive is a single grammatical unit, it should not be separated by an adverbial modifier:

SPLIT INFINITIVE: He used *to frequently go* to the theater.
REVISED: He used to go frequently to the theater.
or
He used to go to the theater frequently.

The split infinitive is sometimes defensible as an aid to clarity in certain constructions. Such constructions are infrequent, however, and the safest rule is to treat the infinitive as a single inviolate structure.

8. Faulty Subordination Faulty subordination, sometimes called "upside-down" subordination, occurs when the writer fails to place the most important idea of a sentence in the main clause. Context and the writer's intention will, of course, dictate the idea to be stressed. Like all the errors in sentence structure that we have discussed, faulty subordination is usually the result of carelessness and haste:

FAULTY SUBORDINATION: On a cloudy day in July, Joe Hunt was flying over the front lines when his plane exploded. (Presumably, unless the context clearly rules otherwise, the important information in the sentence is the explosion of the plane.)

IMPROVED: On a cloudy day in July, Joe Hunt's plane exploded as he was flying over the front lines.

FAULTY SUBORDINATION: Mildred has a smile which clutches at most men's hearts.

IMPROVED: Mildred's smile clutches at most men's hearts.

FAULTY SUBORDINATION: He had just become president of his company when his wife left him.

IMPROVED: His wife left him just as he became president of his company.

Exercise 10: Review

Revise the following sentences:

1. He was hit by a car on the way to the post office.
2. Thrown into a rage by the insult, I saw him strike his tormentor.
3. I only know that before his death he was an intensely frustrated man.
4. Horace loved Phala more than Francis.
5. If you want to make not only a good impression on your hostess but also to please your mother, arrive on time.
6. By trying to turn that corner at seventy is a good way never to turn another.
7. The reason that Baxter failed the course was because Geraldine had a passion for Coke dates.
8. To make a swift but wise decision, it is necessary to have experience and poise.
9. He was to never fully and finally realize his error until it was too late.

189

10. At twenty-seven, a kindergarten class was my next assignment.
11. A professor's salary seldom equals a business executive.
12. Mrs. Gamp is dowdy, incorrigible, and has an immense appeal for most readers of Dickens.
13. She ran to catch the train from the drugstore.
14. Catching my hand, I was urged by Mary not to fight.
15. He worked as much, or perhaps even more than any other man on the crew.
16. Bennett decided to not even try to get a passing mark.
17. He looked at the dog, trembling with fear.
18. I would like you to think of Shakespeare and how humble was his upbringing.
19. Torn by conflicting emotions, the situation was almost too much for Melton.
20. There only are two ways to perform this task effectively.

SENTENCE EFFECTIVENESS

So far in this chapter we have explained how sentences are made up of certain components called words, phrases, and clauses arranged in certain grammatical patterns, and we have noted some common violations of these basic structural principles. In a sense, of course, we have been considering "sentence effectiveness" throughout: a badly constructed sentence can hardly be an effective one. There are, however, major rhetorical and stylistic principles that distinguish superior writing from mediocre. These principles may be conveniently grouped under the headings "Variety," "Emphasis," and "Logic."

Variety

Many sentences, perfectly correct in grammatical structure, are ineffective because of monotony. Sentence will follow sentence of the same pattern and type, inducing sluggishness in the ideas and somnolence in the reader. Of course, an exaggerated striving for the sake of variety is worse, perhaps, than the boring monotony of the unvaried style. Plodding prose is at least not contrived and pretentious. Here, as elsewhere in writing, common sense and good judgment must prevail. The following practical suggestions, however, should help you achieve an effective expository prose through an unforced variety in sentence length, pattern, and type.

9. Variety through Sentence Length   Nobody knows how long the ideal sentence should be; in fact, despite the "sentence readability" formulas of Rudolf Flesch and others, there is no single ideal length. Though it is true that sentence length varies somewhat with the formality of usage— the average sentence in a formal paper read before a convention of philosophers would surely be considerably longer than one in a football pep talk—one cannot prescribe the length that anyone ought to use. It is said that when Abraham Lincoln was asked how long he thought a man's legs should be, he replied without hesitation, "Long enough to reach the floor." So it is with sentence length. Passages chosen at random from the work of two contemporary writers demonstrate this fact.

The lights flicked away; the screen glowed silver, and soon life began to unfold, beautiful and passionate and sad, while still the young men and girls entered, scented and sibilant in the half dark, their paired backs in silhouette delicate and sleek, their slim, quick bodies awkward, divinely young, while beyond them the silver dream accumulated, inevitably on and on. (60 words)

—WILLIAM FAULKNER, "Dry September."

He had decided now that to break would be much easier. He would eat, then, by himself and could read a book with his meals. They would eat by themselves. He would see them through the safari on a very formal basis—what was it the French called it?

—ERNEST HEMINGWAY, "The Short Happy Life of Francis Macomber."

191

The point to be made here, however, is that the writer may and should vary the length of his sentences to attain variety. The experienced writer will make these variations automatically; the inexperienced writer, at least for a time and especially in revisions, should vary sentence length consciously. In the following characteristic expository paragraph from a student theme, the writer has used sentences consisting of, respectively, fifteen, thirteen, twenty-four, eighteen, thirty-two, eighteen, thirty-five words.

Weather is stuff that is happening all the time, even at night and on Sundays. Sometimes we are apt to forget about it, but it is still there. Weather is the sum total of the manifestations of the atmosphere that surrounds our planet, and these manifestations are varied and unpredictable in form. Weather is an important commodity, and it behooves all of us to make an attempt to understand it. It is one thing to be caught in the rain unexpectedly; it is an entirely different situation to know that it is going to rain and then to get caught in it. Weathermen are misled by their scientific knowledge and equipment; they do not realize the simplicity of atmospheric conditions. Actually, weather is not difficult to understand if you analyze it with an open mind and the help of a very few instruments: your grandmother, a rusty barometer, a broken hygrometer, and your roommate's encyclopedia.

10. Variety through Subordination   Perhaps the most important stylistic mark of mature, varied prose is the skillful use of subordination. (See S-15 for the use of subordination to gain emphasis.) The consistent use of simple and compound sentences is appropriate on occasion, it is true, to gain emphasis or dramatic effect. A study of the King James' version of the Bible, or, in our own time, the work of Ernest Hemingway will demonstrate the effectiveness of consistent simple and compound constructions. But the vast majority of competent writers reserve the independent clause for important ideas and subordinate less important ideas by the use of modifying clauses, phrases, or words.

INEFFECTIVE: Many business executives are subjected to nervous strain. This strain is relentless and exhausting.

IMPROVED: Many business executives are subjected to relentless, exhausting nervous strain.

INEFFECTIVE: The State U. football team was completely demoralized. This trouble was caused by the actions of two players. These two players cared nothing for their teammates, their coach, or their university.

IMPROVED: The State U. football team was completely demoralized by the actions of two players who cared nothing for their teammates, their coach, or their university.

INEFFECTIVE: Many students never master the art of studying. Yet they complain about low grades. Such students have no right to complain.

IMPROVED: Students who never master the art of studying have no right to complain about low grades.

Exercise 11

The following paragraphs are taken from a student theme. Improve the sentence structure through subordination.

In February of 1957, our family bought a new house. It was located in a new addition near Moline. The yard was not landscaped in any way. The house was only finished on the first floor. The basement was not finished and the attic did not even have a floor.

We started with the yard. We had it leveled, and then we put the fertilizer and grass seed on. Later we added a few shrubs and flowers. The basement was next. We put two walls in so we could get three rooms. Then water started to leak in around the floor, but the man who sold us the house fixed it for us. After the basement dried out, we painted the walls and floor in the big room. My sister painted a mural on one wall. Then Dad fixed up a woodshop and utility room.

193

11. Variety through Word Order   The usual word order of the English sentence, as we noted early in the chapter, is subject-verb-object, with the adverbial modifiers following the verb or object. Though a natural order for the English sentence, this basic pattern, when constantly used, results in monotony. A simple means of attaining variety in the sentence is to make the adverbial elements introductory words, phrases, or clauses. (See "Periodic Sentences," S-16.)

Introductory Adverb

Fruitlessly, he searched through his pockets.
Amazingly, the West Germans have achieved a great prosperity.
Magnificently, the old stag turned to face his tormentors.

Introductory Prepositional Phrase

Out of the depths of the ocean, we obtain thousands of species of fish.
To this period belongs one of the great discoveries of medical science.
At last, he had found his niche.
In 1930, the Butlers moved from the country to the city.

Introductory Verbal Phrase

To illustrate his point, the instructor cited many concrete examples.

Introductory Adverbial Clause

As he passed the doorway, two men ran through the alley.
When we saw him flinch, we knew the bullet had struck him.

The participial phrase, which is essentially an elliptical adverbial clause, can also be used for variation. (Beware of dangling participles.)

Passing the doorway, he saw two men run through the alley.
Seeing him flinch, we knew the bullet had struck him.

Variation in word order, however, should be used with discretion. In the following paragraph concerning the Salem witch trials, the first sentence begins with an adverbial clause. The following sentences are in natural order until the last, which begins with a prepositional phrase, with a short adverbial phrase introducing the second main clause.

As they received more and more attention, the girls became more adept in their game of being possessed. They added new screams of pain and began to ward off spiritual shapes which they said tempted them to sign away their souls to the devil. It seems incredible that the village people could have believed these girls unquestioningly, but they did. The few who took time to consider sensibly the actions and the accusations of the girls were squelched by the indignant champions of the possessed. Some of these champions were themselves imagining that they too felt pains and saw visions so that they could be placed among that honored group of girls who acted as accusers for the whole town. In fact, it came to be quite dangerous for anyone to admit that he believed there could be anything deceptive about the strange actions of the girls, for if he did, he soon found himself among the many accused of being witches.

12. Variety through Parenthetical Elements   Variety may be added to the sentence by inserting a parenthetical element between subject and predicate. Of course, an awkward interruption is to be avoided.

MONOTONOUS: King Edward VIII abdicated his throne and he married Mrs. Simpson in spite of all the opposition.

IMPROVED: King Edward VIII, abdicating his throne, married Mrs. Simpson in spite of all the opposition.

MONOTONOUS: The spring formal was the place I met the most important person of my life. How well I remember it.

IMPROVED: The spring formal—how well I remember it—was the place I met the most important person in my life.

MONOTONOUS: During 1946, I thought only of being discharged from the service and returning home, as so many others did.

IMPROVED: During 1946, I, as did so many others, thought only of being discharged from the service and returning home.

MONOTONOUS: Marcus is the person to be blamed. Thomas had nothing to do with it.

IMPROVED: Marcus, not Thomas, is the person to be blamed.

Note how the parenthetical elements in the second and fifth sentences add variety to the following paragraph.

People lived in constant fear, not only of the curses of the witches, but of being accused of some sort of sorcery themselves. They saw their neighbors, close friends, and even relatives, people they knew and loved well, sent to prison, and still they did not doubt the word of the "poor afflicted children." Instead they remembered all the petty quarrels, mishaps, and freaks of nature which they could now blame on evil powers and added their testimony to condemn the accused. Trials were held in which the sole evidence was the testimony of the possessed girls about the spiritual shapes of the accused witches. Many people, unable to prove where their shapes had been at specific times, confessed to witchcraft and were sent to prison to be used as witnesses against other witches rather than being hanged right away. Many times their confessions and accusations of others were wrung from them by torture.

13. Variety through Questions, Commands, Exclamations The occasional use of a question, a command, or an exclamation is a simple and effective means of achieving sentence variety. This suggestion, it should be unnecessary to warn you, may very easily be carried to excess, with the result that your writing will seem pompous, stilted, and unnatural. But used in moderation, it is excellent. Note the following possibilities:

DECLARATIVE: America will continue to grow stronger.

INTERROGATIVE: Will not America continue to grow stronger?

IMPERATIVE: Make America continue to grow stronger.

EXCLAMATORY: Make America stronger!
              A stronger America!

The student theme on the Salem witch trials ends effectively with a question:

The people of Salem, including ministers and even the judges who tried the accused, were so blinded by the general hysteria and superstitious fear that they did not stop to consider how people who had led upright lives for years could suddenly become evil. It was not until after nineteen men and women had been hanged and one hundred and fifty more had been put in prison to await trail that the hysteria began to wear off and people began to realize that so large a number of their neighbors could not suddenly become possessed of evil powers. The effects of the affair, however, were felt for many years. Silent feuds between families continued for several generations, and some of the girls who had started all the trouble suffered pangs of conscience that were worse than any they had professed to endure during their seizures. Considering this dismal history, in which wise and upright men played the roles of devils, can one wonder that man's inhumanity to man persists as tenaciously as his humanity?

Emphasis

Emphasis in the sentence means an ordering of the component elements so that stress is placed on the major idea and, at the same time, less emphasis is placed on unimportant elements. Certain clear-cut rhetorical principles enable the writer to gain effective emphasis in his sentences.

14. Emphasis through Position In every sentence you write, one or more ideas will naturally have greater importance than others. Since it is your object to emphasize the important sentence elements, you must place them in the positions of greatest prominence and stress. These emphatic positions have long been recognized as the beginning and especially the ending of each sentence. Your object, then, should be to place your key idea or word either at the beginning or ending of the sentence. By the same reasoning, you should take care to put the relatively unimportant elements, such as parenthetical expressions, somewhere in the middle. Place first things *first*—and especially *last*. Obviously, it would be mistaken zeal to try to make all of your sentences equally emphatic; indeed, to make such an attempt would be to defeat your purpose. Even the mighty oak would no longer give the impression of might if all the trees of the forest were mighty oaks.

UNEMPHATIC:	This team will not win a game, in all probability.
EMPHATIC:	In all probability, the team will not win a game.
UNEMPHATIC:	Dr. Wilberforce was arrested for perjury after he escaped from China.
EMPHATIC:	Dr. Wilberforce, who recently escaped from China, was arrested for perjury.
UNEMPHATIC:	Southerners want to be understood as much as people in other parts of the country.
EMPHATIC:	Southerners, as much as people in other parts of country, want to be understood.

Exercise 12

Improve the emphasis in the following sentences:

1. In my opinion, Senator Thristleburt is eminently well qualified for the Presidency of our Republic, in case he makes up his mind to run.
2. The world will be blown up in two years, three months, and twenty-two days, according to his view.
3. Milton decided that he would withdraw from the club, however.
4. He may eventually achieve distinction by pure hard work.
5. He embezzled $50,000 as a last resort.

15. Emphasis through Subordination We have discussed subordination in S-10 as a means of achieving variety. Since judicious subordination relegates relatively unimportant ideas to subordinate constructions and emphasizes important ideas by placing them in main constructions, subordination is an excellent device for achieving emphasis as well as variety. Nothing is more unemphatic than the "chain sentence":

UNEMPHATIC: We would generally go to the movies on Friday afternoon, and afterward we would have Cokes at the drugstore, and then if we had time enough we would dance awhile before dinner.

EMPHATIC: Friday afternons we generally go to the movies, drink a Coke afteward, and, if there is time, dance awhile before dinner. (Proper subordination is achieved principally through the use of a compound verb.)

UNEMPHATIC: The Duke of Windsor spends the winter at Palm Beach; he likes its climate.

EMPHATIC: The Duke of Windsor spends the winter at Palm Beach because he likes its climate. (The second independent clause is subordinated properly to a dependent clause.)

UNEMPHATIC: The Duke of Windsor spends the winter at Palm Beach, and he plays golf there.

EMPHATIC: The Duke of Windsor spends the winter playing golf at Palm Beach. (The second independent clause is subordinated to a participial phrase.)

UNEMPHATIC: The Duke of Windsor spends the winter at Palm Beach, and he plays golf there.

EMPHATIC: The Duke of Windsor spends the winter golfing at Palm Beach. (The second independent clause is subordinated to a single word.)

16. Emphasis through Periodic Sentences In our discussion of variety in the sentence, we considered manipulation of word order as a means of attaining an effective variety (see S-11). The *periodic sentence* is one which withholds the full meaning until the end. It is a result of a change in the normal word order of the sentence and is an effective means of gaining emphasis, since it creates suspense. A sentence cast in the normal subject-verb-object order is called a "loose" sentence:

LOOSE: Paul Bunyan came to a land of clear blue lakes and primeval forests, which had not yet known the logger's ax.

Note how this sentence gains in dramatic emphasis when the adverbial elements, which, in the loose sentence, follow the verb, are brought to the beginning of the sentence, and the normal order of the subject and verb is reversed.

PERIODIC: To a land of clear blue lakes and forest, which had not yet known the logger's ax, came Paul Bunyan.

Consider another example of the increase in emphasis between the loose and periodic sentence:

LOOSE: Education remains the greatest hope of democracy, one in which we all have a stake, in spite of all its shortcomings and failures in America today.

PERIODIC: In spite of all its shortcomings and failures, the greatest hope of democracy, in which we all have a great stake, is education.

As these examples illustrate, the loose sentence is not a *bad* sentence. The loose sentence, in fact, does and should predominate overwhelmingly in writing. A prose loaded with periodic sentences would, except, perhaps, in impassioned oratory, seem affected and pretentious. But it is for this very reason—the relative rarity of the periodic sentence—that it is extremely effective in emphasizing those sentences that warrant emphasis.

The following paragraph opens an autobiographical sketch concerning a student's boyhood during the depression. The first sentence is periodic; all the other sentences in the paragraph are loose.

Among large, black, noisy, smelly factories, in soot-blackened homes, lived the people who, because of the depression, could not afford to move. They worked hard, these people, and tried to make each penny stretch to help carry them over the bad times. We, their children, didn't realize the need for such tight-fistedness. We missed our penny grab-bags of candy, our chewing gum, and nickel picture shows. It was useless to ask "Pop" for "dough." He never had any. And "Ma" wouldn't give any because there was always a need for it somewhere else. It wasn't impossible to earn money; you could sell papers or magazines, but then the "big guys" would take your money from you. You could call on Pop to convoy you, but he wasn't always available, and rather than have you get hurt, he would forbid you to sell anything. One of the gang solved the financial problem: "Let's collect junk and sell it to the junkman. The big guys won't touch us if we all take the stuff to the junkyard and come home together."

17. Emphasis through Parallelism   Parallelism in the sentence means putting similar or contrasting ideas into similar grammatical constructions, thus giving equal grammatical rank to ideas of equal importance. In parallel constructions, a phrase is parallel with a phrase, a clause with a clause, a noun with a noun, or a participle with a participle, and so on. (For a discussion of faulty parallelism, see S-1.) The result of these balanced elements is a sentence of great emphatic quality. Since few people naturally talk or write in parallel, balanced structures, however, this kind of sentence, like the periodic, loses, if overused, in spontaneity and naturalness as much as it gains in emphasis. There is, however, probably little need to warn you against excessive parallelism and its peril of artificiality. By writing balanced sentences occasionally, you may secure special attention for ideas you wish to emphasize.

Many famous writers have found the parallelism of a balanced sentence an unfailing means of attaining emphasis. Consider, for example, the following:

1. He [the poet] must, therefore, content himself with the slow progress of his name, contemn the applause of his own time, and commit his claims to the justice of posterity.

—DR. SAMUEL JOHNSON.

He must, therefore,	content himself with the slow progress of his name,
	contemn the applause of his own time,
	and commit his claims to the justice of posterity.

2. Some books are to be tasted, others to be swallowed, and some few to be chewed and digested.

—FRANCIS BACON.

Some books are	to be tasted,
others	to be swallowed,
(and)	
some few	to be chewed and digested.

3. Reading maketh a full man; conference a ready man; and writing an exact man.

—FRANCIS BACON.

Reading maketh	a full man;
conference	a ready man;
(and)	
writing	an exact man.

4. No man is an island, entire of itself; every man is a piece of the continent, a part of the main. If a clod be washed away by the sea, Europe is the less, as well as if a promontory were, as well as if a manor of thy friend's or of thine own were: any man's death diminishes me, because I am involved in mankind, and therefore never send to know for whom the bell tolls; it tolls for thee.

—JOHN DONNE.

No man is	an island, entire of itself;
every man is	a piece of the continent,
	a part of the main.

If a clod be washed away
   by the sea

        Europe is the less
        as well as if a promontory were
        as well as if a manor of thy
           friend's
        or of thine own were:

any man's death di-
   minishes me

        because I am involved
          in mankind,

(and)
therefore never send
   to know

        for whom the bell tolls;   it tolls for thee.

5. If the people believe that independent thought and criticism are essentials of society, if they think that universities are centers of such criticism and that the rest of the educational system is intended primarily to prepare the citizen to think for himself, then academic freedom will not be a problem, it will be a fact.

                     —ROBERT M. HUTCHINS.

If the people believe that
   independent thought and
   criticism are essential to
   the program of society,
if they think that universities are centers of such
   criticism
   (and)
that the rest of the educational system is intended
   primarily to prepare the
   citizen to think for himself

        then   academic freedom will
             not be a problem,
         it will be a fact.

6. Begin the morning by saying to thyself, I shall meet with the busybody, the ungrateful, arrogant, deceitful, envious, unsocial.

                     —MARCUS AURELIUS.

203

Begin the morning by saying to thyself, I
shall meet with   the busybody,
the ungrateful,
arrogant,
deceitful,
envious,
unsocial.

7. We are under-bred and low-lived and illiterate; and in this respect I confess I do not make any very broad distinction between the illiterateness of my townsman who cannot read at all and the illiterateness of him who has learned to read only what is for children and feeble intellects.

—HENRY DAVID THOREAU.

We are   under-bred
(and) low-lived
(and) illiterate;
and in this respect

I do not make any very
broad distinction between   the illiterateness of my townsman who cannot read at all
(and) the illiterateness of him
who has learned to read only
what is for children and
feeble intellects.

8. To abandon the struggle for private happiness, to expel all eagerness of temporary desire, to burn with passion for eternal things—this is emancipation, and this is the free man's worship.

—BERTRAND RUSSELL.

To abandon the struggle for private
happiness,
to expel all eagerness of temporary desire,
to burn with passion for eternal things—   this is emancipation
and this is the free
man's worship.

9. He knew that in our system of things the conferring of authority on particular individuals is largely accidental, that its compliment is slight, and that the man who exercises it is no different from his fellow men or from what he was himself before he assumed the role of leadership.

—ADLAI STEVENSON.

He knew   that in our system of things
           the conferring of authority
           on particular individuals is
           largely accidental,
         that its compliment is slight,
         (and) that the man who exer-
                  cises it is   no different from
                                                 his fellow men
                                                 or from what he
                                                 was himself be-
                                                 fore he assumed
                                                 the role of lead-
                                                 ership.

Exercise 13

Discuss the use of parallelism in the following theme:

THE WORLD I LEFT BEHIND ME

The sky was a deep blue, and the flowers were intense in their
colors. The grass was green, all shades of green, and here and
there a browned old leaf lay decaying quickly in the lost dry
air. The roses lent a heavy odor which mingled with the light
scent of the violets beneath. The dogs lay sleeping in a patch of
shade while the kitten on the porch licked its paw thoughtfully.

Outside the fence, out in the serene and sleepy world, a little
boy drove a few chickens ahead of him into the market place. A
few minutes behind, leading a little burro loaded down with fire-
wood, was an old man who stopped at the gate and rang the bell.

Out of the house walked a white-coated man, but he slouched
when he saw who was ringing. The rhythm and song of his voice
droned on the air, and got lost in the sound of the bee-hum. The
wind quietly rustled the leaves of the trees, and a leaf came drift-
ing down on the kitten, who sleepily pushed it aside.

On the swing sat a little girl, dressed in a starched and neatly
pressed white dress, swinging back and forth in the loud silence
with a slow, steady motion. She looked on the scene with sleepy
eyes, and thought of home.

Ever since she could remember, this had been her home, but
she knew that she was an American from the United States, not
Mexico. And soon she would be going back there, and she would

go to school. What would it be like? she wondered. Would it be all like unboiled milk, nice and smooth and fresh tasting, or would it be boiled and make her mouth dry and sour? But this afternoon was too lovely to spoil with such unanswerable questions.

How about gathering some pansies for Mother? She was not feeling very well this morning. Oh, but it would be too much trouble, and anyhow Mother was asleep now, and the pansies would die before she woke up. Now I'm only making excuses, she thought, but I don't care.

The sun moved on, high overhead in the cloudless sky. The wind drifted a leaf off another tree, and a ripe apricot fell to the ground. A car went slowly by, as it maneuvered around the flock of cows and sheep now being herded down the street. Somewhere a bird chirped, and next door the sprinkler started, giving another soft sound upward to the air.

18. Emphasis through Repetition Many people have been so strongly warned against repeating a word too close to its earlier use that they deny themselves one of the major devices that skilled writers use for emphasis. Of course there is a great deal of difference between the awkward, unintentional repetition of words by inexperienced writers and the purposeful, repeated use of certain key words by competent authors. You should have no difficulty whatever in detecting the ineffective repetitiousness of the following excerpt from a student theme:

This book is called *The Search for Bridey Murphy* and was written by Morey Bernstein. It was the most *wonderful book* that I have read for years. It tells the story of a Mrs. Simmons' previous existence as Bridey Murphy in nineteenth century Ireland. The author wrote this *book* in a *wonderful* style of writing, very clear and easy to read. I enjoyed reading it very much and feel that it would be a *wonderful book* for all college students to read.

There is nothing haphazard, accidental, or ineffectual about such fine examples of repetition as these:

Everything which another man would have hidden, *everything* the publication of which would have made *another man* hang himself, was matter of gay and clamorous exultation to his weak and diseased mind. *What* silly things he said, *what* bitter retorts he provoked, *how at one place* he was troubled with evil presentiments which came to nothing, *how at another place,* on waking from a drunken doze, he read the prayer-book and took a hair of the dog that had bitten him, *how* he went to see men hanged and came away maudlin. . . .

—THOMAS BABINGTON MACAULAY,
Review of *The Life of Samuel Johnson, LL.D.*

My argument is in outline as follows: that that absolute *certitude* which we were able to possess, whether as to the truths of natural theology, or as to the fact of a revelation, was the result of an assemblage of concurring and converging *probabilities,* and that, both according to the constitution of the human mind and the will of its Maker; that *certitude* was a habit of mind, that *certainty* was a quality of propositions: that *probabilities* which did not reach to logical *certainty,* might create a mental *certitude*; that the *certitude* thus created might equal in measure and strength the *certitude* which was created by the strictest scienific demonstration; and to have such *certitude* might in given cases and to given individuals be a plain duty, though not to others in other circumstances.

—CARDINAL NEWMAN,
Apologia Pro Vita Sua.

The moon blazed down on the vast desolation of the American coasts, and *on all the* glut and hiss of tides, *on all the* surge and foaming slide of waters on lone beaches. *The moon blazed down on* 18,000 miles of coast, *on the* million sucks and scoops and hollows of the shore, and *on the* great wink of the sea, that ate the earth minutely and eternally. *The moon blazed down* upon the wilderness, it fell on sleeping woods, it dripped through moving leaves, it swarmed in weaving patterns on the earth, and it filled the cat's still eye with blazing yellow. *The moon* slept over mountains and lay like silence in the desert, and it carved the shadows of great rocks like time.

—THOMAS WOLFE,
Of Time and the River.

We shall go on to the end, *we shall fight* in France, *we shall fight* on the seas and ocean, *we shall fight* with *growing* confidence and *growing* strength in the air, we shall defend our Island, whatever the cost may be, *we shall fight* on the beaches, *we shall fight* on the landing grounds, *we shall fight* in the fields and in the streets, *we shall fight* in the hills; we shall never surrender, and even if, which I do not for a moment believe, this Island or a large part of it were subjugated and starving, then our Empire beyond the seas, armed and guarded by the British Fleet, would carry on the struggle, until, in God's good time, the New World, with all its power and might, steps forth to the rescue and liberation of the old.

—WINSTON S. CHURCHILL,
Blood, Sweat and Tears.

When one has understood this, he no longer *puts his hope* on earth in anything less than that *good will* of which the Gospel speaks—it speaks of *good will*, not of good velleity; he *puts his hope* in those obscure energies of a little real *goodness* which persist in making life *germinate* and *regerminate* in the secret depths of things.

—JACQUES MARITAIN,
"Confession of Faith."

I have seen many noses that I should have liked to tweak, but never once have I *yielded to the impulse*. But this, like everything else, is a matter of degree. *If you always yield to impulse,* you are mad. *If you never yield to impulse,* you gradually dry up and very likely become mad to boot. In a life which is to be healthy and happy, *impulse,* though not allowed to run riot, must have sufficient scope to remain alive and to preserve that variety and diversity of interest which is natural to a human being.

—BERTRAND RUSSELL,
"The American Way Is Dour."

Humbly born, after a stormy life of democratic leadership and great achievement he *humbly* died. Yet it has been too often true that the very *humbleness,* even the disadvantages, of a man's beginnings has led him to abuse authority subsequently attained.

—ADLAI STEVENSON, "Memorial
Address of Philip Murray."

19. Emphasis through Climax   One of the standard methods of attaining an emphatic sentence is to arrange material in the order of climax, i.e., from the less important to the most important words and ideas. Though many periodic sentences have a somewhat climatic effect, as we have already seen, the genuine sentence of climax is even more effective. Observe the following sentences:

For a man to write well, there are required three necessaries—to read the best authors, observe the best speakers, and much exercise of his own style.

—BEN JONSON, *Timber.*

To see wise men degraded, fools preferred, one govern towns and cities, and yet a silly woman over-rules him at home; command a province, and yet his own servants or children prescribe laws to him, as Themistocles' son did in Greece. . . . To see horses ride in a coach, men draw it; dogs devour their masters; towers build masons; children rule; old men go to school; women wear the breeches; sheep demolish towns, devour men, etc. And in a word, the world turned upside downward.

—ROBERT BURTON,
Anatomy of Melancholy.

Is life so dear or peace so sweet as to be purchased at the price of chains and slavery? Forbid it, Almight God! I know not what course others may take, but as for me, give me liberty, or give me death!

—PATRICK HENRY, "Speech at the
Virginia Convention, 1775."

And the entire object of true education is to make people not merely *do* the right things, but *enjoy* the right things:—not merely industrious, but to love industry—not merely learned, but to love knowledge—not merely pure, but. to love purity—not merely just, but to hunger and thirst after justice.

—JOHN RUSKIN,
The Crown of Wild Olive.

For in proportion as it [the university] is truly liberal and vital, all its members, as younger and older scholars, will be intensely

209

concerned with the most urgent problems of mankind—with scientific and technological advance, with political power and social justice, with the multiple threats of war and the conditions of peace, with art past and present, with man's moral rights and duties, and with the challenges of religious aspiration and belief.

—THEODORE M. GREENE,
Liberal Education Reconsidered.

20. Emphasis through Active Voice   One of the most certain ways to make a sentence more emphatic is to change its verb from the passive into the active voice. Though there are, of course, circumstances under which it is entirely proper to use a passive verb, far too often we use the passive voice as a result of timidity or in a mistaken attempt to give our writing an unnecessary formality of tone. By changing all such passive uses to active, your writing may be made more positive and emphatic in tone. This is one of the basic laws for writing effective sentences: stay in the active voice everywhere you possibly can.

UNEMPHATIC: Attention is called to our new price list enclosed.

IMPROVED: May we call your attention to our new price list?

UNEMPHATIC: He was made the recipient of an honorary degree by Maypole College.

IMPROVED: Maypole College gave him an honorary degree.

21. Emphasis through the Short Sentence   An effective device for securing emphasis is the occasional statement of a key idea in a very brief sentence. In writing in which most of the sentences are fairly long, whether loose or periodic, the especially terse, succinct statement inevitably stands out, thus making it emphatic. But this device is useful only if the average sentence is fairly long. A passage of short, choppy sentences could never be emphatic. Note how emphatic are the short sentences in the concluding paragraph of William Faulkner's Nobel Prize Acceptance Speech:

Until he relearns these things, he will write as though he stood among and watched the end of man. *I decline to accept the end of man.* It is easy enough to say that man is immortal simply because he will endure: that when the last ding-dong of doom has clanged and faded from the last worthless rock hanging tideless in the last red and dying evening, that even then there will still be one more sound: that of his puny inexhaustible voice, still talking. *I refuse to accept this.* I believe that man will not merely endure: he will prevail. He is immortal, not because he alone among creatures has an inexhaustible voice, but because he has a soul, a spirit capable of compassion and sacrifice and endurance. *The poet's, the writer's, duty is to write about these things.* It is his privilege to help man endure by lifting his heart, by reminding him of the courage and honor and hope and pride and compassion and pity and sacrifice which have been the glory of his past. The poet's voice need not merely be the record of man, it can be one of the props, the pillars to help him endure and prevail.

Exercise 14: Review

Discuss the following theme in terms of the variety and emphasis of its sentences.

SOUTH DAKOTA

For the first time in over a month the scorching sun and dry, dusty winds of summer have slackened their vengeance on our withered land. We have had thirty-eight consecutive days on which the sun set in a clear sky, blazing forth a last promise of the hell we could expect on the next day. For more than five weeks we cursed the sun as it rose in the morning, sweltered under it until exhaustion overcame us, and prayed at twilight that the next day might not be the same.

Yesterday at sunset, clouds rose into view on the northwest horizon. In a beautiful display of yellow, red, and purple, the forerunners paraded solemnly toward us. By the time night turned them blue-black, they had advanced half the way to us from that point where the sky meets the endless prairie.

At three o'clock in the morning I awoke from a hopeful slumber to a thunderstorm which lasted for more than an hour. I lay awake, listening to the diminishing sound of the thunder as the storm moved eastward over the prairie. The rain came down steadily, pattering lightly on the veranda outside my window. A

211

cool breeze rustled the curtains, and the fresh smell of ozone and rain filtered into my room. At last I fell asleep, secure in the knowledge that the drought was really ended.

Around eight o'clock in the morning we arose to a transformed world. The sun was shining once more, but this morning it was sparkling on the droplets of rain still clinging to our pale trees and brown grass, and on the little puddles which covered the land as far as one could see. The few birds which made their home at our little oasis were singing. The robins hopped about the lawn and shrubs, searching out the stranded earthworms between concertos. Our one pair of wrens nesting in the orchard warbled among the apples and pears which we had saved.

After a late breakfast Dad and I decided to go out to survey our reborn acres. The little garden beside the orchard had responded to our care and would soon be yielding fresh vegetables for the table once more. The plants were lifting their foliage again, a feat which we had not been able to inspire by a heavy irrigation every evening during the drought, although we had managed to keep them alive. We walked together across the once-green meadow and were delighted to find that we could get our feet wet from the curled, brown combination of bunch grass and sandburrs.

Half a mile out on the range, we descended into a slight ravine and discovered the herd of Angus splashing in the muddy water of the creek which only yesterday had been bone dry. Old Rocky, the huge, black, broad-shouldered herd bull, meandered over to us, water dripping from his legs and muzzle, to have his back scratched. Two calves dashed in a race that sent their worried mothers galloping after them, lowing for them to return.

The willows which grew on either side of the creek were as green as in springtime, probably because their roots had penetrated to the strata of sand which kept us supplied with water back at the house. A few hundred yards down the creek, an earthen dam created an artificial lake. The lake was now full, and the water was pouring over the spillway in the middle of the dam. Yesterday our cattle had drunk from a muddied spring which seeped up through an alkali pond bed.

We walked down the creek for a quarter of a mile and started back to the house. The sight of the wheat stubble made us feel good. We had been able to combine the wheat before the drought ruined the kernels. Next we walked over what had been our corn field. The young plants, not a foot tall, were sprawled grotesquely in every direction, their remains bleached white by the sun. The day got hotter, and we were glad to reach the shade of the two pale elms and the single yellow-leaved cottonwood growing in the yard.

Now the long afternoon is ended. Once more the sun is setting —behind a new bank of clouds. Tendrils of gold, scarlet, purple, and black radiate from the place where the sun is hidden. The sky is colored in an abstract design reaching almost to the zenith. Beyond, the darkness increases. Soon the eastern horizon is shrouded in the blue-black of evening. In the west the brilliant colors fade to darker hues. A robin on the gatepost intones the evening Angelus. Far away, out on the range, a coyote wails his greeting to night, and Old Rocky's deep-throated voice bellows defiance. Silence and darkness descend over the prairie.

Logic

We can well end our discussion of the effective sentence with a consideration of the necessity for logic in the sentence. Variety and emphasis are essential for effective prose, but even more basic is the need for each sentence to bear clearly and consistently the current of thought which the writer is attempting to communicate. The three basic principles of rhetorical effectiveness—variety, emphasis, and logic—are, of course, interrelated and cannot really be placed in isolated compartments. Certain matters of logic in the sentence, however, can be profitably discussed, especially those that are likely to create difficulty for the student in the basic composition course.

The purpose of grammatical rules, if they are good ones, is to bring logic and order to the spoken and written sentence. We have already discussed in Chapters 3 and 4 and the first part of this chapter the principles of grammar and structure necessary for clear, unequivocal meaning. You should note especially these sections with reference to logical grammatical relationships within the sentence:

Problems of Number in the Pronoun, G-9–G-11.
Vague, Indefinite, and Split Reference in the Pronoun, G-20–G-22.

Consistency of Person in the Pronoun, G-23.
Consistency of Tense in the Verb, G-36.
Tense Sequence in the Verb, G-35.
Problems of Sentence Structure, S-1–S-8.

A few other principles essentially grammatical in nature may be added.

22. Logical Consistency in Subject and Voice In general, maintain the same subject throughout the sentence. A shift in the subject usually involves a shift from the active to the passive voice or vice versa.

SHIFTED: George Washington set out on a mission to warn the French, and their forts also received his close investigation. (Subject shifts from *George Washington* to *forts.*)

CONSISTENT: George Washington set out on a mission to warn the French, and he closely investigated their forts.

SHIFTED: In the morning, we rode our bicycles; in the evening, our roller skates were given a good workout. (Subject shifts from *we* to *roller skates*; voice shifts from active to passive.)

CONSISTENT: In the morning, we rode our bicycles; in the evening, we gave our roller skates a good workout.

23. Logical Consistency in Verb Mood This error occurs chiefly in connection with the process theme, in which the careless writer will shift back and forth between the indicative and imperative mood of the verb:

SHIFTED: Cook the mixture slowly, and you should stir it until the sugar is dissolved. (Shift from imperative to indicative mood.)

CONSISTENT: Cook the mixture slowly and stir it until the sugar is dissolved.

24. Logical Consistency in Discourse Avoid needless shifts from indirect to direct discourse, or vice versa:

SHIFTED: He told me a special delivery letter had just arrived and asked would you like to send it out. (Shift from indirect to direct discourse.)

CONSISTENT: He told me a special delivery letter had just arrived and asked if I would like to send it out.

SHIFTED: Lincoln asked General McClellan whether his army was well supplied with arms and provisions, and is it ready to take to the field.

CONSISTENT: Lincoln asked General McClellan whether his army was well supplied with arms and provisions, and whether it was ready to take to the field.

Exercise 15

Point out faults in logical grammatical relationships in the following sentences.

1. Peel, quarter, core, and slice the apples, and then the cook leaves them to stand while he makes the crust.
2. Martin likes to play tennis, but baseball is much preferred by him.
3. The battalion toiled slowly up the mountain, but soon the top came into view.
4. Mary asked me to come to the party and would I bring a friend of her sister?
5. Make your exit, and then you should run around to the other side of the stage.

25. Logical Reasoning   A full discussion of logical reasoning and the most common logical fallacies belongs to a consideration of the argumentative or persuasive theme. The illogical sentence, however, occurs frequently enough to warrant brief mention here. The student who writes: "I am convinced that drinking is on the increase on this campus, because I notice that Joe's Campus Tavern draws bigger crowds every year" is guilty of poor reasoning. There are several things wrong with his statement. The mere fact that the patronage of the tavern has increased is no sound reason to assume that drinking has increased; the reason may be that word of Joe's fine pizzas is beginning to circulate. The most serious fallacy in the sentence, however, is what is called a *hasty generalization,* by far the most frequent fallacy in both student writing and writing in general. The writer has "jumped to a conclusion." Careful, extensive research would have to be done before one could safely make the sweeping generalization that the amount of drinking in a student body of any size is on the increase.

Other rather frequent fallacies are the *non sequitur,* drawing an inference that does not necessarily follow from the evidence ("He's a rich man; he couldn't have any sympathy or understanding of the laboring classes") and *ignoring the question,* digressing into irrelevant argument ("You shouldn't vote for Easton; he's been divorced two times"). All these fallacies are best avoided by careful thought before you write.

Exercise 16

Examine the following sentences for logical fallacies:

1. The reason that more boys have trouble with college English than girls is that most high school English teachers are women.
2. My friends tell me that the big companies had rather hire good social mixers than a man with high grades.
3. The fraternity system on this campus is the main reason for racial discrimination.
4. If the girls in our house were allowed to date independents, our social rating would go down.
5. When I saw that the driver of the car behind me was a woman, I knew I was in trouble.

26. Logical Consistency in Thought Sometimes a sentence may be logical in grammatical relationships, contain no logical fallacies, and still be unsatisfactory on logical grounds.

ILLOGICAL: These people will remember this incident the rest of their life. (People . . . their . . . *life*?)

LOGICAL: These people will remember this incident the rest of their lives.

ILLOGICAL: We were told that there was a conflict between our personality. (We . . . our . . . *personality?*)

LOGICAL: We were told that there was a conflict between our personalities.

A more serious error is an inadvertent blunder in logic that results in an absurdity of statement. These "boners," although a source of considerable amusement to your instructor and classmates, will completely destroy any serious intention in a given passage.

It is the story of a man set apart from his own race by sensitivity and intelligence, who at the age of six tried to burn his grandmother's house.

With a small amount of care from their parents, these juveniles can be prevented.

These children may be male, female, or both.

The danger of tornadoes is very great, as the hundreds of people killed by them will testify.

Since power was his main goal, and his people were against him, it was to Caesar's advantage to be killed.

Our enemies have one great advantage over us which we will probably never have, and that is people.

I have had a very hard life because my mother died at two.

Men and women at the age of seventeen are not developed similarly.

Exercise 17

Comment on logical inconsistencies of thought in the following sentences:

1. Our instructor told us that we would fail unless we worked out the lesson during the year.
2. Soon my many belongings were sitting among the jumbled mass of my roommates.
3. Seventy-four victims of relentless cruelty passed away every day, or nearly two every hour.
4. At the completion of the school year, all the students wend their way to their home.

5. Mr. Johnson's condition was quite bad and was taken to a hospital.

Exercise 18: Review

One of the best ways to improve the effectiveness of your sentences is to imitate deliberately the sentences of masters of English prose. The imitation should not be verbatim or slavish; instead, you should attempt to express a different idea, at the same time retaining the design, structure, and profundity of the model sentence.

MODEL: To the man with an ear for verbal delicacies—the man who searches painfully for the perfect word, and puts the way of saying a thing above the thing said—there is in writing the constant joy of sudden discovery, of happy accident.

—H. L. MENCKEN,
A Book of Prefaces.

IMITATION: To the man who really desires truth—the man who seeks always the reality behind the illusion, and is courageous enough to face that reality when he finds it—there is in life a sense of constant adventure, of thrilling discovery.

Base sentences of your own on the following models:

1. To die at the height of a man's career, the highest moment of his effort here in this world, universally honored and admired, to die while great issues are still commanding the whole of his interest, to be taken from us at a moment when he could already see ultimate success in view—is not the most unenviable of fates.

—WINSTON S. CHURCHILL.

2. I forget who it was that recommended men for their soul's good to do each day two things they disliked, but it is a precept that I have followed scrupulously: every day I have got up and I have gone to bed.

—SOMERSET MAUGHAM,
The Moon and Sixpence.

3. Publishing a volume of verse is like dropping a rose petal down the Grand Canyon and waiting for the echo.

—DON MARQUIS, *The Sun Dial.*

4. But when in modern books, reviews, and thoughtful magazines I read about the Needs of the Age, its Complex Questions, its Dismays, Doubts, and Spiritual Agonies, I feel an impulse to go out and comfort that Bewildered Epoch, to wipe away its tears, still its cries, and speak edifying words of Consolation to it.

—LOGAN PIERSALL SMITH, *Trivia.*

5. Criticism is properly the rod of divination: a hazel-switch for the discovery of buried treasure, not a birch twig for the castigation of offenders.

—ARTHUR SYMONS, Preface to *An Introduction to the Study of Browning.*

6. Talk to every woman as if you loved her, and to every man as if he bored you, and at the end of your first season you will have the reputation of possessing the most perfect social tact.

—OSCAR WILDE, *Lady Windemere's Fan.*

7. When I hear people say they have not found the world and life so agreeable or interesting as to be in love with it, or that they look with equanimity to its end, I am apt to think they have never been properly alive nor seen with clear vision the world they think so meanly of, or anything in it—not a blade of grass.

—WILLIAM HENRY HUDSON, *Far Away and Long Ago.*

8. You have not converted a man because you have silenced him.

—JOHN MORLEY, *On Compromise.*

9. Even in America, the Indian Summer of life should be a little sunny and a little sad, like the season, and infinite in wealth and depth of tone—but never hustled.

—HENRY BROOKS ADAMS, —*The Education of Henry Adams.*

10. If some great Power would agree to make me always think what is true and do what is right, on condition of being turned into a sort of clock and wound up every morning before I got out of bed, I should instantly close with the offer.

—THOMAS HENRY HUXLEY,
Materialism and Idealism.

6.

The Paragraph

The most important division within the theme or short essay is the paragraph. A knowledge of how a good paragraph is constructed is indispensable to any writer who wishes to make his written expression clear and effective. There are, of course, many kinds of paragraphs—expository, narrative, descriptive, to name a few—and each kind has its own characteristics. In this chapter, however, we shall concentrate upon the expository paragraph, since most of your writing in the basic composition course will be expository—factual and informative rather than imaginative—in nature. The expository paragraph can be conveniently considered from three aspects: *length*, *development*, and *function*.

Length

It is important to remember that the paragraph is essentially a form of punctuation. Indeed, the very term "paragraph" is derived from the Greek words *para*, meaning "by the side of," and *graphos*, meaning "writing." "Paragraph" originally meant, then, "by the side of writing." And in the old texts the sign of the paragraph (of which our symbol ¶ is a remnant) was used in the margin of the text to indicate divisions in the thought.

Today, we mark the first line of the paragraph by beginning a fresh line in the manuscript or text with a clear indention. Ordinarily the last line of the paragraph remains partially unfilled. These devices are simply punctuation marks to indicate to the reader divisions of thought within the text.

1. Appropriate Length You should remember that you as a writer have the length of the paragraph largely under your own control. One of the basic principles governing paragraph length is that a solid block of text without paragraph divisions is forbidding to most readers, since they assume, usually with justification, that a greater intellectual effort will be necessary to follow the course of the writer's thought. You have probably received sales letters and noted the extreme brevity of the paragraphs, especially the first, usually not more than a sentence or two and covering at the most four lines of text. The writers of such letters, of course, deliberately shorten the length of the paragraph in order to attract the reader. Another example is the paragraph divisions in newspapers, especially on the front page. One reason for paragraph brevity in news writing is that most newspapers aim at the general reader, who prefers the short paragraph because it calls for less intellectual effort. Another reason, however, is the format of the usual newspaper page. The narrowness of the news columns necessitates the relatively short paragraph, since a paragraph of even reasonable length within normal margins would run unbroken in a newspaper column from the top to the bottom. Consider this example. Enclosed within the margins of this page, the following introduction to a news story appears almost infantile:

Eight firemen were killed and three hurt Thursday when a brick wall collapsed on them during a fire at 820 East Vine.

Two walls of the eight-story structure were blown out by exploding gases on the inside of the building.

Witnesses said there was an explosion—a large dull thud.

"Look out for the wall!" one fireman screamed. "Here she comes!"

But if we reduce the column width to the approximate width of a newspaper column, the paragraph length appears completely normal.

> Eight firemen were killed and three hurt Thursday when a brick wall collapsed on them during a fire at 820 East Vine.
>
> Two walls of the eight-story structure were blown out by exploding gases on the inside of the building.
>
> Witnesses said there was an explosion—a large, dull thud.
>
> "Look out for the wall!" one fireman screamed. "Here she comes!"

We see, consequently, that the paragraph is not only a unit of thought within the theme, but also a device for adjusting the appearance of any given piece of writing to the audience for which it is intended. The writer should feel free to manipulate paragraph length accordingly.

The standard expository paragraph, however, as opposed to the specialized types we have discussed so far, does have a somewhat more predictable length. A practical suggestion is that the expository paragraph have a minimum length of 100 to 150 words and a maximum of 350 to 400 words. The paragraphs in the body of the theme usually run two or four to the page, depending upon whether the theme is handwritten or typewritten. This length, of course, is subject to variation—as we shall see when we consider the functions of paragraphs—but will often hold true. Certainly you should avoid, on the one hand, writing your entire theme in one paragraph or, on the other, breaking your page into seven or eight paragraphs. At all times, however, the compactness of paragraph development is more important than its length.

Exercise 1

I. Examine the paragraphing in an expository essay in *The Atlantic* or *Harper's* and compare it with the paragraphing In a similar essay in the *Reader's Digest*. Is there a difference? If so, what reason can you give for that difference?

II. In your newspaper, compare the length of the paragraphs in the news stories on the front page with the paragraph length on the editorial page. How do you account for the difference?

III. Examine the paragraph division in the sample themes in T-12. Does paragraph length vary markedly in the different themes? Can you account for differences in length in terms of the author's purpose?

Development

Since the standard expository paragraph develops an idea of some consequence, there are certain basic structural principles which we can apply. Most expository paragraphs are actually compositions in brief, and the same principles govern them that govern the theme or essay. In fact, if you can write an effective expository paragraph, you are capable of fulfilling almost any writing assignment effectively. The three most important principles of good paragraphs are *unity, coherence,* and *completeness.*

2. Unity   In the discussion of the theme, we placed a great deal of emphasis on the *central idea.* The paragraph too must have a central idea, and this idea is almost always contained in the *topic sentence.* The idea contained in the topic sentence is the *subject* of the paragraph, and other details in the paragraph must be concerned with this subject. Because of its importance, the topic sentence usually stands at the very beginning of the expository paragraph. The alert student soon finds that he can review assignments in many textbooks very quickly by reading only the first sentence in each paragraph, although he will occasionally find it necessary to read within the paragraph for explanatory detail.

Here are a number of paragraphs taken from general expository material. Note that in each paragraph the subject dealt with is stated in the very first sentence, which, therefore, is the topic sentence.

The deliberate cultivation of the gift of putting yourself into another person's place is the beginning of wisdom in human relations. The practice of this gift will change the very flavor of life. Its influence on the other person is magical—he feels at once that he is being understood; but its influence on oneself is almost equally magical. When you understand a person, realize his circumstances, desires, difficulties, you appreciate him, you like him. You like him because you *become* him. You make excuses for him. You turn his flank instead of offering a frontal attack. You are in the citadel before he knows where he is, and he feels glad to have you there. His life is sweetened, and so is yours.

—ARNOLD BENNETT,
How to Make the Best of Life.

The psychological consequences of the spread of white culture have been out of all proportion to the materialistic. This world-wide cultural diffusion has protected us as man had never been protected before from having to take seriously the civilizations of other peoples; it has given to our culture a massive universality that we have long ceased to account for historically, and which we read off rather as necessary and inevitable. We interpret our dependence, in our civilization, upon economic competition as proof that this is the prime motivation that human nature can rely upon, or we read off the behaviour of small children as it is moulded in our civilization and recorded in child clinics, as child psychology or the way in which the young human animal is bound to behave. It is the same whether it is a question of our ethics or of our family organization. It is the inevitability of each familiar motivation that we defend, attempting always to identify our own local ways of behaving with Behaviour, or our own socialized habits with Human Nature.

—RUTH BENEDICT,
Patterns of Culture.

Every language has two standards of usage,—the colloquial and the literary. By "colloquial language," we mean the language of conversation; by "literary language," that employed in literary composition. Everyday colloquial English admits many words, forms, phrases, and constructions that would be out of place in a dignified essay. On the other hand, it is an error in taste to be always "talking like a book." Unpracticed speakers and writers should, however, be conservative. They should avoid, even in informal talk, any word or expression that is of doubtful propriety. Only those who know what they are about, can venture to take liberties. It is quite possible to be correct without being stilted or affected.

—GEORGE LYMAN KITTREDGE and
FRANK EDGAR FARLEY, *An Advanced
English Grammar.*

The proboscis of the mosquito is a conspicuous projection from the head. It consists essentially of a soft, fleshy rod, ending in a pair of small lobes termed *labellae.* The rod is deeply grooved dorsally, and in this groove there lie (a) a pair of needle-like *maxillae;* (b) a pair of lancet-like structures, the modified *mandibles;* and (c) a median tube consisting of (i.) a long grooved incomplete tube, in section like the outer cover of a bicycle tire, that is to say, incomplete ventrally, and (ii.) a blade-like structure that fits against this ventral slit and converts it into a tube; this blade-like structure is termed the *hypopharnyx;* the ventrally grooved structure against which it fits is termed the *labrum epipharnyx.*

—ROBERT A. WARDLE, *The Principles
of Applied Zoology.*

Although the topic sentence is placed at the beginning of most expository paragraphs, it may come at any point, or it may be only implied.

Topic sentence at the end:

In the movie story of mankind, the man who writes to Mother, steps aside for his friend, or places his sweetheart's happiness above his carnal desires is pretty sure to end as the ecstatic bridegroom, the president of the company, or the composer whose genius the audiences at Carnegie Hall acclaim by beating their palms into a pulp. The cad who kicks a dog, cheats at cards, betrays a friend, or attempts to seduce a maiden, is headed straight for the Big House, death, and eternal perdition beyond. To movie heroes, of course, death is no more than the passport to eternal joy, its occurrence usually being accompanied by a majestic chorus of unseen angels hurling triumphant hosannahs at the audience while the screen swarms with moving clouds. It is surely consoling to discover that in the special logic of the movies, self-sacrifice always ends in successful (if unplanned) self-aggrandizement; and that selfishness is utter folly, doomed to a terrible fate.

—LEO C. ROSTEN, *Hollywood: The Movie Colony—The Movie Makers.*

Topic sentence in the middle (fifth sentence):

Because of these discoveries a new conception of the atom was necessary. It came from Ernest Rutherford, Niels Bohr, and others. Textbooks on physics had to be rewritten and physicists lost their old jaunty cocksureness. In Verne's prime everything was interpreted in terms of mechanism and laws of nature; today chance rules in the universe, and the laws of nature are recognized for what they are—mere statements of statistical averages. There are now doubt and uncertainty in physics. The Bohr-Dirac-Heisenberg school of scientists studied equations that were supposed to reveal the secrets of the atom and hence of reality, only to find that reality had vanished and that trees, houses, and stars were not what they seemed to be but only indications or "pointer readings" of a deeper something that was real, something that science could never reach. Is it just a coincidence that the same uncertainty prevails in art, in economics, in international relations?

—WALDEMAR KAEMPFFERT, *Explorations in Science.*

Topic sentence implied ("The American people have derived many tangible and intangible benefits from World War II"):

Probably never in the history of this country have its people, as a whole, eaten so well as during the past three years [1941–

1944]. There's practically no unemployment. The soldiers and sailors are the best paid and fed in the world. The thrill, and even the joy of living has much increased. The nation is healthier. (The death toll in the current war and the number maimed by the war are of the same order of magnitude as the automobile casualties before the war.) The people have rather willingly adopted healthy restraints, constructive collaboration, unified determination, a national spirit of worthy sacrifice. Sensational advances in the treatment of certain diseases, new knowledge of food, new accomplishment in a million new home gardens, new and widespread instruction in world geography—all of these have come also. Without the war, most of them would yet have been totally missing, and the others of slow maturing. The women in the offices, factories, and armed services have discovered abilities and self-assurance heretofore unrealized. Elementary applied sciences have been taught to about a million young men who would otherwise have been deprived of a practical training that is important in a civilization highly dependent on applied science. The political and social prestige of labor has increased remarkably in three years of war; and millions of citizens have billions in savings—establishing a policy heretofore unknown, unpracticed, or impossible.

—HAROLD SHAPLEY,
"A Design for Fighting."

You should, to assure unity, make certain that your own expository paragraphs contain topic sentences or that a topic sentence is clearly implied. Probably the safest procedure at this stage is to place the topic sentence at the very beginning. Actually, most writers of exposition begin their paragraphs almost instinctively with a topic sentence, so in general you can trust your natural inclination, especially if you have written an outline before your first draft. If, however, you find that one or more of your paragraphs seem vague and without particular point, it would be well to revise the paragraph, making certain that you have expressed the main idea concisely in the first sentence of the paragraph.

A far greater danger is the inclusion in the paragraph of more than one major topic. In practice, however, such lack of unity is most often the result of an improper statement of the main idea. The following student paragraph, for instance, breaks in two at the seventh sentence.

(1) I have discovered that college is a great change from high school. (2) While attending high school, I was given considerable attention and guidance by the members of the faculty. (3) In college I find myself on my own in the classroom. (4) Also, now that I am away from home, I am on my own in another respect. (5) It is up to me to make my own decisions. (6) It has not been so before for the simple reason that my parents chose to make my decisions for me. (7) The month of September is offering still another change in my way of living. (8) This is the change that faces every fraternity pledge. (9) Instead of being more on my own as I am as a student and offspring, I will, as a pledge, be subjected to more personal controls and regulations than I have ever known before.

Note that the paragraph immediately gains unity upon revision of the topic sentence so that it states the topic for the entire paragraph.

(1) My first month in college has brought three important changes in my life. (2) While attending high school, I was given considerable attention and guidance by the members of the faculty. (3) In college I find myself on my own in the classroom. (4) Also, now that I am away from home, I am on my own in another respect. (5) It is up to me to make my own decisions. (6) It has not been so before for the simple reason that my parents chose to make my decisions for me. (7) Still another change, and probably the most important, is the one that every fraternity pledge must face. (8) Instead of being more on my own as I am as a student and offspring, I will, as a pledge, be subjected to more personal controls and regulations than I have ever known before.

Exercise 2

Here are examples of student paragraphs which violate the principle of paragraph unity. See if you can provide unity in each paragraph by either the addition of a topic sentence or the restatement of a topic sentence already present.

What does a rainy day mean to you? Does it mean boots, umbrellas, raincoats, and bother? Does it mean slippery sidewalks, missed buses, and edgy tempers? Does it mean a day in which nothing you have planned comes out properly? To many people a rainy day means a lost day. I am fond of rain. I like to hear the noise of rain on a roof, I like to see the trees glistening and shimmering with wetness, and I like to smell the fresh scent of cleanliness during the rain. I enjoy walking in the rain; it gives me a feeling of freedom and life. I relish looking through my window and seeing the flowers bowed down with the weight of the moisture.

Argumentative writing should make the reader think about or act upon the viewpoints stated in the writing. This first requirement demands much experience and study on the part of the writer. It is not an easy task to create a piece of writing to which the reader will have a reaction. It is a skill acquired through practice and careful consideration on the writer's part. Observation also plays an important part, because through observation the writer is able to judge the reactions of his reader in advance. The writer's purpose should not be too obvious. The reader should be persuaded gently, not forced. Many readers will emphatically resist too much pressure.

My chief goal in college is to attain a respectable grade average. This is not my only goal, but it is a very important one. In the first place, my parents are spending quite a bit of their money on my education, and in fairness to them I should do as well in my studies as possible. I am sure, also, that college work and life will be a great asset to me personally in the future. In addition to being better educated, I should have a better knowledge of human nature, since I will meet in college people from all parts of the country. The living away from home will also teach me how to be on my own. There will be nobody around telling me when to work and how to do it.

3. Coherence   "Coherence" means essentially "to hold together" and this cohesiveness in writing comes largely from effective organization. Later we shall consider conventional methods of organizing and developing expository paragraphs; there is little question that a knowledge of these various schemes is valuable to the writer. But first let us consider the actual *writing* of the paragraph. Probably no writer before he begins a paragraph thinks, "Shall I develop this paragraph by an enumeration of details, by cause and effect, by comparison and contrast, or by example?" and then proceeds to make a conscious choice. The development of the paragraph is dictated almost always by the nature of the material with which the writer is working and his particular approach to it. We can take as our basic rule in achieving paragraph coherence the following: *A coherent paragraph is one in which the main idea is clearly stated and the writer's particular approach to that idea clearly developed.*

Here is a paragraph that lacks coherence:

(1) Living away from home for any length of time can be quite an ordeal for some people because of homesickness. (2) A person's home becomes a part of that person; when he has to leave his home he leaves part of himself behind. (3) But the gap can be filled to some extent with the help of new friends, new experiences, and new surroundings. (4) This process of adjustment can be quite difficult or fairly simple, depending on the individual involved. (5) In some cases proper adjustment is never really made. (6) For the child or adolescent, living away from home for the first time can be particularly disturbing. (7) But on the other hand, it can be very beneficial because it gives him a chance to become more self-reliant and mature.

The first three sentences of this paragraph are satisfactory. Sentence 1 states the topic, "homesickness"; sentence 2, a major reason for homesickness. Sentence 3 indicates that the writer will develop the rest of his paragraph in terms of the various means of relieving homesickness. But sentences 4 and 5 veer off to another aspect of the topic—the difficulty of adjustment to strange surroundings. Sentence 6 particularizes the persons most susceptible to homesickness. Sentence 7 brings in still another aspect of the topic: the beneficial effects of homesickness. We see, consequently, that although the paragraph deals with only one topic, homesickness, the development of the writer's approach to that topic is confused and uncertain. In other words, the paragraph lacks coherence.

Coherence can be restored to the paragraph by the judicious use of transitional devices and rearrangement of details to emphasize and clarify the writer's approach.

(1) Living away from home for any length of time can be quite an ordeal for some people because of homesickness. (2) For the child or adolescent in particular, the first separation from home may be very disturbing. (3) His home has become a part of him; when he has to leave, he leaves part of himself behind. (4) The process of adjustment to this new situation can be quite difficult or fairly simple, depending on the individual involved. (5) In some cases, proper adjustment is never really made. (6) But for most of us the gap can be filled, to some extent at least, with new friends, new experiences, and new surroundings. (7) And homesickness can actually be beneficial, since it forces us to become more self-reliant and mature.

In the revised version, sentence 1 again states the topic. Sentences 2-5 elaborate upon the topic. Sentence 6 introduces a turn in thought, marked clearly by the transition word "but."

The great majority of expository paragraphs are developed by a simple elaboration of the idea stated in the topic sentence. In such a development, you should take care that the relationship of the amplifying details to the topic sentence is completely clear. This clarity is achieved through logical order, as we have seen in the revised paragraph on homesickness, and through transition words (see T-10 for a full discussion of transitions).

In revising your own paragraphs, be certain that your train of ideas concerning the topic of the paragraph is developed logically and clearly. If you are simply elaborating upon a single, clearly defined aspect of the topic, the coherence of the paragraph will probably take care of itself. But any definite turn or digression in the thought or development of the topic must be indicated clearly to the reader by the use of transitional words or phrases.

Patterns in Paragraph Construction. A useful and convenient means of developing your own sensitivity to the various ways in which paragraphs are developed is the study of isolated paragraphs by professional writers. As we have said, writers rarely, if ever, consciously decide before writing, "Now, I shall construct this particular paragraph in this particular way." The paragraph, after all, is a part of the larger composition, and the way in which a writer develops the paragraph will depend upon the manifold and subtle influences exerted by the context in which the paragraph appears. But the analysis of the paragraphs of the professional writer is an excellent way to gain a proper perspective toward your own paragraphs and, especially in revision, to improve them.

Statement and Amplification. Most expository paragraphs are developed by the statement and amplification of the topic sentence. The topic of the paragraph is stated in the first or second sentence; the rest of the paragraph is devoted to the amplification of the topic idea through the addition of particulars and details, as in the following examples:

There is a hasty way of writing which is a counterpart to the hasty way of reading. It is becoming more common every year and raising less and less protest. A speech, or an article, has to be written by a certain day; there are the usual interruptions and distractions. The writer is hurried but confident, with a fairly clear notion of what he wants to say. He dashes down or dictates a first draft, reads it through quickly, or has it read back to him, makes a few verbal alterations, calls it done and immediately turns to some other business. The greater the haste in which the draft is written, the closer will it come to his ordinary conversational style; and will therefore have a certain intimate charm of expression, unless of course he has trained himself to think wholly in clichés. But it is likely to contain repetitions, contradictions, muddled sequences of ideas, dropped threads, hastily chosen phrases, irrelevancies, queer variations of tense and case—especially when he is writing on a topic new to him and not merely repeating his own or someone else's remembered phrases.

233

And phrases that seemed good enough to him in his haste—useful stand-ins for the star phrases he could not quite command—will often not only fail to convey a particular meaning to the reader but will make a blank of the whole passage.

—ROBERT GRAVES and ALAN HODGE,
The Reader over Your Shoulder.

Institutions and patterns of thought and feeling can no more escape their past than can individuals. Our American colleges and universities are lineally descended from the universities of the later Middle Ages: they have always been, and today remain, essentially guilds (*universitates*) of clerks. Many of their peculiarities, both superficial and fundamental, can be understood only in terms of their historical origins. When professors dress up for parade they put on black clerical cassocks, monastic hoods and a headgear which can be demonstrated to be a priest's berretta rather than a hat: one wears it in church, removing it only during prayer. Until recently our diplomas were in Latin, and the degrees granted were still medieval. To be sure, in the United States we got a bit mixed up in this matter. During the Middle Ages, since the *universitas* was a guild, it gave a journeyman's—or bachelor's—degree, and a master's sometimes called the doctorate because it entitled one to teach (*docere*). The former term became habitual in Britain, and the latter on the Continent. Since this country was subjected to two waves of educational colonization, one from England and the other from Germany, we decided to out-medievalize the Middle Ages, and ended by granting three degrees instead of two: the bachelor's, the master's and the doctor's. No one has yet really decided what our American master's degree means. The main point is that we have tended to compound our educational tradition rather than to rethink it.

—LYNN WHITE, JR.,
Educating Our Daughters.

Definition. The paragraph concerned with definition is usually an approximation and amplification of a formal definition—the term to be defined, the class to which the term belongs, and a differentiation between the term and other members of its class. (See pages 56–62 for a discussion of the formal and informal definition.)

Identification is a method of tension reduction through the achievement of another person or of a group of people. An individual employing this mechanism is said to "identify himself" with the person, organization, or activity concerned. Identification appears early in life in the relationship between a child and a parent. Since a young child achieves many of his adjustments only through the help of his parents, he establishes a habit of regarding their qualities as assets of his own. A boy's strongest identification is usually with his father, who satisfies many of his needs for strength and knowledge. Many traits, ranging from inconsequential mannerisms to important social attitudes, are learned through the operation of the identification mechanism. In that sense, identification is one of the basic factors in character formation.

—L. F. SHAFFER, E. J. SHOBEN, JR.,
The Psychology of Adjustment.

Lime, properly speaking, is a metal, which goes among chemists by the name of calcium. But it is formed, as you all know, in the earth, not as a metal, but as a stone, as chalk or limestone, which is a carbonate of lime: that is, calcium combined with oxygen and carbonic-acid gases. In that state it will make, if it is crystalline and hard, excellent building stone. The finest white marble, like that of Carrara in Italy, of which the most delicate statues are carved, is carbonate of lime altered and hardened by volcanic heat. But to make mortar of it, it must be softened and then brought into a state in which it can be hardened again; and ages since, some man or other, who deserves to rank as one of the great benefactors of his race, discovered the art of making mortar. This discovery was probably very ancient; and was made probably, like most of the old discoveries, in the East, spreading westward gradually.

—CHARLES KINGSLEY, *Town Geology.*

Now just what is meant by sensations and perceptions?—and how does the mind change the former into the latter? By itself a sensation is merely the awareness of a stimulus; we have a taste on the tongue, an odor in the nostrils, a sound in the ears, a temperature on the skin, a flash of light on the retina, a pressure on the fingers: it is the raw crude beginning of experience; it is what the infant has in the early days of its groping mental life; it is

235

not yet knowledge. But let these various sensations group themselves about an object in space and time—say this apple; let the odor in the nostrils, and the taste on the tongue, the light on the retina, the shape-revealing pressure on the fingers and the hand, unite and group themselves about this "thing": and there is now an awareness not so much of a stimulus as of a specific object; there is a perception. Sensation has passed into knowledge.

—WILL DURANT,
The Story of Philosophy.

Comparison or Contrast. Like definition, comparison or contrast, either alone or in combination, is usually employed in a paragraph to give a precise meaning to a term or concept. Contrast is especially effective in distinguishing between true and false conceptions, as in the first paragraph below, or between terms commonly confused. Comparison of an unfamiliar object or idea with one familiar to the reader, as in the second paragraph below, is a standard rhetorical device in expository writing.

True patriotism is quiet, simple, dignified; it is not blatant, verbose, vociferous. The noisy shriekers who go about with a chip on their shoulders and cry aloud for war upon the slightest provocation belong to the class contemptuously known as "Jingoes." They may be patriotic,—and as a fact they often are,—but their patriotism is too frothy, too hysteric, too unintelligent, to inspire confidence. True patriotism is not swift to resent an insult; on the contrary, it is slow to take offense, slow to believe that an insult could have been intended. True patriotism, believing fully in the honesty of its own acts, assumes also that others are acting with the same honesty. True patriotism, having a solid pride in the power and resources of our country, doubts always the likelihood of any other nation being willing carelessly to arouse our enmity.

—BRANDER MATTHEWS,
Parts of Speech: Essays on English.

The navigators' answer to the compass problem [at the North Pole] is radical: don't use a compass. Polar flying is done by memory: an artificial memory, of course, consisting of a gyro-scopic instrument, but still merely a direction-keeping device, not a direction-finding one. You start out in the right direction and then you simply hold your course. The gyro works like a tourist's so-called sense of direction in a strange city, which is also merely a memory, and says: "I'm going down the avenue my hotel is on. Now I have turned right. Now I have turned left and am going on a street that's parallel to that avenue my hotel is on." Your initial direction may be that of your take-off runway. Actually, most polar flights start in regions where the compass works, so you take it from the compass. Then you set your gyro, throw a switch, and your gyro starts remembering.

—WOLFGANG LANGEWIESCHE, "The
Polar Path: Where Every Direction
Is South."

And it is when we are considering Hardy's power of creating men and women that we become most conscious of the profound differences that distinguish him from his peers. We look back at a number of these characters and ask ourselves what it is that we remember them for. We recall their passions. We remember how deeply they have loved each other and often with what tragic results. We remember the faithful love of Oak for Bath-sheba; the tumultuous but fleeting passions of men like Wildeve, Troy, and Fitzpiers; we remember the filial love of Clym for his mother, the jealous paternal passion of Henchard for Elizabeth Jane. But we do not remember how they have loved. We do not remember how they talked and changed and got to know each other, finely, gradually, from step to step and from stage to stage. Their relationship is not composed of those intellectual appre-hensions and subtleties of perception which seem so slight yet are so profound. In all the books love is one of the great facts that mould human life. But it is a catastrophe; it happens sud-denly and overwhelmingly, and there is little to be said about it. The talk between the lovers when it is not passionate is practical or philosophic, as though the discharge of their daily duties left them with more desire to question life and its purpose than to investigate each other's sensibilities. Even if it were in their power to analyse their emotions, life is too stirring to give them time. They need all their strength to deal with the downright blows, the freakish ingenuity, the gradually increasing malignity

of fate. They have none to spend upon the subtleties and delicacies of the human comedy.

—VIRGINIA WOOLF,
The Second Common Reader.

Analogy. Analogy is essentially comparison, but unlike
the comparison we have considered previously, it uses the
metaphor and simile (see D-12). Comparison and contrast
in paragraph development is straightforward, realistic, and
practical; analogy is imaginative, inventive, and even poetic.
But, executed skillfully, the analogy is highly effective, and
every student of writing should attempt it.

The effect of historical reading is analogous, in many respects,
to that produced by foreign travel. The student, like the tourist,
is transported into a new state of society. He sees new fashions.
He hears new modes of expression. His mind is enlarged by con-
templating the wide diversities of laws, of morals, and of manners.
But men may travel far, and return with minds as contracted as
if they had never stirred from their own market-town. In the same
manner, men may know the dates of many battles and the
genealogies of many royal houses, and yet be no wiser. Most
people look at past times as princes look at foreign countries.
More than one illustrious stranger has landed on our island amidst
the shouts of a mob, has dined with the king, has hunted with
the master of the stag-hounds, has seen the Guards reviewed, and
a knight of the Garter installed; has cantered along Regent Street;
has visited St. Paul's, and noted down its dimensions; and has
then departed, thinking that he has seen England. He has, in fact,
seen a few public buildings, public men, and public ceremonies.
But of the vast and complex system of society, of the fine shades
of national character, of the practical operation of government
and laws, he knows nothing. He who would understand these
things rightly must not confine his observations to palaces and
solemn days. He must see ordinary men as they appear in their
ordinary business and in their ordinary pleasures. He must mingle
in the crowds of the exchange and the coffee-house. He must
obtain admittance to the convivial table and the domestic hearth.
He must bear with vulgar expressions. He must not shrink from
exploring even the retreats of misery. He who wishes to understand the condition of mankind in former ages must proceed on

the same principle. If he attends only to public transactions, to wars, congresses, and debates, his studies will be as unprofitable as the travels of those imperial, royal, and serene sovereigns who form their judgment of our island from having gone in state to a few fine sights, and from having held formal conferences with a few great officers.

—THOMAS BABINGTON MACAULAY,
"History."

Whoever attempts to forecast the course systems of government will take must therefore begin from the two propositions that the only thing we know about the Future is that it will differ from the Past, and that the only data we have for conjecturing what the Future may possibly bring with it are drawn from observations of the Past, or, in other words, from that study of the tendencies of human nature which gives ground for expecting from men certain kinds of action in certain states of fact. We cannot refrain from conjecture. Yet to realize how vain conjectures are, let us imagine ourselves to be in the place of those who only three or four generations ago failed to forecast what the next following generation would see. Let us suppose Burke, Johnson, and Gibbon sitting together at a dinner of The Club in 1769, the year when Napoleon and Wellington were born, and the talk falling on the politics of the European Continent. Did they have any presage of the future? The causes whence the American Revolution and the French Revolution were to spring, and which would break the sleep of the peoples in Germany and Italy, might, one would think, have already been discerned by three such penetrating observers, but the only remarks most of us recall as made then and for some years afterwards to note symptons of coming dangers were made by a French traveller, who said that the extinction of French power in Canada had weakened the tie between the American colonies and Great Britain, and by an English traveller who saw signs of rottenness in the French Monarchy. Men stood on the edge of stupendous changes, and had not a glimpse of even the outlines of those changes, not discerning the causes that were already in embryo beneath their feet, like seeds hidden under the snow of winter, which will shoot up under the April sunlight.

—JAMES BRYCE,
Modern Democracies.

Example. Paragraph development by example is a means of achieving concreteness. It is especially useful in dealing with abstract terms, as in the first paragraph below. The term is stated, and then its meaning is illustrated by an example, usually a familiar one.

Curiosity is as clear and definite as any of our urges. We wonder what is in a sealed telegram or in a letter in which some one else is absorbed, or what is being said in the telephone booth or in low conversation. This inquisitiveness is vastly stimulated by jealousy, suspicion, or any hint that we ourselves are directly or indirectly involved. But there appears to be a fair amount of personal interest in other people's affairs even when they do not concern us except as a mystery to be unraveled or a tale to be told. The reports of a divorce suit will have "news value" for many weeks. They constitute a story, like a novel or play or moving picture. This is not an example of pure curiosity, however, since we readily identify ourselves with others, and their joys and despair then become our own.

—JAMES HARVEY ROBINSON,
Mind in the Making.

Of a speech it may be said that it is admirable but incomprehensible to those who do not know the language in which it is delivered. A speech delivered in Chinese may be excellent, and yet remain incomprehensible to me if I do not know Chinese; but what distinguishes a work of art from all other mental activity is just the fact that its language is understood by all, and that it infects all without distinction. The tears and laughter of a Chinaman infect me just as the laughter and tears of a Russian; and it is the same with painting and music, and also poetry when it is translated into a language I understand. The songs of a Kirghiz or of a Japanese touch me, though in a lesser degree than they touch a Kirghiz or a Japanese. I am also touched by Japanese painting, Indian architecture, and Arabian stories. If I am but little touched by a Japanese song and a Chinese novel, it is not that I do not understand these productions, but that I know and am accustomed to higher works of art. It is not because their art is above me. Great works of art are only great because they are accessible and comprehensible to everyone. The story of Joseph translated into the Chinese language touches a Chinese. The story of Sakya Muni (Buddha) touches us. And there are, and must be, buildings, pictures, statues, and music, of similar power. So that if art fails to move men, it cannot be said that this is due to the spectators' or hearers' lack of understanding, but the conclusion to be drawn may be, and should be, that such art is either bad or is not art at all.

—LEO TOLSTOY, *What Is Art?*

Classification. Like the full expository analysis, the paragraph developed by classification organizes its material into clear, logical divisions. (For a discussion of classification and division, see pages 67–72.)

The cloud classification in general use at the present time is based on one devised by Luke Howard, a London chemist, who specified four types and gave to each a Latin name that its appearance suggested. The high wisps of clouds that reminded him of a lock of hair, he called *cirrus.* The cloud that spread itself like a sheet became *stratus;* the cloud that gathered itself into a heap became *cumulus;* and the shapeless, ragged threatening low cloud that gives us most of our rain and snow he dubbed *nimbus,* which simply means cloud. But any classification limiting us to a lock of hair, a heap, and a sheet quickly involves us in trouble when we come up against clouds "backed like a weasel, or very much like a whale." Ideally, something more elastic and comprehensive is required, yet the International code is based upon the same key words. By combining them variously it does succeed in giving us ten major types instead of four, and is about as satisfactory as any other scheme that has been devised. For convenience, rather than precision, we can group the ten types under three heads, thus:

High clouds: cirrus, cirrocumulus, cirrostratus.
Middle clouds: altocumulus, altostratus.
Low clouds: stratocumulus, stratus, nimbostratus, cumulus, cumulonimbus.

—GEORGE KIMBLE and RAYMOND
BUSH, *The Weather.*

Bravery, honesty, strength of character are the stuff for hero-worship. At the boy's level, this worship gravitates toward the

241

doer of spectacular deeds; on the average adult level, toward the wielder of power; and in the eyes of a more critical judgment, toward idealism and moral qualities. The most universal hero is he who can fill all these specifications. This, by the many shapes of their courage, integrity, and strength, Washington and Lincoln and Lee are able to do. When the dust of partisanship has settled, another leader in two great crises, economic and military—Franklin D. Roosevelt—will probably join their august company. But Jefferson the sedentary man, Ben Franklin the opportunist, and Andrew Jackson the rough-hewn soldier fail to satisfy everybody. Upon a still lower rank, men like Daniel Boone and Crockett and Buffalo Bill and Edison remain almost juvenile heroes. They do not have all the dimensions of our few supreme symbols. Was it not Emerson who suggested that we Americans were the shattered pieces of a great mould?

—DIXON WECTER,
The Hero in America.

Combined Methods. Many paragraphs, of course, especially long and complex ones, employ a combination of some or all of the patterns of structure that have been discussed thus far. The first paragraph below uses particulars and details, classification, example, and comparison and contrast in its development. The second paragraph is developed largely by example, but also by statement and amplification.

The dreadful cocksureness that is characteristic of scientists in bulk is not only quite foreign to the spirit of true science, it is not even justified by a superficial view. It is of course quite possible to write the history of science as one long crescendo, whose ultimate glorious achievement is the present—and what wonderful people we must be. It is always given in this way, in teaching, as part of a little introduction which is a pep talk for the particular science being dealt with. The Greeks were very clever people, the introduction will go, and they thought of many ingenious theories, but they were lazy, and did not do experiments with their hands. Their foremost philosopher was Aristotle, and it is now the fashion to say that he was not altogether too bad, but the medievals were bad who believed things on Authority, the authority of Aristotle. Modern Science began with Galileo and Newton, and has run steadily ahead ever since, with a great acceleration of progress in the last fifty years, with radioactivity, the discovery of X rays, Einstein, Bohr, the strucure of the atom, Oppenheimer, the Manhattan Project and the Atomic Energy Commission (leaving out the Un-American Activities Committee). But the same story can be told with a humiliating reverse English on it: if the climax and pinnacle of science is our knowledge of the atom *now*, then what was known ten years ago must have been decidedly imperfect, for science has made great strides since then. What was known twenty years ago was even more imperfect, and the science of fifty years ago hardly worth knowing. Using a little imagination, we can ask what will become of the science of today, some twenty or thirty years from now? Unless the rate of scientific advance shows a notable slacking off (and there are no signs of this) our best knowledge of today will become decidedly frowsy.

—ANTHONY STANDEN,
Science Is a Sacred Cow.

In the atmosphere which envelops the world to-day it is perhaps timely to emphasize the fact that the part played by science in making war more destructive and more horrible was an unconscious and unintended by-product of scientific activity. Lord Rayleigh, president of the British Association for the Advancement of Science, in a recent address points out in detail how the folly of man, not the intention of the scientists, is responsible for the destructive use of the agents employed in modern warfare. The innocent study of the chemistry of carbon compounds, which has led to infinite beneficial results, showed that the action of nitric acid on substances like benzene, glycerine, cellulose, etc., resulted not only in the beneficent aniline dye industry but in the creation of nitro-glycerine, which has uses good and bad. Somewhat later Alfred Nobel, turning to the same subject, showed that by mixing nitro-glycerine with other substances, solid explosives which could be safely handled could be produced—among others, dynamite. It is to dynamite that we owe our progress in mining, in the making of such railroad tunnels as those which now pierce the Alps and other mountain ranges; but of course dynamite has been abused by politicians and soldiers. Scientists are, however, no more to blame than they are to blame for an earthquake or a flood. The same thing can be said of poison gas. Pliny was killed by breathing sulphur dioxide in the eruption of

Vesuvius almost two thousand years ago. Chlorine was not isolated by scientists for warlike purposes, and the same is true of mustard gas. These substances could be limited to beneficent use, but when the airplane was perfected, men whose hearts were poisoned and whose brains were addled perceived that the airplane, an innocent invention, the result of long disinterested and scientific effort, could be made an instrument of destruction, of which no one had ever dreamed and at which no one had ever deliberately aimed.

—ABRAHAM FLEXNER, "The Usefulness of Useless Knowledge."

4. Completeness One of the major faults of student writing is the incompletely developed paragraph. These paragraphs may have a topic sentence and be coherent as far as they go, but they lack the specific and concrete details that characterize superior writing. Consider the following paragraph from a student book report on *The Grapes of Wrath:*

The most appealing part of the book is its capacity to express to the reader the emotions and thoughts of the characters. After reading the book, one feels as if these are people he has known and lived with. There are times, in fact, when the reader's sympathy with the Joads causes him to resent Steinbeck's determination to show their case as hopeless.

As the paragraph stands, it gives the reader no concrete evidence to support the writer's statements concerning this book. The statements may be sincere and discerning, but they need substantiation through specific and concrete detail. An improved version might be something like the following:

The reader feels that the characters in *The Grapes of Wrath* are people he has known and lived with. Tom Joad's determination to bring the Joad family to California to what he thought would be a new and better way of life is the determination of almost any elder brother who is given the responsibility of saving his family from poverty and want. Ma Joad could be any mother who strives grimly to hold her family together against forces that seem bound to drive it apart. The Rose of Sharon, turning from her dead baby to give sustenance to a starving man, is woman personified in her selfless generosity. A weakness of the book may be that the reader finds it difficult to believe that human beings like these could be so completely helpless in these particular circumstances.

The following paragraph also lacks completeness of development:

In committing a person to an asylum, a judge makes one of three decisions. First, the patient may be discharged as not mentally ill. Second, he may be discharged as not mentally ill, but in need of psychiatric treatment. Finally, the patient may be found mentally ill and be committed to an institution for treatment.

More completely developed, the paragraph might read as follows:

In committing a person to an asylum, a judge makes one of three decisions. First, the patient may be discharged as not mentally ill. Such a patient usually has had merely an emotional upset, or was brought in by the police for sanity tests before coming to civil trial. Second, he may be discharged as not mentally ill but in need of psychiatric treatment, and released on probation to his family for treatment in a private sanitarium, or he may be sent to a state institution if that action is desired. A patient discharged in this manner may be an alcoholic or a marked neurotic. Finally, the patient may be found mentally ill, and be committed to an institution for treatment until the time he can be proclaimed cured by the action of another court hearing. The patient thus committed may suffer from a mental illness which is incurable. If so, he will spend the rest of his life in an institution.

Complete development of a paragraph does not mean intentional padding or the repetition of the same idea again and again in different words. Complete development comes from careful planning and thought. The stunted, underdeveloped paragraph occurs usually in the theme that has been composed hastily and carelessly with very little thought behind it. Writing is something like shooting a gun: unless you are loaded, nothing much happens.

Exercise 3

The following paragraphs are taken from the themes of students in composition courses. Examine them closely and be prepared to discuss the extent to which they achieve or fail to achieve unity, coherence, and completeness.

Expository writing is noncreative. It is more science than art and is never art for art's sake. No short story, poem, or novel can be called expository writing, unless it has a purpose outweighing the form. Excellent examples of purposeful writing are everywhere available. The grocery list has the purpose of reminding the forgetful shopper that the refrigerator is low on milk and eggs, that a box of cake mix must be purchased for the party coming up, that now is the time to pick up the two pairs of trousers at the cleaners, and that it would be good to buy a few light bulbs—one hundred watts.

Oklahoma is a pretty state in the spring. At that season, the beauty of no other state is quite like it. The ranges on the rolling plains are green with grass not yet browned by the sun. The oaks and blackjacks on the knolls are pretty and welcoming. The prairie breeze is gentle and it carries scents of things green and growing, and of lands newly planted. Tall cottonwoods and elms, assisted by willows, line the streams and mark their location from afar. God is generous to Oklahoma in the spring. Perhaps His generosity is an award in atonement for the extremes of the summer and winter that have passed or are to follow, for the torrential rains and the bitter droughts and dust, for the almost unbearable heat and the extreme cold, for the stifling stillness of the summer air and the turbulent violence of electrical storms and tornadoes, for these and the other reasons that white men were slow to want Oklahoma and the Indians fought to leave it.

The "decline of attention" in American life is particularly exemplified in advertising and entertainment as expressed in their common media, radio, television, and periodicals. The trend is characterized by programs and articles the absorption of which requires the least possible amount of effort. The stimulus which appeals to the least discriminating of the senses, the eye, is assured success. The magazine article or advertisement that is not generously embellished with pictures or reduced to utter simplicity is likely to be unnoticed by the fleeting glances of time-conscious America. Magazines that cram their pages with pictures and relegate prose to captions seem to be most popular today. Even the heretofore unchallenged circulation statistics of the wordy news magazines have been threatened by the advent of news digests and digests of the digests. The significance of *Quick* is not only its compact size and compressed reports, but also its name. Quite possibly if the trend continues we may see a *Quicker* and ultimately a *Quickest*.

The jazz man is a modern maestro, and mood music is his business. From dusk to dawn he wraps his soul around a mournful tune, weaving a soft, magical pattern in blue as his skillful fingers ripple fiddle-faddle on the heartstrings of barflies and patrons of dingy nightspots. He stands, a tall, black Joshua, pouring his lonely, liquid melodies into each bleak corner, floating them across the bar where, night after night, a million miseries and heartaches are ground into the polished mahogany or whisked away with a swish of the bar rag. The jazz man is a bit of flotsam in a frantic world. A sad-eyed trumpeter with a ragged tune and a honey-colored horn, he fashions a new tonight for faceless puppets in smoke-filled basements and pieces together the remnants of yesterday's happiness. Transient in mind and body, he carries his heart in a trumpet case, and his home is a bandstand in a noisy, obscure room in a nameless city. Where he goes there is sweat and smoke and stomping feet—and laughter.

Materialism has tragically colored man's intellectual approach to the solution of his problems. We limit our inner creativeness with external constraints and insignificant anxieties at the mercy of constant interruptions by telephone and television and insistent print, timing our lives to the movement of a production belt we do not control. As man's inner life has withered, he has recovered a sense of stability and purpose by releasing the most primitive elements in his unconscious. Today man is concerned with the present and future, and the past is looked upon only with academic interest. It is no longer looked upon as a foundation of life. Meditation and a gradual growth to maturity are non-existent to the modern mind. The world is "realistic." There is no money in the classics. Obtaining spiritual nourishment from the present chaos of events and sensations is the equivalent of trying to pick a garbage pile for food. In the end, as Samuel Butler prophesied, man may become just a machine's contrivance for reproducing another machine.

Exercise 4

Indicate the most logical structural pattern for developing the following topic sentences into paragraphs.

1. Wit and humor are frequently confused, but there is actually a marked difference between the terms.
2. A day's hike consists of three stages.
3. Nuclear disarmament is essential to world survival.
4. Fathers are nice but mothers are nicer.
5. Getting along with a roommate is a delicate business.
6. There are two major causes for academic failure.
7. A "date," in the social sense, is difficult to define.
8. Inductive reasoning is best understood in terms of Thomas Huxley's anecdote of a man faced with a tray of green apples.
9. The fielding of a first class shortstop is poetry in motion.
10. Peace is no longer an impossible dream, but an absolute necessity.

Function

The paragraph, of course, is not an isolated unit. It is a unit *within* the whole composition and serves as an integral and functional part of the composition. So far we have discussed the paragraph largely in terms of its unified and coherent internal development within the body of the expository theme. But this treatment should not obscure the flexible and versatile nature of the paragraph in the hands of the competent writer. Its length and development have almost an infinitive variety in terms of its special functions within the composition. The most important of these functions are as follows.

5. Introductory Paragraphs We have already considered the qualities of the effective introduction to the theme in Chapter 2 (T-9). The introductory paragraph, in addition to introducing the main thesis of the theme, should be relatively short and should engage the reader's interest. Most readers, even your instructor, need as much inducement as possible to begin a piece of writing. A long, labored introductory paragraph will frequently make such a poor first impression that the rest of the theme, no matter how competent, will suffer.

Note the following examples of effective, engaging introductory paragraphs.

CLICK . . . CLICK . . . CLICK, CLICK, CLICK, CLICK—faster and faster, an ominous signal is heard. The atomic alarm has sounded. It can be a warning, in time, against atomic bombs—or it can be the death rattle of our civilization: a harsh, staccato noise emitted from an electronic device that scientists call a Geiger counter. It clicks out its warning of radiation, such as that emitted from radium, or more pertinently from the mother stuff of atomic bombs, uranium. Whenever dangerous radioactivity is sprayed out in radiations—X-ray-like gamma rays, alpha particles which are helium hearts, beta rays which are fleet electrons—the Geiger counter clicks.

—RON ROSS, in *Science News Letter*.

No region in the United States has created so many legends about itself—and had so many created for it—as the South. The very word carries with it a multitude of connotations and scenes, romantic or realistic, pleasant or unpleasant, according to one's personal temperament and prejudices, but often utterly at variance with facts, historical or physical. At the present moment that region is the focus of a new wave of myth-making, and this crop of legends and beliefs may have tragic consequences for the efforts of men of good will to achieve just relations between Negroes and whites in the land below the Potomac.

—LOUIS B. WRIGHT,
in *A Southern Vanguard*.

6. Transitional Paragraphs In the longer theme especially, an entire paragraph may be used to make a transition from one major division of a paper to another division. (See T-10 for a discussion of transitions.) The transitional paragraph may be lengthy, including a summary of the material that has gone before and introducing material that will follow; or it may be short, consisting sometimes of only one transitional sentence, or even a single word.

. . . Like Freud, [Dr. Ernest] Jones is unable to see the dramatic facts: that in the players' scene Hamlet makes sure of the King's guilt, and the King finds out that Hamlet has somehow discovered the truth about the murder. So Hamlet is now watched because he knows too much. If the "curiosity" of a King about a man plotting against his life is infantile, then we can say with Jones that Shakespeare is developing an "infantile curiosity theme."

What did Shakespeare's audience see? [*Transitional paragraph*]

After the players' scene, the play is no longer concerned with Hamlet's finding the facts of the murder, but with the attempts of Hamlet and the King to kill each other. . . . Almost as soon as Hamlet is in the same country with the King, after he has made sure that the King committed the crime, Hamlet kills him. Yet the name "Hamlet" has come to mean the weak-willed dreamer, the "scholarly" anaemic procrastinator.

Why? [*Transitional paragraph*]

Two reasons for confusion seem very simple. Neither nineteenth century scholars and actors nor Freud had the intellectual equipment to understand Shakespeare.

—JOHN ASHWORTH,
"Olivier, Freud, and Hamlet."

This brings us to another kind of thought which can fairly easily be distinguished from the three kinds described above. It has not the usual qualities of the reverie, for it does not hover about our personal complacencies and humiliations. It is not made up of the homely decisions forced upon us by everyday needs, when we review our little stock of existing information, consult our conventional preferences and obligations, and make a choice of action. It is not the defense of our own cherished beliefs and prejudices just because they are our own—mere plausible excuses for remaining of the same mind. On the contrary, it is that peculiar species of thought which leads us to *change* our mind. [*Transitional paragraph*]

—JAMES HARVEY ROBINSON,
The Mind in the Making.

7. Short Paragraphs for Emphasis   In the first quoted passage above, from Ashworth's "Olivier, Freud, and Hamlet," we see examples of short paragraphs used not only as transitional devices, but also as a means of achieving emphasis. The first transitional paragraph consists of a single sentence, the second of a single word. Although effective as Ashworth employs them, short paragraphs should be used sparingly by the inexperienced writer. They can be merely a cheap way of gaining emphasis.

8. Paragraphs in Dialogue   Direct quotations of the speech of persons engaged in dialogue are usually placed in separate paragraphs in order to make clear to the reader a change in speaker:

Marjorie unpacked the basket of supper.
"I don't feel like eating," said Nick.
"Come on and eat, Nick."
"All right."
They ate without talking, and watched the two rods and the fire-light in the water.
"There's going to be a moon tonight," said Nick. He looked across the bay to the hills that were beginning to sharpen against the sky. Beyond the hills he knew the moon was coming up.
"I know it," Marjorie said happily.
"You know everything," Nick said.
"Oh, Nick, please cut it out! Please, please don't be that way!"
"I can't help it," Nick said. "You do. You know everything. That's the trouble. You know you do."
Marjorie did not say anything.

—ERNEST HEMINGWAY,
"The End of Something."

9. Concluding Paragraphs   The concluding paragraph is the writer's last chance to impress his idea or ideas upon the reader, and consequently serves an important function in the whole composition. (See T-11 for a discussion of effective conclusions to themes.) The introductory paragraph should make a favorable first impression on the reader; the concluding paragraph should make a favorable and enduring last impression. The concluding paragraph may consist of a concise summation of the points made in the body of the theme, a generalized statement of the significance of what has gone before, or an extension of the particular idea developed in the theme to a more general and far-reaching context. Above all, it should not be forced. If your theme comes naturally to an end at a given point, do not feel that you must tack on a concluding paragraph because your instructor expects it. Such endings are almost invariably artificial and weak.

The following passages, each in its own way, are examples of effective concluding paragraphs.

Communism and Fascism claim to be theoretical formulations of a "new order" in the world. But as revealed in their works they are no more than the recurrence of old political forms, that is to say, the recurrence in practice of what is variously known as tyranny, dictatorship, absolute monarchy; the recurrence in theory of what is known as divine right. As such they are alike, and alike at war with the fundamental values and assumptions which liberal-democracy, if it is to retain any significance, must preserve.

—CARL BECKER, *Modern Democracy*.

I have not here been considering the literary use of language, but merely language as an instrument for expressing and not for concealing or preventing thought. Stuart Chase and others have come near to claiming that all abstract words are meaningless, and have used this as a pretext for advocating a kind of political quietism. Since you don't know what Fascism is, how can you struggle against Fascism? One need not swallow such absurdities as this, but one ought to recognize that the present political chaos is connected with the decay of language, and that one can probably bring about some improvement by starting at the verbal end. If you simplify your English, you are freed from the worst follies of orthodoxy. You cannot speak any of the necessary dialects, and when you make a stupid remark its stupidity will be obvious, even to yourself. Political language—and with variations this is true of all political parties, from Conservatives to Anarchists—is designed to make lies sound truthful and murder respectable, and to give an appearance of solidity to pure wind. One cannot change this all in a moment, but one can at least change one's own habits, and from time to time one can even, if one jeers loudly enough, send some worn-out and useless phrase —some *jackboot, Achilles' heel, hotbed, melting pot, acid test, veritable inferno* or other lump of verbal refuse—into the dustbin where it belongs.

—GEORGE ORWELL,
Shooting an Elephant.

Exercise 5

In the specimen reference paper, "Exploration in Antarctica," page 404, consider the functions of the paragraphs. Note especially the introduction and conclusion, and examine the paragraphs within the paper for transitional and emphatic functions.

7.

The Formal Outline

We have seen in Chapter 2 the use one student made of the topic outline in completing a writing assignment. That outline might be called a "private" outline, since the student used it for his own private purposes. But in many writing assignments your instructor may expect you to present a formal outline with your paper. In such a situation, your outline must conform to certain rules.

1. The Outline Form Formal outlines follow a system of indention to show divisions of subject matter and their levels of importance. These indentions can be represented graphically as follows.

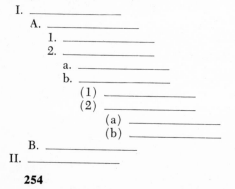

I. _____

   A. _____

      1. _____

      2. _____

         a. _____

         b. _____

            (1) _____

            (2) _____

               (a) _____

               (b) _____

   B. _____

II. _____

Note that major divisions are marked with Roman numerals, major subdivisions under those topics with capital letters, and further subdivisions with Arabic cardinal numbers, lower-case letters, then Arabic cardinal numbers and lower-case letters in parentheses. The subdivisions are also indicated by indentions, each subordinate division being indented about five spaces.

There are three types of formal outline: the topic outline, the sentence outline, and the paragraph outline.

2. The Topic Outline   The most common type of outline is the topic. The topic outline uses phrases or single words to designate the major and minor divisions of the composition for which the outline serves as a blueprint. As a concrete example, consider the following topic outline prepared for a theme of approximately 900 words.

BIRD MIGRATION

Thesis sentence: In spite of many decades of observation, naturalists are still in doubt concerning the cause and nature of bird migration.

I. Seasonal Movement of Birds a Puzzle for Centuries

    A. Early theories

    B. Concept of migration

II. Theories of Original Cause of Migration

    A. Prehistoric glacial movements

    B. Overpopulation in native homeland

III. Factors Affecting Time of Annual Flights

    A. Weather changes

    B. Mating instinct

IV. Means of Navigation

    A. Prominent geographical features

    B. Food supply.

    C. Geosensitive instinct

V. Flight Schedules
  A. Continuous migrants
    1. Ducks
    2. Geese
  B. Daytime migrants
    1. Hawks
    2. Swallows
    3. Chimney swifts
  C. Nighttime migrants
    1. Thrushes
    2. Flycatchers
    3. Warblers
    4. Sparrows
  D. Nighttime migrants in majority because of convenience of feeding

VI. Length of Flight
  A. Nonmigratory birds
    1. Game birds
    2. Cardinal
    3. Carolina wren
  B. Semimigratory birds
    1. Blue jays
    2. Robins
  C. Migratory birds
    1. Intracontinental United States
      a. Chippings
      b. Vespers
      c. Field sparrows
    2. Canada and Northern U.S. to Central and South America
      a. Tanagers
      b. Warblers
      c. Thrushes
    3. Extreme Global Ranges
      a. Nighthawks
      b. Barn swallows
      c. Arctic terns

VII. Bird Migration a Continuing Challenge for Ornithologists

Remarks.

1. The indention of subordinate divisions is carefully observed and margins maintained. Clear indention of logical subdivisions of thought is the keystone of the effective, informative outline.

2. Divisions of the same rank are parallel in grammatical structure. In other words, those divisions marked by Roman numerals and those marked by capital letters are all noun phrases; the divisions marked by cardinal numerals are single nouns, with the exception of Division VIC, under which a separate major classification is made. The noun phrase outline is by far the most common in formal topic outlines. The important thing to remember, however, is that topics of equal rank should have the same grammatical structure.

3. Each division contains at least two subdivisions. Avoid single subdivisions for topics. You can always incorporate a single subdivision into the major topic to the improvement of the logic and clarity of the outline.

4. The outline contains full and adequate detail. The major fault of most student outlines is that they are too general and too brief. The thought required for the inclusion of specific and concrete detail in the outline is always rewarded by the comparative ease in writing the theme that follows.

5. Do not use broad, vague topics like "Introduction" and "Conclusion." Instead, use phrases which state the opening and closing ideas of the theme. Outlines for papers over six or seven thousand words may have need of separate sections with these titles, but even in those, the subdivisions should be specific and informative. In shorter papers, there is no need for such general labels. They serve simply as a postponement of work that must be done when the theme is written. Concrete topics at the beginning and the end of the outline are far more helpful in the act of writing than the general terms "Introduction" and "Conclusion."

In actual practice the final outline and the theme usually evolve together. Seldom is the original outline so perfect that the writer will not see some worthwhile changes in his topics and organization as he writes the theme. But the outline carefully prepared before writing is begun will assure the final theme of many virtues that a good composition must have. Let us look at the theme written from the topic outline we have examined.

BIRD MIGRATION

[I]. The true nature and cause of bird migration have been subjects of speculation for centuries. In very early times fanciful theories were formulated to account for the seasonal disappearance of many birds. Some typical ideas were that they hibernated in muddy stream bottoms or secluded themselves in hollow trees. Careful observation soon displaced these superstitions with the concept of migration. Although migration has been recognized for over one thousand years, its causes and many aspects of its nature are still in doubt.

[IIA]. There are at present two theories accepted as probable. According to the first theory—generally considered the more plausible—before the onset of the glacial movements of the Great Ice Age, all of the bird fauna of North America were nonmigratory. As the ice sheet appeared, inclement weather conditions, insufficient food supplies, and a lack of nesting locations forced the birds southward. They consequently traveled with each glacial movement, going south as the glaciers moved down and returning north with their subsequent recession. By the end of the Pleistocene or Ice Age, migrational movement had become such an integral habit with the birds that it was continued.

[IIB]. The second theory assumes the tropical regions to be the birds' natural home. As is the case with most animal forms, the birds tended toward overpopulation. At the end of the glacial periods, because of population pressures, there was a natural radiation of birds during the mating season into the vast spans of virgin northern country where the competition for food was less intense. Yet because the southland was their native home, they returned as soon as the brood could fend for itself.

[III]. There are other aspects of bird migration unexplained as yet. One in particular: what is the local element which causes the birds to leave their southern homes at the approximate termination of a winter several thousand miles away? The most obvious answer, weather, is actually not the chief cause of migration. During the flight the weather may well change from the favorable conditions under which the birds left to decidedly adverse local weather. But by affecting the food supply and indirectly the mating season, the weather does determine the mean date of departure and consequently the mean date of arrival. Another possible trigger for migration is the increasing length of the days at the termination of the winter months. This lengthening is believed to cause an increase in endocrine secretion by the tropical migrators, thus engendering the mating urge and consequently migration.

[IV]. The question of how migratory birds find their way is another problem unsolved as yet. Not all of the birds return to the same nesting regions; yet there are many that return even to the same nests. A favorite popular theory is that they follow coast lines, mountain ranges, and rivers. This may be true in part, but in a major sense it must be incorrect, for not only are few species ever observed following rivers, but for the most part birds fly straight southward, invariably crossing and completely ignoring these supposed guiding marks. Food rather than geographical terrain seems to be the determining factor in migrational routes, since birds usually take the shortest route over which there is sufficient food. There is also the possibility that through some physiological means migrating birds are geosensitive and can perceive northerly or southerly directions. This mechanism probably functions in relation to the direction of the sun's rays.

[V]. Concerning some aspects of bird migration, our information is much more specific. We know from the observations of both professional and amateur ornithologists that the time of day at which flights are made varies with the species. Waterfowl—ducks and geese—fly for the most part continuously. The daytime migrants include chiefly swallows and chimney swifts. The nighttime travelers are the thrushes, flycatchers, warblers, sparrows, and the majority of bird families. The reason for this preference for nighttime flying is that feeding periods can thereby be closer together. For example, if a bird flew continuously for twelve hours during the day because of some barrier such as a sea, it would not arrive at its destination until nightfall and would not, consequently, feed until morning—a lapse of approximately thirty hours between feedings. Obviously, if it flew at night, there would be a lapse of only twelve hours.

[VI]. Perhaps the most variable factor among individual species is the length of flight. The nonmigratory birds are chiefly the game birds—quail, grouse, pheasants—and the cardinal and Carolina wren. There are certain birds, of which the robin and blue jay are the best representatives, which might be classified as semimigratory. As individuals, all these birds migrate, but as a species they may not. Certain robins, for example, are more hardy than others. When winter comes, say in southern Illinois, the robins there move southward while the more northerly and more hardy individuals move to southern Illinois. Flight-length variations also exist among the true migrants. The chipping, vesper, and field sparrow migrate from northern United States to the Gulf Coast. The tanagers, warblers, and thrushes travel from the United States and Canada to Central and South America. There are also birds which have exceedingly long ranges. Barn swallows go from Alaska to South America. The champion, however, is the Arctic tern, which has a migratory range of over eight thousand miles, from the Arctic to the Antarctic, and, therefore, often travels over sixteen thousand miles in one year.

[VII]. We can see, consequently, that although ornithologists have cleared away much of the mystery that has cloaked bird migration in the past, many gaps remain in our present knowledge of exactly why and how birds migrate. Certainly there are enough puzzles yet to be solved to challenge amateur and professional ornithologists for many years to come.

We have considered before, in Chapter 2, the importance of the thesis sentence in establishing unity in the entire composition. We can see that each major subdivision in "Bird Migration" is related to the central idea of the theme as stated in the thesis sentence. As you have already noticed, the thesis sentence is outside the divisions of the outline. It must be the unifying idea for all divisions. At this point, however, let us pay particular attention to the relationship between the internal units, the paragraphs, of the theme and the major and subordinate divisions of the outline.

The most immediately apparent relationship is in paragraph division. The major divisions of the outline (I, II, III, . . .) correspond exactly with the paragraph division of the theme, with the exception of Division II, which the writer considered of sufficient importance for two paragraphs.

The topic sentence of each paragraph is a restatement of the topic of each major division of the outline. One of the great values of the topic outline is that it forces the writer to formulate a specific and definite idea for each division of the theme. Of necessity when he comes to the writing of the theme, his material is organized into focal points which naturally serve as the topics of his paragraphs. The writer who prepares his outline carefully before he writes will seldom need to worry about unified paragraphs.

Finally, internal paragraph organization is clearly sketched by the subordinate divisions of the topic outline. Irrelevance of detail will show much more clearly in the outline than in the fullness of the actual theme. The conscientious development of the outline serves not only as a guide for the major divisions of the theme, but also as insurance that the details within the major divisions will be coherent and relevant.

All this is not to say, of course, that the preparation of a satisfactory topic outline is complete assurance of an excellent theme. The actual writing of the theme is the most difficult and demanding part of the writing process. But the form skeleton of a logical, detailed topic outline is an extremely important step in creating the unity, coherence, and relevance that good expository writing must have.

3. The Sentence Outline The sentence outline is more time consuming than the topic outline in that complete sentences are used to indicate major and minor subdivisions instead of phrases or single words. But this disadvantage is offset by the increased clarity of the sentence outline and the more explicit formulation of the major ideas in the composition. Here is a sentence outline of "Bird Migration."

I. The seasonal movements of birds have been a puzzle for centuries.

   A. Various early theories were formulated to account for these movements.

   B. Careful observation soon displaced these superstitions with the concept of migration.

II. There are at present two theories concerning the original cause of migration.

   A. The first, and more plausible, is that migration was caused by the glacial movements of the Great Ice Age.

   B. The second theory is that overpopulation in the native homeland was the original cause of migration.

III. The factors affecting the time of flight are as yet unexplained.

   A. Weather is a contributing cause, but not the chief one.

   B. The inception of the mating urge is another possible cause.

IV. The means of navigation is also still in question.

   A. Coast lines, mountain ranges, and rivers are only a partial answer.

   B. Food supply is certainly an important factor.

   C. Migrating birds may also be geosensitive, probably in relation to the direction of the sun's rays.

V. Flight schedules vary with the species.

   A. Continuous migrants include most waterfowl.

   B. Daytime migrants include chiefly swallows and chimney swifts.

   C. The majority of bird families are nighttime travelers since birds require daylight for feeding periods.

VI. Perhaps the most variable factor among individual species is the length of flight.

   A. The nonmigratory birds are chiefly game birds.

   B. The semimigratory birds migrate for relatively short distances as individuals, but may not migrate at all as a species.

   C. The true migrants fly distances ranging from intracontinental to global.

VII. Bird migration will remain a continuing challenge for ornithologists.

4. The Paragraph Outline   The paragraph outline is
largely a summarizing device, since it is composed of the
topic sentence of each paragraph of a work that has already
been written, as in the following paragraph outline of "Bird
Migration."

BIRD MIGRATION

1. Early superstitions about the seasonal movements of birds
   have been replaced by the concept of migration.
2. Of the two theories concerning the causes of migration, the
   more plausible is that of the glacial movements of the Great
   Ice Age.
3. A second theory is that overpopulation in the native homeland
   was the original cause of migration.
4. The time of flight of migratory birds may be explained at least
   in part by weather and the mating urge.
5. The means of navigation used by migrating birds is probably
   a combination of geographical features, adequate food supply,
   and perhaps an obscure geosensitive mechanism in the birds
   themselves.
6. The various species of migrating birds may be classified by
   their flight schedules as continuous, daytime, and nighttime
   migrants.
7. Length of flight among migratory birds ranges from intrastate
   to global.
8. Although much has been learned about bird migration, many
   puzzles still remain.

Exercise

Examine the following outlines for errors in formal outline
structure.

HOW TO GROW AND PROCESS TOBACCO

THESIS: Tobacco can be grown in every Southern state. The art
of growing and processing tobacco was one of the
early discoveries of the American settler.

I. Good soil is essential for the growth of tobacco.

   A. Tobacco can be grown in many types of soil as long as it is well drained.

      1. The tobacco field must be well nourished and not worn out.

      2. The tobacco field will need great amounts of potash.

   B. The soil determines the texture of the tobacco.

   C. The climate affects the aroma of the tobacco.

   D. Protective measures must be taken by the farmer to control diseases.

      1. Insect pests attack the tobacco plant and cause great losses.

      2. Tobacco must have protection from certain weather conditions.

II. The tobacco crop is harvested four to six months after the planting period.

   A. When the tobacco leaves start to turn yellow or brown, it is time for the plant to be harvested.

   B. The most popular way of harvesting the tobacco plant is to cut each leaf as it ripens.

   C. The tobacco leaves are strung together for curing.

III. One way of curing tobacco is the open-air method.

   A. The tobacco to be left outside for curing by the sun.

   B. The tobacco to be placed in open air-ventilated barns and allowed to mature naturally.

IV. Tobacco may also be fire-cured.

   A. The tobacco is hung in barns that are airtight.

   B. Fires are built on the floor of the barn.

   C. The smoke and heat from these open fires cure the tobacco.

   D. After curing, the tobacco leaves are subjected to moisture to prevent cracking or breaking.

V. After curing, the tobacco is made ready for the market.

   A. The tobacco leaves are sorted into various standard grades based on size, color, and quality.

B. The tobacco is placed in cases, bales, or hogsheads for shipment to a central warehouse.

C. The tobacco is sold directly to companies and dealers.

Conclusion: After this long process is completed, the tobacco and the many products that are formed from raw tobacco go to better the lives of people in every corner of the world.

THE UNDERGROUND RAILROAD

I. Introduction.

II. Causes for the Negroes' flight.

A. Suppressed by the whites.
  1. Inadequate amount of food.
  2. Poor clothing.
  3. Poor living quarters.

B. Want for freedom by the Negro.
  1. Negroes wanted the freedom to live and have families belonging to them and not the owner of the plantation on which they (Negroes) lived.

III. Aid for the Negroes' escape.

A. Underground Railroad.
  1. Reasons for organizing.
    a. White men displeased with the treatment of the Negro organized this organization.
    b. The organizers' reasons for the most part patriotic.
  2. Attempts to hinder Underground Railroad.
    a. Proslavery forces managed to pass the fugitive slave law.
    b. They organized man-hunting leagues.
  3. Methods used to combat those measures.
    a. Private homes were used as hiding places for the fugitives.
    b. Transportation, food, and clothing were provided by sympathizers of the cause.

B. Other aids.
  1. Vigilance Committee.
  2. Anti-Man Hunting League.
  3. Women's Sewing Circle.
  4. Anti-Slavery Society.

IV. Towns and communities noted for their aid.

    A. Only three towns noted for unreserved support.
        1. Princeton, Illinois.
        2. Newport, Indiana.
        3. Sandusky, Ohio.
    B. Canada was the fugitives' destination.

V. Expense in aiding fugitives.

    A. Most expense carried by individuals who harbored slaves.
        1. Little or no outside help in currency was received by "conductors."
        2. Clothing was given more than any other aid.
    B. Different organizations raised some money.
        1. This money usually received from inactive members.
        2. Money kept for the most part to spread the news of this organization over the country.

VI. Conclusion.

8. Diction

Diction means essentially the choice of words to express our ideas. Words to the writer are the same as colors to the painter, notes to the musician: they are the staple of his craft. Versatile, judicious use of words is the mark of the good writer.

We shall consider first in this chapter the use of the dictionary—the word treasury of our language, the basic tool in the effective use of words. We shall then consider the various specific principles of good diction—appropriateness, exactness, vividness, directness—and end with a glossary of words frequently confused.

The Dictionary

1. Selecting a Dictionary   The following dictionaries are recommended for the college student:

One-volume, desk-size dictionaries:

Webster's Seventh New Collegiate Dictionary, G. & C. Merriam Co., Springfield, Mass.

The American College Dictionary, Random House Inc., New York.

Webster's New World Dictionary of the American Language, College Edition, World Publishing Co., Cleveland, Ohio.

New College Standard Dictionary, Funk & Wagnalls, New York.

Thorndike-Barnhart Comprehensive Desk Dictionary, Doubleday & Co., Garden City, New York.

Concise Oxford Dictionary of Current English, Clarendon Press, Oxford.

One-volume unabridged dictionaries:

Webster's Third New International Dictionary of the English Language, G. & C. Merriam Co.

New Standard Dictionary, Funk & Wagnalls.

Multivolume dictionaries:

A New English Dictionary on Historical Principles in 10 vols. and supplement, Clarendon Press, Oxford, reissued in a corrected edition in 1933 as *Oxford English Dictionary*, 12 vols. and supplement.

Dictionary of American English on Historical Principles in 4 vols., University of Chicago Press, Chicago.

You should consult the unabridged and multivolume dictionaries in your college library. These volumes are extremely useful when you wish information concerning a word that the desk-size dictionary, for lack of space, must exclude. The *Oxford English Dictionary* (OED), for instance, traces the change in meaning of every English word from its earliest known occurrence in the language. The *Dictionary of American English* traces the use of words by American writers since 1620. You will find indispensable, however, a personal copy of a good desk-size dictionary, which is in itself a storehouse of lexical information. The following considerations in the selection and use of your personal dictionary will help you derive full benefit from it.

Publication Date. A dictionary should not be considered in the same light as the family Bible, to be handed down from one generation to another. The language changes: new words appear, old words drop out, old meanings change, new meanings come in—even the spelling of some words alters. Consequently, the older a dictionary, the less dependable it is as a reference book for contemporary diction. When you buy your dictionary, choose the most recent edition of one of the desk-size dictionaries listed above.

2. Using the Dictionary *Arrangement.* Dictionaries do not have a uniform arrangement. In *Webster's Seventh New Collegiate,* definitions are arranged in chronological order— the first definition given under a particular part of speech represents the oldest meaning of the word, not the present meaning. *Webster's New World* uses a similar arrangement which it calls a "semantic order." *The American College Dictionary,* on the other hand, lists the common, present-day meaning of a word first. There is also an important difference in the arrangement of entries in the various dictionaries. *Webster's Seventh New Collegiate,* for instance, has separate sections for the general English vocabulary (including technical words and foreign phrases), biographical names, and geographical names. Other dictionaries, such as *Webster's New World* and the *American College,* arrange all entries in one alphabetical list. You should read carefully the table of contents and introductory material in your dictionary for full information as to its contents and most efficient use.

On pages 271–273 is given a sample from a page of *Webster's Seventh New Collegiate Dictionary.* That page, with the following comments, illustrates the kind of information you may expect to find in a good desk-size dictionary.

Meanings. Dictionaries, as we have noted, arrange definitions in different orders, and you must know the particular principle of arrangement used in your own dictionary. (In the sample page from *Webster's Seventh New Collegiate,* definitions are in a numbered list representing approximate chronological order, following the etymology or "word story," which is in brackets.) But regardless of the order of the definitions, you should examine *all* of them. Then, on the basis of the context in which the word is used, either in your own writing or in another's, you can select the appropriate definition.

Spellings. The dictionary is useful for checking spellings about which you are in doubt. The main entry in boldface type is the correct spelling of the word (you should not, of course, copy the accent marks or the centered periods within the word to indicate syllable division). When there are optional spellings, the preferred form is given first. Avoid (except in Canada) the optional spellings labeled *Brit.*, such as *labour, honour,* and *pyjamas.*

Etymologies. In *Webster's Seventh New Collegiate,* the etymology is given in square brackets immediately preceding the definition(s). Other dictionaries, however, reverse the order. The *American College Dictionary,* for instance, places the etymologies after the definitions. The etymology includes the ultimate source of the word and sometimes some of the intermediate sources. Much valuable, even entertaining, information about word origins and development may be found in the etymology. The source, for example, of our word *curfew* is Old French *cuevrefu,* from Old French *covrir,* "to cover," and *feu,* "fire." The word originated from the medieval French custom of sounding a bell each night at a certain hour in order to tell the inhabitants of the town it was time to cover their fires as a precaution against conflagrations. Our almost colorless adjective *nice* came into Middle English from Old French *nice,* which was derived from Latin *nescius,* meaning "ignorant," which came from Latin *ne + scire,* "not to know." Thus the original meaning of a *nice* person was one who did not know, who was ignorant of certain matters. Subsequent developments in the meaning of this word make a fascinating etymological study. For full etymologies and historical examples of meanings at different times in a word's development, you should consult the *Oxford English Dictionary* or the *Dictionary of American English,* both listed at the beginning of this section.

Pronunciations. The dictionary is indispensable for finding the conventional pronunciation of unfamiliar words encountered in reading. The phonetic pronunciation of a word

Centered Period for Syllabic Division

Pronunciation

Definition

Functional Label

satin stitch *n* : an embroidery stitch nearly alike on both sides and worked so closely as to resemble satin

satin weave *n* : a weave in which warp threads interlace with filling threads to produce a smooth-faced fabric

sat·in·wood /'sat-°n-,wu̇d/ *n* **1** : an East Indian tree (*Chloroxylon swietenia*) of the mahogany family; *also* : its lustrous yellowish brown wood **2** : a tree (as several yellowwoods) with wood resembling true satinwood; *also* : its wood

sat·iny /'sat-nē, 'sat-°n-ē/ *adj* : having the soft lustrous smoothness of satin

sat·ire /'sa-,tī(ə)r/ *n* [MF, fr. L *satura, satira,* fr. (*lanx*) *satura* full plate, medley, fr. fem. of *satur* sated; akin to L *satis* enough—more at SAD] **1** : a literary work holding up human vices and follies to ridicule or scorn **2** : trenchant wit, irony, or sarcasm used to expose and discredit vice or folly **syn** see WIT — **sa·tir·ic** /sə-'tir-ik/ *or* **sa·tir·i·cal** /i-kəl/ *adj* — **sa·tir·i·cal·ly** /-i-k(ə-)lē/ *adv*.

sat·i·rist /'sat-ə-rəst/ *n* : one that satirizes; *esp* : a satirical writer

sat·i·rize /-,rīz/ *vi* : to utter or write satires ~ *vt* : to censure or ridicule by means of satire

sat·is·fac·tion /,sat-əs-'fak-shən/ *n* [ME, fr. MF, fr. LL *satisfaction-, satisfactio,* fr. L, reparation, amends, fr. *satisfactus,* pp. of *satisfacere* to satisfy] **1 a** : the payment through penance of the temporal punishment incurred by a sin **b** : reparation for sin that meets the demands of divine justice **2 a** : fulfillment of a need or want **b** : the quality or state of being satisfied : CONTENTMENT **c** : a cause or means of enjoyment : GRATIFICATION **3 a** : compensation for a loss or injury : ATONE-MENT, RESTITUTION **b** : the discharge of a legal obligation or claim **c** : VINDICATION **4** : convinced assurance or certainty

sat·is·fac·to·ri·ly /-'fak-t(ə-)rə-lē/ *adv* : in a satisfactory manner

sat·is·fac·to·ri·ness /-t(ə)rē-nəs/ *n* : the quality or state of being satisfactory

sat·is·fac·to·ry /,sat-əs-'fak-t(ə-)rē/ *adj* : giving satisfaction : ADEQUATE

sat·is·fi·able /'sat-əs-,fī-ə-bəl/ *adj* : capable of being satisfied

Etymology

sat·is·fy /'sat-əs-ˌfī/ *vb* [ME *satisfien*, fr. MF *satisfier*, modif. of L *satisfacere*, fr. *satis* enough + *facere* to do, make—more at SAD, DO] *vt* **1 a :** to carry out the terms of (as a contract) : DISCHARGE **b :** to meet a financial obligation to **2 :** to make reparation to (an injured party) : INDEMNIFY **3 a :** to make happy : PLEASE **b :** to gratify to the full : APPEASE **4 a :** CONVINCE **b :** to put an end to (doubt or uncertainty) : DISPEL **5 a :** FULFILL, MEET **b :** to make true by fulfilling a condition ⟨values that ∼ an equation⟩ ⟨∼ a hypothesis⟩ ∼ *vi :* to be adequate : SUFFICE; *also :* GRATIFY

Discriminated Synonyms

syn SATISFY, CONTENT mean to appease one's desires or longings. SATISFY implies full appeasement esp. of a need or requirement; CONTENT implies gratification to the point where one is not disturbed or disquieted even though every wish is not fully realized **syn** see in addition PAY

Regional Label

sa·to·ri /sə-'tōr-ē, -'tȯr-/ *n* [Jap] : a state of intuitive illumination sought in Zen Buddhism

sa·trap /'sā-ˌtrap, 'sa-/ *n* [ME, tr. L *satrapes*, fr. Gk *satrapēs*, fr. OPer *xshathrapāvan*, lit., protector of the dominion] **1 :** the governor of a province in ancient Persia **2 a :** RULER **b :** a subordinate official : HENCHMAN

Primary Stress

sa·tra·py /'sā-trə-pē, 'sa-, -ˌtrap-ē/ *n* : the territory or jurisdiction of a satrap

Secondary Stress

sat·u·ra·ble /'sach-(ə-)rə-bəl/ *adj* : capable of being saturated

sat·u·rant /'sach-(ə-)rənt/ *n* : something that saturates

¹**sat·u·rate** /'sach-ə-ˌrāt/ *vt* [L *saturatus*, pp. of *saturare*, fr. *satur* sated — more at SATIRE] **1 :** to cloy with overabundance : SURFEIT **2 :** to treat, furnish, or charge with something to the point where no more can be absorbed, dissolved, or retained ⟨water *saturated* with salt⟩ **3 a :** to infuse thoroughly or cause to be pervaded : STEEP **b :** to fill completely : IMBUE **c :** to load to capacity **4 :** to cause to combine till there is no further tendency to combine : NEUTRALIZE **syn** see SOAK — **sat·u·ra·tor** /-ˌrāt-ər/ *n*

Verbal Illustration

²**sat·u·rate** /'sach-(ə-)rət/ *adj* : SATURATED

sat·u·rat·ed /'sach-ə-ˌrāt-əd/ *adj* **1 :** steeped in moisture : SOAKED **2 a :** being the most concentrated solution that can remain in the presence of an excess of the dissolved substance **b :** being a compound that does not tend to unite directly with another compound — used esp. of organic compounds containing no double or triple bonds

Usage Note

sat·u·ra·tion /ˌsach-ə-'rā-shən/ *n* **1** : the act of saturating : the state of being saturated **2** : SA-TIETY, SURFEIT **3** : magnetization to the point beyond which a further increase in the intensity of the magnetizing force will produce no further magnetization **4 a** : chromatic purity : freedom from dilution with white : INTENSITY **b** (1) : degree of difference from the gray having the same lightness—used of an object color (2) : degree of difference from the achromatic light-source color of the same brightness — used of a light-source color **5** : the supplying of a market with all the goods it will absorb **6** : an overwhelming concentration of military forces or firepower

Word Story

Capitalization

Sat·ur·day /'sat-ərd-ē/ *n* [ME *saterday*, fr. OE *sæterndæg;* akin to OFris, *sāterdei;* both fr. a prehistoric WGmc compound whose first component was borrowed fr. L *Saturnus* Saturn and whose second component is represented by OE *dæg* day] : the seventh day of the week — **Sat·ur·days** /-ēz/ *adv*

Sat·urn /'sat-ərn/ *n* [L *Saturnus*] **1** : an ancient Roman god of agriculture held to have reigned during a golden age **2** : the planet 6th in order from the sun — see PLANET table

Plural Form

sat·ur·na·lia /ˌsat-ər-'nāl-yə, -'nä-lē-ə/ *n pl but sing or pl in constr* [L, fr. neut. pl. of *saturnalis* of Saturn, fr. *Saturnus*] **1** *cap* : the festival of Saturn in ancient Rome beginning on Dec. 17 **2** *sing, pl* **saturnalias** *also* **saturnalia a** : an unrestrained often licentious celebration : ORGY **b** : EXCESS, EXTRAVAGANCE — **sat·ur·na·lian** /-'nāl-yən, -'nä-lē-ə-ən/ *adj*

Usage Label

Sa·tur·ni·an /sa-'tər-nē-ən, sə-/ *adj* **1** : of, relating to, or influenced by the planet Saturn **2** : *archaic* : of or relating to the god Saturn or the golden age of his reign

sa·tur·ni·id /-nē-əd/ *n* [deriv. of NL *Saturnia,* genus of moths, fr. L, daughter of the god Saturn] : any of a large family (Saturniidae) of stout strong-winged moths with hairy bodies — **saturniid** *adj*

sat·ur·nine /'sat-ər-ˌnīn/ *adj* **1 a** *archaic* : born under or influenced astrologically by the planet

ə abut; ᵊ kitten; ər further; a back; ā bake; ä cot, cart; j joke; ŋ sing; ō flow; ȯ flaw; ȯi coin; th thin; t͟h this;

273

is given in parentheses immediately after the boldface entry. In some dictionaries, a short pronunciation key is placed at the bottom of each page; in some, it is provided on the inside of one or both of the front and back covers. The introductory pages also generally contain an explanation of the phonetic system used. Mastery of these phonetic symbols is rewarding, since it will save you time and increase the accuracy of your pronunciation. But you must remember that standard pronunciations may vary from one section of the country to another. These variants are reflected in first and second pronunciations recorded in dictionaries.

Furthermore, the editors of the *Webster's Third New International Dictionary*, who may be considered representative dictionary-makers, do not consider the dictionary a *standard* of usage, but a *record* of usage. Consequently, merely putting one pronunciation "first" does not make it the only "correct" one.

Subject and Geographical Labels. Subject labels, like naut. for "nautical," sometimes occur after technical words or common words used in a technical sense to indicate to what branch of knowledge the word belongs. Geographical labels, such as *U.S., Brit.,* indicate the region in which the spelling or particular meaning of a word is most commonly used.

Usage Labels. Such italicized labels as *colloq.* (appropriate only in familiar conversation or writing), *slang,* or *dial.* (a local or provincial word) indicate the level of usage of a particular word. Words no longer used are labeled *obs.,* for "obsolete"; and words no longer used except in special contexts, as in Biblical expressions or poetry, are labeled *archaic*—see meaning 2 of *Saturnian* in the insert. Foreign words in some dictionaries are preceded by vertical parallel lines, and should be italicized. In general writing, all words bearing labels are to be avoided, or at least subjected to serious scrutiny, since they are not regarded as standard, contemporary English. Of course, words with *subject* labels are correct when used in appropriate technical writing. Colloquialisms, though inadvisable in formal English, are perfectly acceptable in conversation and informal writing (see D-4 to D-6).

The usage designations of words have been the main points of disagreement among dictionaries. *Webster's New Collegiate*, for instance, labeled "smart aleck" as *colloq. U.S.;* the *American College Dictionary* listed the word as standard. On the other hand, *Webster's New Collegiate* listed "hucksters" as standard; the *American College Dictionary* labeled it as *U.S. slang.* All of which goes to prove that dictionaries are made by human beings. When you find disagreements, let common sense be your guide, although the more conservative interpretation is usually the safer one in formal writing.

Grammatical Designations. The dictionary is a valuable reference for grammatical facts about a word. The grammatical classification or classifications of the word are usually given in an italicized abbreviation, as *n.* for noun, *v.t.* for transitive verb, *adj.* for adjective (see "satiny" in the sample page). Principal parts are given for strong verbs (those that have unusual past tenses or past participles), and unusual plurals or nouns are supplied, as well as alternative plurals for those nouns that have them.

Idiomatic Phrases. The dictionary may be profitably used in checking the correctness of idioms (see D-10 for a full discussion of idioms). Since it is difficult to keep in mind all idioms, one at least occasionally must depend on the dictionary. It is especially useful in finding exactly which preposition may be idiomatically used with a certain verb.

Synonyms and Antonyms. At the end of an entry, after the last meaning has been supplied, synonyms are frequently given, and, depending on the importance and frequency of use, the difference in meaning is explained. For example, at the end of the entry "satisfy" in the sample page, we find an explanation of the difference between the use of satisfy and a synonym, *content,* with a cross reference to *pay.* After the synonyms have been given, the antonym, or word of opposite meaning, is often suggested.

Hyphenation. The dictionary is also useful to the writer in the troublesome problem as to whether certain compound words are written separate, solid, or hyphened: notebook, self-control, drive-in, wellborn, high school.

Syllabication. The dictionary also indicates the proper syllabic division when you find it necessary to break a word at the end of a line. In *Webster's Seventh New Collegiate,* as illustrated in the sample page, the syllabic division is indicated in the main entry by a centered period. In the *American College Dictionary,* syllabic division is marked consistently by centered periods within the main entry. (See the discussion of syllabication, P-23.) Words may usually be divided at these points, but in the past tense of verbs or past participle forms—*ed* can be written on the next line only when it is pronounced.

Miscellaneous Information. Various dictionaries will contain supplementary information in prefaces and appendixes. *Webster's Seventh New Collegiate,* for instance, provides fifteen appendixes, including spelling rules, a vocabulary of rhymes, and a pronouncing gazeteer. The *American College Dictionary* includes six prefaces and two appendixes covering such matters as British and American usage and common signs and symbols. Almost all recent editions of college dictionaries contain lists of American colleges and universities. Be certain to check the table of contents of your dictionary in order to be aware of the miscellaneous information the dictionary contains.

3. Vocabulary Improvement A large vocabulary is the hallmark of an educated man or woman. We cannot even think of a complicated or abstract concept until we have a word for it. For this reason, the vocabulary test remains one of the most dependable indexes of intelligence. A common misconception is that the large vocabulary is an attribute restricted to intellectuals, "eggheads." Nothing could be more false. The great majority of men and women of real attainment in any field possess unusually large vocabularies.

Your dictionary is the principal means for the improvement of your vocabulary. You should develop immediately, if you have not already done so, the "dictionary habit." Never sit down to read, or write, without your dictionary in easy reach. Never allow an unknown meaning to escape you. At the start, this practice may be tedious; in reading difficult material, you will spend nearly as much time consulting your dictionary as you spend in actual reading. But time lost now will be time gained later.

As you add new words to your vocabulary, you should use them. All of us have "active" and "passive" vocabularies. Our active vocabulary consists of words we use in our speaking and writing. Our passive vocabulary, by far the larger of the two, includes those words we understand, at least vaguely, when we see or hear them, but which we never use in speech or writing. The old admonition that a person should learn and use three new words every day still makes good sense. The constant effort of every literate person should be to transfer words from his passive to his active vocabulary.

As you learn new words and put them to use, your dictionary is an indispensable tool.

Exercise 1

I. Use your dictionary to determine the origin of the following words:

1. hussy	11. heathen	21. dimity
2. wedlock	12. doom	22. flannel
3. wassail	13. buxom	23. leather
4. villain	14. lewd	24. nylon
5. termagant	15. recreant	25. rayon
6. tawdry	16. penthouse	26. damask
7. sponsor	17. pander	27. cotton
8. carnival	18. lieutenant	28. linen
9. assassin	19. yankee	29. wool
10. disaster	20. sophistication	30. muslin

II. Write a paragraph on the development of the meaning of any one of the words listed in I, using the *Oxford English Dictionary* as a reference.

III. Distinguish carefully the following groups of synonyms:
1. animated, lively, vivacious
2. long, yearn, hanker, pine, thirst, hunger
3. ill will, malice, malevolence, spite, grudge
4. approve, certify, endorse, sanction, accredit
5. beautiful, handsome, fair, beauteous, pretty, pulchri-tudinous, lovely, good-looking
6. desire, appetite, lust, passion, yen
7. effrontery, temerity, gall, cheek, audacity, nerve
8. praise, laud, acclaim, extol, eulogize
9. quarrel, wrangle, altercation, squabble, spat, tiff
10. salient, conspicuous, outstanding, noticeable

IV. Using a desk dictionary, find at least three meanings for each of the following words, and determine which meaning is currently most common:

1. liaison
2. malignant
3. retrograde
4. clever
5. admire

V. Determine the plurals of the following nouns:

1. appendix
2. sister-in-law
3. alumna
4. datum
5. phenomenon
6. banjo
7. perch
8. index
9. hippopotamus
10. mongoose

VI. Determine the suitability of the following words for use in formal writing. Do you find differences in opinion among dictionaries? If a word does not appear in the dictionary, should the word never be used in speaking or writing?

1. categorize
2. detritus
3. bogus
4. bamboozle
5. regurgitation
6. structure (verb)
7. conflagration
8. stuck-up
9. phony
10. boot (profit)
11. sock (stocking)
12. punk
13. rumrunner
14. old maid
15. cranky

VII. Determine the pronunciation of the following words:

1. precedence
2. precedent
3. derogatory
4. denigrate
5. desultory
6. *risorgimento*
7. centenary
8. exigencies
9. calumnies
10. indemonstrable
11. melancholia
12. Twickenham

Appropriateness: The Levels of Usage

There is no single standard of "correct" English. Instead, a word is correct if it is appropriately used: i.e., if its level of usage is appropriate to the circumstances in which it is used. Thus the choice of vocabulary in a paper to be read to an engineering society would surely differ from that of an address to your fraternity brothers on "The Ideals of Kappa Sigma." And though you might very well use the word "gal" in a letter to a close personal friend, you would surely not want to include it in a sociology term paper.

In the English language there are three general levels of usage: formal, informal, and substandard. Though they overlap to some extent, it is nevertheless useful to understand them. *Standard English*, consisting of the first two levels, is the language used generally by the educated community. The words in Standard English are in present, national, and reputable use. Use of the third level, the substandard, is characteristic generally of the uneducated community.

4. Formal The formal level is marked by Standard English words, including a rather high proportion of polysyllabic words, a rather elaborate sentence structure, and a complete absence of all dialectal words (local in use or meaning), slang, contractions, and colloquialisms (those words and constructions restricted largely to familiar conversation and writing). It is appropriately used in scientific writing, scholarly books, learned journals, formal essays and addresses, and formal invitations and replies. It is characterized by a serious tone and intention. The student should have a mastery of formal usage, since it is the level of most writing done in the professions and business.

5. Informal   A great deal of writing is now informal; you will probably write most of your themes on this level. Informal usage is marked by correct grammar and standard English words, except that colloquialisms and an occasional dialectal or slang word are permitted. Informal English generally contains fewer technical or "big" words than does formal; sentence structure is simpler; the average sentence is shorter; and there is a higher percentage of loose sentences than in formal English. Personal letters, popular books, both novels and nonfiction, mass-circulation magazines, and most newspapers are written on the informal level.

6. Substandard   Substandard English should be avoided by the college student in speech and certainly in writing except in dialogue representing uneducated speech. The substandard vocabulary includes dialectal words, slang, and colloquialisms. Substandard grammar is unconventional and sentence structure unpredictable. It is the vernacular speech of great masses of Americans. In printed sources, it is found in comic strips, in some popular songs, and in the speech of many fictional characters. The sophisticated writer and speaker uses substandard English only for a specific purpose.

The three levels of English—formal, informal, and substandard—can be illustrated by synonyms:

Formal	Informal	Substandard
revolver, pistol	gun	rod, gat
young woman, girl	girl	dame, moll, tomato
money, financial resources	money	dough, lettuce, moolah
intoxicated, inebriated	drunk	stewed, pickled, pied, stoned
minister	preacher	rev
opportunity	chance	break
automobile	car	jalopy, clunker
electricity	electricity	juice

You should strive for the appropriate word, the word suitable to the circumstances in which you are using it. Except for very special effects, do not mix the levels.

INAPPROPRIATE: A good secretary must be willing to assume almost an infinite number of responsibilities. She must strive continually to relieve her boss of all routine jobs. (The words *boss* and *jobs* belong on the informal level and are out of place in a formal context. *Employer* and *duties* would be more appropriate.)

INAPPROPRIATE: John Marsten is a nice fellow. He likes to have a good time—we've had some wonderful fishing trips together—but when a job's to be done, he's willing and eager to participate. (*Participate* is a bit formal for this informal context. *Do his part* would be better.)

EMPHATIC: Men do not sit in prisons as long as they used to; the parole boards shove them out almost as fast as the cops shove them in.
—H. L. MENCKEN, *Prejudices.*

Exercise 2

Designate the level of usage to which each of the following passages from student themes belongs:

From the failure of "The People's Will" and his brother's execution, Lenin derived two principles that were to guide his plan of revolution: first, he saw that terrorist attempts were futile against the might of the Czar, and second, that the peasants of Russia were not receptive to revolutionary incitement. As a supplement to these principles he observed that Russia was quickly becoming industrialized and that factory workers were becoming an important class. The workers were illiterate and discontented with the conditions imposed upon them. They suffered the hardships of long hours, low wages, and poor living conditions. Lenin realized the potentialities of this group and endeavored to direct their discontent and ill feeling toward the Czar's government.

281

That night, the eighteen of us got little sleep. We had a royal bull-session which ended, as bull-sessions often do, with a heated discussion about religion. Those who had "hit the sack" were rudely aroused by the merciless C.Q.'s whistle. In considerable confusion, we loaded into two six-by-sixes and shivered all the way to the airport. After the guards at the airport entrance waved us on, we pulled onto the runway and stopped under the wing of a C-54. Down the strip we could dimly see the forms of B-25's, laid out like men on a chessboard—pawns to be played by the Tenth Air Force in the battle of Burma.

Next, you'll have to go along with me in saying that those of less than average I.Q. add very little to the common welfare (I'm not referring to production of material wealth). Naturally, there are exceptions but I think you'll find that this is generally true. Very few in this classification are avid readers of the news section and editorials of papers, are religious frequenters of libraries, are well educated, or are members of civic or charitable organizations. Since it is these activities that contribute most to any degree of civilization which we now enjoy, I find these below-averagers guilty not only of failing to pull their own weight but of actually dragging the whole ship of state down.

About half way through dessert the blonde gets up from the table bawling and heads home. You have to talk real sweet to get that kind to cry. Probably he told her, "Turn in the furs and get someone else to pay the rent."

Jack Morrison is a photographer for the *Mirror*, and he often works with Miller. Jack comes in with a girl on his arm. Every guy in the place starts thinking and drinking. Morrison takes his girl over to Miller's table and introduces them. Miller does not rise, but Morrison and his date sit down. The chit-chat is running to dry goods. I can tell because Mike gives Jack's suit the fabric test. The suit must not have passed because bighearted Mike offers Jack a fist of bills to start him on the way to being well-clad. Morrison and the doll get up and depart like rabbits.

One of the aims of a democratic society is to enable all of its members to participate in the economic and cultural life of the community to the fullest extent of their natural capabilities. In accordance with this aim, class barriers should not be perpetuated; a democratic society should be a fluid society. But occupational training in high school for semi-skilled jobs helps to intensify class barriers. A student in the lower income group, no matter what his intellectual abilities, finds it difficult to reconcile his family's economic needs with his desires either for a college education or for additional courses in the humanities while he remains in high school. If he is forced by circumstances into the occupational program, he then spends a large part of his school day perfecting relatively simple physical skills. Upon graduation he enters an occupation and a way of life commensurate with his meager training. He is destined to remain near or at the social-economic level of his parents.

Exactness

Many a student in the composition course has come to an instructor with a graded theme and said, with reference to the instructor's comments on a particular sentence or passage, "That is not what I meant at all." The instructor's answer is usually something to the effect that the writer's intention means nothing if he fails to communicate it to the reader. Words are slippery things. They sometimes have multiple meanings and synonyms with subtle gradations of meanings. They have connotations that are as important as denotations, frequently even more important. Different contexts will give different meanings to the same word. Certain traditional combinations of words called *idioms* cannot be violated without distracting and confusing the reader. One of the most important injunctions to the beginning writer is: *Choose the exact word.* Not only must you be certain that you will be understood; you must be certain that you will not be misunderstood.

7. Connotation and Denotation The denotation of a word is its central core of meaning, roughly equivalent to its dictionary meaning. The connotation of a word is that atmosphere of suggested or emotional meaning which invests the word. The denotation of Christmas is "December 25, celebrated annually by the Christian church in commemoration of the birth of Jesus." The connotation of Christmas is what Christmas means to most of us beyond the denotation of the word, including the happiness, joy, and festive gaiety of the season. A cowboy is a mounted herder of cattle, generally in the western U.S.A. This is the denotation of the word. Its connotation includes all of the romance of the old West, the silver spurs and sombreros, and the swashbuckling bravado of countless western movie heroes. Many words carry a derogatory or unfavorable connotation —*gangster, collaborator* (since World War II), and *dictator*. Although every word necessarily has denotation, there are many words that arouse very little emotional response, either favorable or unfavorable, and hence have little if any connotation: *radiator, automobile, supermarket, ink bottle, typewriter* are examples.

Since many words are so charged with connotation, it is important to choose the word that has not only the right denotation, but also the exact connotation that you wish to communicate to your reader. Many times a carelessly chosen word will arouse an unfavorable reaction or a feeling of antipathy which makes communication with the reader difficult or misleading. There is, for example, a difference between referring to your neighbor's pet as a "dog" and calling it a "mongrel." Similarly in war, communiqués generally do not mention the word *retreat*, which might arouse the unwanted emotion of fear; instead, they generally refer to "strategic withdrawal to previously prepared positions," or to "strategic shortening of lines." Similarly, our soldiers always fight bravely, but our enemies sometimes fight "with suicidal fury." The word *automobile* has little connotation compared to a *convertible* (favorable), or *jalopy* (unfavorable), or *hot-rod* (favorable or unfavorable, depending on the writer's age).

To write well you must carefully choose words with the exact denotation and connotation that you wish to convey.

8. Context The context of a word is the environment in which it is used, including the statements preceding and following it, the circumstances under which the statement is made, the speaker or writer who makes the statement, and the hearer or reader. The real meaning of any word is not actually its dictionary definition plus connotation, but its dictionary definition plus connotation plus context. Since, strictly speaking, no two contexts are ever identical, the meaning of a word varies slightly every time it is used. One might compare the use of words in their evershifting contexts with the ancient Greek philosopher's statement that it is impossible to dip one's foot into the same river twice since the water will never be exactly the same. Perhaps, philosophically speaking, words can never have the same meaning exactly, but for all practical purposes their meaning can be determined and used repeatedly. Yet an awareness of the importance of contexts is worth cultivating if one would understand the use of words. The significance of the context is particularly well illustrated in the use of certain abstract nouns like *democracy* and *freedom,* which surely mean vastly different things to the U.S.S.R's Premier Kosygin and to President Lyndon B. Johnson.

9. Synonyms The English language contains over a quarter of a million words and thus provides us with a vocabulary unusually rich in synonyms. Synonyms are words which have the same, or nearly the same, denotations, but which often differ in connotation. To use words exactly, you should choose the synonym which conveys the exact meaning desired. Sometimes the difference between synonyms is great; between others, the difference is small. Consider, for example, *quarrelsome, pugnacious, belligerent,* and *warlike.* Though they all mean basically much the same thing, *belligerent* could not be applied to sailors in a Saturday night brawl. Nor could *pugnacious* be applied to nations, though *warlike* would be excellent. The dictionary is an invaluable aid in differentiating among synonyms. In addition to the dictionary, special books devoted to synonyms are available, such as *Roget's Thesaurus* and *Webster's Dictionary of Synonyms.* The serious writer will find these books very helpful. President Franklin D. Roosevelt, a skillful wielder of words. kept a copy of *Roget* on his office desk.

A carefully discriminating use of synonyms is one of the surest marks of a good writer, for only the skillful craftsman knows the nuances of meaning that lie between some of the closely related synonyms, like *continually, continuously,* and *incessantly.* Learn to discriminate among synonyms and to use the one which exactly suits the meaning you wish to communicate.

Exercise 3

Using your own desk-size dictionary or *Roget's Thesaurus* as a reference, distinguish between the pairs of synonyms following each number:

1. composure, nonchalance
2. currently, presently
3. doubt, skepticism
4. indemnify, gratify
5. informer, informant
6. luxuriantly, luxuriously
7. masterful, masterly
8. possibility, probability
9. saturnine, sullen
10. savage, barbarian

10. Idioms Students are usually aware of the fact that modern foreign languages like Spanish and French contain idioms, but they are often mildly surprised to learn that their own native tongue also contains many idioms. Thus they are like the title character in Molière's *Bourgeois Gentleman,* who was surprised to find that he had spoken prose for forty years without ever having suspected it. The reason we are not aware of idioms in our native English is simply that they are the native, natural, normal, characteristic way of saying the thing in English. In fact, we are aware of them only in their violation, for when the proper idiom has not been used, the result sounds awkward and unnatural to sensitive ears.

Idioms are not only the natural and characteristic form of English expression; they are often the only way to make a statement intelligible. For example, the English idiom requires the use of the expletive *there* in this sentence:

There will be a dance in Vanderbilt Field House next Saturday night.

Only a foreign speaker or writer would dispense with the expletive; the result, though entirely grammatical and even logical, is unidiomatic:

A dance will be in Vanderbilt Field House next Saturday night.

Many idioms, such as the following, cannot be translated literally into a foreign language:

Take the floor, please.
To make good.
To catch sight of.
To take in hand.

But by far the most troublesome idioms are those formed by the coupling of certain verbs with certain prepositions. Whenever the wrong preposition is used with the verb an unidiomatic expression results; for example:

The jury *acquitted* Robinson *from* murder.

This sentence is unidiomatic because the verb *to acquit* must be followed by the preposition *of* to form the idiom *to acquit of*. There are, of course, many verbs which are used with a number of prepositions, each use forming a slightly different meaning.

It would be impossible, and indeed unnecessary, to memorize all correct English idioms. The native-born writer will instinctively choose the right idiom most of the time. When in doubt whether you are using the correct idiom, or when the expression does not sound quite right to you, consult your dictionary. Here is a sample list of English idioms:

abide with (remain)	acquiesce in, to
abide by (to stand by, keep)	acquit of
	addicted to
abstain from	adept in
accede to	adequate for
accuse of	adhere to

agree in (an opinion)
agree to (a proposal)
agree with (a person)
agreeable to
angry at (a thing)
angry with (a person),
  not *at*
averse to
buy from
capable of
careless of, about
characteristic of
compare to, with
comply with
concern in (be
  interested)
concern with (to study
  qualities)
concerned with (involved
  in)
concur in (opinion)
concur with (person)
confide in (entrust a secret)
confide to (entrust)
conform to, with
contrast with
desire for
desirous of

die of
differ from (things)
differ with (person)
different from
disagree with
expert in
foreign to
guard against
identical with
independent of
infer from
negligent of
oblivious of, to
place in
plan to
prefer to
protest against
reason with
revel in
rob from
sensible of
sensitive to
separate from
sympathy with
try to
unmindful of
vexed at, with

Exercise 4

Improve the exactness of the diction in the following sentences:

1. He is much different than what I had expected.
2. Bobby hesitated to join our church because she didn't like the prospect of being dunked.
3. The new governor proved inadequate to the responsibilities of his position.
4. The robber's automobile made a cloud of dust that blinded the sheriff's deputies.
5. The frenzied animal jumped up on top of the shed.

6. In London society at the close of the last century, the custom was to eat dinner at eight o'clock.
7. Thristleburt eagerly agreed with the plan.
8. The new student frequently finds it somewhat difficult to comply to the regulations of the college.
9. I disagreed violently with the implication he drew from your remarks.
10. Maximilan was oblivious about the shouting in the rear seat.
11. Marguerite is considered a real beauty by the townspeople, but I personally feel that she is too big.
12. The professor felt that 99 percent of the people are too dull to benefit from an education.
13. Martin refused to admit that Griselda could be angry at him.
14. Let's see you try and do it.
15. Trooper Jackson stoutly maintained that he was capable to perform the job.
16. The instructor was quite sober when he discussed with the class the semester's program.
17. The board of trustees felt that the survey would help them a lot in coming to a decision about the budget.
18. The visiting speaker was an expert of linguistics.
19. Lawford shows little concern with our problems.
20. The proposal is agreeable with me.

Vividness

We have noted before that writing can be impeccable in grammar, mechanics, and organization, yet still be ineffective. One of the most frequent faults in writing of this sort is a lack of vividness. Such writing is often generalized and abstract; the writer offers little or nothing in the way of concrete detail to make his ideas vivid and interesting to his reader. No metaphors or similes flavor the arid stretches of limp, unappetizing prose. Or if they do, the figures are shop-worn and stereotyped—the kind that come easily to the mind but have no effect on the reader, except, perhaps, to increase his ennui.

You should realize, however, that there are dangers in attempting to enhance the vividness of your diction. Like other rhetorical properties of writing, vividness is achieved only through careful and discriminating effort. The figure of speech especially is difficult for the inexperienced writer to handle effectively and should be used, at least in expository prose, with great moderation. Even the attempt to make your writing more concrete can, if overdone, lead to wordiness and "fine or stilted writing," which we shall discuss in the next major division of this chapter, "Directness." Nevertheless, with these warnings in mind, consider carefully the following suggestions for increasing the vividness of your diction. Vividness, or the lack of it, is often the difference between excellent and mediocre writing.

11. Concrete Words Concrete, or specific, words are those which make a direct appeal to one of the five senses—taste, touch, smell, sight, or hearing. Abstract, or general, words are those which do not make this appeal to one of the five senses. The greater number of concrete, specific words you use, the more effective and vivid your writing will become. Of course there are no concrete synonyms for many abstractions, which must of necessity be used, like *toleration, sovereignty, choice, opportunity, inflation,* and countless others. But the constant use of a high proportion of concrete rather than abstract words is one of the greatest secrets of successful writing. It has been employed by all the masters from Homer to Hemingway. Look, for example, at the concreteness of Shakespeare's song:

> When icicles hang by the wall,
>   And Dick the shepherd blows his nail,
> And Tom bears logs into the hall,
>   And milk comes frozen home in pail,
> When blood is nipped and ways be foul,
> Then nightly sings the staring owl,
>   Tu-who;
> To-whit, tu-who!—a merry note,
> While greasy Joan doth keel the pot.
>
> When all aloud the wind doth blow,
>   And coughing drowns the parson's saw,

And birds sit brooding in the snow,
  And Marian's nose looks red and raw,
When roasted crabs hiss in the bowl,
Then nightly sings the staring owl,
    Tu-who;
To-whit, tu-who!—a merry note,
While greasy Joan doth keel the pot.

Probably the most effective—and safest—means of achieving vividness is through the verb:

GENERAL: The old woman moved toward the counter.

CONCRETE: The old woman (crept, limped, staggered, hobbled, darted) toward the counter.

GENERAL: He walked out the door.

CONCRETE: He (slipped, stalked, strode, ambled, lurched) out the door.

GENERAL: The horse ran past the stable.

CONCRETE: The horse (galloped, cantered, pounded, shot) past the stable.

A specific, concrete noun is usually preferable to a generalized, abstract noun:

GENERAL: The driveway was lined with beautiful trees.

SPECIFIC: The driveway was lined with beautiful (elms, birches, poplars).

GENERAL: A bird sang at my window.

SPECIFIC: A (robin, mockingbird, meadow lark) sang at my window.

Adjectives are the easiest means of providing vividness. But you should take great care not to overuse them.

GENERAL: Beneath the ridge wound a river.

SPECIFIC: Beneath the razorback ridge wound a sluggish river.

GENERAL: We went to a good movie.

SPECIFIC: We went to an (entertaining, exciting, absorbing, informative) movie.

Consider these additional examples of increased vividness in diction:

ABSTRACT AND GENERAL: The man walked down the road.

CONCRETE AND SPECIFIC: The gnarled old man, crippled with rheumatism, hobbled down the icy road.

ABSTRACT AND GENERAL: The house was set in the midst of trees.

CONCRETE AND SPECIFIC: The palatial country home was set in the midst of a grove of huge elm trees.

ABSTRACT AND GENERAL: He is also influenced by a priest (Karl Malden), who is wonderful in his part.

CONCRETE AND SPECIFIC: He is also influenced by a priest, played by Karl Malden, who interprets his part with understanding and skill.

ABSTRACT AND GENERAL: One of the officers of our organization has proved unworthy of our trust.

CONCRETE AND SPECIFIC: Ed Boyles, our treasurer, has absconded with our funds.

12. Figures of Speech (See "Mixed Figures of Speech," S-5)

To express yourself more vividly, use an occasional figure of speech. The two most frequently used figures are the simile, in which a comparison is generally stated using *like* or *as*, and the metaphor, a figure in which the comparison is assumed and not actually stated.

SIMILE: My love is like a red, red rose.

METAPHOR: The Lord is my shepherd. . . .
You are my sunshine.

You should not, however, consider the figure of speech a pure embellishment or ornament. A forced or trite figure is worse than none at all. Consider the following examples from student writing:

Her beautiful eyes were like deep pools in the moonlight. (This basic simile has been used so often that it has lost its strength.)

He was as quiet as a cat walking through mashed potatoes. (A cat walking through mashed potatoes would certainly be quiet, but the circumstance is so rare as to be outlandish).

Sunshine danced on the water and seemed to laugh at the world. (The personification of sunshine on the water is strained and forced.)

The gay, happy mood of the lake changed to one of defiance and strength. (One does not think of a lake, even in a storm, as being defiant and strong.)

The stars and the moon peeked from under cloudy bedclothes. (The stars and the moon are *over* clouds, not under them.)

Observe the integral, effective figures in the following passages:

The train pulls away, faster now, and the woman is back there in the house, where she is going to stay. She'll stay there. And all at once, you think that you are the one who is running away, and who had better run fast to wherever you are going because it will be dark soon. The train is going pretty fast now, but its effort seems to be through a stubborn cloying density of air as though an eel tried to swim in syrup, or the effort seems to be against an increasing and implacable magnetism of earth. You think that if the earth should twitch once, as the hide of a sleeping dog twitches, the train would be jerked over and piled up and the engine would spew and gasp while somewhere a canted-up wheel would revolve once with a massive and dreamlike deliberation.

—ROBERT PENN WARREN,
All the King's Men.

The Model T was distinguished from all other makes of cars by the fact that its transmission was of a type known as planetary —which was half metaphysics, half sheer friction. Engineers accepted the word "planetary" in its epicyclic sense, but I was always conscious that it also meant "wandering," "erratic." Because of the peculiar nature of this planetary element, there was always, in Model T, a certain dull rapport between engine and wheels, and even when the car was in a state known as neutral, it trembled with a deep imperative and tended to inch forward. There was never a moment when the bands were not faintly egging the machine on. In this respect it was like a horse, rolling the bit on its tongue, and country people brought to it the same technique they used with draft animals.

—LEE STROUT WHITE,
"Farewell, My Lovely."

The steersman dug his paddle into the stream, and held hard with stiffened arms, his body thrown forward. The water gurgled aloud; and suddenly the long straight reach seemed to pivot on its center, the forests swung in a semicircle, and the slanting beams of sunset touched the broadside of the canoe with a fiery glow, throwing the slender and distorted shadows of its crew upon the streaked glitter of the river. The white man turned to look ahead. The course of the boat had been altered at right-angles to the stream, and the carved dragon-head of its prow was pointing at a gap in the fringing bushes of the bank. It glided through, brushing the overhanging twigs, and disappeared from the river like some slim and amphibious creature leaving the water for its lair in the forests.

—JOSEPH CONRAD, *Tales of Unrest.*

13. Trite Expressions Trite phrases are those which have been worn out by the overuse of generations of writers. Originally they were clever or effective expressions—a means of enhancing vividness. Now they merely have a deadening effect on writing, detracting markedly from vividness and originality. Inexperienced writers are constantly tempted to use clichés, for to do so is, using the cliché expert's own phrase, "to follow the line of least resistance." Thinking is always hard work; so many of us find it easier to use ready-made phrases or verbal counters than to think of fresh expressions of our own.

Students may think they, too, can use trite phrases because they see them used in much newspaper and magazine writing and because they frequently find them in the public utterances of speakers who ought to know better. It is true that use of trite expressions and clichés is not a hanging, or even a fining, offense, yet the superior student who seriously wants to improve his writing can readily make great improvement simply by deleting these phrases. The following is not an exhaustive list, but it is extensive enough to suggest the kind of hackneyed expression you must try to eliminate:

the acid test	all work and no play
last but not least	nip it in the bud
white as snow	a long-felt need
sober as a judge	at a loss for words
slow but sure	caught like rats in a trap
black as ink	to smell a rat
tired but happy	better late than never
blissfully ignorant	busy as a bee
in the last analysis	conspicuous by his absence
in the final analysis	doomed to disappointment
each and every	goes without saying
for better or worse	easier said than done
this mortal coil (life)	equal to the occasion
preside at the piano	weaker sex (the female)
a sumptuous repast	festive occasion
traffic snarled	few and far between
traffic slowed to a snail's pace	irony of life
better half (wife, usually)	irony of fate
holy matrimony	method in his madness
hostages of fortune (children)	mother nature
filthy lucre (money)	psychological moment
among those present	ripe old age
rich and varied experience	sadder but wiser
venture a suggestion	wrought havoc

Though it is impossible to avoid all trite expressions in conversation, most of them should be removed from writing in the process of revision. Train yourself to be alert to their appearance and to eliminate them. Students who sometimes fear they cannot write without the assistance of these verbal crutches are often surprised to find after their initial feeling of loss that they can get along very well without them.

Exercise 5

Make the diction in the following passages more vivid:

1. After receiving the colonel's reprimand, the captain saluted, turned, and walked out the door.
2. I have wonderful memories of my home. The house was on a side street that was lined with trees. Flowers filled the window boxes, and in the backyard was a huge tree, with a rope swing attached to the strongest limb.
3. My brother is a professional gambler, but tell it not in Gaul.
4. On our vacation, we traveled to New England, then up to Canada, back through the Midwest, and finally south to our home.
5. We should view with alarm the subversive activities of our political opponents.
6. Whipped by a brisk breeze, the tiny wavelets rose to rough hills of water.
7. The boys in the leather jackets left their motorcycles, walked into the dance hall, and stood looking at the crowd.
8. When Mother Nature frowned, all the landscape frowned with her.
9. Since we knew how dishonorable his intentions were, we nipped them in the bud.
10. He dropped into the arms of Morpheus shortly after the shades of night had fallen.
11. She knocked on his door; when he opened it, she told him she hated him and never wished to see him again.
12. The quarterback faded to the right and rifled a long pass into the end zone.
13. The native called out in fear as the alligator closed in on him, its jaws opened wide.
14. The scenery affected me deeply.
15. It goes without saying that all work and no play makes Jack a dull boy.
16. Our team will be put to the acid test tonight when it meets Snibleyville for the championship.
17. It was a nice day. We were certain we would have a fine picnic.
18. All of us sobbed as he breathed his last breath.

19. The Wilstons were happy when they won a new house and station wagon.
20. They were two tired but happy boys.

Directness

Students too often look upon writing as a sort of trick. They make the mistake of thinking that the more florid and elaborate their diction, the more they will impress the reader. But this idea is directly opposed to the major stylistic tendency of English expository prose in the last century or more. Directness, with its companion virtue of sincerity, is the quality for which the modern writer strives. This is not to say that good modern English prose is flat and monotonous. It exhibits the positive rhetorical qualities that we have discussed under "Vividness." But effective prose is direct: it is notably free of the jargon and wordiness that typify "fine writing."

14. Sincerity If you would write well, you must be honest and sincere. For dishonesty (even of the unintentional, subconscious variety) and insincerity are the great roadblocks in communication. If you would reach your readers, write what you mean, and mean what you write. The greatest single cause of ineffectiveness is pretending to believe something that you really do not believe, or at least that you do not care about very much. Feel it, mean it, write it, and you will be effective. You may even be eloquent. Students' personal letters are frequently much better written than their themes and term papers because their letters are sincere attempts to communicate their thoughts as well as they are able. Many papers prepared for class, on the other hand, are unsuccessful because the authors do not really have anything to say, do not really care very much about their subjects, and try too hard to make a good impression to be natural.

15. Jargon The late Sir Arthur Quiller-Couch, Professor of English Literature at Cambridge University, gave the name "jargon" to a certain kind of expression which is especially dear to government bureaucrats. Representative Maury Maverick liked to call it "gobbledegook." Still others have called it "federalese," since it is the style rather habitually employed by the various departments of the federal government. But it can be found almost anywhere: in textbooks, committee reports, even in some student themes. Jargon never uses a clear, straightforward statement; instead it talks around the point. It does not say "yes" or "no"; instead it says "my answer is in the affirmative," or "my answer is in the negative." Jargon is a pompous kind of expression which habitually uses a cumbrous, mouth-filling phrase rather than a simple, direct expression. It prefers the Latinate word to the common English one. It uses euphemisms instead of simple words. A spade is not a spade, but "an agricultural implement"; a person does not die, he "passes away" or "passes on." The writer of jargon says, "He was conveyed to his place of residence in an intoxicated condition," when he actually means "He was carried home drunk." Jargon also uses certain roundabout phrases such as *as regards to, with respect to, in regard to* instead of simple prepositions.

> Dean Parker wanted to see Evangeline *in regard to* the Russell Scholarship. (*about*)
>
> My feelings *with respect to* Russia are of a suspicious *nature.* (I am suspicious of Russia.)

George Orwell gives an excellent illustration of jargon in his valuable essay on writing, "Politics and the English Language." First he quotes this passage from the Book of Ecclesiastes in the Bible:

> I returned, and saw under the sun, that the race is not to the swift, nor the battle to the strong, neither yet bread to the wise, nor yet riches to men of understanding, nor yet favor to men of skill; but time and chance happeneth to them all.

Then Orwell turns the passage into modern jargon:

> Objective consideration of contemporary phenomena compels the conclusion that success or failure in competitive activities

exhibits no tendency to be commensurable with innate capacity, but that a considerable element of unpredictability must invariably be taken into account.

16. "Fine Writing" The kind of writing which has been sarcastically labeled "fine writing" attempts to be too flowery and literary. It tries too hard and succeeds in being unnatural, stilted, and artificial. It is usually marked by a heavy concentration of poetic, archaic, or uncommon words, instead of ordinary, everyday words. For example:

place of residence	for	home
dwell	for	live
damsel	for	girl
mayhap	for	perhaps
amongst	for	among
institution of learning	for	university
law enforcement officer	for	policeman
greensward	for	lawn
repast	for	dinner
eftsoons	for	soon afterward

These expressions may of course be properly used in certain contexts. The point to be emphasized is that a passage which contains a number of these becomes vague, poetic, and too ornate; in a word, it becomes "fine writing." This sort of writing is often also marked by overuse of trite figures of speech, circumlocutions, and perhaps by a recurrence of words with similar initial sounds (alliteration). For example:

Our forefathers built this ship of state so sturdily, so staunchly that it weathered the stormy waters of the Civil War. When the storm ceased and the calm ensued, the high ideals and standards, character, and truth that they carefully and patiently built, were not found tossed aimlessly about like bits of driftwood, but were standing in unity, in one strong, everlasting monument—like a coral island, strong every inch.

17. Wordiness The undesirable stylistic qualities of *triteness, jargon,* and *fine writing* are, of course, often special aspects of *wordiness,* the violation of the fundamental principle of economy in writing. Using more words than are necessary for the exact expression of an idea weakens effect because unnecessary words tend to obscure more important ones. Telegraphic brevity, the opposite extreme of wordiness, is, of course, no better, but, within reason, the more "deadwood" you can eliminate from your writing, the better it will be. *The general rule, then, is to strike out in revision all words which do not contribute anything either to the thought or to the smoothness of expression.*

In addition to the wordiness often inherent in jargon and fine writing, inexperienced writers will frequently use unnecessary words in the following ways:

Redundancies

It was a *free* gift which he received absolutely *gratis.*

The saying that "Movies are better than ever" is one of the *false* illusions that Hollywood has created among the American people.

How silly and yet how serious are these feelings of the average American *person.*

You have the same trouble here as *you do* in public schools.

The Russians are probably just as puzzled over our plans for the future as we are *concerned about their intentions.* Therefore, I do not believe anyone knows the true answer to the unhappy state of relations *between the two countries.*

Unnecessary Clauses

The military planes *which are* manufactured in this country are superior to the Russian ones.

During Garden Week, *which is* held every April in Virginia, thousands of tourists visit the state.

Overuse of Articles

When I arrived at *the* college, I found that *the* students were required to stay on *the* campus over *the* week ends.

Shall *the* Negroes be given *the* opportunities they desire?

Circumlocutions

My information is that he was suspended in his junior year.
(I hear he was suspended in his junior year.)
I came to college to learn the ancient and honorable arts of
animal husbandry and horticulture.
(I came to college to learn farming.)

Exercise 6

In the following paragraphs, written by a Latin American
journalist, show how one writer has ranged from simple, direct
statements through increasingly vivid description and use of
figures of speech to what finally becomes "fine writing" when
the author resorts to clichés. Identify his specific strengths and
flaws.

. . . Irazú is the highest and most active of Costa Rica's nine
volcanoes. . . .

Irazú is a familiar figure to both tourists and residents. It is
not a feared volcano that vomits lava and shoots fire, demanding
human victims. It is, on the contrary, a cool peak where visitors
take pictures and build bonfires. . . .

Irazú has been unloading ashes almost every day since March
18, 1963. Some days the eruptions are sporadic; others, the discharge is constant, unending, like tropical rain. . . .

Some mornings . . . the clouds of ashes rise majestically,
like atomic mushrooms, to a height of 33,000 feet. Other times
the billows, less voluminous but still at precise intervals, appear
like smoke from an incredible pipe of a cosmic giant, far out in
the infinite. On sunny afternoons . . . the columns of smoke
resemble irridescent polychrome images that run quickly but
not recklessly westward, always on the move. . . .

Before your eyes, almost within reach, you see the rising and
growing of a solid, amorphous, lead-colored mass that thrusts
forth from the unknown and reaches toward infinity, in fine
particles carried by the wind. . . .

Exercise 7

Make the diction in the following sentences more direct:

1. Those young teenage delinquents rioted all through the night.
2. As people grow up and marry, they take on more and more responsibility; and as time goes on, the restless urge to be forever on the go dies in a person as he grows older.
3. This is the current controversial issue which confronts actors of the motion picture field.
4. A stammer is frequently an evaluative disability arising in societal situations wherein speech is the foci of anticipatory energy responses leading to behavioral manifestations of control disintegration.
5. My childhood was very *triste*, a conjunction of sordid circumstances exquisitely designed, or so it seemed, to destroy all the finer qualities of my nature.
6. For many hundreds of years, there have been wars among the countries of the world.
7. A point where I differ in opinion from the author is his view of the general educational systems of Europe and America, scholastic and social being the two main divisions.
8. These two apparently different systems of education in Europe and America have the same objectives, but achieve their goals in unparallel methods of management.
9. The European system concentrates the efforts of the student at an earlier age than does that of the American counterpart.
10. The European student is pushed hard at scholarship, leaving a blank side to his education of things other than scholarship.
11. Paris lies spread before you in dusky vastness, domed and fortified, glittering here and there through her light vapors, and girdled with her silver Seine.
12. Her sophomore year was marked by an increased participation in extracurricular activities.
13. If the colleges want to play their part in the contemporary life of America today, they must be revived, revitalized, and restored to the status they deserve.
14. It was in Presbyterian Hospital, Memphis, Tennessee, that little Barbara Jean first saw the light of day.
15. What is the nature of your objection to planning our dance for New Year's Eve?

16. I differ with you, Professor Flatbush, in regard to your analysis of existentialism.
17. Spring is almost here; eftsoons violets in all their beauty will peep through the verdure.
18. The committee should be made aware of the fact that our objections to the report are on the basis of careful, mature consideration and not from any personal predilections or concerns.
19. All employees are requested to extinguish illumination devices upon quitting a room.
20. As a rule pledges are usually required to spend a certain period each night at study.

Accuracy

18. Words Frequently Confused The pairs or groups of words in the following list are frequenly confused and hence misused. It is important that all college students learn to use words accurately.

Word	Meaning	Illustrative Sentence
accept	verb: to receive, usually with approval	We are delighted to *accept* your invitation to dinner.
except	preposition: excluding, or with the exclusion of	The decision met with the approval of all *except* Miss Berg.
affect	verb: to change or influence	The widespread use of oil and gas furnaces has *affected* the coal mining industry.
effect	usually a noun meaning result, but occasionally a verb meaning to put into action	As noun: The coal miners feel the *effects* of dieselization. As verb: As a result of this agreement, plans for a guaranteed annual wage will be *effected* immediately.

303

Word	Meaning	Illustrative Sentence
all together	in unison or in a group	The juniors and seniors went to the beach *all together*.
altogether	adverb: entirely or completely	Your estimate is *altogether* correct.
already	adverb: at a prior time	I had *already* paid the mortgage when the bank announced a higher interest rate.
all ready	two words: all prepared	We are *all ready* to go to the hockey meet.
allusion	a reference to something	In *Lycidas* there is an *allusion* to Atropos, one of the three Fates.
illusion	an error in vision or mental conception	The mirage in the desert is an *illusion*.
delusion	a fixed aberration of the mind	An insane person often suffers from a *delusion* of persecution.
ascent	noun: upward climb or movement	The *ascent* of the rocket was unbelievably fast.
assent	noun: agreement	The dean of men gave his *assent* to our plans for a gala masquerade ball.
censor	noun: an official who rules on the morality or suitability of books, plays, cinemas, etc., for public production	The State Board of *Censors* had to delete a good many yards of celluloid from Marilyn Roman's latest movie.
censure	noun: a public expression of disapproval verb: to censure publicly	In 1955 the United States Senate by an overwhelming majority voted *censure* of Senator Joseph McCarthy.

Word	Meaning	Illustrative Sentence
cite	verb: to refer to	How many authors did you *cite* in your term paper?
sight	noun: ability to see, or that which is seen	Though he has astigmatism, his *sight* is only slightly impaired.
site	noun: a location	This is the *site* of the Indian village.
continual	adjective and adverb (continually): occurring in steady, rapid, but not unbroken, succession	Her sarcastic remarks were a *continual* irritation to him.
continuous	adjective, adverb (continuously), and noun (continuousness): continued without cessation or interruption	For a period of three days, the troops shivered in a *continuous* rain.
consul	noun: a diplomatic representative	Mr. F. B. C. Rundall is the British *consul* in New York.
council	noun: an appointed or elected governing body	Why don't more good men run for the City *Council?*
counsel	(1) noun: advice or those giving advice; (2) verb: to advise	As noun: For legal *counsel,* the accused burglar chose the firm of Bradbury, Oglethorpe, Burnstein, and McGinnis. As verb: As your accountant, I *counsel* you to report your full and true income.
formally	adverb: in a formal manner	"Mr. Brathwaite, I do not believe we have ever met *formally.*"

Word	Meaning	Illustrative Sentence
formerly	adverb: at a prior time	It was *formerly* the policy of this university to hand out football scholarships.
imply	verb: to indicate or suggest	Mr. Collins, addressing a meeting of the Farm Bureau, *implied* that the government has solved the problem of the food surplus.
infer	verb: to draw a conclusion from	I *inferred* from Mr. Collins's speech that he approved of the administration's farm policy.
incredible	adjective: unbelievable, or almost unbelievable	His excuse for failing was *incredible*.
incredulous	adjective: skeptical, unbelieving	When his teacher heard it, his face broke into an *incredulous* smile.
ingenious	adjective: clever	He contrived an *ingenious* device which automatically turned on the lights at dusk.
ingenuous	adjective: frank, open; naïve, innocent	His *ingenuous* smile inspired confidence.
irritate	verb: to excite to anger or impatience; to make sensitive or sore	The dean of women's remarks about sororities surely *irritated* the Chi Omegas.
aggravate	verb: to make worse, or to intensify	Bill's smoking only *aggravates* the soreness of his throat.
exasperate	verb: to irritate to the point of losing restraint	The habitual irregularity of buses in New Haven is *exasperating*.

Word	Meaning	Illustrative Sentence
it's	contraction of *it is*	*It's* a long road that never turns.
its	neuter pronoun, possessive case.	Each case must be treated on *its* own merits.
liable	adjective: subject to something unpleasant or undesirable, as a fine or penalty	Drivers convicted of speeding a second time are *liable* to a fine of $50.
likely	adjective: that which is probable	It is *likely* to rain tomorrow.
apt	adjective: readily teachable; suited to the purpose; inclined	George is an *apt* pupil. His teacher often makes an *apt* remark.
loose	(1) adjective: not tight; (2) verb: to set free	As adjective: Hecuba, wearing a *loose* gown, enters from the left. As verb: *Loose* the prisoner at once, or take the consequences!
lose	verb: to suffer loss of	Did the depositors of the First National Bank *lose* any money when the cashier absconded with $143,000?
precede	verb: to go before	The Middle Ages *precede* the Renaissance.
proceed	verb: to go forward	Let us *proceed* with the regular business of the Dahlia Hill Garden Club.
principal	(1) adjective; first or highest; (2) noun: head of a school; sum of money	Edward's *principal* ambition was to become a crooner. Mr. Smithers, who formerly taught biology, was made *prin-*

Word	Meaning	Illustrative Sentence
		cipal of Upper Darby High School. You owe me $1,000 *principal*, plus three years' interest at 6 percent.
principle	noun: a fundamental; a fixed rule	The *principles* of geometry never change.
quiet	(1) adjective: noiseless; (2) noun: lack of noise; (3) verb: to make quiet	As adjective: I'd do anything for a *quiet* life. As noun: The *quiet* of the morn is refreshing. As verb: We told Mr. Miller that he should *quiet* his barking dog.
quite	adverb: completely, wholly, entirely	All in all, I'm *quite* satisfied with myself as I am.
respectively	adverb: to each his own	Letters of credit were issued to Andrews, Smith, and Burbank, *respectively*.
respectfully	adverb: in a respectful manner	All members of the House of Representatives must address each other *respectfully*.
statue	noun: a piece of sculpture	In the forum stands a *statue* of Caesar.
statute	noun: a law or ordinance	The *statute* of limitations allowed him to escape paying his clothing bill.
stature	noun: height (usually of a person), or rank	No man can increase his *stature* by wishing.
tenet	noun: fixed opinion or belief	Such were the *tenets* of the Nazis.

Word	Meaning	Illustrative Sentence
tenant	noun: "the holder or possessor of property"	The *tenant* shall be liable for all damage beyond ordinary wear.
to	preposition or part of infinitive	Shall we go *to* the concert? I am not inclined *to* answer.
two	adjective: numeral	Who caught *two* fish on one hook?
too	adverb: in addition; to an excessive degree	Emily is *too* fond of clothes.

Exercise 8

Choose the correct form in each of the following sentences:

1. Where did Myrtle (*loose*) (*lose*) her purse?
2. The (*principle*) (*principal*) of Jones Junior High School then arose to state his position in the school controversy.
3. (*Precede*) (*Proceed*) on this road with extreme caution.
4. Firmly but (*respectively*) (*respectfully*) we intend to make our case against the school trustees.
5. What were the (*principle*) (*principal*) beliefs of the Transcendentalists?
6. How could a general of Lee's (*statue*) (*stature*) (*statute*) have done otherwise?
7. The town of Marlborough has enacted a (*statue*) (*statute*) (*stature*) prohibiting the riding of motorbikes on its sidewalks.
8. Violators of this ordinance are (*likely*) (*liable*) (*apt*) to a fine of $20.
9. All the citizens wanted was a little peace and (*quiet*) (*quite*).
10. I (*imply*) (*infer*) from your remarks that you intend to call me a crook.
11. Mr. Roderick McBundy (*inferred*) (*implied*) that the Commissioner was not scrupulously honest.
12. Later on in the business meeting the (*council*) (*counsel*) (*consul*) voted (*censor*) (*censure*) of McBundy's conduct.

13. I believe Miss Carol Swan has a few screws (*lose*) (*loose*) in her head.

14. Bandaging a first-degree burn may (*irritate*) (*aggravate*) (*exasperate*) tissues.

15. Did you mean to (*infer*) (*imply*) that Virginia is not the only Mother of Presidents?

16. Each day has (*it's* (*its*) own problems, and (*its*) (*it's*) certain that all of them can never be anticipated.

17. You are (*apt*) (*likely*) (*liable*) to be right if you predict rain in Oregon.

18. In the course of his remarks the speaker (*cited*) (*sighted*) (*sited*) the examples of Caesar, Cicero, Pliny, and Aristotle.

19. The (*illusions*) (*allusions*) of the metaphysical poets were most often nonliterary ones.

20. She was (*formally*) (*formerly*) a beauty queen in South Carolina, it is said.

21. I am pleased to (*accept*) (*except*) your kind invitation to the President's reception.

22. How has the guaranteed annual wage plan (*affected*) (*effected*) prices?

23. After much persuasion the dean of women finally gave her (*ascent*) (*assent*) to the Panhellenic Council.

24. The (*afteraffects*) (*aftereffects*) of rheumatic fever are sometimes serious and permanent.

25. There are (*altogether*) (*all together*) too many parasites in British society.

9.

Spelling
Difficulties

If you come to this chapter with a weakness in spelling, you should realize that you are certainly not alone. Extremely literate people—eminent journalists, writers, and scholars—have been plagued with spelling difficulties. It is not easy, in fact, to find many individuals who will boast of spelling prowess. And considering the illogical relationship between some of the spoken words of our language and their written symbols, the wonder is that people are able to master English spelling to the extent that they do.

A perfect language—if there ever is such a thing—will have one specific written symbol to represent each sound. The letter *a*, for instance, would represent a single sound and not the multiple sounds exemplified in br*a*zen, f*a*sten, and pleas*a*nt, to name a few. *Victual* would be pronounced "viktual" and not, of all things, "vittel." But as unsatisfactory as English is in this respect, the faults will quite probably not be remedied in your lifetime. Consequently, if you have a spelling weakness—and most students have to a greater or lesser degree—the best you can do is learn to live with it.

But living with a spelling weakness does not mean resigning yourself to it—not, that is, if you consider yourself at least potentially a well-educated and literate person. It is a sad fact but a true one that of all errors in composition the spelling error is the most universally condemned. It would be interesting to know, for instance, how many letters of application have been buried in filing cabinets because of two or three obvious misspellings. The weakness should be faced, not with resignation, but squarely, with a determination to overcome it. There is no question that spelling skill is best developed from the early grades through constant drill and practice. But even at this stage in your educational career you can, with patience and persistence, develop your ability to spell to the point that misspellings will not offer a serious impediment to your effectiveness in writing.

Your attack on your spelling difficulty should be in terms of these four resolutions:

1. Form the dictionary habit.
2. Pronounce words correctly.
3. Learn the four standard spelling rules.
4. Learn to spell common words.

Form the Dictionary Habit

Every college student should own and use a good college dictionary, but if you feel that you have a spelling difficulty, you must consider a dictionary absolutely indispensable. It should be at your elbow every time you sit down to a writing assignment. If you are in the slightest doubt concerning the spelling of any word, you should check with your dictionary. If you form this basic habit, you have won half the battle at the very beginning. At first the practice of checking every doubtful word may seem laborious, but the result is well worth the pains, especially since with increased proficiency in spelling and use of the dictionary, less and less time will be required for the process.

In looking up a word, you should be certain that you understand the correct use of a dictionary (see D-2 for a full discussion). The spelling of the word is indicated by the main entry, printed in boldface type. This entry is usually divided into syllables by spacing and centered periods. Before transcribing the word (do *not* transcribe the centered periods and spacing between syllables), check the pronunciation, which is indicated in parentheses immediately following the main entry. Although pronunciation is not a completely reliable guide to spelling, it does offer a valuable aid to the correct spelling of a large proportion of English words.

Be certain to transcribe accurately the dictionary spelling to your paper. Countless students have discovered to their dismay that even though they conscientiously checked the dictionary for spelling of a word, all their work has come to nothing because of a faulty transcription. A more important reason for care in transcription is that your visual image of the word must be correct. The best spellers probably are guided almost entirely by visual images; that is, the word will simply not "look" right unless it is spelled correctly. Instructors in college composition have frequently been disconcerted by a deterioration in their spelling ability because in reading hundreds of themes and seeing certain words spelled many ways, they have lost the correct visual image of those words and are unable to distinguish, without checking, between correct and incorrect forms.

If you have a good deal of trouble with spelling, you might well buy a pocket dictionary for the express purpose of looking up words when you are writing. The smaller dictionary will involve less time than the larger and will probably contain most of the words in your active vocabulary. But do not consider the pocket dictionary a replacement for your college dictionary. It will be almost useless, for instance, in expanding your vocabulary.

Pronounce Words Correctly

Correct pronunciation is, as we have noted, by no means a completely accurate guide to correct spelling. But mispronunciation is a frequent cause of incorrect spelling. If you say "quanity" you are likely to spell the word that way instead of spelling it correctly, "quantity." If you say "*per*scription" instead of "*pre*scription," the chances are that you will spell the word incorrectly. The following words are especially susceptible to misspelling through mispronunciation. Dictionaries allow alternate pronunciations of some of these words, but it is to your advantage—especially if the spelling of the word gives you trouble—to adopt that pronunciation which is most phonetically true.

accidentally	mathematics
arctic	mischievous
athlete	occasionally
boundary	optimistic
candidate	perseverance
cavalry	perspiration
children	prefer
disastrous	prescription
drowned	preserve
February	probably
formerly	quantity
generally	similar
grievous	sophomore
handling	strictly
height	suffrage
hindrance	temperament
hundred	temperature
introduce	temporary
irrelevant	used (used to)
liable	usually
library	valuable
lightning	veteran
literature	visualize

Learn the Four Standard Spelling Rules

Spelling rules are undoubtedly a help in mastering the spelling of certain classes of frequently used words. But before you attempt to apply the rules, remember that "a little knowledge is a dangerous thing." To apply the rule correctly, you must know it thoroughly and be aware of the inevitable exceptions. A half knowledge of the rule and its application is worse than no knowledge at all.

1. The I-E Rule Of the four standard spelling rules, the most useful is the i-e rule. It is easy to understand and to apply, there are few exceptions, and it eliminates one of the most irritating difficulties in English spelling. It is best remembered by a short rhyme:

> If the sound is *ee*
> Use *i* before *e*
> Except after *c*.

Thus we know how certain words are spelled:

achieve	brief	piece	shriek
belief	chief	priest	thief
believe	niece	relieve	yield

but others, when the *ee* sound follows the *c*, are spelled thus:

ceiling	conceive	deceive	receipt
conceit	deceit	perceive	receive

The most important exceptions to this rule are *either, neither, seize, weird, leisure, financier, species*. These words may be combined into a sentence for easy memorization: At his *leisure, neither financier* would *seize either weird species*.

2. The Final Y Rule Another rule that works with a high degree of regularity, especially in forming the plural of nouns and the third person singular of verbs, is the final *y* rule. Words ending in *y* preceded by a consonant change the *y* to *i* before any suffix except one beginning with *i*.

baby—babies	fly—flies	vary—varied
carry—carries	try—tries	copy—copies
mercy—merciful		*but*
lovely—loveliness		copy—copyist

EXCEPTIONS: A good many alternative spellings still remain in general use:

shy—shier or shyer; shiest or shyest
fly—flier or flyer
dry—dryly or drily

On the other hand, words ending in *y* preceded by a vowel retain the final *y*:

obey—obeyed   attorney—attorneys   chimney—chimneys
valley—valleys   enjoy—enjoys   toy—toys

EXCEPTIONS: day—daily   slay—slain   say—said
               lay—laid   pay—paid   gay—gaily

3. The Final E Rule   A useful rule that will eliminate many of your misspellings of common words is the final *e* rule. It is applied to words ending in silent *e* to which a suffix is to be added. When the suffix begins with a *vowel, drop* the final *e*. When the suffix begins with a *consonant, retain* the final *e*. You should note, however, that there are numerous exceptions to this rule.

Drop the e

admire *a*tion	=	admiration
admire *a*ble	=	admirable
arrange *i*ng	=	arranging
care *i*ng	=	caring
desire *a*ble	=	desirable
move *a*ble	=	movable

EXCEPTIONS

a. The final *e* is retained to distinguish between words of similar spelling:

dye = dyeing (as opposed to *dying*)
singe = singeing (as opposed to *singing*)

b. The final *e* is retained in words ending with *ce* or *ge* before suffixes beginning with *a* or *o*. This exception preserves the soft sound of *c* and *g*.

notic*e* *a*ble = noticeable
(but notic*e* *i*ng = noticing)
manag*e* *a*ble = manageable
(but manag*e* *i*ng = managing)

c. The final *e* is either retained or dropped in a few words
with the suffix *able*:

lik*e* *a*ble = likable or likeable
us*e* *a*ble = usable or useable
sal*e* *a*ble = salable or saleable
siz*e* *a*ble = sizable or sizeable

The tendency to retain the final *e* in these words can be
credited to the desire to maintain the long sound of the previous
vowel.

Retain the e

arrang*e* *m*ent = arrangement
car*e* *f*ul   = careful
mov*e* *m*ent   = movement

EXCEPTION

In certain frequently used words in which the final *e* is preceded by a vowel, the final *e* is dropped before a suffix beginning
with a consonant:

argu*e* *m*ent = argument
tru*e* *l*y   = truly
aw*e* *f*ul   = awfully (but aw*e*some)

This exception also applies, in American English, to words in
which the combination *dg* forms a single consonant:

abrid*ge* *m*ent   = abridgment
acknowled*ge* *m*ent = acknowledgment
jud*ge* *m*ent   = judgment

British practice retains the final *e* in all these words.

4. The Double Consonant Rule Words of one syllable,
and polysyllabic words with the accent on the last syllable,

ending in a single consonant preceded by a single vowel, double the final consonant before suffixes beginning with a vowel. Although fairly complicated, this rule is of enough help in eliminating misspellings of common words to warrant your learning it.

hop (one-syllable word) + ing (suffix beginning with a vowel) = hopping

begín (two-syllable word with accent on last syllable) + ing = beginning

prófit (two-syllable word with accent on first syllable) + able = profitable

commít + ment (suffix beginning with consonant) = commitment

One-syllable words:

cram	crammed	clan	clannish
drag	dragging	red	reddish
grip	gripped	sad	sadder
bud	budding	stab	stabbed
drop	dropped	fog	foggy
cut	cutter	glad	gladdened

Words with accent on final syllable:

recur	recurrence	equip	equipped
admit	admittance	infer	inferred
control	controlled	compel	compelled
submit	submitted	confer	conferred

Words with accent on other than last syllable:

benefit	benefited	sever	severance
prefer	preference	inherit	inheritance
refer	reference	listen	listening
happen	happening	profit	profiting
marvel	marvelous		

EXCEPTIONS

a. *Excellence* is a definite exception to this rule.

b. Apparent exceptions like *prefer, refer* actually conform to the rule:

prefér—preférred, but préference

refér—reférred, but réference

c. A few alternative spellings violate the rule:

travel —traveling or travelling

worship—worshiping or worshipping

The double consonant rule does not apply to suffixes beginning with a consonant:

commit	commitment		sad	sadness
equip	equipment		glad	gladly

Exercise 1

A knowledge of the four rules just discussed should enable you to spell correctly all the words in the following list. On a separate sheet of paper, fill in the missing letters in the blanks where letters are needed.

The I-E Rule

1. ach——ve
2. br——f
3. c——ling
4. ch——f
5. conc——t
6. dec——tful
7. f——nd
8. gr——ve
9. l——sure
10. rec——ve

The Final Y Rule

1. bur——d
2. dela——d
3. famil——s
4. fl——s
5. librar——s
6. modif——s.
7. obe——d
8. pit——d
9. sk——s
10. tr——s

319

The Final E Rule

1. advantag——ous
2. definit——ly
3. desir——able
4. forc——ful
5. immediat——ly

6. liv——able
7. mov——able
8. peac——able
9. wast——ful
10. writ——ing

The Double Consonant Rule

1. bag——age
2. benefit——ed
3. intermit——ent
4. occur——ence
5. omit——ed

6. prefer——ence
7. quarrel——ing
8. quiz——es
9. refer——ence
10. stop——ing

Learn to Spell Common Words

It is highly doubtful, no matter how poor a speller you consider yourself, that you will ever misspell the word *pyrrhuloxia*. In the first place, you will probably go through life without having any occasion to use the word. In the second place, if an occasion does arise, you will check your dictionary very carefully before attempting to write it. The long and comparatively rare words in the language are a very minor hazard to the student with a spelling weakness. The villains are the words in common usage, the words that are indispensable in normal written communication, words like *interest, occasion, recommend,* and *similar*. These common words are the ones you must master before you can develop any confidence in your ability to spell and your capacity to produce a really effective composition.

The Private Spelling List   As a student in a composition course, you should always keep a private list of your own misspellings. You may keep this list in the flyleaves of the textbook or in a separate notebook; the important thing is that it be convenient for daily use. You should enter in this list any word that you must check for spelling in the process of your writing. Also, and more important, you should enter any misspellings marked by your instructor in a completed theme. Before writing the next theme, you should go over your list carefully to make certain that you do not repeat misspellings from the previous theme. If a word appears on your list twice, you should underscore that word in red as a habitual misspelling and take drastic means to correct it. Probably the best remedy is the old-fashioned process of writing the correct spelling fifteen or twenty times, for which we can give the newfangled reason that correct arm and pen "motor memories" will reinforce the correct mental image.

If you keep your private word list current and use it conscientiously, you should be able to eliminate the great majority of the habitual misspellings in your everyday word stock by the end of your course in composition.

5. A List of Words Frequently Misspelled   The following list of seven hundred words has been compiled from studies of the words most frequently misspelled by college students in their writing. The italicized words within the list are a further refinement, in that they represent the two hundred words most frequently misspelled by college students. Your best procedure is probably to learn the two hundred italicized words first. But you should not be satisfied until you master the entire list. This may seem a formidable task, but remember that you already know a great many of them.

absence	accurately	admit
absurd	accuses	adolescence
abundance	accustom	advantageous
academy	*achievement*	advertisement
accept	acknowledgment	*advice*
accessible	*acquaintance*	*advise*
accidentally	*acquire*	*affect*
acclaim	acquitted	afraid
accommodate	across	against
accompanied	actuality	aggravate
accomplish	address	aggressive
accumulate	adequate	alleviate

alley
allotted
allowed
all right
already
altar
altogether
always
amateur
among
amount
analysis
analyze
annual
anticipate
anxiety
apologize
apology
appall
apparatus
apparent
appearance
applies
applying
appreciate
approach
appropriate
approximately
arctic
area
argue
argument
arising
arrangement
article
artistically
ascend
assassin
assent
athlete
athletic
attendance

audience
author
auxiliary
awkward

balance
balloon
barbarous
barring
basically
basis
becoming
before
beginning
believe
beneficial
benefited
boisterous
boundaries
breadth
breath
brilliant
Britain
Britannic
budget
bureau
bureaucracy
business
busses

calendar
camouflage
candidate
canvas
canvass
capital
capitol
carburetor
career
careless
caricature
carrying

casualties
category
ceiling
cemetery
censor
ceremony
challenge
changeable
chaperon
character
characteristic
chargeable
chauffeur
chimney
choose
chord
chose
cloth
clothes
coarse
colloquial
column
comfortable
comfortably
coming
commission
commit
commitment
committed
committee
companies
comparable
comparative
comparatively
compelled
competition
competitive
complement
completely
complexion
compliment
comprehension

compulsory
conceivable
conceive
concentrate
concur
condemn
condescend
conferred
confident
confidential
conqueror
conscience
conscientious
conscious
considerably
consistent
conspicuous
contemptible
continually
continuous
control
controlled
controversies
controversy
convenience
convenient
coolly
cooperation
coordinate
corps
corpse
correspondence
council
counterfeit
counsel
courageous
course
courteous
criticism
criticize
cruelty
cupful

curiosity
curriculum
cylinder

dairy
dealt
deceit
deceive
decision
defendant
deferred
deficient
definite
definitely
definition
dependent
descend
descendant
describe
description
desert
desirability
desirable
despair
desperate
dessert
destroy
deter
devastate
develop
development
device
devise
diary
dictionary
dietitian
difference
different
dilemma
dining
disappear
disappearance

disappoint
disapprove
disastrous
discipline
disease
dissatisfaction
dissatisfied
dissipate
doesn't
dominant
dormitories
during

ecstasy
effect
efficiency
efficient
eighth
eligible
eliminate
embarrass
embarrassment
eminent
emphasize
endeavor
enforce
enormously
entertain
environment
equaled
equipped
erroneous
especially
exaggerate
exceed
excellent
except
exceptionally
excusable
exercise
exhaust
exhilarate

323

existence
experience
explanation
extraordinary
extremely
exuberance

familiar
fascinate
faucet
feasible
February
fiend
fiery
finally
financial
financier
flirtatious
forcible
foreign
formally
formerly
forth
forty
fourth
frantically
fraternities
friend
fulfill or fulfil
fundamental
fundamentally
further

gaiety or gayety
gauge
generally
genius
genuine
gorgeous
government
governor
grammar

gray
grievance
grievous
gruesome
guard
guidance

handkerchief
haphazard
happily
happiness
harass
haven't
having
heartily
height
heinous
hereditary
heroes
heroine
hesitancy
hindrance
holiness
hopeful
huge
humorous
hundredths
hurriedly
hypocrisy
hypocrite

illegible
illiterate
illusion
imaginary
imagination
imitate
immediately
immensely
imminent
implement
impromptu

incidentally
incredible
indefinite
independent
indictment
indigestible
indispensable
inevitable
influence
ingenious
ingenuous
innocence
inseparable
intellectual
intelligence
intercede
interest
interpret
involve
iron
irrelevant
irresistible
it's
its
itself

jealous
judgment

kindergarten
knowledge

laboratory
laborer
laid
later
latter
lavender
lead
led
legitimate
leisure

lenient
liable
library
lightning
likable
likely
literature
livable
livelihood
loathe
loneliness
lose
losing
lovable
loveliness
luscious

mackerel
magnificence
maintain
maintenance
manageable
manufacturer
marriage
massacre
mathematics
meant
mediocre
merely
mileage
millionaire
mimicked
miniature
minute
miracle
miscellaneous
mischievous
missile
misspelled
mistletoe
moccasin
modifier

momentous
monopolize
moral
morale
mortgage
mosquitoes
mountainous
murmur
muscle
mustache or
   moustache
mysterious

naïve
necessarily
necessary
necessities
necessity
Negro
Negroes
neighbor
neither
nevertheless
nickel
niece
nineteen
ninetieth
ninety
ninth
noisily
noticeable

obedience
obstacle
obstinate
occasion
occasionally
occupying
occur
occurred
occurrence
o'clock

omission
omit
omitted
oneself
operate
opinion
opponent
opportunity
oppose
optimism
origin
original
outrageous

paid
parallel
paralysis
paralyze
parliament
particularly
passed
past
peace
peaceable
peculiar
pedestal
pennant
perceive
perform
permanent
permissible
perseverance
persistence
personal
personnel
persuade
phenomenon
philosophy
physical
physician
picnicking
piece

pierce
plague
planned
pleasant
pneumonia
poisonous
populace
possess
possession
possibility
possible
potatoes
practical
prairie
precede
precedence
preceding
prefer
preference
preferred
prejudice
preparation
prepare
prevalent
principal
principle
privilege
probably
procedure
proceed
professor
prominent
pronounce
pronunciation
propaganda
prophecy
prophesy
psychiatrist
psychoanalyze
psychology
purchase
pursue

pursuing

quantity
quiet
quite
quizzes

readily
realistically
really
receive
receptacle
recommend
refer
reference
referred
referring
regard
relief
relieve
religion
religious
reluctant
repellent
repetition
repetitious
representative
rescind
reservoir
resistance
resource
respectfully
respectively
response
restaurant
rhetoric
rhyme
rhythm
ridiculous

sacrilegious
safety

satiric
satisfactorily
scandalous
scarcely
schedule
scissors
secretary
seize
sense
sensitive
separate
sergeant
serviceable
severely
shining
shoulder
shriek
shuffle
siege
significance
similar
sincerely
skeptical
solemn
solos
soluble
sophistication
sophomore
souvenir
specimen
speech
sponsor
spoonful
stagnant
stationary
stationery
statue
statute
stomach
stopped
strengthen
strenuous

326

stretch	tentative	*unnecessary*
strictly	*than*	*useful*
studying	*their*	*using*
subscribe	*then*	usually
subsistence	*there*	
subtle	therefore	*various*
succeed	*they're*	vengeance
success	*thorough*	vigilance
successful	*to*	*villain*
summarize	together	
superintendent	*too*	*weather*
supersede	tragedy	*weird*
suppose	transferred	*whether*
suppress	*tries*	*whose*
surprise	truly	*women*
syllable	Tuesday	*writing*
	two	*written*
technique		
temperament	unanimous	*you're*
tendency	*undoubtedly*	

Exercise 2: Review

Select the correct spelling in the following groups of variants:

1. a. temperment
   b. temperament
   c. temperement
2. a. benefitted
   b. benifited
   c. benefited
3. a. pronounciation
   b. pronunciation
   c. pronuntiation
4. a. succeed
   b. suceed
   c. succeede
5. a. similar
   b. similer
   c. similiar
6. a. amature
   b. amatuer
   c. amateur
7. a. reccommend
   b. reccomend
   c. recommend
8. a. dissappointed
   b. disappointed
   c. dissapointed
9. a. analize
   b. annalyse
   c. analyze
10. a. schedual
    b. schedule
    c. skedual
11. a. inseparable
    b. inseperable
    c. insepareble
12. a. undoubtedly
    b. undoubtably
    c. undoubtly
13. a. omission
    b. ommission
    c. ommision
14. a. catagory
    b. categorey
    c. category
15. a. desend
    b. descend
    c. decend
16. a. tentitive
    b. tenative
    c. tentative
17. a. embarrasment
    b. embarrassment
    c. embarassment
18. a. permissible
    b. permissable
    c. permisible

327

19. a. pleasant
    b. pleasent
    c. plesant
20. a. inteligence
    b. intelligents
    c. intelligence
21. a. independence
    b. independants
    c. independance
22. a. convient
    b. convenient
    c. convenent
23. a. conqueror
    b. conquror
    c. conquerer
24. a. superintendant
    b. superintendent
    c. superentendant
25. a. severely
    b. severly
    c. sevearly
26. a. unnecessary
    b. unneccessary
    c. unecessary
27. a. conscence
    b. conscience
    c. concience
28. a. proceding
    b. preceeding
    c. proceeding
29. a. achievement
    b. acheivement
    c. achievment

30. a. irresistable
    b. irresistible
    c. irresistble
31. a. persistent
    b. presistent
    c. persistant
32. a. accomodates
    b. accommodates
    c. acommodates
33. a. developemunt
    b. development
    c. developmant
34. a. tendency
    b. tendancy
    c. tendencey
35. a. enviornment
    b. environment
    c. envirement
36. a. paralell
    b. parralel
    c. parallel
27. a. inveterate
    b. invetrate
    c. invetterate
38. a. seize
    b. sieze
    c. sieize
39. a. conceiveable
    b. conceivable
    c. concievable
40. a. fascinating
    b. facinating
    c. fascinateing

41. a. successful
    b. sucessful
    c. succeful
42. a. fiery
    b. firey
    c. firy
43. a. hindrance
    b. hinderance
    c. hinderence
44. a. suppress
    b. supress
    c. suppres
45. a. immediately
    b. immediatly
    c. immediatley
46. a. apparant
    b. aparrant
    c. apparent
47. a. ocurrence
    b. occurrence
    c. occurence
48. a. laboratory
    b. labratory
    c. laborotary
49. a. vengeance
    b. vengance
    c. vengence
50. a. incidently
    b. incidentally
    c. incidentaly

10.

Punctuation and Mechanics

PUNCTUATION

Punctuation marks are symbols used to clarify writing. The purpose of punctuation is to provide in writing roughly the same signals we use in speech to set apart one word or group of words from another, or to emphasize one word or a group of words. In speech we use the pause to separate; in writing we use the comma, the semicolon, the period, and so on. In speech we use voice pitch or stress to emphasize; in writing we use the exclamation point, the question mark, and so on. The study of punctuation, then, is a study of symbols designed to aid the reader to understand the meaning of your writing.

Punctuation rules are general formulations of certain situations in a sentence in which a particular mark of punctuation is needed for clarity. One rule for comma punctuation, for instance, states: "When two independent clauses are joined by coordinating conjunction, a comma should be placed before the conjunction." This rule is not simply a convention thought up by English teachers for the harassment of students. It is based on the solid grammatical fact that coordinating conjunctions connect not only independent clauses, but also individual words. Although a comma is not always vital for clarity in compound sentences, many times the omission of the comma before the conjunction causes real confusion:

> I sent the letter to Tom and Jerry, who thought he should have been consulted, hasn't spoken to me since.

Without the comma before the coordinating conjunction "and," the reader is likely to misinterpret the sentence completely, at least until he reaches the verb in the second independent clause. Correctly punctuated according to rule, the sentence is completely clear at first reading:

> I sent the letter to Tom, and Jerry, who thought he should have been consulted, hasn't spoken to me since.

The punctuation rules that follow are actually descriptions of those situations in composition in which you will need a certain mark of punctuation. Punctuation, like most of the elements of English composition, is not a rigid, inflexible system. The professional writer can use unorthodox punctuation to achieve unusual and dramatic effects. But your writing in college and later in business and the professions should conform to the established conventions of English punctuation.

The Comma

The most frequently used, and misused, mark of punctuation in writing is the comma. The plethora of rules concerning the comma in many books is enough to make any student despair. Actually the use of the comma falls into four main divisions:

1. To separate independent clauses
2. To separate elements in a series
3. To separate introductory elements
4. To separate parenthetical elements from the rest of the sentence

A thorough understanding of these four aspects of comma usage will eliminate most of your difficulties with the comma.

1. To Separate Independent Clauses   When two independent clauses are joined by a coordinating conjunction (*and, but, for, nor, or yet, so*), a comma should be placed before the conjunction.

> The forest looked green and cool, but we were forced to continue trudging along the dusty road.
>
> He resented the implication of complacency, for he had always been aware of the danger of subversion.
>
> Bidwell had been away a long time, and he expected to see a good many changes in his home town.

Note that these sentences, like most compound sentences, are comparatively long. The reader needs a clear indication of the point at which the first independent clause ends and the second begins. This indication the comma provides.

Sometimes elimination of the comma in the compound sentence, as we have noted earlier, will lead to actual misreading.

> Mr. Stanfield directed the questions to Bill and Tom, who knew the answers, sat smugly and watched Bill squirm.

The reader is quite likely to take "Bill and Tom" as the compound object of the preposition "to" and consequently misread the sentence, at least momentarily. Notice how the proper use of the comma immediately clears up the difficulty.

> Mr. Stanfield directed the questions to Bill, and Tom, who knew the answers, sat smugly and watched Bill squirm.

In the example just cited, the second independent clause contains internal commas. On the grounds of clarity, some writers would use correctly a semicolon between the independent clauses. (See P-7.)

> Mr. Stanfield directed the questions to Bill; and Tom, who knew the answers, sat smugly and watched Bill squirm.

The comma before the conjunction is optional if the compound sentences are extremely short, if they are closely related, or if they have the same subject.

> I saw him and I ran.
> He laughed, and his friend smiled.

Exercise 1

Punctuate the following sentences where punctuation is needed:

1. His latest book is an excellent one and I am sure everyone in the club will enjoy reading it.
2. He looked frantically through the drawers for he was certain the key was in one of them.
3. Last night I saw Thomas and Harold had seen Vernon the night before.
4. Two is company but three's a crowd.
5. Give her credit for her courage or admit that she is simply stupid.
6. Two years ago we were told that each of us would be given an increase in rank but now the same people who were so encouraging then refuse even to recognize us.
7. When he found that all his work had come to nothing, this great man turned to another task and from his failure in the first, he drew strength for his glorious victory in the second.
8. Western told us that the time had come for action.
9. He had never visited California nor had he ever had the desire to do so.
10. The real secret of success is caring enough to make the necessary sacrifices.

2. To Separate Coordinate Elements in a Series *Elements in a Series.* The individual elements in a series of words, phrases, or clauses without internal comma punctuation should be separated by a comma.

> This furniture is attractive, comfortable, and expensive.
>
> On our vacation, we went to Colorado Springs, to Denver, and to a small mountain town called Gunnison.
>
> We had no idea who he was, where he came from, or what he wanted from us.

Note that the final two elements in these series are connected by coordinating conjunctions, but still the comma is used. Some writers consider the comma in this position optional, but it is best to use a comma before the conjunction for the sake of consistency and, sometimes, clarity.

Coordinate Adjectives. Coordinate adjectives—two or more adjectives modifying the same noun—should be separated by commas.

> The brisk, sunlit day was a delight to the senses.
> He was a sick, disappointed, weary man.

In some instances, an adjective and a noun are used so often together that they became a virtual noun compound. In such constructions, the adjectives are *not* coordinate (of equal rank—capable of being joined by *and*) and therefore are not separated by a comma.

> She is a strange old woman.
> The Brightons live in the big white house on the corner.
> He is a fascinating little fellow.
> The jet stream was sharp white against the clear blue sky.

The question whether or not adjectives are coordinate is sometimes a difficult one. The best test is to read the construction aloud to determine whether there is a natural pause between the adjectives in question. If so, a comma is needed; if not, the adjectives require no separation. Remember, however, that the adjective immediately adjacent to the noun is never separated from the noun by a comma.

Dates, Addresses, Geographical Items. In dates, addresses, and geographical items containing more than one element, the elements should be separated by a comma. If the combination ends within the sentence, a comma is placed after the final element.

DATES

They were married June 2, 1942. (The month and day are considered one element.)

They left the United States in August, 1945.

On January 1, 1947, they arrived in Cannes.

ADDRESSES AND GEOGRAPHICAL ITEMS

For two years he lived at 18 West Clark Avenue, Cleveland, Ohio. (The street and the number are considered a single element.)

His address now is 107 North Westlawn, Chicago 7, Illinois. (The city and postal region are considered a single element.)

Their postal address is now 383 Madison Avenue, New York, New York 10017. (The state and zip code are considered a single element.)

Martinsville, Pennsylvania, is my home.

Exercise 2

Punctuate the following sentences:

1. The wind was cold the ground was muddy and the scenery was atrocious.
2. She is a lovely friendly and charming girl.
3. His wife reminds me of the wicked old witch in *Hansel and Gretel.*
4. I used to live at 410 Meadow Drive Chicago 7 Illinois.
5. On December 8 1955 William Templeton was murdered at the door of his home.
6. The attractive white house on the corner belongs to his grandmother.

7. Most of us would admit that candor honesty and frankness are desirable traits in a human being.
8. Max lived in Madison California for two years.
9. The bright yellow flowers nodded over the ramshackle old fence.
10. They spent their vacation in Colorado and Wyoming.

3. To Separate Introductory Elements   Introductory adverbial and verbal elements are used out of their normal order in the sentence and should be set apart from the rest of the sentence by a comma.

Introductory Adverbial Clauses and Verbal Phrases   Introductory adverbial clauses and introductory verbal phrases are set off from the rest of the sentence by a comma.

adv. cl.
Although he confessed his crime, we were not certain that he was the guilty man.

v. phr.
Singing a mocking ditty, he swaggered down the trail.

adv. cl.
As far as he was concerned, the matter was closed.

adv. cl.
If he goes, I shall never forgive him.

Introductory Transitional Elements. Introductory adverbs and adverbial phrases used as transition devices (see page 157) are set off from the rest of the sentence by commas. (See P-4 for the punctuation of these elements within the sentence.)

Unfortunately, we failed to see his great potential as a writer.
First, let us consider the origin of the species.
In fact, I doubt that he realized he was cheating.

Introductory Prepositional Phrases. Introductory prepositional phrases are preferably set off from the rest of the sentence by a comma unless the normal order of subject and verb is inverted.

        prep. phr.
In New York, he found his true destiny.

           prep. phr.
At the sound of the bell, it will be ten o'clock.

       prep. phr.
During March, the first robins usually appear.

      prep. phr.
Out of the mist came the huge freighter. (Subject *freighter* and verb *came* inverted.)

Exercise 3

Punctuate the following sentences where punctuation is needed:

1. In the fall we usually hunt ducks along the Mississippi River.
2. If you wish to see him you should come early.
3. After searching for a place to stay we finally found the Dunne Hotel.
4. Luckily he was not at all disturbed by the accident.
5. At the most he won fifty dollars.
6. Although I have read this book many times I still enjoy it.
7. On the other hand you will find that professional football is a very exciting sport to watch.
8. Lastly we must decide on the time of our next meeting.
9. After classes I like to drop by the Union for a cup of coffee.
10. Indeed this is the best examination paper I have ever received.

4. To Separate Nonrestrictive Elements from the Rest of the Sentence

Appositives. A noun or noun phrase immediately following a noun and providing additional information about it is set off by commas.

Marstow, my roommate, is the leading character in the play.
This figurine, one of the most expensive in the shop, was created by a boy of twelve.
Jane, his sister, is much more attractive than he is.

Note, however, that when the first of two adjacent nouns is used in an adjectival sense, the second noun is not set off by commas.

His sister Jane is much more attractive than he is.
My roommate Marstow is the leading character in the play.
The novel *Babbitt* is one of my favorites.

Nonrestrictive Adjective Clauses. When an adjective clause serves only to provide additional information concerning the noun or pronoun it modifies, it is set off from the rest of the sentence by commas.

John Smith, *who is married*, lives on Buford Avenue.

A restrictive adjective clause, however, is not set off by commas.

The John Smith *who is married* lives on Buford Avenue.

In the first example, the adjective clause simply provides additional information. In the second example, the adjective clause restricts its noun to one particular person and is necessary to the meaning of the sentence.

Frequently, an adjective clause is restrictive or nonrestrictive according to the writer's intention.

The apples, which were spoiled, were thrown out. (All of a given lot of apples were thrown out. The fact that they were spoiled is added information.)
The apples which were spoiled were thrown out. (Of a given lot of apples, only those apples which were spoiled were thrown out. The adjective clause here restricts the meaning of the noun it modifies.)

Nonrestrictive Adverbial Clauses. Adverbial clauses following the main clause in a sentence are usually restrictive and are not set off by commas. In some instances, however, clauses which add a reason or concession are plainly nonrestrictive. These clauses usually begin with *because, since, as,* or *though.*

NONRESTRICTIVE: I gave him the money, *although I doubt that he will appreciate it.*

NONRESTRICTIVE: He threw away the letter, *since he couldn't bear to think of the answer.*

RESTRICTIVE: We went *because we were invited.*

RESTRICTIVE: The burglar waited *until the house was dark.*

Parenthetical Words, Phrases, and Clauses. Any element which interrupts or breaks the normal order of the sentence should be separated from the sentence by commas.

Conjunctive adverbs (see G-45) are set off by commas:

It is quite true, *however,* that he refused to go.
The result, *consequently,* was not what Brown had expected.
William was, *on the other hand,* delighted at the prospect.

Words or phrases of direct address should be set off by commas:

Call me, *Warren,* if you need help.
My advice, *my friend,* would be to forget the whole matter.
You, *sir,* are a cad.

Directive, qualifying, or emphatic elements used parenthetically should be set off by commas:

We were, *to tell the truth,* positive that you would not come.
This report, *for example,* is almost illegible.
It was, *indeed,* our last attempt to restrain him.

Quotations are set off from the words that introduce or follow them:

Jill answered, "I must study for my examination."
"Beginning tomorrow, a new grading policy will go into effect," the instructor announced.

Interpolations within quotations should be set off by commas:

"How often," *he asked,* "must I tell you this?"
"Yes," *Mary replied,* "I am sorry."
"The trouble with you," *he said,* "is that you are incapable of recognizing your own mistakes."

Absolute constructions should be set off by commas:

His attitude being what it is, I have no concern about the outcome.
We were disappointed when we missed him, *that being our reason for coming to town.*

5. The Comma for Clarity The preceding rules cover the great majority of the situations in which the comma is needed. But you should remember that the comma may be used wherever it is necessary for clarity. Among the most common situations in which such punctuation may be needed are the following:

Identical words immediately conjoined:

Whatever is, is right.

Simple sentences with a compound verb when the first verb carries a compound complement:

The standard written sentence must contain a subject and a verb, and must be grammatically independent.

Contrasted elements:

He was told that he should consider the offer, not that he should accept it immediately.

6. Unnecessary Commas Most instructors in composition would much prefer that their students use too few commas rather than too many. Overpunctuation with the comma is actually a more common fault than underpunctuation. You may have been told at some point in your scholastic career that you should use a comma to mark a natural pause in the sentence. If so, disregard that advice. Punctuation by rule is by far the safest practice. Here are some examples of overpunctuation with the comma:

Separating subject and verb:

The reason that he failed, was his outside activities.

Separating compound subjects:

The research assistant in the laboratory, and the lecturer in the auditorium were probing the same problem.

Separating compound verbs:

The path wound to the left, and descended sharply into the valley.

Separating compound direct objects:

The university bought four more city blocks, and the buildings standing on them.

Separating compound prepositional phrases:

The freshmen registered for a physical science sequence, and for a premedical program.

Setting off restrictive elements:

He was the man, who chased us last night.
Masterson has been in Europe, since the beginning of World War II.

Separating adjective and noun:

It was a bleak, cold, day.

Separating conjunction from clause:

But, I did not go.

Exercise 4

Punctuate the following sentences where punctuation is needed:

1. Next comes social life which I consider the most important.
2. We realized however that our cause was lost.
3. Maximilian Tightlow the eminent poet will speak tonight in the auditorium.
4. I have already told you Warren that you must abide by the rules.
5. Disciplining offenders who have lost their sense of community responsibility is useless unless we try also to remove the causes of their delinquency.
6. An accident which brought home to me the perils of drunken driving occurred yesterday in Birmingham Alabama.
7. We are not certain he committed the crime although it is true that he did confess.
8. We stayed at Brookfield Manor which is an ideal place for tourists.
9. John C. Thomas the mayor spoke to a crowd of over four thousand people.
10. He gave us wisdom and patience and led us with firmness and courage.
11. The most practical thing a girl can take no matter what she does in the future is accounting.
12. He used to say that his wife who was also a writer was his best critic.
13. My aunt Mary Jane always dropped her r's.
14. "I have found" he said "that you are the guilty party."
15. Mr. Brown whom we were forced to leave behind may be trusted to make everything all right with the five others who could not go.
16. The Bensons will write the first chapter of the book unless you have strong objections.
17. Semantics which everyone who wishes to understand language must study is concerned with the meanings of words.
18. His latest book is an excellent one although I am not sure that everyone in this club will enjoy reading it.
19. This opera which is the most elaborate to appear in this century was written by an obscure Russian.
20. The box which was lost contained valuable papers.

The Semicolon

The semicolon is needed as a punctuation mark much less frequently than the comma; it remains, nevertheless, an extremely important mark of punctuation. An understanding of its use will enable you to avoid two serious and fundamental errors, the comma splice and the run-together sentence (see BE-4–BE-5).

7. To Separate Independent Clauses   Two or more independent clauses in a compound or compound-complex sentence *unconnected by a coordinating conjunction* should be separated by a semicolon.

> The ability to take infinite pains is the mark of the genius; the ability to delegate those pains to subordinates is the mark of the executive.

If the two independent clauses in the preceding sentence are separated by a comma only, a comma splice results. If no punctuation is used between the two clauses, a run-together sentence results. These errors can be corrected in three ways:

a. By using a semicolon between the clauses, as in the foregoing example.

b. By connecting the two clauses with a coordinating conjunction:

> The ability to take infinite pains is the mark of the genius, but the ability to delegate those pains to others is the mark of the executive.

c. By making the two independent clauses separate sentences:

> The ability to take infinite pains is the mark of the genius. The ability to delegate those pains to others is the mark of the executive.

Do not confuse coordinating conjunctions (*and, but, for, nor, or yet*, and *so*) with the conjunctive adverbs (*therefore, nevertheless, however*, and so on). See page 157. Independent clauses connected by conjunctive adverbs must be separated by a semicolon before the conjunctive adverb.

COMMA SPLICE: He renounced his responsibilities, therefore, he must renounce his privileges.

CORRECT: He renounced his responsibilities; therefore, he must renounce his privileges.

8. To Separate Elements with Internal Commas
Clauses or phrases of equal rank with internal comma punctuation should be separated by semicolons in the interest of clarity:

These instructions, as I have told you, are of extreme importance; and I shall expect you to follow them explicitly. (The internal comma punctuation within the first independent clause makes a semicolon desirable between the two independent clauses for the sake of clarity.)

Mr. Thomas, the superintendent; Mr. Jones, the principal; and Mr. Leland, the instructor in science, will attend the meeting.

Seated in the car were my sister, who still wore her wedding dress; my cousin, his face a fiery red; and my new brother-in-law, a picture of despondency.

The meeting last night, one of the most chaotic I have attended, lasted until midnight; and unless something happens in the meantime, I fully expect the next one to last until dawn.

9. The Semicolon Fragment
The semicolon is used in connection with sentence elements of equal grammatical rank. It should not be used to separate unequal elements.

SEMICOLON FRAGMENT: We were glad to see them go; although we had enjoyed their visit very much.

343

CORRECTED: We were glad to see them go, although
                      we had enjoyed their visit very much.

SEMICOLON FRAGMENT: When we saw the object appear on the
                      horizon and start its slow, majestic
                      course across the sky; we knew that
                      we were safe.

CORRECTED: When we saw the object appear on the
                      horizon and start its slow, majestic
                      course across the sky, we knew we
                      were safe.

Exercise 5

Punctuate the following sentences where punctuation is needed:

1. These principles are basic to the process, all other considerations are comparatively minor.
2. The parcel contained the following: a pair of men's shoes, size 9C, two men's coats, a woman's summer dress, size 16, and a child's raincoat.
3. In the summer—my favorite season—we go to our cottage on Lake Burns, but in the winter we remain in the city.
4. Mark Hostettler was told he had only a year to live, therefore he decided to live life to the hilt.
5. Thristleburt, a man of strong purpose, shouldered his shovel and followed the other convicts along the dusty road.
6. Burton, who lived across the street from me for years, Willis, who was my brother's best friend, Stanton, who received his start in life from my father—all these turned against me.
7. I don't really care for him however I would not oppose his promotion.
8. In the midst of life is death, in the midst of joy is sorrow.
9. When the wind begins to veer to the east and the clouds come low over the lake, the villagers disappear into their sod houses.
10. Branson looked up and saw the bomber, a single black object came hurtling down toward him.

Other Marks of Punctuation

10. The Period   The period is used as follows:

To mark the end of a declarative or imperative sentence:

General Electric carries on a great deal of scientific research.
George, go feed the dogs.

To mark the end of an indirect question:

Frances asked whether we had received our application blanks.

To punctuate abbreviations. (See P-20.) Most abbreviations require a period:

Mr.	St. (street)	M.A.	A.D.
Mrs.	St. (saint)	A.B.	B.C.
Dr.	Jan.	Jr.	N.Y.
Ave.	Ph.D.	etc.	Ill.
ft.	in.	A.M.	P.M.

There are some abbreviations, however, which are customarily used without periods:

MS (manuscript); MSS (manuscripts); CBS (Columbia Broadcasting Company); *PMLA* (Publications of the Modern Language Association of America); *NED* (*New English Dictionary,* another name for the *Oxford English Dictionary, OED*), and so on.

Abbreviations of the names of certain organizations (acronyms) omit periods:

NATO, CARE, WAVES, WACS, WASPS, SEATO, UNESCO

To separate dollars from cents in sums of money:

$23.84 $600.27

To mark a decimal fraction:

Ivory soap is said to be 99.44% pure.
The newest jet speed record is 1042.26 mph.

To indicate an ellipsis. See P-25.

11. The Question Mark The question mark is used as follows:

To conclude every direct question:

What are we having for lunch, Mabel?
Have you ever visited Banff and Lake Louise?

To conclude a sentence consisting of a declaration followed by a short, dependent question:

This is your fourth ticket for speeding, isn't it, Sonny?
You have already qualified for the Naval Reserve, haven't you?

To punctuate questions which occur in the middle of a sentence:

The Speaker of the House said—or did I misunderstand him?—
    that the Legislature had passed the standard measure legal-
    izing ownership of securities by minors.
Did the President sign the bill? veto it? allow it to become a
    law without his signature?

Note, however, that *the question mark is never used after an indirect question:*

He wondered whether Dr. Rice was still in debt.

To indicate an uncertain date or fact:

The first part of *Henry IV*, 1597 (?), introduces Shakespeare's
    greatest comic figure, Falstaff.

You should note that *requests worded as questions merely as a matter of courtesy may be followed either by a question mark or by a period:*

Will all members of the senior class return their blanks at once (.) (?)

12. The Exclamation Mark   The exclamation mark is used as follows:

To express strong emotion.   It concludes all exclamatory sentences, and it may be used after an emphatic interjection whether it be a phrase, clause, word, or sentence.

Help! Fire! Fire! Save our house!
Ouch! I've scalded my hand!
- - - -! That fish got away!

Overuse of exclamation marks.   The exclamation mark must be saved for statements that really are strong exclamations. For example, after the mild interjections "well" and "oh," the use of the comma is sufficient.

Well, since I have no alternative, I have decided to accept the offer.

The excessive use of the exclamation mark is one of the characteristics of what is sometimes called "schoolgirl punctuation." Adolescent girls are often fond of using this mark where it is unnecessary, just as they like to use quotation marks to express irony or sarcasm, and dashes where terminal marks properly belong.

Exercise 6

Punctuate the following sentences where punctuation is needed:

1. He is a brilliant musician, isn't he
2. Winston your house is on fire
3. The principal told us—or have you already heard—that he has canceled the spring formal
4. Mrs Miller asked us if we were willing to cut our vacation short

5. She said she would pay us $200 an hour to whitewash her trees
6. Will all members of the football team report for practice at two o'clock this afternoon
7. When are you leaving, George
8. Your father has fallen and broken his hip
9. Run
10. You dislike me very much, don't you

13. The Dash The dash is a perfectly respectable mark of punctuation when used according to rules. All too often, however, as we have noted, it is capriciously used in "schoolgirl punctuation," which places a dash almost anywhere according to whim. The indiscriminate use of the dash is to be avoided. The correct use is as follows:

To introduce a list or enumeration where a mark less formal than the colon is wanted:

Jane had a world of good qualities—sweetness, understanding, warmth, and vivacity.

To introduce a summarizing statement after an enumeration:

Jane had sweetness, understanding, warmth, and vivacity—in a word, charm.

To indicate an abrupt break in the structure or the thought of a sentence:

This reminds me of something that happened to us at Chaco Canyon in the Navajo country—but, no that's another story.
Celeste was too pure, too naïve, too sensitive—oh, how shall I say it?—for life in a sorority house.

To separate a parenthetical statement from the rest of the sentence. There are three ways of setting off parenthetical matter in a sentence: (1) parentheses are used for something completely parenthetical (see P-24); (2) commas are used for an element that is only slightly parenthetical (see

P-4); (3) dashes are used to emphasize an abruptly parenthetical element, or a parenthetical element that contains
internal commas.

> Dr. Judson—emaciated, pale, and fever-racked—finally escaped
> from the China coast aboard a tramp steamer.
> How glad we were to see him—our scout leader of long ago—
> we shall never be able to tell you.

14. The Colon   The colon is correctly used as follows:

To introduce a formal listing:

> The box contained the following objects: a thermometer, an
> old pair of trousers, and a tattered calendar.
> He was told that he must cultivate three qualities for the job:
> perseverance, fairness, and discretion.
> The pay of the soldier in earlier times usually consisted of
> these: loot, lust, and liquor.

The colon is used incorrectly before a listing not formally
introduced.

INCORRECT: His favorite sports are: football, basketball, and
golf.

CORRECT: His favorite sports are football, basketball, and
golf.

INCORRECT: The items included were: three books, two note-
books, and a ream of typing paper.

CORRECT: The items included were three books, two note-
books, and a ream of typing paper.

To introduce a formal quotation or explanation:

> More people should remember Emerson's statement: "A fool-
> ish consistency is the hobgoblin of little minds."
> He told us exactly what we wanted to hear: that the factory
> would open soon and immediately resume full-time pro-
> duction.
> Throughout the war, this statesman worked with one objec-
> tive in mind: a just peace.

Note that a capital letter is used after the colon if the subsequent material is a complete statement. If the material that follows is a simple series or a dependent clause, a lower-case letter is customary.

To join two independent clauses when the second is a restatement, explanation, or amplification of the first:

The future may not be completely prosperous: there may be periods of violent economic adjustment.

By refusing to face up to these realities, he placed himself in a painful dilemma; he could neither return to his old way of life, with its simplicities and veracities; nor could he endure his new existence, with its sophistications and hypocrisies.

Be cautious in using the colon for this purpose, however. You should not use the colon when a semicolon is clearly appropriate.

The colon has the following special uses:

AFTER THE FORMAL SALUTATION IN A LETTER:
Dear Sir:
Dear Mr. Jones:

IN TIME NOTATIONS:
4:45 P.M.
12:00 noon

BETWEEN THE TITLE AND SUBTITLE OF A BOOK:
Walt Whitman: A Study in Realism

IN BIBLICAL REFERENCES:
Genesis 3:4–6

15. The Apostrophe   The principal uses of the apostrophe are as follows:

To form the possessive case of nouns and indefinite pronouns. (See G-6–G-8, G-17.)

The possessive singular of the noun is formed by adding an apostrophe and *s* to the singular form of the noun:

350

Mary's coat
the sun's rays
Bruce's tie

If the singular form of the noun ends in *s*, either the apostrophe and *s* or the apostrophe alone may be used to indicate singular possession:

Keats's poems or Keats' poems
Charles's father or Charles' father
Thomas's book or Thomas' book

If the noun forming the possessive ends in *s*, contains two or more syllables, and modifies a noun beginning with *s*, the apostrophe alone is commonly used to indicate possession:

Dickens' sentences
the princess' slipper

The *possessive plural* of the noun is formed by adding the apostrophe alone to the *s* plural form of the noun:

the Smiths' car
the boys' playground

If the possessive plural of the noun does not end in *s*, the apostrophe and *s* are added to indicate plural possession:

the men's club
the children's laughter
women's voices

The possessive of *compound nouns* is formed by the apostrophe *s* combination on the last element of the compound:

my brother-in-law's house
my brothers-in-law's houses
someone else's glove
Gilbert and Sullivan's operettas
      but
Bruce's and Henry's books (individual ownership)

The possessive of *indefinite pronouns* is formed by the apostrophe and *s*. The possessives of all other pronouns, however, are self-contained, and *the apostrophe should never be used.*

RIGHT: nobody's hat, everybody's favor, one's appearance
WRONG: it's wings, who'se hat, of your's, of their's
RIGHT: its wings, whose hat, of yours, of theirs

To mark omissions in contracted words and numerals:

doesn't, couldn't, they're, it's (it is), o'clock, '55

To form plurals of figures, letters, and words referred to as words:

There were six *and*'s in one paragraph.
The word "accommodate" contains two *m*'s and two *o*'s.
His *5*'s and *3*'s are indistinguishable.

Exercise 7

Punctuate the following sentences where punctuation is needed.

1. There are two shirts, a tie, and a handkerchief in the package.
2. The last time the Brentons camped it was several years ago Mr. Brenton came down with pneumonia.
3. Its true that a cat will forget its master much sooner than a dog will.
4. Warners case may be summed up as follows "He loved wisely but not too well."
5. There were two soldiers, three sailors, five airmen in the crowd all in all a motley crew.
6. Morton peeked at his cards and saw three 7s and two 5s.
7. They knew exactly what he wanted permission to build a tennis court on the vacant lot.
8. Winston turned to adjust he stopped in amazement.
9. The Joneses have two new cars; one is Bills, the other Marys.
10. Be careful not to overuse buts and ands.

16. Quotation Marks Double quotation marks are correctly used as follows:

To enclose direct quotations in dialogue:

"I am," said Paula, "simply mad about Proust. He has a wonderful insight into a woman's mind."

"I've never heard of him," he said.

"Oh, you have." She looked at him incredulously. "The Frenchman who wrote *Remembrance of Things Past.*"

"You mean—" He thought for a moment. "I think his name is usually pronounced—" Finally he said, "Yes, I have heard of him."

The passage illustrates the following principles of punctuating dialogue:

a. The words of each successive speaker are indented as for a paragraph.

b. Interpolations like *he said* are not enclosed within the quotation marks.

c. In an unbroken speech of several sentences by one person, quotation marks are placed at the beginning and end of the entire quotation, not around each sentence.

A quotation of the speech of one speaker extending over several paragraphs should have quotation marks at the beginning of each paragraph but at the end of only the last paragraph.

To enclose a quotation not a part of dialogue.

As Emerson said, "A foolish consistency is the hobgoblin of little minds."

I shall always remember something my professor in philosophy said: "A real education is a process of constructive disillusionment."

Though most of us recognize that "reading maketh a full man," many of us are not quite willing to turn off *Bonanza* to read the books we never have time for.

Is it practicable, do you think, in dealing with the Russians "to negotiate from a position of strength"?

Quoted passages of poetry do not require quotation marks since the verse form sets them apart from the text. Long passages of prose—which may be defined arbitrarily as pasages of more than fifty words—are set off from the text by smaller type in print and by single-spacing and indention in typewritten manuscript. Quotation marks are not used to enclose such quotations:

> The Smithsonian Institution lent art objects to the Pan American Union for an exhibit called "Chancay—Neglected Civilization of Potters and Weavers." The magazine *Americas* defined Chancay pottery thus:
>
>> Chancay ware is thin and highly porous. It was fired completely in an oxidizing atmosphere to a tan, orange, or orange-red hew. Frequently there is a creamy-white wash, or slip, poorly and unevenly applied, on which designs have been painted in a strongly contrasting sepia or black. Forms include bowls, jars, bottles with spouts, canteen- and football-shaped vessels, and, frequently, human figurines.

Quotation marks are *not* used with indirect quotations:

> My philosophy professor maintained that a real education is a process of constructive disillusionment.

When you use a verb with *that*, as in *maintained that* . . . or *said that* . . ., follow it with an indirect quotation, not the "direct" wording and punctuation. Let a direct quotation follow the verb:

> My philosophy professor maintained: "A real education is a process of constructive disillusionment."

To enclose words used as words. Italics are similarly used; however, one never uses both italics and quotation marks (see P-18). Likewise, letters and figures referred to as such are often placed in quotations.

> The word "lady" is of Old English origin and may perhaps be derived from words which meant in Old English "the loaf-kneader," that is, "the bread maker."
> He made the figure "5" so that it looked like "2."

To enclose the titles of stories, poems, essays which are shorter than book length, works of art, parts of books, and articles. Use italics for titles of books, magazines, newspapers, names of ships, long musical compositions, plays, and long or book-length poems. (See P-18.)

These recommendations state the best American practice and should be followed by college students. It is only fair to point out, however, that some highly regarded periodicals, especially *The New Yorker* and *Harper's*, consistently follow another style in which all titles are given in quotation marks.

Many students have enjoyed "The Secret Life of Walter Mitty" and "A Rose for Emily." (short stories)

I prefer James's "The Real Thing" to *The Ambassadors.* (The first is a story; the second, a book.)

John L. Lowes's *The Road to Xanadu,* a book about the mind of Coleridge, is considered by many the greatest work of literary scholarship written in the twentieth century.

Housman's "When I Was One and Twenty" and "Loveliest of Trees" were both published in his famous volume, *A Shropshire Lad.*

One of Thurber's most popular essays is "University Days."

The Detroit *Free Press* is regarded as a leading American newspaper.

To enclose slang expressions and words used in a special sense:

He prefers the company of his "beatnik" friends to mine.

A certain class of people like to talk about "inferior" races.

Be careful, however, of the "coy quote":

All of us girls are just "crazy" about that "divine" convertible.

Use of single quotation marks. Single quotation marks are correctly used to enclose quotations within quotations.

Churchill said, "My countrymen, it is fitting that we celebrate this great day by singing 'God Save the King.'"

An exception—double quotation marks to enclose a quotation within a quotation—occurs only in a blocked paragraph quote which appears without quotation marks:

> George Washington was called the "Father of His Country."
> Thomas Jefferson was the "Author of Independence." . . .

17. Quotation Marks with Other Marks of Punctuation

With periods and commas. When a period or a comma falls at the same place with a closing quotation mark, either double or single, the period or comma is invariably placed inside the quotation mark. This is an arbitrary convention of punctuation and printing. Though books printed in England frequently follow a practice quite opposite, in America this is standard practice. College students should learn to follow it without deviation.

> Shelley wrote "Ozymandias," "Ode to the West Wind," and "Queen Mab."
> Very few Americans seem to know the words of their national anthem, "The Star-Spangled Banner."

With colons and semicolons. The colon and semicolon go outside closing quotation marks.

> A good many cultural snobs say, "There is nothing good on television"; but how can they say this about Noel Coward, Mary Martin, Sir Laurence Olivier, and Leonard Bernstein?
> That evil child denounced the following people as "collaborationists": his mother, his two sisters, and his uncle.

With question marks, exclamation marks, and dashes. The question mark, exclamation mark, and dash go inside or outside a closing quotation mark depending upon whether the question mark, exclamation mark, or dash belongs to the quoted matter. If it belongs, the mark goes inside; if it does not belong, the mark goes outside.

> Does anybody know who wrote "Frankie and Johnnie"?
> Was it Byron who wrote the cruel little poem, "Who Killed John Keats?"

356

Can you name the colleges included in the so-called "Ivy League"?

With statements introducing quotations and interpolations within quotations. Statements introducing quotations (see P-16) and directive interpolations within quotations (see P-16) are punctuated according to the demands of their particular structure.

"Please let me alone," he said, "since there is nothing you can do."

"Please let me alone," he said. "There is nothing you can do."

It is a trite but true statement that "the road to hell is paved with good intentions." (Note that the quotation is here an integral part of the sentence; consequently, no punctuation is needed before the quote.)

I heard him say, "Don't do that!"

I was shocked to hear him make the following statement: "Don't do that!" (Whether to use the comma or colon after the statement introducing the quotation is frequently the writer's choice. In general, as illustrated in the two examples above, if the introductory statement is short, a comma is used; if the statement is long and somewhat formal, a colon is used.)

Exercise 8

Punctuate the following sentences where punctuation is needed.

1. I know I have been here before he said. She looked at him questioningly. Don't you remember exactly when? It seems strange that you wouldn't recall exactly a place so beautiful. He looked out over the valley. I know. But it's so. He stopped. Then he said It's vague, but I know I have seen it.
2. Warren asked Wasn't it Roosevelt who said all we have to fear is fear itself
3. My professor's favorite short story is Faulkner's The Bear.
4. Robert's mother told him that his father wanted him to become a doctor.
5. Robert's mother said Your father wanted you to become a doctor.

6. The World War II generation of students has often been called the silent generation.
7. The student replied The only thing I have read by Joyce is his short story The Dead, and I must say that I was not impressed.
8. Slang expressions like real gone and cool have no place in polite conversation.
9. She said out of sight, out of mind is a trite but true expression.
10. If you want to be simply one of the boys, you have no business trying for a graduate degree.

MECHANICS

18. Italics   Italic type is indicated in handwritten or typed manuscripts by a single underline. Italics are used as follows:

For titles of books, magazines, newspapers, and other complete works published separately. Names of ships, planes, and titles of motion pictures are also italicized.

Time, Gone with the Wind, Hiawatha, Paradise Lost, The Washington Post, Othello, Every Man in His Humour, Picnic, The Man in the Gray Flannel Suit, The Saturday Evening Post, the *Queen Mary,* the *Viscount, Bridge on the River Kwai*

Titles of shorter works not issued as separate publications, such as short stories, essays, and poems, are enclosed in quotation marks. (See P-16.)

For words used as words, letters as letters, and figures as figures (see also P-16):

Bogus, a genuine Americanism, originated as a slang word, but it is now considered standard.
The origin of *O.K.* is somewhat in dispute.
Be sure you dot your *i*'s and cross your *t*'s.

For foreign words and phrases not yet considered part of standard English:

Hitler was always pleading for more *Lebensraum*. Every time *Der Führer* used the word, the crowd would always cheer wildly.

For some reason or other she always treated me as if I were *persona non grata*.

The common house cat, *Felis domestica*, is easily housebroken.

For strongly emphatic words or statements. Students should be warned, however, that it is very easy to overuse italics for emphasis, and thus actually weaken the statement.

I cannot emphasize too strongly the difference in law between *possession* and *ownership*.

Exercise 9

Punctuate the following sentences where punctuation is needed (for the use of quotation marks, see P-16):

1. Her chatter ran on ad infinitum.
2. Hemingway's short story, The Short Happy Life of Francis Macomber, first appeared in Cosmopolitan Magazine.
3. Keep this axiom firmly in mind: Never underestimate a competitor.
4. My favorite newspaper is The New York Times.
5. He sailed to Europe on the Carnovan Castle.
6. The decision is already a fait accompli.
7. Chapter 10 of The University Handbook is entitled Punctuation and Mechanics.
8. Mike Todd's movie, Around the World in Eighty Days, is a happy conjunction of travelogue and melodrama.
9. He used the word continual, not continuous.
10. Critical opinion is sharply divided on Cozzens' novel, By Love Possessed.

19. Capitalization Capital letters are used correctly as follows:

For the first word of every sentence and the first word of each line of poetry:

There is something I must tell you, George.

"Time present and time past
Are both present in time future,
And time future contained in time past."—T. S. ELIOT

For each important word and the last word in a title.
Articles, conjunctions, and short prepositions are not capitalized except as beginning or ending words, or when a preposition is an integral part of the title or is important in itself.

Gone with the Wind, Of Human Bondage, Of Time and the River, The Man in the Gray Flannel Suit, "Two Tramps in Mud Time," "Death of the Hired Man," "Under Which Lyre," "The Short Happy Life of Francis Macomber," *What Men Live By*

For all proper nouns and derivatives of proper nouns, including:

NAMES OF PERSONS AND PLACES, AND ADJECTIVES MADE FROM THEM:

Shakespeare, Virginian, Canadian, Roman, Vesuvius, Crater Lake, Jasper Park, Wood's Hole, Manchester, Chicago, Housman, Hemingway, Cummings, Spenserian, Cartesian, Jesuit, Arian

EXCEPTIONS: Some derivations, through frequent use, are now considered common and are no longer capitalized:

pasteurized milk, derby hat, herculean task, leghorn hat, chinaware

ALL ORGANIZATIONS, INCLUDING RELIGIOUS:

Lions, Kiwanians, Mormons, Seventh-Day Adventists, Episcopalians, Future Farmers of America, The Chase Manhattan Bank, General Motors Corporation, The Soil Conservation Commission, Elks, Moose, Catholic, Buddhist, Protestant, Unitarian

ALL RACES, ETHNIC GROUPS, AND LANGUAGES:

Hottentots, French, Lithuanian, Celt, Celtic, Slavic, Old High German, Spanish, English, Russian, Negro, Persian, Indian

DAYS OF THE WEEK, MONTHS, HOLIDAYS:

Tuesday, January, Labor Day, Mother's Day, Christmas, Easter, Columbus Day

HISTORICAL PERIODS AND EVENTS:

Stone Age, War of the Roses, Spanish-American War, Edict of Nantes, the Magna Carta, the Civil War, Reformation.

PERSONIFICATIONS:

"How soon hath Time, the subtle thief of youth,
Stolen on his wing my three and twentieth year!"
—JOHN MILTON

WORDS PERTAINING TO THE DEITY, INCLUDING PRONOUNS:

God, Lord, Jehovah, the Trinity, the Blessed Virgin, the Almighty, Allah, Heavenly Father, Prince of Peace, Redeemer, Saviour, He, Him

For all titles preceding proper nouns or used as substitutes for proper nouns:

Judge Blue, President Johnson, Chief Justice Warren, Admiral Byrd, General Grant, Dr. Smathers, Governor Clinton, Secretary Rusk

When the title follows the name, it is not capitalized unless it is a title of exceedingly high rank:

Lewis W. Douglas, Ambassador to the Court of St. James's, but John W. Smith, principal of Lonesome River High School

Most abbreviations used after names are capitalized, such as Ph.D., LL.D., Esq., M.A., K.C.B., S.J., Jr., Sr. See P-20.

For words of family relationship. Father, Mother, Brother, Sister, Aunt, Cousin are generally capitalized when they stand alone or with a Christian name. When they are used as common nouns with possessive pronouns, as *my father, my brother, my uncle,* they are not capitalized.

For names of courses when they are used as proper nouns. When they refer to specific courses, as Forestry 33B or Comparative Literature 20, the names should be capitalized. When these are used as subjects, not courses, they are common nouns: forestry, engineering, comparative literature, and so on. But note carefully that *the names of languages are always proper nouns,* and hence capitalized:

He is majoring in engineering (forestry, literature).
He is majoring in English (French, Russian).

For directions designating geographical or political regions. Do not capitalize the directions north, south, east and west, unless you use them to designate geographical or political regions.

St. Louis is southwest of Chicago.
Dallas is one of the largest cities in the Southwest.

Do not capitalize school, college, university, street, river, and the like, unless they are used as part of a proper noun.

Exercise 10

Capitalize where capitalization is necessary:

1. I heard him say, "I am sorry, mother, but I did the best I could."
2. He decided to take mathematics instead of spanish.
3. He was born in Phoenix, Arizona, and could not imagine living outside the southwest.
4. The main staple of his diet after his marriage was lima beans and vienna sausage.
5. A novel that impressed him a great deal was Maugham's *of Human Bondage.*

6. John W. Estey is the Superintendent of Schools in Frederick, Oklahoma.
7. This community was visited by president Eisenhower and senator Lyndon Johnson.
8. Since he was interested in the natural sciences, he chose as electives biology 232 and zoology 345.
9. The one person he treasured above all others was his sister.
10. One can tell by her accent that she is from the south.

20. Abbreviations In ordinary writing (not formal social correspondence), the following uses of abbreviations are standard:

For titles before proper names. Mr. Messrs., Mrs. Mmes., Dr., St. (Saint), Col., Gen., Rev., and Hon. The last two should be preceded by the article "the" and followed by the person's Christian name.

RIGHT: Mr. Vanderbilt, Dr. Johnson, Mrs. Busch, St. Teresa, the Rev. Richard Potter

WRONG: Rev. Potter

For titles after proper names: A.B., M.A., Ph.D., LL.D., D.Litt., M.D., Esq., Jr., Sr.

For dates. The abbreviation A.D., "Anno Domini," is always used before the year; B.C., "before Christ," is always used after the year. The abbreviations A.M. and P.M. are used with precise designations of the time and are not to be used as substitutes for "morning" and "afternoon."

For certain words in addresses, footnotes, bibliographies, and the like. St., Ave., p., vol., no., *ibid., op. cit.*

For certain conventional expressions (except in formal social correspondence): e.g. (for example), i.e. (that is), viz. (namely), etc. (and so forth).

For names of many governmental bureaus and agencies: SS, CD, FHA, HOLC, TVA, UNESCO, CIA, UN. Note that such abbreviations should not begin a sentence.

Indiscriminate abbreviation. Do not abbreviate indiscriminately.

INAPPROPRIATE: He has an appointment with the prof. later this A.M.

APPROPRIATE: He has an appointment with his professor later this morning.

INAPPROPRIATE: He dreaded his math exam more than any other.

APPROPRIATE: He dreaded his mathematics examination more than any other.

INAPPROPRIATE: On our vacation, we visited Nev., Cal. and S. Dak.

APPROPRIATE: On our vacation, we visited Nevada, California, and South Dakota.

WRONG: His house is two sts. over from mine.
We went to the mts. for a vacation.
He decided to read fifty pp. a day.

21. Numerals *For numerical notations.* If the number requires fewer than three words, it should be spelled out; if it requires three or more words, numerals are used.

A basketball team consists of five players.
We asked twenty-five people to the party.
There were more than seventy thousand people in the stadium.
There were 70,562 people in the stadium.
He registered 375 students in History 105.
Chicago is approximately 310 miles from St. Louis.

This convention is standard in general expository prose. It will vary, however, with the writer's purpose. In statistical reports, for instance, numbers may be used consistently instead of their written equivalents.

For a series of numbers. In a series of numbers, consistency should be the guide.

The parcel contained 282 pencils, 31 typewriter ribbons, and 18 erasers.

For numbers beginning a sentence. Numbers beginning a sentence should be written out.

364

Four and twenty blackbirds were baked in a pie.
Two hundred and thirty-two students dropped out of the
sophomore class at St. Trinian's.

If the number is very large, it is better to change its position
in the sentence so that it will not come first:

$1,150,000,000 in sales were made by International Harvester.
International Harvester had sales of $1,150,000,000 last year.

For dates (except in formal notes):

POOR: President F. D. Roosevelt took office March fourth,
nineteen hundred and thirty-three.

CORRECT: President F. D. Roosevelt took office March 4, 1933.

For street numbers and apartment numbers:

The Coopers live at 188 McLean Street.
The police have been investigating Apartment 204A, Lincoln
Hall.

For decimals and percentages:

The shocking absence rate in English 33 last semester was
4.05 per cent.

For page and chapter numbers of books:

You will find this information in Chapter 15, page 479.

For time, when used with A.M. *or* P.M.:

Faculty meetings are generally held at 7:30 P.M. on the first
Tuesday of each month.

Exercise 11

Correct the following sentences:

1. There were 2,000 people at the rally.
2. 5,054 tickets were sold for the homecoming dance.

3. He informed the prof. that he didn't want a lab course this semester.
4. Milford was a frosh at State U. last year.
5. He thought back to the time when one could go to a movie for 25 cents.
6. His birthday is on October twenty-ninth, nineteen forty-four.
7. John Robert won the county tennis championship yesterday for the 4th time.
8. In the course of his travels, he developed a taste for Ala., but a great distaste for Minn.
9. Doctor Jones is the family doctor of Mister Worthington and his family.
10. He read 30 pp. a day for 2 years.

22. Hyphens *Between two or more words used as a compound adjective modifying a following noun*:

He was confronted by a *six-foot* wall.
Johnson is a *well-known* chemist.
The crowd pressed through the *wide-open* gate.
He fished in the pockets of his *worn-out* coat.

But compounds involving two proper nouns or an adverb ending in *ly* are not hyphenated:

The South Carolina farmers met in indignation.
Chrysler has a generously planned retirement program.

Between compound numbers from twenty-one to ninety-nine:

Sixty-six Rotarians went to the convention.
One hundred forty-three dollars is absolutely my best offer.

Miscellaneous usage:

a. Words with prefixes *ex, self,* and so on: *ex-president, self-made man, all-knowing*
b. Similar words or those with an awkward union of letters: *re-creation* as opposed to *recreation; re-formation* as opposed to *reformation; bull-like; semi-independent*

c. Noun compounds: *daughter-in-law, son-in-law, mother-in-law*

It is extremely difficult to know whether many compound words are written separate, hyphened, or solid. When in doubt consult your dictionary. Many can be written several ways.

drugstore	bookstore	basketball
notebook	weekend (adj. and n.)	football
goodby *or*	post office	textbook
good-bye *or*		undergraduate
goodbye		

23. Syllabication If it becomes necessary to divide a word at the end of a line in either a handwritten or a typewritten paper, the following rules should be observed:

The hyphen is placed at the end of the line, not at the beginning of the following line.

Do not divide words of one syllable: breathe, hence, march. Do not separate the *ed* suffix from the root in such words as *weighed, talked,* for the *ed* suffix is not a separate syllable.

Always divide words between syllables. Make the division between double consonants in words that have them: lit-i-gate, lit-er-a-ture, com-pel-ling, sub-mit-ted. Do not, however, allow a single letter to stand alone: a-lone, e-licit, man-y, tin-y.

Miscellaneous usage:

COMPOUND WORDS MAY BE DIVIDED AT THE HYPHEN: *all-American, good-by.* Words with a prefix or a suffix may be divided between the prefix and the root or between the root and the suffix: *predica-ment, destitu-tion, semi-classical, ante-bellum* (n.). None of these words is ordinarily written with a hyphen.

AVOID THE DIVISION OF PROPER NOUNS.

AVOID THE DIVISION OF FIRST AND LAST NAMES, OR LAST NAMES AND INITIALS.

AVOID THE DIVISION OF THE LAST WORD OF A PARAGRAPH OR PAGE.

CONSULT THE DICTIONARY WHEN IN DOUBT ABOUT SYLLABICATION.

Exercise 12

I. Indicate the proper division of each word, if the word can be divided.

adoption	dilettante	strolling
arbitration	disarray	terribly
bringing	disturbance	tomorrow
committee	engagement	unconquered
defiled	existence	undercurrent
detrimental	lately	unluckily
difficult	maximum	

II. With the aid of a dictionary, indicate which of the following should be hyphenated, which should not.

all around	foot ball	past master
anti Communist	forth right	ready made
best loved	full back	rest room
base ball	half starved	room mate
book store	in as much	semi circle
day break	non partisan	week end party
dry goods	north west	

24. Parentheses and Brackets Parentheses are used to enclose parenthetical matter—material that is explanatory, or supplementary, as figures interpolated in a text to number parts of a statement. There are three ways of punctuating parenthetical matter: (1) with commas, which make the least break in the sentence (see P-4); (2) with dashes, which mark a fairly abrupt break, and emphasize the material they enclose (see P-13); and (3) with parentheses, which are primarily for extraneous material, either supplementary, interpretive, or explanatory. If a mark of punctuation is used with the closing parenthesis, it should follow the parenthesis. When an entire sentence is in parentheses, the end punctuation is placed inside the closing parenthesis. A comma should never precede a word or phrase in parentheses.

The ancient Celts (Brythonic and Goidelic) painted their bodies blue—nobody knows why.

The Sioux patrol suddenly broke off the attack and galloped over the hill. (This strange action will be explained later in detail.)

Brackets are used by a writer to enclose his own interpolated remarks in a quotation, whether these be corrective, illustrative, or explanatory:

"All that I have been saying is summed up in a few characteristic words of the great Philosopher [Aristotle]."
—CARDINAL NEWMAN.

Here the writer, quoting Cardinal Newman, interpolates the identification of the philosopher.

The use of *sic* in brackets in a quotation means that an erroneous statement or spelling is actually *thus* in the original, and is not an error in transcription.

He who waits for a dead man's shoon [*sic*] will long go barefoot.

Brackets often are necessary and useful when using quotations in a research paper needing explanatory terms of your own.

25. Ellipsis Periods   Three spaced periods, called ellipis periods, are used to indicate the omission of one or more words within or at the beginning of a quoted sentence. Four spaced periods are used to signify an ellipsis and a terminal period. Do not let yourself be confused by advertising writers who use dots for their own purposes of getting attention and perhaps even of arranging material attractively on the page or billboard.

The pursuit of perfection, then, is the pursuit of sweetness and light. He who works for sweetness and light works to make reason and the will of God prevail. He who works for machinery . . . works only for confusion.

—MATTHEW ARNOLD.

. . . a steeple pricked up out of a knoll of trees, above a snuggle of gothic villas; then there was the sad stare of what looked like an orphanage.

—ELIZABETH BOWEN.

It used to be I thought of death as a man something like Grandfather a friend of his a kind of private and particular friend. . . .

—WILLIAM FAULKNER.

Brackets and ellipses together help you to use a shortened form of an extended quotation:

And those two Americanists [Pelayo and Valera] awarded the chairs to Miguel de Unamuno Jugo de Larragn, which was the full name of the young man from Bilbao. . . .

—GASTÓN BAQUERO.

26. Manuscript Form   Theoretically, good writing is good writing whether it is expertly typed on expensive paper or scrawled on used wrapping paper. But actually, this is rarely the case. The competent writer will make certain that his finished work is both legible and neat. He knows that although sometimes inspiration may be laggard and ideas less than original, the physical appearance of his writing is consistently and completely under his control. It is only common sense to make certain that one's writing is appealing in appearance and consistent with prescribed manuscript form.

Your instructor will quite probably give you explicit instructions as to the mechanics of appearance and manuscript form that you should follow in your themes. There are, however, a number of generally accepted principles that we can profitably discuss here. Remember, however, that your instructor is the final authority in these matters.

Type or write legibly, neatly, and correctly. Whether you type or handwrite your themes, be certain that they are legible. If you handwrite, use a fountain pen with dark blue or black ink. You should do your revision in an earlier draft, not on the final copy of your theme. If you must make a correction in the final copy, do it neatly by crossing out the error with horizontal lines and inserting the correction immediately above the error. If your instructor allows you to use pencil on impromptu themes, use a pencil with a relatively soft lead, and make certain that your eraser is good.

If you can type, the final copy of your outside themes should be typewritten. The typewriter ribbon should be fresh and the type clean. Typewritten themes should always be double-spaced and the margins consistent (see below). Paragraphs should be indented five spaces, words should be separated by one space, and sentences by two spaces. Be certain that the copy is free of typographical errors, for usually your instructor cannot distinguish between such errors and misspellings. In fact, if you cannot type well enough to avoid typographical errors, you should handwrite your themes.

Use standard paper. If you typewrite, use regulation typing paper (8½ x 11 inches) of good quality. If you handwrite, use ruled paper with broad lines. Use one side of the paper only. Many English departments require special paper for themes, in which case you will receive specific directions from your instructor.

Make margins consistent and generous. Your themes in the basic composition course are instructional devices, and your instructor must have adequate space for his comments and corrections. Whether you type or handwrite, leave margins of at least one inch at the top, bottom, and sides of your text. Again, many English departments will require specially designed paper with the margins for your text clearly marked. Do not encroach into those margins.

Label your themes correctly. All themes should have a title, which is centered at the top of the first page. All *important* words in the title are capitalized (see P-19). Do not use a period after the title, but a question mark or exclamation mark should be used if appropriate. Page numbers should be placed at the top right-hand corner of the page. Your instructor will give you specific directions for the placement of such information as your name, the date, the course number and title, the instructor's name, the theme number, and so on. Most instructors prefer regular themes to be folded to the right with the identification on the upper side.

Revise your manuscript carefully. You should turn to Chapter 2, "Writing the Theme," and review the case study of the writing of a theme (pages 17–30), which illustrates the process of writing from the preliminary outline to the final copy. The importance of meticulous, careful revision cannot be overemphasized.

Exercise 13: Review

Supply all marks of punctuation in the following passages:

(1) She glanced at the houses tried not to see what she saw gave way in Why do these stories lie so They always make the brides home coming a bower of roses Complete trust in noble spouse Lies about marriage Im not changed And this town O my God I cant go through with it This junk heap

Her husband bent over her You look like you were in a brown study Scared I dont expect you to be crazy about it at first But youll come to like it so much lifes so free here and the best people on earth

She whispered to him while Mrs Clark considerately turned away I love you for understanding Im just Im beastly over sensitive Too many books Its my lack of shoulder muscles and sense Give me time dear

—SINCLAIR LEWIS, *Main Street.*

(2) The average American was more intelligent than the average European and was becoming every year still more active minded as the new movement of society caught him up and swept him through a life of more varied experiences On all sides the national mind responded to its stimulants Deficient as the American was in the machinery of higher instruction remote poor unable by any exertion to acquire the training the capital or even the elementary textbooks he needed for a fair development of his natural powers his native energy and ambition already responded to the spur applied to them

—HENRY ADAMS.

(3) Months later the cowboy was frying pork over the stove of a little ranch near the dakota line when there was a quick thud of hoofs outside and presently the easterner entered with the letters and the papers

Well said the easterner at once the chap that killed the swede has got three years Wasnt much was it

He has Three years The cowboy poised his pan of pork while he ruminated upon the news Three years That aint much

No it was a light sentence replied the easterner as he unbuckled his spurs Seems there was a good deal of sympathy for him in Romper

If the bartender had been any good observed the cowboy thoughtfully he would have gone in and cracked that there dutchman on the head with a bottle in the beginnin of it and stopped all this here murderin

Yes a thousand things might have happened said the easterner tartly

—STEPHEN CRANE.

(4) In time allen even generated a sort of charm and besides he was an eligible bachelor the sort you think of as a bright young man even when he has reached the age of forty There was once a piece of gossip for there are always those who hate success that he practiced before a mirror At any rate he achieved his charm He developed a way of holding a book and of marking the place with his long forefinger carelessly but lovingly at the same time resting his elbow upon the table and gesticulating gently with the book It was a pose suitable for a portrait which may have been southbys intention originally He also took pains with his dress When he came to harvard from minnesota he brought his trunk with him but allen was quick to see that the

garments within it were not correct right from the beginning he had an unfailing instinct for doing what was suitable He ended by wearing harris tweeds and flannel trousers and by smoking an english pipe wtih a special mixture although he did not like tobacco

He also took to drinking beer out of a pewter mug By the time he was taken into the berkley club he had developed a way of banging the mug softly upon the table informally and without ostentation He used to say that there was nothing like good pewter in fact he had a fair collection of it in a colonial pine dresser but he never did like beer

—J. P. MARQUAND, *Wickford Point.*

Exercise 14: Review

Copy the following sentences, replacing the blanks with the proper punctuation marks if they are needed:

1. Hadn't I better stop the sale___Oh___Mary___what should I___What do you think I should do___
2. It will not do to boast___but it is well to be true to the facts___and to see that___apart from these purely mortal troubles___the race has enjoyed conditions in which most ills have been averted.
3. The beautiful elms that shaded a great part of the way massed themselves in the___groves of academe___and showed pleased glimpses of___Old Harvard's scholar factories___then far fewer than now.
4. I knew of the dinner à la Russe___as it was then called___ only from books___and it was a sort of literary flavor that I tasted in the successive dishes. When it came to the black coffee___and to the petits verres of cognac with lumps of sugar set afire atop___(omission)
5. Dr___Holmes said___Ah___well___I don't know that you will ever feel you have really met him___He is like a dim room with a little taper of personality burning on the corner of the mantel___
6. Celeste might never have been a first-century Christian___ I think she's really a pagan at heart___but she would have made it awfully uncomfortable for the other unbelievers.
7. By act of the Legislature___upon prayer and petition___ Hadleyburg was allowed to change its name to___never mind

what___I will not give it away___and leave one word out of the motto that for many generations had graced the town's official seal.

8. A door opened, and Scully himself entered. He paused in surprise as he noted the tragic attitude of the Swede. Then he said___What's the matter here___

9. The Swede answered him swiftly and eagerly___These men are going to kill me___

10. ___Kill you___ejaculated Scully___Kill you___What are you talkin___The Swede made the gesture of a martyr.

11. Scully wheeled sternly upon his son___What is this___ Johnnie___

12. O ye that love mankind___Ye that dare not only oppose the tyranny but the tyrant___stand forth___

13. "Millions in New England have suffered from flood damage___actually according to Red Cross statistics the number is 83,000___without any effective flood-control suggestion from the Department of Interior."

14. Dr___Rice then asked___Did I understand you to say that Bridey pronounced Sean___See-an___on the tape recording___

15. These voters were once termed___Independents___a vague term indeed___but descriptive if not accurate.

16. These victories for the New Guard___the___moderns___the relative___liberals___or whatever one may choose to call them___were fundamental.

17. The perception of real affinities between events___that is to say___of ideal affinities___for those only are real___enables the poet___(omission) to assert the predominance of the soul.

18. Men very naturally seek money or power___and power because it is as good as money___the___spoils___so called___of office___

19. Professor Pedant then asked___Class___how would you punctuate this sentence___Tennyson wrote both___The Lotus Eaters___and___Tears Idle Tears___

20. Confound it___now look what you've done.

11.

The Research Paper

Writing the research paper is regarded in many first-year English courses as a very important and meaningful part of the year's work. In preparing this paper, students have an opportunity to learn some of the basic principles of research: how to set up a problem, how to find material in the library relevant to this problem, how to weigh and evaluate material, and how to come to a considered conclusion.

Mastery of the techniques of using the library and of properly preparing a research paper is of great value to you not only in your first-year English course, but also in your advanced college courses, since many of these normally require the preparation of a research paper. After graduation you will likewise find these skills invaluable in business, where research assumes constantly increasing significance, and in working as a member of clubs and organizations. Thus by mastering these techniques now, you will effectively serve both your immediate and long-range interests.

Though concepts of what the term paper should be differ widely from campus to campus, and your own instructor will doubtless wish to set the standards to which your paper will conform, there is an area of general agreement which we can profitably discuss.

Preliminary Considerations

Nature of the Research Paper The research paper does not deal with personal experiences and is not written out of the student's own store of knowledge, as are many themes. It is not to be spun out of himself as a spider spins her web. Rather, it is to be based on information gathered from many different sources in the library and elsewhere. This does not mean, however, that all the student has to do is to put his borrowed material together into a sort of patchwork quilt of quotations, into what one writer has called "an inane compilation of encyclopedia articles." Taking one paragraph on penicillin or Napoleon from the *Encyclopaedia Britannica,* another from the *Encyclopedia Americana,* another from the *Reader's Digest,* and another from a text-book does not constitute research. Far too often so-called "research papers" tend to support the writer who remarked that "cribbing from one source is plagiarism, but cribbing from enough sources is research."

Since this concept of the research paper is quite common, many students feel there is no room whatsoever for original-ity in their term papers. On the contrary, there is ample scope for the most original student to display his talent by the manner in which he handles or utilizes the material that he has drawn from his sources. If the student has thought about his materials, if he has weighed and evaluated them, if he knows what he is trying to do in his paper, then his material will become building units out of which he can form a structure recognizably his own. Arranging the facts found in research in such a way as to throw new light on a subject is one definition of a research paper.

Choosing and Limiting the Subject Subjects may, with the approval of your instructor, be chosen from almost any area of learning. You should choose for investigation a subject in which you are interested, about which you would like to learn more; for if you yourself are not interested, it is a fair assumption that you will not succeed in interesting anyone else.

Having found a general subject matter with which you wish to work, next try to formulate some specific aspect of, or *problem* or *question* within, the subject that you would like to investigate. Perhaps the most effective way of limiting the scope of your paper is to restrict the subject to a problem you would like to solve or to a question you would like to answer. By making this limitation, you will also give purpose and a sense of direction to your research. Too often papers fail because they attempt to treat impossibly broad subjects, suitable only for a book, or perhaps even a series of volumes. For example, no student paper could possibly hope to deal satisfactorily with subjects as large as Canada, the Soviet Union, communism, the race question, the modern American novel, antibiotics, modern poetry, or the labor movement. These are tremendous subjects which have to be narrowed to a size with which a student can cope. Within these broad topics, however, lie countless problems and questions that students are capable of handling: for instance, "The Development of the Oil Industry in Canada since World War II," "An Evaluation of the Contemporary Canadian Novel," "The Hungarian Rebellion against Russia," "The Effect of the Smith Act on the Communist Party in America," "A Study of School Integration in Little Rock," "A Literary Evaluation of Hemingway's Short Stories," "The Reputation of Sinclair Lewis in the Late 1950's," "The Literary Discovery of William Faulkner," "Waksman or Fleming, Father of the Wonder Drugs?" "A Critical Evaluation of the Major Poems of Dylan Thomas," "The Literary Reputation of Wallace Stevens at the Present," and many more. These are definite, workable subjects, of a scope that students can treat.

Clearness of Purpose   The reason many term papers are dull, and hence at least in part unsuccessful, is that their writers never discover exactly where they want to go. Without a clearly defined purpose, there is little wonder that the writer gets nowhere, that he reaches no conclusion. As the late Dean Greenough of Harvard often remarked, "The worst thing that can be said about any research paper is 'so what?'" In order to avoid the error of getting nowhere, you need above all to have a clearly defined purpose in your own mind. In order to establish your clearness of purpose, as well as to indicate the exact nature and scope of the paper to your readers, you may want to include an introductory paragraph stating forthrightly the purpose and scope of the study you are undertaking. Such a statement of objectives frequently helps you to proceed more logically in the body of your paper. State your purpose clearly in one sentence.

NOT: I am going to discuss explanations of the Arctic.

BUT: Polar expeditions are a symbol of man's restless and courageous quest for knowledge.

The Research Attitude Once you have found a proper subject, you seek material bearing evidence upon it, usually in the library. All relevant information in books, magazines, newspapers, pamphlets, and encyclopedias becomes evidence which you will want to examine, evaluate, and consider. Before you can make an informed, or even adequate, judgment, you must acquire the important research attitudes of the open mind, a desire to handle material impartially, and the desire to pursue a free search for truth wherever it may lead. You ought to start your investigation without any preconceived prejudices. It is the purpose of your research to find evidence leading to an answer or to a solution. If you have already made up your mind at the outset, there can be no fair examination of the evidence: you become both a prejudiced jury and an unjust judge. To pursue truth freely, you must be objective and scientific, as unprejudiced and unbiased as possible.

If your serious reading has hitherto been largely limited

379

to the use of one or two textbooks in a course, you may be puzzled to find in the process of your research that there are often legitimate differences of opinion among intelligent, competent experts and that there is no absolute consensus among them. Though you may be confused and baffled at first, you may be assured that your confusion is a vital part of your education, since from it you may learn, if you will, that truth is not always simple or clear, that there is not always an easy, completely satisfactory answer even to simple problems. But if you learn to weigh divergent views and to come at last to your own working solution of the problem, you will have mastered one of the most valued techniques that educated men have discovered.

In evaluating your evidence, you should strive to use your material critically; i.e., you should try to read between the lines wherever possible. You should be suspicious of any author who is prejudiced for any reason or who obviously has an ax to grind. Not all material is of equal value, by any means; some authors are far more competent and authoritative than others. You should, accordingly, try to make a selection of the best material on your subject. There is no necessity whatever to present *everything* in print on the subject—indeed it would be an impossibility, even were it desirable—but this should not be made an excuse for suppressing evidence on one side or the other.

A few words of caution: wherever possible you should draw material from special studies rather than from general encyclopedias. Remember that in college the *Encyclopaedia Britannica* does not carry quite the same awesome authority that it did in high school, for now a great many more books, monographs, and articles in the learned journals are available to you. And whenever possible, endeavor to use the material that is the most recent and most modern available. Why quote from a critical treatise on Shakespeare written in 1892 or 1907, when you can use works published in the last several decades? After all, there has been progress in scholarship and research as well as in automobiles and electronics. Though the truth may be unchanging, every generation has a different notion of what the truth is. And in many of the sciences progress has been so rapid in recent years that even the most reputable treatises of a generation ago are now obsolete.

A preference for recent scholarship and a reliance upon it should not, however, lead you to ignore the really great or classic writers of the past, whose opinions somehow manage to escape the usual erosion of time. For example, the historian Gibbon, the scientists Harvey and Darwin, the economist Adam Smith, and the literary critics Dryden, Dr. Johnson, Coleridge, and Matthew Arnold may appear "dated" in some respects, but they will never become obsolete or unimportant, no matter how many brilliant books our contemporaries may publish.

Remember, then, that you choose your broad subject for your interest in it; you have a tentative point of view toward it in order to limit the subject and guide your reading; you explore the ramifications your material leads you to; and you reappraise your own assumptions in the light of what you read. Your final point of view will grow out of your reading and your reaction to it.

Using the Library

The Card Catalogue   The card catalogue is the heart of the library. It consists of a great many filing cabinets containing drawers of alphabetically arranged 3 x 5 cards, indicating the holdings of the library in books, periodicals, and pamphlets. There are usually at least three cards, filed in the proper drawers, for each book: (1) an author card, filed alphabetically under the author's surname; (2) a title card, filed alphabetically according to the first important word in the title of the book; and (3) a subject card, which alphabetizes the book according to the subject of its contents. The following is a sample author card:

639.2
R650

Robertson, Robert Blackwood, 1913–
 Of whales and men. [1st ed.] New York, Knopf, 1954.

 299 p.   illus.   22 cm.

 1. Whaling.   I. Title.

 SH381.R59   *639.28   53–6858 ‡

 Library of Congress   [25]

The title and subject cards are exactly the same as the author card, except that the title card lists the title of the book, *Of Whales and Men* (in lower case and without italics), above the author's name, and the subject card lists the subject of the book, *Whaling* (without italics), above the author's name.

A careful examination of the sample author card reproduced here can save time and effort, for it gives much valuable information. First comes the "call number," in the upper left-hand corner of the card. This number indicates the location of the book on the shelves. It is also necessary to use this number, of course, in checking out the book. The call number is based either upon the Dewey Decimal System or upon the Library of Congress system. There are, however, a few libraries, including the Harvard College Library, that do not use either system. In the Dewey Decimal System, the following classification is used:

000–099   General Works
100–199   Philosophy and Psychology
200–299   Religion

300–399	Sociology
400–499	Philology
500–599	Natural Science
600–699	Useful Arts
700–799	Fine Arts and Recreation
800–899	Literature
900–999	History and biography

The Library of Congress, on the other hand, uses the following categories:

A	General Works
B	Philosophy, Religion
C	History
D	Foreign History
E, F	American History
G	Geography, Anthropology
H	Social Science
J	Political Science
K	Law
L	Education
M	Music
N	Fine Arts
P	Language and Literature
Q	Science
R	Medicine
S	Agriculture
T	Technology
U	Military Science
V	Naval Science
Z	Bibliography, Library Science

The author's name, surname first, is in boldface print at the top of the sample card. The date of birth and death follow the name, the date of death being blank in this instance, since the author was still alive when the card was printed. Under the author's name is listed the title of the book (remember that in transferring the title to your note card you should capitalize the first letter of each important word and underline the entire title), the edition, the place of publication, the publisher, the date of publication, and on the next line, the number of pages, an indication that the book is illustrated, and its size. The first line at the bottom of the card gives the heading of the subject card and indicates that there is a separate title card. The next line gives in order the Library of Congress classification, the Dewey Decimal classification, and the Library of Congress card number. The last line contains the name of the publisher of the card, and a special code number.

You will probably begin your research by consulting the subject cards appropriate to your subject. But you should be resourceful. If you are writing on a subject having to do with "segregation," you should look not only under that particular subject but also under such related subjects as "integration," "racial issues," "racial prejudice," and so on. Remember also that almost all libraries these days have a highly trained staff who can help immeasurably with difficult problems. Do not hesitate to consult them.

A List of Standard Reference Works *General Encyclopedias and Yearbooks.* The general encyclopedias are useful in college research chiefly because they give a panoramic view of the area in which the subject for investigation lies. They also serve as a point of departure for more specialized study. Give special attention to the bibliographies, for they will direct you to the special studies. The annual yearbooks are valuable for information on events too recent for inclusion in the encyclopedia proper.

> *Collier's Encyclopedia,* 20 vols., 1958. Vol. 20 contains bibliographies and an index.
>
> *The Columbia Encyclopedia,* 3rd edition, 1963. Perhaps the best single-volume desk encyclopedia.
>
> *Encyclopedia Americana,* 30 vols., 1962. Supplemented by *Americana Annual.*
>
> *Encyclopaedia Britannica,* 24 vols., 1961. Supplemented by *Britannica Book of the Year.*
>
> *Information Please Almanac,* 1947 to date.
>
> *New International Encyclopedia,* 27 vols., 1930. Supplemented by *New International Year Book.*
>
> *World Almanac,* 1868 to date.

Subject Reference Works. The special encyclopedias and indexes usually give more detailed information than can be found in general encyclopedias. The following are major reference works in their respective subject fields, although the list is by no means exhaustive. You should consult the card catalogue for further references. See also:

Winchell, *Guide to Reference Books,* 1951, plus Supplements, 1950–.
Shores, *Basic Reference Sources,* 1954.

AGRICULTURE

Agricultural Index, 1916–.
Bailey, *Cyclopedia of American Agriculture,* 4 vols., 1907–1909.
Wilcox, *Modern Farmer's Cyclopedia of Agriculture,* 1952.

ART AND ARCHITECTURE

Art Index, 1929–.
Bryan's Dictionary of Painters and Engravers, 2 vols., 1903–1905.
Gardner, *Art through the Ages,* 1948.
Hamlin, *Architecture through the Ages,* 1953.
Harper's Encyclopedia of Art, 2 vols., 1937.

BUSINESS AND ECONOMICS

Encyclopedia of the Social Sciences, 15 vols., 1930–1935.
Larson, *Guide to Business History,* 1948.
Manly, *Business Information: How to Find and Use It,* 1955.
Munn, *Encyclopedia of Banking and Finance,* 1949.

EDUCATION

Education Index, 1949–.
Monroe, *Cyclopedia of Education,* 3 vols., 1926.
Monroe, *Encyclopedia of Educational Research,* 1955.

ENGINEERING

Engineering Encyclopedia, 2 vols., 1943.
Engineering Index, 1906–.
Industrial Arts Index, 1913–.

HISTORY

Adams, *Dictionary of American History,* 5 vols., 1940.
Cambridge Histories (*Ancient,* 12 vols., 1923–1939; *Medieval,*
    8 vols., 1911–1936; *Modern,* 14 vols., 2d ed., 1926).
Langer, *Encyclopedia of World History,* 1952.
    12 vols., 1949–50.

MUSIC

Grove's Dictionary of Music and Musicians, 9 vols., 1954.
The Oxford History of Music, 7 vols., 1929–1934.
Scholes, *Oxford Companion to Music,* 1950.
Thompson, *International Cyclopedia of Music and Musicians,*
    1959.

PHILOSOPHY AND PSYCHOLOGY

Baldwin, *Dictionary of Philosophy and Psychology,* 3 vols.,
    1928.
Bibliography of Philosophy, 1934.
Drever, *A Dictionary of Psychology,* 1952.
Psychological Index, 1894–1933. Replaced by *Psychological
    Abstracts,* 1927–.

RELIGION

Catholic Encyclopedia, 15 vols. and 2 supp., 1907–1922.
Hastings, *Encyclopedia of Religion and Ethics,* 13 vols., 1911–
    1928.
Index to Religious Periodical Literature, 1949–1952, 1953–
    1954.
Latourette, *History of Christianity,* 1953.
*The New Schaff-Herzog Encyclopedia of Religious Knowl-
    edge,* 12 vols., 1949–1950.

SCIENCE

Biological Abstracts, 1926–.
Chemical Abstracts, 1907–.
Chronica Botanica, 1935–.
Hawkins, *Scientific, Medical, and Technical Books,* 1953.
Hutchinson's Technical and Scientific Encyclopedia, 4 vols.,
    1935–1936.

Kirk and Othmer, *Encyclopedia of Chemical Technology*, 1963–.

Parke, *Guide to the Literature of Mathematics and Physics*, 1947.

Physics Abstracts, 1898– (Section A of *Science Abstracts*).

Van Nostrand's Scientific Encyclopedia, 3rd ed., 1958.

SOCIAL SCIENCES

Burchfield, *Student's Guide to Materials in Political Science*, 1935.

Encyclopedia of the Social Sciences, 15 vols., 1930–1935.

Fairchild (ed.), *Dictionary of Sociology*, 1944.

Kroeber, *Anthropology Today: An Encyclopedic Inventory*, 1953.

Social Science Abstracts, 1929 to present.

REFERENCE BOOKS FOR LITERATURE

Annual Bibliography of English Language and Literature (Modern Humanities Research Association), 1921 to present.

Arms and Kuntz. *A Checklist of Poetry Explication.*

Bartlett's Familiar Quotations, 13th ed., 1955.

Bateson (ed.), *Cambridge Bibliography of English Literature*, 4 vols., 1941.

Baugh (ed.), *A Literary History of England*, 1948, 4 volumes or 1-volume edition.

This is the best short history of English literature available. Since it relies on recent scholarship, it is frequently better than more extensive treatments.

The Cambridge History of American Literature, 4 vols., 1917–1921.

The Cambridge History of English Literature, 15 vols., 1907–1927.

Much information here given has been superseded by later scholarship; nevertheless, it remains the most encyclopedic treatment of English literature.

Essay and General Literature Index, 1900–1933, plus yearly supplements since 1934.

Gayley, *Classic Myths in English Literature and in Art*, 1939.

Hamilton, *Mythology*, New American Library and Universal Library.

Mencken (ed.), *A New Dictionary of Quotations*, 1942.
The Oxford Companion to American Literature, 2d ed., 1948.
The Oxford Companion to Classical Literature, 1937.
The Oxford Companion to English Literature, 3d ed., 1946.
  An invaluable one-volume reference work with material ar-
  ranged in dictionary order.
PMLA Annual Bibliography.
Spiller (ed.), *A Literary History of the United States*, 3 vols.,
  1948.
  This is more reliable than *The Cambridge History* since it
  is based on more recent scholarship.
The Year's Work in English Studies (The English Associa-
  tion), 1920–.

BIOGRAPHICAL REFERENCES

American Men of Science, 1960–1962.
Biography Index, 1946–.
Current Biography, 1940–.
The Dictionary of American Biography, 20 vols. and index,
  1928–1936. Supplements, 1944, 1958.
This work covers famous Americans no longer living.
The Dictionary of National Biography, 22 vols., 1885–1901;
  supps., 1901, 1912, 1927, 1937, 1949.
  This work covers permanent British subjects no longer
  living.
Directory of American Scholars, 4 vols., 1963–.
Kunitz, *American Authors of the Nineteenth Century*, 1936.
Kunitz, *American Authors, 1600–1900*, 1938.
Kunitz and Haycraft, *Twentieth Century Authors*, 1942.
Webster's Biographical Dictionary, 1956.
  It includes 40,000 brief biographical sketches of famous
  people of all countries and ages.
Who's Who, Who's Who in America, International Who's Who,
  etc.
  Separate books, each published annually, giving brief ac-
  counts of living men and women.

GAZETTEERS AND ATLASES

Collier's New World Atlas and Gazeteer, 1953.
Encyclopaedia Britannica World Atlas, 1958.

Hammond's Ambassador World Atlas, 1954.
Rand McNally's Commercial Atlas and Marketing Guide, 1958.
Webster's Geographical Dictionary, 1955.

SPECIAL DICTIONARIES

(General dictionaries are listed on pages 267–268.)

Bergen and Cornelia Evans, *A Dictionary of Contemporary English Usage,* 1957.

Brewer's Dictionary of Phrase and Fable, 1953.

Crabb's English Synonyms, 1945.

Fowler, *Dictionary of Modern English Usage,* 1937.

Partridge, *Dictionary of Slang and Unconventional English,* 1961.

Roget's Thesaurus of Words and Phrases, 1961.

Periodical Indexes Much of the most valuable material in the library is not available in books and must be obtained from magazines, periodicals, and newspapers. This material is often more valuable than similar treatments in books simply because it takes time for material to find its way into books; the periodical literature is thus more likely than older books to represent the modern or current scholarly view on a subject.

Readers' Guide to Periodical Literature, 1907 to Date. This index, arranged by author, title, and subject is one of the most useful periodical indexes for first-year college students. It is brought up-to-date monthly by the publishers; material of former years is accumulated in permanently bound volumes. The *Readers' Guide* gives the title of the magazine, the volume number, date, and exact page reference to material. Note the following entries from the *Readers' Guide,* which have been numbered and lettered for convenience in the explanations given below:

1. Weymouth, Martha Hays
     Magic sugar bowl. Farm J 77:113 + O '53
2. Weyranch, Martin Henry
     Tort liability. Am City 68:114–15 O '53

3. Whale meat
   From whaler to platter. H. Mitgang. il N.Y. Times **Mag**
   p 34 + N 14 '54
4. Whaleboats. See Boats and Boating.
5. Whalen, Robert G.
   Old Dr. Aspirin. N Y Times Mag. p. 20 + Je 14 '53
   Problem of problem drinkers. N Y Times Mag p 20 +
   Ap 11 '54
   Two generals patrol the docks. N Y Times Mag p 20 +
   N 29 '53
6. Whalen, William J.
   Layman looks at Latin. Cath. World 179:449–55 S '54
7. Whales
   a. Blackfish bonanza. L. Chace. il Natur Hist 63:38–
   40 Ja '54
   b. Great sperm whale. il Life 35:118–20 + N 2 '53
   c. Heart of a whale. il Newsweek 43:53 Ja 25 '54
   d. Jonah the second. K. Smith. Coronet 34:39 Je '53
   e. Killer whale. F. Dufresne. il Field & S 59:38–9 + D '54
   f. Killing the killers. Times 64:36 O 4 '54
   g. Reporter at large, on a whaling factory. R. B. Robertson.
   New Yorker 29:36–40 + Jan 23; 31–2 + Ja 30 '54

Explanations

1. Author entry—refers to an article by Martha Hays Weymouth
   entitled "Magic Sugar Bowl," in the *Farm Journal,* volume 77,
   page 113 and continuations, in the issue of October, 1953.
2. Author entry—refers to an article called "Tort Liability" in
   American City, volume 68, pages 114–115, in the issue of
   October, 1953.
3. Subject entry—refers to an article by H. Mitgang entitled
   "From Whaler to Platter," with illustrations, in the *New York
   Times Magazine,* page 34 and continuations, in the issue of
   November 14, 1954.
4. This is a cross reference.
5. Author entry—with three articles by Robert G. Whalen, which
   appeared respectively in the *New York Times Magazine* as
   follows: page 20 and continuations, June 14, 1953; page 20
   and continuations, April 11, 1954; page 20 and continuations,
   November 29, 1953.
6. Author entry—refers to an article, "Layman Looks at Latin"

by William J. Whalen, which appeared in *Catholic World,* volume 179, pages 449–455, in the issue of September, 1954.

7. Subject entry—refers to the following articles: (a) "Blackfish Bonanza" by L. Chace, with illustrations, in *Natural History,* volume 63, pages 38–40, issue of January, 1954; (b) "Great Sperm Whale," with illustrations, in *Life,* volume 35, pages 118–120 with continuations, issue of November 2, 1953; (c) "Heart of a Whale," with illustrations in *Newsweek,* volume 43, page 53, in the issue of January 25, 1954; (d) "Jonah the Second," by K. Smith in *Coronet,* volume 34, page 39, in the issue of June, 1953; (e) "Killer Whale" by F. Dufresne, with illustrations, in *Field and Stream,* volume 59, pages 38–39 and continuations, in the issue of December, 1954; (f) "Killing the Killers," *Time,* volume 64, page 36, issue of October 4, 1954; (g) "Reporter at Large: On a Whaling Factory," by R. B. Robertson, *The New Yorker,* volume 29, pages 36–40 and continuations, in the issue of January 23; pages 31–32 and continuations, in the issue of January 30, 1954.

The usefulness of the *Readers' Guide* in research, it should be carefully noted, is strictly limited by the fact that it indexes only popular magazines and thus ignores much of the scholarly wealth of the library which is contained in the learned journals and periodicals. Students working on scholarly or literary subjects often conclude too hastily after running through the volumes of the *Readers' Guide* that there is nothing on their subjects in the periodicals. Do not make the mistake of jumping to this premature conclusion. Fortunately there is another very important index, of far more significance for scholars than the *Readers' Guide.*

International Index to Periodicals, 1907 to Date. The arrangement of this reference work is similar to that explained above. It is also issued monthly and accumulated in large permanent volumes. Though there may be some overlapping with *Readers' Guide,* the importance of *International Index* lies in the fact that it covers the whole range of learned and scholarly periodicals, even those published in foreign countries. Since the most significant work in many fields of learning is published in this type of journal, rather than in the popular mass-circulation magazines, it is obvious that no good student can afford to ignore this significant research tool.

A few sample entries from *International Index* are given here, with very brief editorial comments in brackets:

DRYDEN, HUGH LATIMER
  Frontiers of aeronautical science and technology Am Philos Soc Proc 97 no 1:56–60 '53 [Author entry referring to *Proceedings of the American Philosophical Society*]
DRYDEN, J. S. and MEAKINS, R. J.
  Electrical conductivity of certain crystalline materials after grinding. Nature 171:307 F 14 '53 [Author entry]
DRYDEN, JOHN [Subject entry]
  Development of the hero in Dryden's tragedies. J. Winterbottom, bibliog f J Engl & Germ Philol 52:161–73 Ap '53 [Refers to the article of this title by Winterbottom in the *Journal of English and Germanic Philology*, volume 52 (April, 1953), pp. 161–173. A bibliography is included.]
  Dryden and the encomium musicae. J. Kinsley. bibliog f R Engl Stud ns 4:263–7 Jl '53 [Refers to an article with this title by J. Kinsley in the *Review of English Studies*, New Series, volume 4, pages 263–267, July, 1953.]
  Dryden's prologue and epilogue to Mithradates, revived with text. J. H. Smith, PMLA 68:251–67 Mr '53 [Refers to article of this title by J. H. Smith in *Publications of the Modern Language Association of America*, volume 68, pp. 251–267, March, 1953. Dryden's text is reprinted.]

Poole's Index to Periodical Literature, 1802–1881, with Supplements, 1882–1886, 1887–1891, 1892–1896, 1897–1901, 1902–1906. This work is less useful to most college students than are *Readers' Guide* and *International Index*, yet since the need to use it occasionally arises, students should be aware of its existence and know something about it. *Poole's Index* is a guide to material in the periodicals, both British and American, from 1802 through 1906, which means that when it is used with the two modern indexes, materials on any subject can be traced from the present time back to 1802. This index is arranged only according to subject.

The New York Times' Index, 1913 to Date. This is an index to subjects appearing in the New York *Times*. It is issued monthly and accumulated in annual volumes. It is often of considerable use in research because it serves to guide the reader not only to material in the *Times* itself, but also to news stories in many other American newspapers, since they presumably cover events at approximately the same date as the *Times*. Used this way, it can be made to serve as a partial index to local newspapers.

Other Periodical Indexes. In addition to these frequently used indexes, there are a number of other, more specialized, guides to material in periodicals, a list of which follows:

Art Index, 1929–: a guide to material on the fine arts.

Agricultural Index, 1916–: a guide to material on agriculture.

Bibliographic Index, 1937–: a guide to bibliographies in books and periodicals.

Biography Index, 1946–: a guide to biographical material in books and periodicals.

Book Review Digest, 1905–: a guide to the location of book reviews in the periodicals.

Dramatic Index, 1909–: a guide to periodical articles about all aspects of the British and American drama.

Education Index, 1929–: a guide to books and articles on all phases of education.

Engineering Index, 1906–: a guide to material in all branches of engineering.

Index to Legal Periodicals, 1908–: a guide to material on the law; it includes book reviews.

Industrial Arts Index, 1913–: principally a guide to material in trade and engineering journals.

Public Affairs Information Service, 1915–: a subject guide to material, including books, on politics, government, economics, etc.

Gathering the Evidence

Writing the research paper is basically the same as writing the theme, a process we discussed in some detail in Chapter

2, with one important difference. The theme deals mostly with subjective reactions. You may, of course, include in a theme information gained from your reading, but the primary emphasis usually falls on your personal reactions to that reading. But in the research paper you are primarily concerned with knowledge you have gleaned from sources other than your own mind. It is extremely important, therefore, that you gather information systematically as you examine the sources for your paper, and that the information is transmitted accurately and clearly to your reader.

How to Take Notes While reading about your subject, take notes on material that you think will be of possible use in your paper. Each note should be made on a separate 3 x 5 or 4 x 6 index card (or similar sheet of paper). Do not make the mistake of taking more than one note on a card, for experienced researchers have learned that this practice inevitably results in confusion and loss of time and effort. Do not write on the back of your note cards; you may later overlook the information there. Likewise, do not try to take notes in a composition book; this, too, will cause trouble.

When you find apparently useful material, take a note by condensing several pages into a paragraph, or even a sentence if possible. Many times you will find that you would like to have a verbatim quotation from the book or article. If so, copy it on the card, taking extreme care to do so accurately. Oddly enough, a great many people cannot copy a passage without error, and to make mistakes in the text or even punctuation of a quotation is to misrepresent what the author really said. Be especially careful to indicate every omission, even of a single word, by using ellipsis periods (see P-25); for if you drop a word, phrase, or sentence from an author's statement without properly indicating the omission, you distort the author's remark and mislead your readers. Above all, be certain to place quotes around phrases, sentences, and passages that you copy verbatim from your source. If you use a verbatim passage in your paper without quotes, you are claiming that passage as your own, and you are guilty of plagiarism.

Plagiarism is a legal as well as an ethical offense, and you should be careful to avoid it. As a matter of integrity and courtesy, you must give credit to the source of your ideas whether you quote or not. If you do not quote your source verbatim, be sure to paraphrase *in your own words*. The following samples may help you to see the difference:

SOURCE:

The world is small and rapidly getting smaller. . . . But if the world is shrinking it is because science is audacious and unsatisfied. And if the Antarctic has shrunk least of all, if it still stands aloof and hidden in glacial fogs, it is because the pack ice and the gales which defend its coasts, and the cold, and the blizzards, and the unutterable lifelessness of the interior regions are not easily to be subdued.[1]

PLAGIARISM:

The world is shrinking because science is audacious and unsatisfied. The Antarctic has shrunk least because the ice and gales and cold are not easily to be subdued.

PARAPHRASE:

According to Richard E. Byrd, science has made the rest of the world seem smaller but not the Antarctic. Its natural barriers isolate it and leave it unchanged.

Form of Notes At the top of each note card write in parentheses your subject heading: i.e., write the subheading of the general subject to which the material on this card will relate. The great advantage in using a subject heading is that it will help you organize and outline your paper. When you have finished your research and note taking, you can then review the notes that you have accumulated and arrange them into stacks according to these subject headings. You will find that the proper treatment and organiza-

[1] Richard E. Byrd, *Discovery* (New York, 1935), p. 40.

tion of your paper will suggest itself to you on the basis of the categories represented by these stacks. Thus notes well taken can greatly facilitate the actual writing of the paper itself, as a great many experienced researchers have found.

Immediately below the subject heading—whether or not the note consists of your paraphrase or whether it is an actual quotation you have copied—you should write the source, giving the following details: the author's name in the order that he would write it (Robert B. Robertson), the title of the work you are drawing upon, the place of its publication, the publisher, the date of publication, and finally the page or pages where the material is found:

Robert B. Robertson, *Of Whales and Men* (New York: Alfred A. Knopf, Inc., 1954), pp. 261–262.

The advantage of writing the correct source in this form on each note card is great, for this information will become a correctly written footnote when you incorporate the note into your term paper.

Here is a sample student note card:

(Whaling in 19th Century New England)

Robert B. Robertson, Of Whales and Men
(New York, 1954), pp. 261 - 262.

Many of the New Bedford whaling
ships of the last century, small by
modern standards, would remain at
sea for 24 to 36 months with a crew
of 50 men. Generally the only woman
aboard was the captain's wife.

Documentation

Since the research paper is a demanding project in manuscript form as well as in content, at least one draft is essential before you make up your final copy. You have probably begun your research with a tentative outline of the material —or perhaps just a hypothesis—in mind. After you have completed your research and have your note cards arranged in their proper order, the construction of your final outline should be a relatively simple matter. (See Chapter 7, page 254 for a discussion of the formal outline.) You are now ready to write your draft.

The actual writing of the paper proceeds in much the same way as the writing of the theme (see Chapter 2). You will, however, have to deal with the placement and form of footnotes. It is extremely important that you indicate to your reader exactly the sources of your information and the extent to which you have used material that is not your own. You will provide the reader this information through a system of annotation of the written text which is called *documentation*. Documentation is achieved principally through *footnotes*.

Footnotes   *Types of Footnotes.* The first and most common type of footnote is a reference to the source of material. The purpose of a reference footnote, or citation, is to enable readers to verify statements, if they desire, and to enable them to read further in the source itself.

The second type, the explanatory footnote, is one in which the author comments upon material in the body of the paper, or presents further information, which, though of interest, is not indispensable to the main discussion.

Placement of Footnotes. You should use the explanatory footnote whenever you feel that you should give additional, though not indispensable, information to the reader. Reference footnotes are needed for (1) every direct quotation from a printed source, and (2) every passage which draws heavily upon a printed source, even though the source may be paraphrased and condensed in the author's own language. Note, however, that information either of common knowledge or of ready accessibility need not be documented; for example, the fact that the Second World War began with the invasion of Poland on September 1, 1939, or that a molecule of water is made up of two atoms of hydrogen and one of oxygen requires no footnote even though it is stated in one of your sources.

In the body of your paper, when you are ready to use a footnote (the note from Robertson's book, for example), all you have to do is to insert a raised Arabic numeral in your text at the place you wish to cite your source—which, of course, will ordinarily be at the end of a sentence, as follows:

_____.[1] _____.

Then drop down to the bottom of the page and insert the citation of source, indenting as much as for a paragraph, and raising the footnote numeral. A period after the numeral is not used either in the body of the text or in the footnote. After indenting and writing the raised numeral, copy down the heading of your note card, assuming you have written it correctly and fully as directed above, and you will have a footnote in proper form.

Footnote Form. Various academic and professional disciplines, such as anthropology, law, linguistics, and literature, have their own systems of documenation. Most of your English instructors in college will ask you to use in their courses the system advocated by the Modern Language Association of America. According to the *MLA Style Sheet*, a footnote is written correctly as follows:

1. The numeral is indented as for a paragraph and raised. It is not followed by a period. A line should separate the footnote from the text proper.
2. The author's name is given in the order that he would sign it. It is followed by a comma.
3. The correct title of the book is underlined to indicate

italics. For treatment of magazines and newspapers, see below.

4. Enclose in parentheses the place of publication followed by a comma, and the year of publication.

5. A comma precedes the page reference. The page or pages cited are abbreviated by "p." for one page, or "pp." for more than one page. These abbreviations are always followed by a period. Then the numeral is given, followed by a period.

If you have more than one footnote on a page, be sure to indent each. If the footnote is too long for one line, return to the margin to begin its second line. Note also that footnotes, unlike the body of the manuscript, are single-spaced. Footnotes may be numbered consecutively throughout a paper, or they may be numbered on each page.

A correct footnote will appear thus:

[1] Robert B. Robertson, *Of Whales and Men* (New York, 1954), pp. 261–262.

This is the first or full reference, for it includes all the data of publication. It is invariably used the *first* time the book is cited in the paper. But if you need to cite the same book again, a shorter form of reference may be used:

1. *Ibid.* (which means "in the same place") may be used to indicate that the note is from the source named in the preceding footnote. If the book is the same, but the material is on another page, write *Ibid.*, and indicate the new page.

2. If you want to refer again to a book previously cited after a reference to another book has intervened, obviously you cannot do it by using *ibid.*, which always refers to the immediately preceding reference. Instead, it is necessary to write a short-reference footnote. If you are using only one book by the same author in the paper, you may use the author's surname and *op. cit.* (which means "the work cited") or the author's surname alone; the short-reference footnote is then written as follows:

⁷ Robertson, *op. cit.*, p. 122.
   or

⁷ Robertson, p. 122.

3. If you are citing from more than one book by the same author, your short-reference footnote includes the author's last name, the title of his book (you may abbreviate the title if it is of considerable length), and the page number:

⁷ Robertson, *Of Whales and Men*, p. 122.

Footnotes for material drawn from books published in more than one volume are similarly handled, except that the volume number in Roman numerals follows the title and precedes the page number. Note well that in citing these works you *do not* use an abbreviation either for *volume* or *page*:

³ William J. Lord, *The New Bedford Whaling Industry* (New York, 1942), III, 87.

In referring to articles in magazines and newspapers, give the author's name, the title of the article in quotation marks, the title of the magazine or newspaper in italics, the volume and number in Roman or Arabic numerals, the date of publication in parentheses, and finally the number of the page you wish to cite.

⁴ Howard Vincent Jones, "Melville's Knowledge of Navigation," *The Saturday Review*, XXX, No. 27 (May 3, 1948), 57.
⁹ *The New York Times*, September 6, 1890, p. 1.

Several consecutive footnotes might appear as follows:

¹ Robert B. Robertson, *Of Whales and Men* (New York, 1954), pp. 261–262.
² *Ibid.*, p. 96.
³ William J. Lord, *The New Bedford Whaling Industry* (New York, 1942), III, 87.
⁴ *Ibid.*, p. 223.
⁵ Robertson, *op. cit.*, p. 33.

[6] Howard Vincent Jones, "Melville's Knowledge of Navigation," *The Saturday Review*, XXX, No. 27 (May 3, 1948), 57.

[7] Lord, *New Bedford Whaling*, II, 24.

[8] "Whaling," *Encyclopaedia Britannica* (1954), XXIII, 672–673.

[9] *The New York Times*, September 6, 1890, p. 1.

Abbreviations in Footnotes. In addition to the most commonly used abbreviations explained on page 399, several others are also useful:

anon.—anonymous
c. or *ca.*—about, used with dates; from Lat. *circa;* Chaucer was born *c.* 1340.
ch. or chs.—chapter, chapters
ed.—edited by, or edition
f., ff.—and the following page, and the following pages: p. 223 f., pp. 267 ff.
l., ll.—line, lines; useful in citing references to poetry
MS, MSS—manuscript, manuscripts
n.d.—no date of publication has been given

Bibliography A bibliography is an alphabetical list of books, magazine and newspaper articles, and pamphlets dealing with a subject. Actually, a complete bibliography of a subject ought to contain all printed references to it, but the bibliography required at the end of your research papers is usually limited to the sources that you used in preparing your paper and to which you refer in your footnotes.

During your reading and note taking, as you find material which you expect to use in your paper, you should prepare a bibliography card for each work. This will ordinarily be a 3 x 5 card giving all of the publication data supplied in a first-reference footnote (see above, page 399), but arranged somewhat differently:

Robertson, Robert B. *Of Whales and Men.* New York, 1954.

Your bibliography should be arranged alphabetically according to the last names of authors. When the name of the author is unknown, the work should be alphabetized under the first word of its title, not counting *a, an,* or *the.*

In preparing your bibliography, remember to give page references to magazines and newspapers; in book entries it is not necessary, however, to give either page references to the material you used or the number of pages the book contains.

In extensive bibliographies, it is customary to make two separate lists, one of books and the other of periodicals. Freshman papers, and most undergraduate term papers, are not generally extensive enough to require this division; consequently, all your material should be alphabetized in one list.

Your bibliography will be prepared from the bibliography cards you made while taking notes. First arrange these alphabetically according to the author's last name or title of the article. Then type each entry, beginning at the margin; if it is too long for one line, continue on the following line, indenting as for a paragraph. Skip a line between entries.

There are several styles of punctuating a bibliography, and you should naturally conform to the style required in your course. The "Simplified Style," the one most widely used today, is illustrated below. In this form, (a) the entry is treated as a whole, and consequently the parts are punctuated with commas; (b) the abbreviations for volume (vol.) and page (p.) are not used if both volume and page numbers are given in a single entry; an abbreviation *is* used if the page or volume number alone is given; (c) Arabic numerals are used exclusively; (d) the date of the magazine article is given in parentheses between the volume and page reference; (e) a second or third entry by the same author does not repeat the author's name; instead, a ———— is entered, followed by a comma, and then followed by the title itself.

SAMPLE BIBLIOGRAPHY

"Can Russia Catch the U.S.?" *U.S. News & World Report,* 32 (February 15, 1952), 64–76.

Cassady, J. J., Deputy Chief of Naval Operations, "First Story of Naval Air Power," *U.S. News & World Report*, 32 (January 18, 1952), 28–33.

Fechteler, Admiral W. M., Chief of Naval Operations, *The Role of the Navy*, Publication No. 40–525, Washington, United States Department of Defense, 1952.

———, "We Can't Be Invaded," *U.S. News & World Report*, 31 (October 5, 1951), 40–52.

Gardner, Admiral M. B., Commander, United States Sixth Fleet, "U.S. Navy at the Gate to Russia," *U.S. News & World Report*, 31 (December 21, 1951), 40–48.

"How We Stack Up against Russia," *Newsweek*, 34 (March 13, 1950), 17–20.

Kerner, R. J., "Russian Naval Aims," *Foreign Affairs*, 24 (January, 1946), 290–299.

Kournakoff, Sergei N., *Russia's Fighting Forces*, New York, 1942.

Low, A. M., *The Submarine at War*, London, 1941.

Mitchell, Mairin, *The Maritime History of Russia, 1848–1948*, London, 1949.

"Our Underwater Defense," *Life*, 31 (December 10, 1951), 133–145.

"Rumors," *Time*, 56 (September 25, 1950), 36.

Smogorsewski, Kazimerz, "Russian Trade," *Britannica Book of the Year*, Chicago, 1950, p. 687.

"Threat of Russia's Snorkels," *The New York Times Magazine*, February 5, 1950, pp. 7–9.

Westcott, Allan, *American Sea Power Since 1775*, Philadelphia, 1957.

Footnote and Bibliographical Styles in Special Fields

In addition to the standard styles of citation that we have considered, many special fields have their own methods. Engineering and scientific papers containing many references to periodicals, for instance, will often abbreviate periodical titles. An excellent list of these titles and their abbreviations is published by the American Chemical Society. Another, and shorter, list is in the *Style Manual of the American Institute of Physics*. The American Medical Association's *Medical Writing* and the *Index Medicus* provide useful lists of periodical titles and abbreviations for writers on medical subjects. A good reference for legal writing is *A Uniform System of Citation*, published by *The Harvard Law Review*.

In term papers or reports in your advanced classes especially, you should make your footnote and bibliographical style conform to the professional standard.

Parts of the Research Paper

A complete term paper should include all of the following parts, if required by your instructor:

Title Page On this sheet the title of the paper, given in capitals, is centered on the page. In the lower right-hand corner, the following information is given on three separate lines: the writer's name, the course and section numbers, and the date.

Outline This should be included only if assigned. For the technique of making an outline, see Chapter 7, page 254, above, where preparing a theme outline is discussed. Exactly the same principles are involved in making a term paper outline; the only difference is length.

Text You should be sure that the text embodies all the principles discussed in Chapter 2, "Writing the Theme." It would, in fact, be an excellent idea to reread Chapter 2 before beginning the final draft of your research paper.

Bibliography

Specimen Reference Paper

EXPLORATION IN ANTARCTICA

Since it was first discovered that the earth was round, men have been seeking the answer to the riddle of what lies at the extreme points of the world, the polar regions. The story of the men who have tried to reach the Poles is one of courage, heroism, and daring far surpassing the best that fiction can offer. Even after the Poles were reached, these brave men continued in their undying efforts to make these cold and silent regions give up their secrets. Man's struggle to reach the Poles and his contribution toward greater knowledge of these regions, the "cold spots of the world" which offer a never-ending challenge and mystery, form one of the most interesting and fascinating chapters in the world's history.

Before explorers actually started making voyages northward and southward, there was no real knowledge of the polar regions. Concerning the Arctic region, the unscientific view was that "there was a happy region, north of the north wind, where the sun was always shining and Hyperboreans led a peaceful life." [1] The popular picture of Antarctica was of a fertile, green, lush land. An 18th century hydrographer, Alexander Dalrymple, predicted the population was more than fifty million. There was almost no realization of the intense cold.

From the first, more men have swung to the southern pole for exploration. This can perhaps be explained by the fact that the North Pole consists mostly of ice and water, whereas the South Pole offers ice and a continent. The South Pole is nevertheless one of the hardest places on earth to reach. Byrd, in the following passage, explains why Antarctica is so hard to penetrate.

The world is small and rapidly getting smaller. . . . But if the world is shrinking it is because science is audacious and unsatisfied. And if the Antarctic has shrunk least of all, if it still stands aloof and hidden in glacial fogs, it is because the pack ice and the gales which defend its coasts, and the cold, and the blizzards, and the unutterable lifelessness of the interior regions are not easily to be subdued. [2]

From 1820, twenty-three leaders have made attempts to subdue Antarctica. Few were successful. The first man to reach Antarctica was Nathaniel Brown Palmer, a twenty-year-old youngster from Connecticut, who in the spring of 1820 reached the tip

[1] "Exploration of Arctic Regions," *Encyclopaedia Britannica* (1951), II, 290.

[2] Richard E. Byrd, *Discovery* (New York, 1935), p. 4.

of Antarctica located at 63° 45′ S. and 60° W. In his honor this tip bears the name of Palmer's Land. Others of importance who made the southward journey are Weddell, 1823, after whom the Weddell Sea is named, and Ross, 1841, who discovered the Ross Ice Barrier. Others periodically made attempts to reach the South Pole up to 1909 but all failed. That year marked the start of a period known as "The glorious and tragic search for the South Pole." [3]

Shackleton was the first of a trio whose primary aim was to conquer the South Pole. A member of Byrd's staff tells of his exploits thus:

> Often we have discussed Sir Ernest Shackleton, another gallant Englishman. His attempts to reach the Pole were always beset by unfortunate and unavoidable incidents which would have discouraged a weaker man. After fighting through almost superhuman obstacles, living for days on short rations and making forced marches, he was obliged to turn back when within ninety miles of his goal.[4]

In the Antarctic summer of 1911–12 shortly after Shackleton's attempt, another Englishman arrived to try his luck at the polar jackpot. Sir Robert Falcon Scott, a British Naval Officer, was like all polar explorers in one respect—he had dedicated his life to reaching the Pole first. But another had that dream also.

Roald Amundsen, the Norwegian sailor, was just ready to start on his long-planned expedition to the North Pole when he was met with the crushing news that Peary had carried the Stars and Stripes to the top of the world. Blocked and frustrated by the news of Peary's exploit, Amundsen met it with "the most astounding move in the history of exploration." [5] Although ill-financed, ill-staffed, and ill-equipped, he started on his proposed expedition. After getting under way, however, he broke the news to his astonished crew that they were on their way, not to the North Pole, but to Antarctica. His reason, to him, was clear. If he could reach the South Pole, it would add greatly to his status as an explorer. Then perhaps he could raise funds for a gigantic North Pole expedition.

[3] Thomas R. Henry, *The White Continent* (New York, 1950), p. 230.

[4] John S. O'Brien, *By Dog Sled for Byrd* (Chicago, 1934), p. 16.

[5] Henry, p. 87.

Otherwise he counted the attainment of the South Pole as of no importance; the Antarctic was simply a barrier to be crossed on the way to the Arctic.[6]

Not even the news that Scott was also on the way to the South Pole deterred him from his purpose of reaching the Pole as soon as possible and then getting back quickly to civilization. "Thus the stage was set for one of the epic tragedies of history." [7]

Scott established his base camp at Cape Evans. After he looked around, his fears of Amundsen's pulling ahead of him were confirmed when he learned the Norwegians were building Framheim, sixty-nine miles closer to the Pole. "Clearly it was to be a race for glory between two explorers and two flags." [8]

Amundsen started for the Pole on October 19, 1911. Scott followed thirteen days later from McMurdo Sound. Perhaps unfortunately for him, Scott followed the unsuccessful Shackleton's route. Amundsen started from what was later to be Byrd's Little America.

The two men's "plans of attack" were radically different. Amundsen followed the old polar tradition of Husky dogs and sledges. Scott tried motor sledges and Shetland ponies. The motor sledges proved useless; they bogged down in the snow. Three of his ponies drowned when the ice broke under them before they even started.

The same luck followed Scott's party on the trail. While they were in the middle of the Ice Shelf, the weather unexpectedly warmed and for fourteen days they wallowed in eighteen inches of slush. Amundsen, with his four companions with thirteen dogs each, had exceptionally good weather. His trip was as easy and effortless as Scott's was hard and plodding.

On December 14, Amundsen reached the South Pole. He stayed for four days. His return journey was fast and easy and was accomplished in thirty-eight days.

On January 17, Scott sighted Amundsen's tents. The Norwegian had left a letter for Scott so that his triumph might be recognized if he himself perished.

Perhaps no man ever suffered a more bitter disillusion than did Scott at the South Pole on January 18, 1912. The proof

[6] *Ibid.*
[7] *Ibid.*, p. 88.
[8] *Ibid.*

of his rival's triumph was indisputable; Amundsen had won the race with less planning, less expense, less equipment. The Englishman could not understand, and did not when he died, how it had been done. For him the flag of the Norwegians was the banner of death.[9]

Scott stayed only long enough to fix the position of the Pole. (As it later turned out, this was practically identical with Amundsen's.)

With heavy hearts, the Englishmen turned for their base—800 miles of solid dragging on foot in the face of a screaming blizzard. They never made it. Eight months later their bodies were found frozen in a tent nine miles from a supply cache. Beside Scott's body lay his diary telling the whole poignant story and ending with the heroic words: "It seems a pity, but I do not think I can write more." [10]

Then came Byrd. Admiral Richard E. Byrd is perhaps the most famous explorer of the cold regions ever known. He was the first man to fly over both Poles. He added more details to the geography of Antarctica than all his predecessors put together. In his four expeditions to Antarctica, Byrd discovered 22 mountain ranges, 26 islands, 9 bays, 20 glaciers, and 5 capes never before seen. He took over 70,000 photographs.[11] A new map detailing one-third of the continent was made possible by him, although the other two-thirds remain unknown. His philosophy and descriptions of the continent have inspired millions of readers who have traveled with him through his books. The following passage shows the strength, the character, and the beliefs of the man who has devoted his life to the science of discovery. Perhaps it shows why he succeeded.

When you look upon such things there comes surging through the confusion of the mind an awareness of the dignity of the earth, of the unaccountable importance of being alive, and the thought comes out of nowhere that unhappiness rises

---

[9] *Ibid.*, p. 91.

[10] Lowell Thomas, "Fifty Years of Exploration," *Popular Mechanics*, 98 (August, 1952), 97.

[11] Henry, pp. 231 ff.

not so much from lacking as from having too much. Like Peter in *War and Peace*, something exclaims, though the words may not form: "All that is mine, all that is in me, is me." [12]

The estimated cost of Byrd's first expedition was $750,000. When he had raised only about two-thirds of the necessary funds, he set out—destination, Antarctica; purpose, scientific exploration. He took two ships, the *City of New York* and the *Eleanor Bolling*. These ships carried five planes, ninety-five Husky dogs, a snowmobile, and large stores of food, radio equipment, and clothing. He was prepared to stay a year.

Christmas, 1928, found the expedition at the Bay of Whales, where they set up a village base called Little America. On November 28, 1929, Byrd made the first flight over the South Pole. The expedition discovered and mapped more than 400,000 square miles. On his return, a special Act of Congress made Byrd a Rear Admiral.

In 1933 the depression was at hand, and Byrd found it difficult to raise money for a second expedition. He raised only $150,000 of the necessary funds. When the expedition reached Antarctica, they had great difficulty in finding a path among the icebergs. Finally they reached Little America.

It was as if they had just stepped outside for a moment instead of nearly five years. As they entered the Old Mess Hall, the scene they had left behind greeted their eyes. Dirty underwear, torn parkas, unmade beds testified to the hastiness of their departure. A coffee pot sat on the table, keeping company with a piece of roast beef with a fork stuck in it. The stove lighted immediately, and the food sitting on it was cooked and eaten. The telephone system they had set up still worked; the record player chimed out "The Bells of St. Mary's." But the most amazing thing of all was that the electric lights worked. The Antarctic cold had preserved everything just as it had been left. Time had stood still in a frozen village.

Byrd and his men hurried to set up more buildings, more conveniences before the Antarctic winter came.

Time was everything, time was nothing, time was something that ran on and on, lacing the dissolving hours with the blinding pain of fatigue; there was no end to it, only a terrible

[12] Byrd, pp. 194–195.

penalty if you allowed it to get the upper hand. Yet time was always the master and you were its creature.[13]

In their race against time, the expedition added ten buildings and two shacks to the village. They installed more lights, telephones, and electric saws and drills. They brought rugs, good mattresses, movies, three cows, and a library. When they finished, the two parallel rows of buildings bore little resemblance to the first sparsely equipped Little America.

Then they settled down to business. During the winter, while the men at Little America prepared exploring parties to be sent out in the spring, Admiral Byrd established himself at Advance Base for the purpose of making meteorological observations. He lived alone for five months in a shack sunk in the ice ninety miles south of Little America. In his second month, just when he was congratulating himself that everything was going well, he was overcome by carbon monoxide fumes from his stove and was left in such a weakened condition it was all he could do to keep alive. He determined not to let the people at Little America know he was sick, however, for he feared they would risk their own lives in the Antarctic night to rescue him. So he said nothing.

Gradually he became too weak even to turn the hand generator of his radio set. Finally the men at the base began to suspect all was not well at Advance Base, and a party was sent out. Three times blizzards drove them back. When they finally reached Byrd, he was gaunt and weak. His life hung in the balance for some days.

While Byrd recovered at Little America, three exploring parties were sent out in the spring. The first, the geological party, was a three-man sledging group sent into the Queen Maud Range. Their target was a geological and paleontological reconnaissance of the explored easterly reaches of the range. Four men comprised the Plateau party, whose purpose was to run a seismic and magnetic survey across the Ross Ice Barrier to the polar plateau. The last party was the four-man sledging unit called the Marie Byrd Land Party. They were sent on a mission of geological reconnaissance into the unpenetrated coastal mountains. All of these reports added to the knowledge of Antarctica's geography.

In 1939–41, Byrd's third Antarctic expedition tackled Antarctica. This one was sponsored by the government. The base was established on the same Little America site, and another was set

[13] *Ibid.*, p. 79.

up far to the east off the Palmer Peninsula. Extensive air and coastal surveys were carried out.

At the end of World War II, Byrd started pressing for a fourth expedition to dwarf all others. The result was Operation High Jump, the largest expedition ever. Rear Admiral Richard H. Cruzen was in charge of the twelve ships and four thousand officers and men. The expedition carried a Navy helicopter and a fleet of the latest landplanes and seaplanes for photomapping the continent. Each plane would carry five cameras—one pointed straight down, two at 30° angles from the horizontal, one on the clock, and the other on the altimeter. These three-dimensional photos could then be put together to form a perfect map of the icecap where no human foot had ever been.

When they reached Little America, they found it had moved approximately one and one-half miles since they had last abandoned it. As before, they found everything perfectly preserved. They set up the fourth Little America, a tent camp with accommodations for three hundred, about two miles north of the old base.

On this fourth expedition, the group made twenty-nine operational and mapping flights, spending 220 hours in the air and covering 27,500 miles.[14]

This fourth expedition was also the occasion of Byrd's second flight over the Pole. When he reached it, he flew around it in a circle (so he could say he had flown around the world non-stop), and dropped a cardboard box containing the multicolored flags of the United Nations.

Besides Byrd, three other men deserve mention for their expeditions to the South Pole. Ellsworth, who flew across the North Pole, flew from the base of Palmer Peninsula to Little America in January, 1936. As a result of this 2,340 mile flight, he laid claim to 80,000 square miles for the United States. This is the region in which American territorial claims could probably be best sustained if any dispute arises. Wilkins also covered a considerable area at the foot of the Palmer Peninsula. He commanded two expeditions and was associated with Ellsworth on three others.

On March 12, 1947, Finn Ronne, who had accompanied Byrd, went ashore with a party of twenty-three (including Mrs. Ronne, the first woman to step on Antarctic ice) on the western

[14] Richard E. Byrd, "Our Navy Explores Antarctica," *National Geographic Magazine*, 92 (October, 1947), 434.

coast of Palmer Peninsula. Ronne determined by altimeter readings that Antarctica is a single continent, not divided by a strait between the Ross and Weddell Seas as many believed. He accurately photographed another 450,000 square miles for the first time.[15]

So ends the story of the men of the past who have tried to reach the Poles. Exploration of the future requires not so much traveling expeditions as fixed stations operating for a year or more to investigate geodetic measurements, gravity determinations, terrestrial magnetism, Arctic meteorology, ice formation and currents, problems of biology, and conditions of life in the polar regions.

Although the days of the long struggle to reach the Poles are over, much remains to be done in the future with polar expeditions. The story of the Arctic and the Antarctic is not yet completed. Men will continue to travel northward and southward to reveal further the nature and effect of these cold and silent regions. As one author so expertly comments on the South Pole:

> Attainment of the mathematical point where every direction is north is no longer of any particular scientific interest, but the Pole will remain for all time a symbol of human courage and endurance.[16]

[15] Henry, pp. 234–235.
[16] *Ibid.*, p. 82.

BIBLIOGRAPHY

Byrd, Richard E., *Alone*, New York, 1938.

———, *Discovery*, New York, 1935.

———, "Our Navy Explores Antarctica," *National Geographic Magazine*, 92 (October, 1947), 429–522.

Commercial and Library Atlas of the World, New York, 1949.

Cook, Frederick A., *Return from the Pole*, New York, 1951.

"Discovery of the Pole," *Life*, 30 (May 14, 1951), 77–82.

"Exploration of Arctic Regions," *Encyclopaedia Britannica* (1951), II, 290–302.

Henry, Thomas R., *The White Continent*, New York, 1950.

O'Brien, John S., *By Dog Sled for Byrd*, Chicago, 1934.

Stefansson, Vilhjalmur, "Claims to Polar Discovery," *Saturday Review of Literature*, 34 (December 8, 1951), 26.

Thomas, Lowell, "Fifty Years of Exploration," *Popular Mechanics*, 98 (August, 1952), 94–99.

12.   The Letter

Writing letters differs very little from other kinds of writing, except that certain special forms and conventions are generally adhered to, as we shall see below. In general, of course, the standard rules of good writing apply to letters. Correctness is especially important, for a letter represents the writer just as surely as our Ambassador to Great Britain represents the United States in England. Very often the recipient is not personally acquainted with the writer; hence he must judge the writer by the letter he holds in his hand. If you send a letter improper in form, marred by mistakes in spelling, grammar, or sentence structure, it is certain that your letter—your ambassador—is going to make a poor impression. It is like sending a diplomat attired in a castoff tweed suit to a state reception at the French Embassy.

Many prominent industrialists and business leaders have complained that college graduates who apply to them for jobs are unable to write a correct letter. Perhaps it is unfair to place so high a value on the ability to write correct letters. After all, the candidates may have other valuable qualities, which, if they were known, might outweigh their inability to write correctly. But the fact remains that, whether it is fair or not, the world sets a high value on literacy as represented in a correctly written letter. Therefore it behooves everyone to master the simple techniques of letter writing.

Style

The style of the letter (except, as pointed out below, in the very formal social letter) should be the same natural and personal style used in any informal writing. Business letters were once characterized by the frequent use of certain clichés which are now considered in poor taste. No longer do we speak of "your favor." Instead we call it what it is, "your letter." Furthermore, current good taste has completely outlawed the telegraphic style which formerly was supposed to stimulate commercial briskness and financial acumen, such as "Yours of the 18th inst. received and contents duly noted." The style of today's business letter is politely personal and even almost conversational.

Kinds of Letters

There are three main kinds of letters: (1) *formal*, (2) *business*, and (3) *personal*.

The Formal Letter　The formal letter is a very specialized type, the writing of which is governed by rules quite different from those covering personal and business letters. Actually, since every passing year in this country marks a greater growth of informality, the average person has little need to know about formal correspondence—and even less opportunity to practice it. The problems posed in writing formal invitations, acceptances, and regrets are more problems of etiquette than of composition. A thorough coverage of them would require far more space in this book than the practical value would justify. For a full account of these matters, you should consult two authoritative works: *Etiquette* by Emily Post and *The Complete Book of Etiquette* by Amy Vanderbilt. In general, the formal note is written in the present tense and the third person, has no heading, inside address, salutation, complimentary close, or signature. All words are spelled out except street numbers and the standard abbreviations *Mr., Mrs.,* and *Dr.* Formal notes of invitation are generally engraved; otherwise they must be handwritten, never typed. The following models of the formal invitation, acceptance, and regret illustrate these basic principles:

Invitation

Miss Celeste Cunningham requests the pleasure of Mr. Arthur Ryan's company for dinner on Saturday, the twenty-fourth of December at seven-thirty o'clock.

One Park Avenue

R.S.V.P.

Acceptance

Mr. Arthur Ryan accepts with pleasure Miss Celeste Cunningham's kind invitation for dinner on Saturday, the twenty-fourth of December at seven-thirty o'clock.

Regret

Mr. Arthur Ryan regrets extremely that a previous engagement prevents his accepting Miss Celeste Cunningham's kind invitation for dinner on Saturday, the twenty-fourth of December.

The Business Letter   Business letters are preferably typed on stationery 8½ x 11 inches, and folded twice horizontally to fit a long business envelope, or once horizontally and twice vertically to fit a smaller envelope. The address on the envelope is written as follows:

Mr. Thomas Jones, Vice President
Martin and Co., Inc.
252 Madison Avenue
New York, New York 10017

In the upper left-hand corner of the envelope, the return address of the writer is always given; generally his name is also included:

Harold Williams
106 Lincoln Hall
University of Illinois
Urbana, Illinois 61803

Every business letter consists of the following parts:

1. Heading
2. Inside Address
3. Salutation
4. Body
5. Complimentary close
6. Signature

Heading. The heading of the business letter consists of the writer's complete address, including the zip code, and date. Very often letters are written on letterhead stationery which gives the firm name and address at the top center of the page. If this is provided, the date is typed either immediately below the printed head or below and to the right. If the business letter is written on unprinted stationery, the heading is generally written as follows, in blocked style with open punctuation:

1212 Springhill Road
Staunton, Virginia 37895
July 7, 1958

The heading might also be written with closed punctuation and indented form, as follows:

1212 Springhill Road,
Staunton, Virginia 37895,
July 7, 1958.

If this type of heading is used, it is necessary to follow this form exactly on the outside address. The indented form with open punctuation is also permissible.

The important thing is, of course, to be consistent in whatever form you use. Unless you have good reason for preferring either of the alternative forms, we suggest that you use the blocked style, presented first above, since the overwhelming preponderance of business letters are now written in this form.

The Inside Address. The inside address gives the complete address just as it is written on the envelope. It is typed about three spaces beneath the heading and even with the left margin. Here again there are three permissible styles, but the first is the preferred.

Mr. Thomas Jones, Vice President
Martin and Co., Inc.
252 Madison Avenue
New York, New York 10017

Mr. Thomas Jones, Vice President,
   Martin and Co., Inc.,
      252 Madison Avenue,
         New York, New York 10017

Mr. Thomas Jones, Vice President
   Martin and Co., Inc.
      252 Madison Avenue
         New York, New York 10017

Whatever form you choose, use it consistently in the inside address and heading.

The Salutation. The salutation appears two lines below the inside address; it is even with the left margin, and it is followed invariably by a colon. Various forms of the salutation are used:

Dear Sir:
Gentlemen:
My dear Sir: (quite formal)
Dear Mr. Arbuthnot:
   (less formal)
 My dear Mr. Arbuthnot:
  (more formal)
Sir: (most formal)

Dear Madam:
Mesdames:
My dear Madam:
  (quite formal)
Dear Mrs. Arbuthnot:
  (less formal)
My dear Mrs. Arbuthnot:
  (more formal)
Madam: (most formal)

There are special salutations required when addressing various officials and dignitaries such as the President of the United States, governors of states, senators, archbishops, monsignors, and others. Correct salutations to be used when addressing such people are listed in dictionaries, etiquette books, and the *Standard Handbook for Secretaries*. No abbreviations except *Mr.*, *Mrs.*, *Messrs.*, *Mmes.*, and *Dr.* are permitted in the salutation. Avoid such abbreviations as *Prof.*, *Rob't*, *Jno.*, *Theo.*, *Sen.*, *Pres.*, and *Rev.*

The Body. The body of the letter is written, as indicated at the beginning of this chapter, according to all the rules of correct composition. There is no special business-letter style. All of the stylistic advice given elsewhere in this book is applicable to the body of the letter. The body of the letter is single-spaced unless extremely short, with a double space between paragraphs. The paragraphs may be either indented five spaces or else blocked.

The Complimentary Closing. The complimentary closing must be below the body of the letter two spaces, and to the right. It should match the salutation in degree of formality, informality, warmth, or lack of warmth. The various complimentary closings are as follows:

Closing	Appropriate Salutation
Yours truly, Very truly yours, Yours very truly,	Dear Sir: *or* Dear Madam:
Sincerely yours, Very sincerely yours, Yours very sincerely, Cordially yours, Sincerely,	Dear Mr. Arbuthnot:
Respectfully yours, Very respectfully yours, Yours very respectfully,	Sir: *or* Madam:

The Signature. The signature must be handwritten in ink just below the complimentary closing. In the business letter, it is customary, if the writer's name does not appear in the letterhead, to type the name beneath the signature. On the line beneath the typed name, the writer's position or office is often indicated. Women sign their own names, not their husband's. If desired, marital status may be indicated in parentheses:

WRONG: Mrs. James W. Arbuthnot

RIGHT: Georgia Belle Arbuthnot
       (Mrs. James W. Arbuthnot)

RIGHT: Georgia Belle Arbuthnot
       or

    (Miss) Georgia Belle Arbuthnot

Letter to a Congressman You may find it advantageous some day to write to a congressman or legislator. You will want to tell him what bill you are supporting, give him succinct reasons for your report, including the reason why the bill matters to you as an individual, and show how the passage (or defeat) of the bill serves the country's welfare.

The Application Letter One of your most immediate and practical needs in business letter writing is the letter of application. In it you have the opportunity to sell yourself with dignity, conscientiousness, and tact.

Whenever possible, address yourself to the person receiving applications by name. State the position for which you are applying and, briefly, why. Refer your reader to your data sheet (sometimes called *vita*) on which you have summarized your personal data, your education, experience, and references.

Be sure to express your willingness and availability to follow through with further correspondence and a personal interview. Be businesslike, direct, and accurate, but try not to sound ponderous or pedantic. Here, more than in any other business letter, your readers will set a high value on the literacy and skill you reveal in your letter.

The Personal Letter The personal letter differs from the business letter chiefly in its greater degree of informality and intimacy. The exact degree will of course vary, depending upon the personal relationship between the writer and the recipient. The inside address is often omitted or placed at the end of the letter, several spaces below the signature and even with the left margin. Though the salutation may be followed by a colon, if the friendship is fairly close, a comma is more common. For example: *Dear Bill, Dear Sally, Dearest, Dear Mr. Arbuthnot,* and so on. Depending on the degree of familiarity, a correspondingly greater informality and a more personal tone may be employed. In the personal letter, the most desirable style to aim at is the conversational. The complimentary closing will likewise correspond in intimacy to that expressed in the salutation.

Specimen Business Letter

410 Montrose Avenue
Chicago, 37, Illinois
July 11, 1966

Mr. George R. Williams, Vice President
Scott, Glore & Co., Inc.
101 Wall Street
New York 2, New York

Dear Mr. Williams:

Thank you very much for your letter of June 30 replying to my request for information about your Solar Electric Generator. Though your brochure and letter have convinced me of the potentiality of converting the rays of the sun into electricity, I am not yet convinced of the practicality of your invention. I am inclined to believe that a cost of $800,000 for the Solar Electric Generator would be prohibitive for the average home owner, even in spite of your assurance that the Generator would be forever free of all operating and repair costs.

Another difficulty with which you have not adequately dealt, in my opinion, is the danger of electrocution which might exist on an extremely clear sunny day such as this. Electrical engineers whom I have consulted tell me that they fear the voltage of your transformer would be totally inadequate to carry the tremendous charge developed on a typical midsummer day, and that to install a transformer of proper size would entail building a special room, which would add materially to the expense of installation.

Though my associates and I feel that your invention has real potential for industrial applications, we are not inclined to invest any money, at least at this time, in your plan to promote the Solar Electric Generator for use in private homes.

Sincerely yours,

J. Andrew Smythe

JAS:bbs

Specimen Letter to a Congressman

Madison Residence Hall
Lafayette College
Mount Vernon, Washington
June 13, 1966

The Honorable Wayne Morse
The United States Senate
Washington, D. C.

My dear Senator:

Because your Senate Subcommittee on Education is holding hearings on public library services, I would like to urge the passage of Senate Bill S.580.

I am a political science major, planning to devote my life to service in local and state government. My friends in this field and I see the public library and the public school together signifying the importance of education in every community. The public library makes knowledge accessible to school children, young adult students, and adults in all occupations. It furnishes needed information to a socially mobile population; it provides information about our democratic traditions; and it enlarges the base of community understanding.

The adequacy and availability of public libraries in each community, as well as the improvement of school and college libraries, are problems which concern government officials, civic leaders, and teachers, who know that a well-informed citizenry is democracy's strength. Passage of S.580, the National Education Improvement Act, is vital to the education of our citizens.

Yours very truly,

Richard S. Mason

Specimen of an Application Letter

                                    11102 Wilshire Road
                                    Chicago, Illinois
                                    July 20, 1966

Mrs. Anne Richter, Director
Book Editorial Department
R. R. Bowker Company
1180 Avenue of the Americas
New York, New York

Dear Mrs. Richter:

    Through John Stensrud, sales representative for
Bowkers in the Chicago area, I have learned that you
are accepting applications for editorial assistants
to work on forthcoming volumes of the <u>Directory of
American Scholars.</u> Because of my undergraduate education in English and journalism, my sustained interest
in these areas, and my experience of the past five
years, I am submitting my application for your consideration.

    The enclosed data sheet summarizes my education,
experience, and references. You will notice that the
kind of detailed, meticulous proofreading, copyread-
ing, and editing I have done qualifies me especially
for work entailed on the tightly summarized, abbreviated, and coded entries used in the <u>Directory of
American Scholars.</u>

    During my vacation from July 27-August 7, I
shall be available for a personal interview either
here in Chicago or at your office in New York or at
the offices of the Jaques Cattell Press in Tempe,
Arizona, at your preference and convenience. You may
write me at my home address or telephone me collect at
my home number. After 5:00 p.m. Monday through Friday and on Saturdays, I am usually at my own apartment.

I enjoy my work here at Lakeside Press and am scheduled for promotion in January, but I feel that the chance to work on the <u>Directory of American Scholars</u> presents an opportunity for professional growth which I may not be able to find here. Mrs. Wilson, my supervisor, knows of my decision to apply for a position with your firm.

Thank you for your consideration of my application. I shall be happy to answer further questions about my qualifications and experience.

Very truly yours,

(Miss) Joanne R. Blanding

Specimen of a Data Sheet

DATA SHEET

<u>Personal</u>
Name and Address

Joanne Renee Blanding (Miss), 11102 Wilshire Road, Chicago, Illinois; telephone: Area Code 312, 944-7227

Birth

August 23, 1940, Mankato, Minnesota

Marital Status

Single

<u>Education</u>
Public Schools
High School
College

Emerson Elementary School, Mankato,
   Minnesota, 1945-1951
Mankato Junior-Senior High School,
   Mankato, Minnesota, 1951-1957
Minnesota State College, Mankato,
   Minnesota, 1957-1961, B.A.

Experience
Proofreader
Copyreader
Editorial Assistant

Mankato Free Press, Mankato,
   Minnesota, 1959-1961
Northwestern Press, Minneapolis,
   Minnesota, 1961-1962
Lakeside Press, Chicago,
   Illinois, 1962-present

Publications Edited
Want Ads, Obituaries, Birth and Death Notices in daily
   issues of the Mankato Free Press for two years
   while in college
Annual Catalogs and Supplements of Northwestern Press,
   publishers of plays, dramatic readings, and
   theater publications
Staff Directories, Intercom Telephone Directories,
   and National Employee Registers for companies
   under contract with Lakeside Press

References
Professor H. W. Gardiner, Chairman, Department of
   Journalism, Minnesota State College, Mankato,
   Minnesota
Mr. J. R. Dale, Managing Editor, Mankato Free Press,
   Mankato, Minnesota
Mr. L. Dennis Stallmann, Executive Vice President,
   Northwestern Press, 1105 South Bryant Avenue,
   Minneapolis, Minnesota
Mrs. Vivian Wilson, Editorial Associate, Lakeside
   Press, 600 North Michigan Avenue, Chicago,
   Illinois

Specimen Personal Letter

674 Ott Street
Orange, Conn.
February 17, 1966

Dear Harry

Betty and I were much surprised to see your picture in the paper last Sunday, and even more delighted by your good fortune in winning the window display contest. How does it feel to be rich, anyway? I suppose you'll be buying that cabin cruiser this spring.

It surely was nice being with you and Isabelle in New York. The best thing about conventions, I think, is the opportunity of seeing old friends. Otherwise those long meetings are a frightful bore.

Let us know when you expect to be in the New Haven area, for Betty and I would love to have you visit us here in Orange.

Sincerely,
Arnold

Exercise

1. Write a letter applying for a position with the General Electric Co. of Schenectady, New York. State your personal qualifications and give a résumé of your education.

2. Write a letter to the dean of your college requesting special permission to graduate *in absentia*.

3. Write a letter to President Charles Wallace McNabie of Maypole College in which you apologize for wearing white buck shoes in the academic procession of the fall convocation. Assume that President McNabie has reprimanded you.

4. Write a thank-you letter to the mother of a classmate who has entertained you in her home over a week end.

5. Write a letter to Dean John Hancock of Maypole College explaining your failure to return from Christmas vacation until four days after resumption of classes.

6. Reply to a letter from the Acme Machine Foundry of 14 Aurora Avenue, Cleveland 18, Ohio, expressing dissatisfaction with the failure of the suspension guides in a recently purchased Acme filing cabinet.

7. Write your congressman requesting him to amend the income tax laws to provide an allowance for human depletion comparable to the allowance for the depletion of mineral resources.

8. As your congressman, write a reply to the letter above.

9. Write a letter to your employer explaining why you must give up your position unless you obtain an increase in salary.

10. Write to the city manager of your home town complaining about the condition of the street in front of your house.

11. Write to a clothing shop calling attention to a mistake made in your monthly bill. (You have been billed for $47.50 worth of clothing you did not buy.)

12. Write to your minister or your high school principal requesting a letter of recommendation to be sent to the Acme Machine Foundry Company of 14 Aurora Avenue, Cleveland 18, Ohio, where you are applying for a position.

13. Write to your home-town newspaper applying for a summer job and asking for an interview with the managing editor.

14. Invite the president of a fraternity (or sorority) on a nearby

campus to address a banquet of your fraternity (or sorority) on your own campus.

15. Reply to a letter inviting you to join an organization.
16. Invite a former classmate to spend a week end with you on campus.
17. Write a letter of condolence to a close friend who has just lost his (or her) father.
18. Write a letter to a close friend thanking him (or her) for introducing you to the person you now love.
19. Reply to a formal invitation to a tea given by Mrs. Charles Wallace McNabie. Accept her invitation.
20. Reply to a formal dinner invitation which you are forced to decline.

Glossaries

A Glossary
of Grammatical Terms

Absolute.   See **Nominative Absolute** and **Independent Element.**

Abstract Noun.   A noun which refers to an intangible, something that cannot be discerned with the five senses: *kindness, sportsmanship, hate.* Cf. **Concrete Noun.**

Accusative Case.   See **Objective Case.**

Active Voice.   See **Voice.**

Adjective.   See G-37–G-39. A word which modifies (i.e., limits or describes) a noun or pronoun. Note that, functionally speaking, possessive pronouns, demonstrative pronouns, interrogative pronouns, indefinite pronouns, articles, and numerals are classified as limiting adjectives:

> *his* plan, *our* investments, *my* mistake (possessive pronouns)
> > *this* candy, *that* monster, *those* peasants (demonstrative pronouns)
>
> *what* settlement? *whose* convertible? *which* vitamins? (interrogative pronouns)
> *some* people, *any* road (indefinite pronouns)
> *a* cyclone, *an* elephant, *the* unicorn (articles)
> *fifty* robins, *six* characters (numerals)

Descriptive adjectives are like the following:

> *gray* suit, *insufficient* evidence, *nasty* cold.

Adjective Clause.   A subordinate clause which modifies a noun or a pronoun and hence functions in the sentence as an adjective.

> Our candidate is a man *who merits sincere admiration*.

Adjective Phrase.   A phrase which modifies a noun or a pronoun and hence functions in the sentence as an adjective.

> The candidate *with the most votes* will win.

Adverb.   See **Conjunctive Adverb** and G-37–G-39. A word which modifies a verb, adjective, or another adverb. Adverbs are used to indicate time, place, manner, and degree.

> Come to me *now*. (time)
> I will meet you *there*. (place)
> Drive *slowly* through the fog. (manner)
> I am *very* happy that you are here. (degree)

Adverbial Clause.   A subordinate clause which modifies a verb, an adjective, or an adverb; hence it has an adverbial function in the sentence. Adverbial clauses may indicate time, manner, place, cause, purpose, condition, concession, comparison, or result.

> Corn should not be planted *until the nights are warm*. (Time—modifies *planted*.)
> Senator Thristleburt campaigned *as vigorously as he could*. (Manner—modifies *campaigned*.)
> He went *wherever the railroads ran*. (Place—modifies *went*.)
> He made this whistle-stop campaign *because he loved a good fight*. (Cause—modifies *made*.)
> He spoke daily *in order that he might educate the voters*. (Purpose—modifies *spoke*.)
> *If you run out of money*, I will lend you some. (Condition—modifies *lend*.)

431

Even though I am old enough to be your father, Evangeline,
   I still want to marry you. (Concession—modifies *want*.)
My uncle is even richer *than other Texans are*. (Comparison
   —modifies *richer*.)
Production of automobiles occasionally is discontinued *so
   that dealers' inventories of new cars may be reduced*.
   (Result—modifies *discontinued*.)

Adverbial Noun.   A noun used adverbially.

He remained *a month*.
At last he returned *home*.

Agreement.   The correspondence in form of one word
with another in gender, number, case, or person.

Agreement in gender: *Mary* went to *her* room.
Agreement in number: *Men are* doomed to die.
Agreement in case: *We*, my brother and *I*, opposed the
   motion.
Agreement in person: *I am* twenty-two years old.

Antecedent.   The noun or pronoun previously mentioned
to which a pronoun refers. The antecedent may also be a
phrase or a clause.

Adlai Stevenson was one *politician who* had literary ability.
   (The pronoun *who* refers to its antecedent *politician*.)
The ancient *Egyptians* were great engineers. *They* constructed the pyramids without modern machinery. (The
   pronoun *they* refers to the antecedent *Egyptians*.)

Appositive.   A noun, pronoun, or other substantive used
beside another noun, pronoun, or other substantive for the
purpose of explanation, and meaning the same person or
thing.

Mr. Arbuthnot, our *lawyer*, explained that the jury, *a group
   of twelve fellow citizens*, was of ancient British origin.

432

(Here *lawyer* is in apposition with Mr. Arbuthnot; and *a group of twelve fellow citizens* is in apposition with jury.)

The poet *Keats* died young.

Article. The words *a, an,* and *the* are articles, the first two being indefinite and the last definite. Their function is adjectival.

Auxiliary. A verb used in the formation of verb phrases, such as *shall, will, may, might, must, can, be, do, have, should,* and *would.*

I *shall* call you early, dear.

Johnson *has been* elected.

Cardinal Number. The numbers *one, two, three, four, five, six,* etc. See **Ordinal Numbers.**

Case. See G-6–G-8, G-12–G-19; also **Agreement.** A change in the form of a noun or pronoun by which a relationship is indicated to some other word or words in the sentence.

Clause. A group of words containing a predication (i.e., a subject and predicate). There are two kinds of clauses: (1) main or independent—those which are independent statements capable of standing alone; and (2) subordinate or dependent—those which depend for their meaning on a main clause and are incapable of standing alone. Dependent clauses function as adjectives, adverbs, or nouns within the complete sentence.

INDEPENDENT: The cannons roared through the night.

DEPENDENT: *As Bill crossed the street,* a truck ran over him.

Collective Noun. See **Noun.**

Colloquialism. A word or expression in national use in informal speaking or writing, but not occurring in formal English.

I *phoned* him yesterday.
Your plans are *O.K.* with me, Bob.
We have an *exam* in *math* tomorrow.

Common Noun.   See **Noun.**

Comparative Degree.   See **Positive Degree.**

Complement.   A word or words necessary to complete the sense of a verb. There are several kinds of complements, as follows:

DIRECT OBJECT:	The mule kicked *Henry.*
INDIRECT OBJECT:	Betty baked *me* a cake.
PREDICATE NOMINATIVE:	I am *he.* Tyler was *President.*
SUBJECTIVE COMPLEMENT:	Same as predicate nominative.
PREDICATE ADJECTIVE:	This pie tastes *sour.* I feel *bad* today. (The predicate adective is also known as a *subjective complement,* or *predicate complement.*)
OBJECTIVE COMPLEMENT:	We painted the house *red.* (Here the predicate adjective *red* refers to the object *house;* hence it is known as an objective complement.)

Complex Sentence.   See **Sentence.**

Compound Sentence.   See **Sentence.**

Compound-Complex Sentence.   See **Sentence.**

Concrete Noun.   A noun which refers to an object or quality which can be discerned by one or more of the five senses: *house, tree, river.*

Conjugation.   The inflection of the verb. See **Verb.**

Conjunction.   See pages 156–160. A word which connects words, phrases, or clauses. The two kinds of conjunctions are coordinating, which join things of equal rank, and subordinating, which connect subordinate clauses to main clauses.

The coordinating conjunctions are *and, but, for, or, nor, so, yet, either . . . or, neither . . . nor.* The subordinating conjunctions are *after, since, although, because, unless, if, though, when, until, whenever, while, where as, that,* etc.

Conjunctive Adverb. See page 157. An adverb which also has the force of a conjunction, since it is used to link main clauses. The principal conjunctive adverbs are *however, moreover, therefore, nevertheless, further, furthermore, hence, then, too, also, consequently, accordingly, thus,* etc.

Consonant. Ordinarily those sounds indicated by the letters *b, c, d, f, g, h, j, k, l, m, n, p, q, r, s, t, v, w, x, y, z.* See **Vowel.**

Construction. The grammatical arrangement of words in a sentence. See **Syntax.**

Coordinate. Of equal rank or value, as two phrases, two dependent clauses, or two verbs.

Coordinating Conjunction. See **Conjunction.**

Copula, Copulative Verb. The linking verbs *be, seem, appear, feel, become, taste, smell, look, sound,* etc., in all their forms. The linking verbs do not take objects; instead they have complements. Thus they serve as links between subjects and complements, which may be either adjectives or nouns. For full discussion, see G-39.

Declension. The change in form of nouns and pronouns to indicate person, number, case, and gender. See **Inflection.**

Demonstrative Adjective. See **Adjective.**

Demonstrative Pronoun. A pronoun which points out the thing it refers to. The demonstrative pronouns are *this, these, that, those.*

Dependent Clause. A subordinate clause. See **Clause.**

Diagraming. A graphic means of showing the syntax of a sentence by arranging the component words on lines. Various systems of diagraming are in use. One of the most widespread systems is as follows:

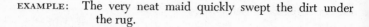

EXAMPLE: The very neat maid quickly swept the dirt under the rug.

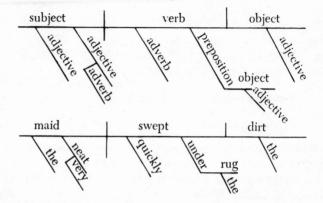

EXAMPLE: Dancing is graceful.

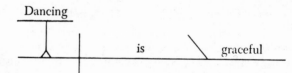

Direct Address. A noun or pronoun directly addressed to a person, used parenthetically, and in the nominative (vocative) case.

Hear our prayer, O *God*.
Let me tell you, *George*, what happened.

Direct Discourse. The exact quotation of words as they were spoken.

Roosevelt said, "We have nothing to fear but fear itself."

INDIRECT DISCOURSE: Roosevelt said that we had nothing to fear but fear itself.

436

Direct Object.   See **Object.**

Double Negative.   Two negative adverbs modifying a verb. See **Can't Hardly** and **Can't Help But** in A Glossary of Usage, page 453.

Ellipsis.   The omission of a word or words necessary for the complete grammatical construction of a sentence but not necessary to the understanding of it.

> "What did your hat cost?"
> "Ten dollars." (i.e., "My hat cost ten dollars.")
> Is Egbert smarter than Harry? (*is smart*, omitted)

Ellipsis Periods.   See P-25. The use of three or four spaced periods (. . .) to indicate the omission of a word or a passage from a direct quotation.

Emphatic Tense.   See **Tense.**

Expletive.   A word necessary to fill out a sentence to make it idiomatic, but without grammatical relation to the rest of the sentence. There are two expletives in English: *it* and *there.*

> *It* is a pity that Laura was expelled.
> *There* will be a dance Saturday night.

Finite Verb.   See G-29–G-31. A verb limited by the number and person of its subject is called finite, i.e., limited. Only finite verbs can make predications. The nonfinite verbs, or verbals, are participles, gerunds, and infinitives.

Future Tense.   See **Tense.**

Future Perfect Tense.   See **Tense.**

Gender.   The grammatical expression of sex is called gender. The three English genders, masculine, feminine, and neuter, are applied to some nouns and pronouns. Actually, however, gender in English is "natural" rather than "grammatical."

actor, actress	but	*painter* (male or female)
he, she, it	but	*who* (male or female)
host, hostess	but	*guest* (male or female)

437

Genitive.   See **Possessive.**

Gerund.   A nonfinite verb, or verbal, usually ending in *ing* and used as a noun.

> *Parting* is such sweet sorrow.
> Alice studied *dancing* in New York.

Gerund Phrase.   A phrase consisting of the gerund, its complement, if present, and modifiers.

> *Swimming across the English Channel* is a great feat.

Idiom.   An expression peculiar to a language; the characteristic way of saying a thing in a language. For full discussion, see D-10.

> *Take the floor,* please. (to a speaker)
> Osgood was *acquitted of* murder.

Imperative Mood.   See **Mood.**

Indefinite Pronoun.   Those pronouns which do not designate a definite person or thing are indefinite, as *anyone, someone, somebody, anything, none, some, few, one, another, either, neither, everybody.* See **Pronoun.**

Independent Clause.   See **Clause.**

Independent Element.   A parenthetical element which is independent of the sentence in which it appears, as far as grammatical relationship is concerned.

> The truth is, *George,* that you are a conservative. (direct address)
> *Night having fallen,* Caesar pitched his camp. (absolute expression)
> This time our advance, *we hope,* will be permanent. (parenthetical)
> *Well,* what's the use? (interjection)

Indicative Mood.   See **Mood.**

Indirect Discourse.   See **Direct Discourse.**

Indirect Object.   See **Object.**

Infinitive. A nonfinite verb or verbal, generally preceded by the sign *to*, though in some constructions the *to* sign is omitted. Infinitives may have the functions of nouns, adjectives, or adverbs.

As a noun:

> *To vote* is an American's duty. (subject)
> I wanted *to mark* my ballot. (object)
> His great desire was *to vote* Democratic. (predicate noun)
> Just as he was about *to vote*, the roof fell. (object of preposition)

As an adjective:

> A judge has the right *to disqualify* himself in cases in which he is interested. (Modifies noun *right*.)

As an adverb:

> Francis is certain *to become* a priest.

The infinitive may take a subject or an object, both of which are always in the objective case. The infinitive may also be modified by an adverb.

> The Oak Grove Players asked *me* to take the lead. (subject)
> I merely wish to advise *her*. (object)
> I asked him to display the advertising *prominently*. (adverb modifying *to display*)

Infinitive Phrase. An infinitive together with its complement, if present, and modifiers.

> He asked us *to go with him*.

Inflection. The changing grammatical forms of words, as in the conjugation of verbs, the declension of nouns, and the comparison of adjectives and adverbs.

Intensive Pronoun.   Pronouns which intensify their antecedents:

> The dean *himself* showed us the building.

Interjection.   A word expressing emotion, but having no grammatical connection to the other words of the sentence. One of the eight parts of speech.

> *oh, well, pish, alas,* and many others

Interrogative Pronoun.   A relative pronoun used in a question.

> *Who* does he think he is?

Intransitive Verb.   A verb complete in itself, taking no direct object. See **Transitive Verb.**

> Birds sing.
> He is sitting on the bench.

Irregular Verb.   A strong verb; i.e., one that forms its past by changing a vowel in its root; e.g., *sing, sang, sung.* See G-28.

Linking Verb.   See **Copula, Copulative Verb.**

Main Clause.   A term synonymous with *independent clause.* A main clause is a group of words containing a subject and verb, expressed or implied, which is grammatically independent.

> main cl.
> Although he was tired, *he knew he must continue.*

Modal Auxiliary.   A helping verb used to express possibility, necessity, permission, etc. The regular modal auxiliaries in English are *can, could, may, might, must, shall, should, will, would.*

Mood or Mode. A form of the verb indicating the attitude of the speaker or writer toward his statement. There are three moods expressed by the modern English verb:

INDICATIVE: I *walked* two miles yesterday. (statement of fact)

IMPERATIVE: *Give* me the book. (statement of command)

SUBJUNCTIVE: If she *were* here, she would understand. (statement contrary to fact)

Nominative Absolute. A nominative absolute is a phrase which is grammatically independent of the rest of the sentence. The construction is almost always composed of a noun or a pronoun (in the nominative case) governing a participle. The construction has limited use in contemporary English.

> *She failing in her promise,* I have been diverting my chagrin.
> —SHERIDAN.
>
> *That being the case,* let's go home.

Nominative Case. The form of the pronoun when it is used as a subject or predicate nominative.

> I am *he.*

Nonrestrictive. See P-4. A modifier which provides additional information about the word it modifies but does not limit its meaning.

NONRESTRICTIVE: My father, *who is fifty years old,* works for the government.

RESTRICTIVE: The man *whom you saw yesterday* is my father.

Noun. Traditionally defined as a word which names a person, place, or thing. See **Abstract Noun** and **Concrete Noun.**

> *John* plays on the *team* coached by *Harold Stone.*

441

A *proper noun* is the name of a particular person, place or thing (*John, New York, America*); all other nouns are designated as *common*. A *collective* noun indicates a collection of persons or things (*team, flock*).

Noun Clause. A dependent (or subordinate) clause used as a noun.

> *That he is sick* is evident.

Noun Phrase. A phrase used as a noun. Such phrases are also named according to the principal element in the phrase, i.e., gerund phrase, infinitive phrase, etc.

> noun phrase, also gerund phrase
> *Walking two miles a day* is sufficient exercise for the middle-aged.

Number. The change in the form of nouns, pronouns, and verbs to show singular or plural number.

Object. A noun, noun phrase or clause, or a pronoun which answers the questions *whom* or *what?* after the transitive verb is called a *direct* or an *indirect object*. See **Complement.**

>   indir.
>   obj.   dir. obj.
> I tossed *Jim* the *ball*.

A noun or a noun construction used after the preposition is called the *object of the preposition.*

> This secret is strictly between *us*.

Objective (Accusative) Case. The form of a pronoun used as a direct or indirect object, as the object of a preposition, or as the subject of a verbal.

> Bart gave *her* the book. (indirect object)
> We saw *him* at the game. (direct object)

John sent the letter to *me*. (object of preposition)
I asked *him* to help me. (subject of infinitive *to help*)

Objective Complement.   A word that completes the meaning of the object.

The Bidwells painted their house *white*.

Of **Possessive (or Genitive).**   See **Possessive.** The possessive formed by the use of the preposition *of* instead of a combination of the apostrophe and *s*.

the home *of* my father
my father's home

Ordinal Numbers.   Numbers designated by the words *first, second, third,* etc. See **Cardinal Numbers.**

Parenthetical Element.   See **Independent Element.**

Participial Phrase.   A group of words containing a participle with its complement, if present, and its modifiers.

Seeing the train just in time, he slammed on the brakes.
Sighing wistfully, she closed the door.

Participle.   A verb form used as an adjective. There are two forms of the participle in English:

a. The *present* participle, a verb form ending in *ing*.
   The *shrieking* child.
b. The *past* participle, a verb form ending in *ed*.
   The *defeated* men.

Participles are also used to form finite verb phrases.

PROGRESSIVE FORM: He was *walking* to town.
PAST PERFECT TENSE: He had *walked* two miles.

Parts of Speech.   Traditionally there are eight parts of speech: *nouns, pronouns, verbs, adjectives, adverbs, prepo-*

sitions, conjunctions, interjections. See appropriate entries in this glossary for a complete discussion.

Passive Voice. See **Voice.**

Past Participle. See **Participle.**

Past Perfect Tense. See **Tense.**

Past Tense. See **Tense.**

Person. A form of the pronoun and, to a lesser degree, the verb, which designates the person speaking, the person spoken to, and the person or thing spoken of.

First person	I am
Second person	You are
Third person	He is

Phrase. A group of words used as a single part of speech. A phrase in contrast to a clause does not contain a finite verb.

Positive Degree. The form of the adjective and adverb which makes no comparison, as opposed to the *comparative degree* and the *superlative degree.*

	Positive	**Comparative**	**Superlative**
Adjective	dull	duller	dullest
Adverb	slowly	more slowly	most slowly
Adjective	beautiful	more beautiful	most beautiful

For a full discussion, see G-37.

Possessive Adjective. A term used frequently instead of *possessive pronoun,* when the pronoun modifies a noun.

He threw a rock at *my* hat.

Possessive (Genitive) Case. The form of the noun or pronoun indicating possession.

That *man's* actions are not *my* worry.

444

The noun usually forms the possessive case by the use of the apostrophe *s* combination.

> man's actions
> boys' hats

Less frequently, and chiefly in those nouns designating inanimate objects, the "*of* possessive" is used. See **Of Possessive.**

> the shoulder of the road
> the top of the mountain

The possessive forms of pronouns may be divided into two categories: possessive adjectives, *my, your, his, her, its, our, their,* and true possessive pronouns, *mine, yours, his, hers, ours, theirs.* For a complete discussion, see G-6–G-8, G-16.

Predicate. The part of the sentence not involving the subject. The predicate contains the verb, its modifiers, and its object or objects with their modifiers.

> pred.
> He *slammed the ball into the corner of the stands.*

Predicate Adjective. An adjective modifying the subject, but used after a linking verb.

> The man is *old.*
> The ground is *hard.*

Predicate Nominative (Or Predicate Noun). A noun or pronoun interchangeable with the subject occurring after the linking verb.

> They are *friends.*

Prefix. An addition to the beginning of a word to change its meaning.

> change: *inter*change.

Preposition. A word which connects its object to some other word in the sentence. A preposition, unlike the conjunction, may correctly relate different parts of speech or unparallel grammatical constructions.

> prep.
> We go often *to* dull plays.

Prepositional Phrase. The preposition with its object and the modifiers of that object.

> prep. phr.
> We go often *to dull plays.*

Present Participle. See **Participle.**

Present Perfect Tense. See **Tense.**

Present Tense. See **Tense.**

Principal Parts. The three forms of the verb upon which all other forms are based.

Present	Past	Past Participle
talk	talked	talked
freeze	froze	frozen

Progressive Tense or Form. See **Tense.** A very common form of the English verb consisting of an auxiliary formed from *to be* plus the present participle of the main verb.

> I am walking.
> I was walking.
> I had been walking.

Pronoun. See G-9–G-23. A word that takes the place of a noun or another pronoun.

> *I* did not know *who* was in *each* of the cabins.

Proper Adjective. A proper noun which functions as an adjective, or an adjective formed from a proper noun.

> The old *Boston* road
> The *Darwinian* theory.

446

Proper Noun. A word that names a particular person, place, or thing.

Milton went to *New York* to see the *Empire State Building*.

Reciprocal Pronoun. The pronouns *each other* and *one another*, the first referring to two people or objects, the second referring to more than two.

Reflexive Pronoun. A pronoun that renames the subject:

He did it *himself*.
She told *herself* that she must go through with it.

Regular Verb. A term used frequently in referring to verbs which form their past and past participle without changing the internal vowel. Such verbs form the past tenses by the addition of *d*, or *ed*.

REGULAR: ask, asked, asked
mark, marked, marked
please, pleased, pleased

Relative Pronoun. A class of pronouns that introduces a dependent clause and functions within the clause as the subject or object. Frequently used relative pronouns are *who*, *whom*, *which*, *that*, and *what*.

I know *whom* you mean.
Do you know *what* you are doing?

Restrictive. A modifier that restricts or limits the meaning of the word it modifies. See **Nonrestrictive.**

The man *whom you just saw* is my uncle.

Retained Object. Normally, when a verb is changed from active to passive voice, the object in the active becomes the subject in the passive.

James hit the *golf ball*.
The *golf ball* was hit by James.

But verbs that take both indirect and direct objects, such as *ask, tell, give* retain their direct objects when placed in the passive voice. These objects are called *retained objects*.

> He asked her a *question*.
> She was asked a *question*.
> John told Max *to leave early*.
> Max was told *to leave early*.

Rhetoric. The study of effective writing.

Sentence. Traditionally, a group of words containing a subject and verb, and expressing a complete thought. Actually, the standard written sentence is a group of words which contains at least one finite verb and stands grammatically independent. Sentences may be divided into four types according to their clausal structure.

1. Simple sentence: A sentence containing one independent clause.

> John and David are names taken from the Bible.

2. Complex sentence: A sentence containing one independent clause and one or more dependent clauses.

> Marston is the man who is guilty.

3. Compound sentence: A sentence containing two or more independent clauses.

> The dog came barking into the yard, and Felix the cat hurriedly ascended the nearest tree.

4. Compound-complex sentence: A sentence containing two or more independent clauses and one or more dependent clauses.

> Mr. Miller, who is a friend of the family, came to visit us last month; and this month we are expecting some distant relatives whom we have not seen for several years.

Simple Sentence.   See **Sentence.**

Simple Subject.   The subject of the sentence separated from its modifiers.

The eerie *tale* that the idiot told was fascinating.

Split Infinitive.   An infinitive with a modifier between the signal *to* and the verb form. See S-7.

He didn't mean *to really do* it.

Strong Verb.   Synonymous with irregular verb. Strong verbs form their past and past participle by changing the root vowel.

ride, rode, ridden
sing, sang, sung

Subject.   The person, place, or thing in a clause or sentence about which an assertion is made.

The *rock* moved slightly.
Mary is going to England.

Subjective Complement.   See **Complement.** A blanket term sometimes used to designate a predicate nominative or a predicate adjective.

Subjunctive Mood.   A class of verb forms used mainly in English to indicate conditions contrary to fact. In isolated instances, however, the subjunctive mood is still used in English to express desire, hope, concession, etc.

If I *were* you, I would not go.
I wish I *were* a millionaire.
I move that nominations *be* closed.

Subordinate Clause.   A clause (a group of words containing a subject and predicate) grammatically dependent

449

upon some other element in the sentence. A *subordinate* clause and a *dependent* clause are the same thing.

subord. cl.
He was told *that he must resign.*

Subordinating Conjunction. A word that relates a dependent or subordinate clause to some other element in the sentence and at the same time subordinates the dependent clause. Subordinating conjunctions have no grammatical function in the clause they subordinate, in contrast to relative pronouns, adjectives, and adverbs.

He was told *that* he must resign. (subordinating conjunction)

I respected him *although* I disliked him. (subordinating conjunction)

He is the one *who* robbed the store. (Relative pronoun. Note that the relative pronoun serves as the subject of the subordinate clause.)

Substantive. A blanket term to indicate any word, phrase, or clause used as a noun. Nouns, pronouns, gerunds, noun phrases, and noun clauses are all designated "substantives" by many grammarians.

Suffix. An addition at the end of a word to change the meaning.

judge: judg*ment*

Superlative Degree. See **Positive Degree.**

Syntax. The relationship of the words in the sentence. The study of the agreement of verbs, for example, would be a concern of syntax.

Tense. The form of the verb which indicates time of action or state. The English verb is usually said to express six principal tenses.

Present tense—present time:	he walks
Past tense—past time:	he walked
Future tense—future time:	he will walk
Present perfect tense—time complete in the present:	he has walked
Past perfect tense—time complete in the past:	he had walked
Future perfect tense—time complete in the future:	he will have walked

The term *tense* in English is also applied to the "progressive" tense (he is walking) and the "emphatic" tense (he does walk). See the conjugation of the verb *work* on pages 134–135.

Transitive Verb. A verb that has a direct object. Think of "transitive" as meaning "go across." In a sentence containing a transitive verb, the action "goes across" the verb, from the subject to the direct object.

> trans. v.
> John *hit* the ball.

Verb. That word, necessary to a sentence, which expresses action, being, or state of being.

Verbal. A form of the verb used as some other part of speech. There are three verbals in English:

Gerund: The present participle form of the verb used as a noun.

> *Swimming* is good exercise.

Participle: The present or past participle form of the verb used as an adjective.

> *Running* water is more sanitary than stagnant water.
> The *defeated* men sat dejectedly on the bench.

Infinitive: The infinitive form of the verb used as a noun, an adjective, or an adverb.

451

He likes *to hunt*. (noun)
There were many things *to do*. (adjective)
She goes to *see* him every day. (adverb)

Verb Phrase.   The main verb with its auxiliaries.

We *could have been gone* long before now.

Verbal Phrase.   The verbal with its object, if present, and modifiers. Gerunds, participles, and infinitives may all take objects.

> ger. phr.
> *Running this town* is a full job.
> part. phr.
> *Being a cautious young man*, he refused to take the leap.
> infin. phr.
> He was forced *to accept the bribe*.

Voice.   A form of the verb indicating whether the subject is the doer or receiver of the action. If the subject does the acting, the voice of the verb is *active*. If the subject receives the action, the voice of the verb is *passive*.

John hit the ball. (active)
The ball was hit by John. (passive)

Vowel.   The sounds represented by the letters *a, e, i, o, u*. All other letters in the alphabet are called *consonants*.

Weak Verb.   Synonymous with *regular verb*. Weak verbs form their past and past participle by adding *d*, or *ed* to the stem verb.

pull, pulled, pulled
dream, dreamed, dreamed

A Glossary
of Usage

The following list is designed mainly to give you aid and comfort in deciding the appropriate level of contemporary usage of a word or phrase—whether a word or phrase is acceptable as formal English or whether it should be restricted to the informal or conversational level. Some items, like *ain't*, are substandard and should not be used on any level by the college student. Before referring to this section, however, you should read carefully D-4–D-6 in Chapter 8, *Diction*, in order to understand fully what the various levels of usage are and in what situations they are appropriate.

This glossary of usage does not attempt to cover all the problems that you will encounter in your speaking and writing. You should consult your dictionary for any items you do not find discussed in this list. We have included, however, those problems that have proved particularly troublesome to students in the basic composition course.

A. The article *a* must never be used before words beginning with a vowel sound. In all such places the article *an* must be used.

INCORRECT: a uncle
             a experience

CORRECT: an uncle
            an experience
                but
            a history
            a one

Above.   Formerly condemned as an adjective preceding a noun, the usage is now generally accepted.

The *above* paragraphs illustrate this point.

Accept, Except.   See D-18.
Affect, Effect.   See D-18.
Aggravate.   Used colloquially to mean "irritate" or "annoy."
In formal use aggravate means "to intensify or increase something unpleasant."
Agree To, Agree With.   Remember that one agrees *with* a person but agrees *to* a plan. One thing agrees *with* another.
Aim.   Avoid as a substitute for intend.

We *intend* (not *aim*) to go tomorrow.

Ain't.   A contraction to be avoided. It is a hallmark of substandard English.
All, All Of.   The injunction to use *all* before a noun rather than *all of* is meaningless in terms of modern usage.

CORRECT: *All of* these children must be cared for.

All The Farther, All The Closer.   The standard forms for these constructions are *as far as, as close as,* etc.
Allow.   Dialectal for *think* or *say.*
Allude, Refer.   *Allude* is an indirect reference, *refer* a direct.

When the professor *referred* to "pearls before swine," I think he was *alluding* to his lectures before his classes.

Allusion, Illusion, Delusion. See D-18.

Almost. Consistently adverbial except in constructions like "Almost everybody invited attended the party," in which *almost* apparently serves as an adjective modifying the indefinite pronoun, *everybody*. The reason for this apparent contradiction is that most of the indefinite pronouns are compounds of adjective and noun (*every body, no body, no one*). *Almost* is felt to modify the adjective, not the noun.

COLLOQUIAL: *Most* all of the girls wear skirts and sweaters until May.

STANDARD: *Almost* all of the girls wear sweaters and skirts until May.

See **Most**.

Already, All Ready. *Already* is an adverb meaning "before or by this time." *All ready* are two separate words meaning "completely ready" or "everyone is ready."

He was *already* gone when we arrived.
They were *all ready* to go.

Alright. This spelling of the standard *all right* should be avoided.

Altho. Avoid this and other simplified spellings, which have never gained general acceptance.

Altogether, All Together. *Altogether* is an adverb meaning "entirely." *All together* refers to a group.

You are *altogether* wrong.
We were *all together* again.

Alumnus, Alumna. See G-3.

Among, Between. See **Between**.

Amount, Number. Use *amount* when referring to the sum total or the whole mass; use *number* when referring to individual, countable objects.

The *amount* of waste was fantastic.
The *number* of men wasted was fantastic.

An. See **A.**

And Etc. Redundant, since *etc.* means *and other things.* Omit *and,* but use *etc.* only where saving space is important, as in a table or a list.

Angle. Inappropriate in formal writing for *point of view, aspect, approach.*

Any More. Colloquial for "no longer."

COLLOQUIAL: We don't go there *any more.*
FORMAL: We *no longer* go there.

Anyone, Any One. These forms are not interchangeable.

Is *anyone* there?
He was not referring to *any one* person.

A similar distinction is made between *everyone—every one, someone—some one.*

Anyways. A dialect word when used to mean *in any case, anyway.*

Anywheres. A dialect form of *anywhere.*

Apt. See D-18.

Around. Colloquial when used for *about.*

COLLOQUIAL: They left *around* noon.

As. Inexact when used in place of *because* or *for*

INEXACT: They could not marry, *as* they were first cousins.
EXACT: They could not marry, *for* they were first cousins.
They could not marry, *because* they were first cousins.

As, So. Many careful writers continue to use *as* with affirmative comparisons, *so* with negative comparisons.

The performance was *as* good as one could expect under the circumstances.
These occurrences are not *so* strange as they seem.

As To.   Overused in the construction "The question *as to* whether . . ." It is better to omit it.

>The question *whether* he is guilty or not is irrelevant.

At.   See **Where At.**

At About.   Redundant. Use only *about*.

>He came *about* nine o'clock (not *at about*).

Awful, Awfully.   These words are colloquial when used as intensives, although they have attained an established place in conversational English.

>She looked *awfully* pretty.
>I feel *awful* bad.

This usage should, however, be avoided in formal writing.

Awhile, A While.   These forms are not interchangeable. *awhile* is an adverb; *while* is a subordinate conjunction or a noun. In the second example below, *while* introduces the adverbial clause. In the third sentence, *while* is the object of the preposition *for*.

>Stay *awhile* and listen to the orchestra.
>Whistle *while* you work.
>We stayed at my mother's house for *a while*.

Badly.   Colloquial for "very much."

>He wanted it *very much* (not *badly*).

Balance.   Colloquial for *rest* or *remainder*.

>He spent the *rest* (not *balance*) of the day in bed.

Bank On.   Colloquial in the sense of *depend on, rely on*.

Because Of.   See **Reason Is Because.**

Being As.   A substandard form for *since* or *because*.

>*Because* (not *being as*) you're here, you might as well help.

457

Beside, Besides.   *Beside* means in space, "by the side of"; *besides* means "in addition to."

> He sat *beside* me.
> There were three persons here *besides* John.

Between, Among.   *Between* is used with two objects or persons; *among* refers to more than two.

> This is *between* the *two* of us.
> This is *among* the *three* of us.

Blame On.   When blame is a verb, the idiom is *blame for*.

COLLOQUIAL: He *blamed* it *on* me.
STANDARD: He *blamed* me for it.

Bust, Busted.   Colloquial or slang verbs for standard *burst, burst, burst.* But note that such forms as *broncobuster, trust buster,* etc., are accepted.

But.   Used with another negative, *but* forms a double negative.

DOUBLE NEGATIVE: He didn't go but once.
CORRECT: He went only once.

But What.   Avoid in place of *that*.

> She had no doubt *that* (not *but what*) they would be there.

Calculate, Reckon.   New England and Southern provincialisms used as synonyms for *suppose*.

Can, May.   It may seem useless to insist upon the old distinction between these two verbs, but many careful writers and speakers still maintain it.

PERMISSION: *May* we have the payment you promised?
ABILITY: Anyone *can* make money if he really works at it.

Can't Hardly. The most common double negative. Standard English uses *can hardly*.

SUBSTANDARD: This anvil is so heavy I *can't hardly* lift it.
STANDARD: This anvil is so heavy I *can hardly* lift it.

Can't Help But, Cannot Help But. These double negative forms are colloquial for *can't help* plus participle.

COLLOQUIAL: People *can't help but* notice a man who hasn't shaved for four days.
STANDARD: People *can't help noticing* a man who hasn't shaved for four days.

Case. See **Factor.**
Censure. See **Criticize.**
Clean. Dialectal for "clear" or "entirely."

They flew *clear* (not *clean*) across the United States.

Company. Colloquial word when used to mean *guest(s)*.
Compare To, Compare With. *Compare to* is used to designate the likenesses alone between objects or persons; *compare with* refers to both likenesses and differences.
Complected. Dialect word. The correct form is *complexioned*.

DIALECT: Shakespeare's ideal woman was dark-*complected*.
CORRECT: Shakespeare's ideal woman was dark-*complexioned*.

Consensus. "Consensus of opinion" is a redundancy, since "consensus" in itself means agreement of opinion.
Considerable. Standard when used as an adjective but colloquial when used as a noun, and substandard when used as an adverb.

COLLOQUIAL: I believe he has *considerable* invested in the market.

459

SUBSTANDARD: Aunt Emma was *considerable* pleased to see her cake had won the blue ribbon.

STANDARD: The injured boy was in *considerable* pain.

Contact.   Although widely used, *contact* as a verb should be avoided in formal speech and writing.

COLLOQUIAL: I will *contact* you as soon as I hear from the Avco Corporation.

STANDARD: I will *get in touch with* you as soon as I hear from Avco.

Continual, Continuous.   See D-18.

Could Of.   Substandard for *could have.*

I *could have* been wrong (not *could of*).

Criticize, Censure.   In a strict sense, *criticize* means to examine and judge as a critic. *Censure* means to concentrate only upon bad qualities. In current colloquial usage, however, *criticize* has come to have essentially the same meaning as *censure.*

Cute.   An inexact, overworked colloquial adjective. Use a more specific word:

She is a *pretty* girl (not cute).
It was a *clever* movie (not cute).

Datum, Data.   For a discussion of foreign plurals, see G-3.

Delusion, Allusion, Illusion.   See D-18.

Different Than.   Formal usage prefers *different from.*

INFORMAL: Your book is *different than* mine.

FORMAL: Your book is *different from* mine.

Disinterested, Uninterested.   *Disinterested* means unbiased, impartial. *Uninterested* means lacking interest.

Done.   Substandard when used for *did*.

SUBSTANDARD: He was her man, but she *done* him wrong.

Don't.   Substandard when used for the third person singular.

SUBSTANDARD: He *don't* care what she does to him.

Dove, Dived.   *Dived* is preferable in formal usage, although *dove* appears to be gaining in general usage.

Drug.   Substandard for *dragged*.

The tractor *dragged* (not *drug*) the car from the ditch.

Due To.   This phrase in formal English should be used only as an adjective.

COLLOQUIAL: *Due* to his illness, he was unable to attend the meeting.

STANDARD: *Because* of his illness, he was unable to attend the meeting.

STANDARD: His clumsiness is *due to* lack of training.

Each Other, One Another.   These two phrases are frequently used interchangeably, but strictly speaking *each other* implies two people or objects, *one another,* more than two:

John and Bill are very fond of *each other*.
The flock of geese called wildly to *one another*.

Effect, Affect.   See D-18.

Elegant.   Colloquial in the sense of *delicious* or *good*.

COLLOQUIAL: What an *elegant* meal!

STANDARD: Melford has an *elegant* manner.

Emigrate.   See **Immigrate.**

Enthuse.   Colloquial for *to be enthusiastic,* or *to become enthusiastic,* or *to make enthusiastic. Enthuse* is not used in formal speech or writing, although it is frequently heard in conversation.

Equally As.   The *as* is unnecessary in such constructions as "The courses were *equally* rewarding."

Etc.   See **And etc.**

Everywheres.   Substandard or dialect word for *everywhere.*

Exam.   A clipped form of the standard *examination,* acceptable only in the most informal writing.

Except, Accept.   See D-18.

Factor, Case.   Avoid the vague, meaningless use of these words.

VAGUE: There were a number of *factors* in his decision.

VAGUE: In *case* of trouble, call on us.

IMPROVED: There were a number of reasons for his decision.

IMPROVED: If you have trouble, call on us.

CORRECT: The following *factors* determine the cost of producing an automobile: the wages of labor, the price of raw materials, overhead expenses, and taxes.

CORRECT: Let us consider the *case* of Martin Whitsitt.

Farther, Further.   Though many careful speakers and writers still differentiate between *farther,* which is applied to distance, and *further,* which expresses the idea of more or in addition, in general American usage this distinction is rapidly leveling out. It appears that *further* now tends to be used in either function.

Faze.   Colloquial for "affect adversely." Not used in formal speech or writing.

Fewer, Less.   *Fewer* refers to numbers; *less* refers to amounts or quantities measured:

Fewer members than usual were at the meeting.
Students spend *less* time on their studies than they should.

Fine.   An overworked, vague adjective of approbation.

He is a fine (decent? attractive? kind?) person.

Firstly.   Illogically enough, *first* is preferable to *firstly* to indicate divisions in a composition, although *secondly* is interchangeable with *second*.

Fix.   Colloquial for standard verb *to repair;* also colloquial as a noun for *predicament*.

COLLOQUIAL: I must have my brakes *fixed*.

COLLOQUIAL: Bill's in a *fix*.

Flunk.   Colloquial for *fail*.

Folks.   Colloquial for *family, relatives*. Note, however, that *folk* is a standard noun or adjective.

COLLOQUIAL: Last Sunday when I was in Toledo, I went to see your *folks*.

STANDARD: Last Sunday when I was in Toledo, I went to see your mother and father.

STANDARD: *Folk* songs are transmitted orally because the *folk* are not literate.

Funny.   Colloquial when used to mean *strange* or *peculiar*. Its standard meaning is *humorous*.

COLLOQUIAL: There is something *funny* about this financial statement.

Further.   See **Farther.**

Gent.   Slang for *man* or *gentleman*.

SLANG: This *gent* gave me a tip on Minesweeper in the third.

STANDARD: A *man* gave me a tip on Minesweeper in the third.

Get, Got, Gotten. The idiomatic use of the verb *get* has become firmly established in conversational and informal English. As yet, however, the usage has not been generally accepted in formal writing.

INFORMAL: I *get* mad whenever I think of him.

INFORMAL: We've *got* to be sure that he is right.

INFORMAL: I've *gotten* tired of his complaining.

FORMAL: We must be certain that he is right.

Good. Substandard when used as an adverb.

SUBSTANDARD: She plays the piano *good*.

STANDARD: She plays the piano *well*.

Gotten. See **Get.**

Guess. Colloquial in the sense of *suppose.*

Guy. Slang for *man.*

Had Of. Illiterate for *had.*

I wish I *had* (not *had of*) passed.

Had Ought, Hadn't Ought. A redundancy for *should* or *ought* or *oughtn't* in substandard English.

SUBSTANDARD: Isabelle *had ought* to stay home and take care of her children.
Mr. Fishback *hadn't ought* to treat her like that.

Hanged, Hung. These are past and past participial forms of two separate verbs.

hang	hanged	hanged
hang	hung	hung

The first verb refers only to death of a human being by hanging; in all other senses of the word, the second form is used.

The criminal was *hanged* yesterday.
The picture *hung* on the wall.

Hardly. See **Can't Hardly.**

Have Got, Gotten. See **Get.**

Healthy, Healthful. *Healthy* means, strictly speaking, to have or possess good health; *healthful* means to promote or be conducive to good health:

> a *healthy* child.
> a *healthful* climate.

Hisself. Substandard for *himself.*

Human. Use as an adjective. The preferred noun form is **human being.**

Illusion, Allusion, Delusion. See D-18.

Immigrate, Emigrate. To *immigrate* means to come into a country to establish permanent residence; *to emigrate* means to leave one's residence in a country to establish residence in another. The same distinction applies to the nouns, *immigrant* and *emigrant.*

Imply, Infer. See D-18.

In, Into. These words are not interchangeable in precise usage.

> He is *in* the water.
> He went *into* the water.

In Back Of. Colloquial for *behind.*

> He ran *behind* the fence (not *in back of*).

Incredible, Incredulous. See D-18.

Infer, Imply. See D-18.

Ingenious, Ingenuous. See D-18.

In Regards To. Do not use in place of the correct idiom *in regard to.*

Invite. Slang when used as a noun for *invitation.*

SLANG: Did you get an *invite* to the Johnson wedding?

STANDARD: Did you get an *invitation* to the Johnson wedding?

Irregardless. Substandard for the standard *regardless*.

SUBSTANDARD: *Irregardless* of what you say, I intend to marry him anyway.

STANDARD: *Regardless* of what you say, I intend to marry him.

Is When, Is Where. A construction to be avoided, especially in definitions.

COLLOQUIAL: Metaphysical poetry *is when* the poet strives for wit rather than beauty.

STANDARD: In metaphysical poetry the poet strives for wit rather than beauty.

COLLOQUIAL: A tragedy is a play *where* the dramatist arouses pity and terror.

STANDARD: A tragedy is a play which arouses pity and terror.

Just. Colloquial and inexact for *simply* or *quite*:

COLLOQUIAL: The sky is *just* beautiful.

Kick. Slang for *complain*.

Kind, Kinds. In formal usage, the modifiers of these forms should be singular and plural respectively.

I prefer *this kind* of shoes.
These kinds of apples are most popular in this area.

Kind Of. Colloquial for *rather* or *somewhat*.

COLLOQUIAL: Clarence became *kind of* disgusted with the local chapter of his fraternity.

STANDARD: Clarence became rather (or somewhat) disgusted with the local chapter of his fraternity.

Kind Of A. A colloquial redundancy.

COLLOQUIAL: That *kind of a* house doesn't appeal to me.

STANDARD: That *kind of* house doesn't appeal to me.

Lady.   The opposite of "gentleman." Should not be used when *woman* is appropriate.

A *woman* (not *lady*) gave me directions to your house.

Lay, Lie.   See G-34.

Learn, Teach.   *Learn* means to receive information; *teach* means to impart knowledge or information.

I'll *teach* (not *learn*) you a lesson.

Leave.   Colloquial when used for *let*, meaning *to permit* or *allow*. Strictly speaking, *leave* means to *depart* or to *abandon*.

COLLOQUIAL: Now, George, you *leave* me go.
STANDARD: Now, George, you *let* me go.

Less, Few.   See **Fewer.**

Let On.   Colloquial when used as a synonym for the standard *pretend* or *admit*.

Let's.   Means *let us*. Consequently, constructions like "Let's you and me go" are colloquial redundancies for "Let's go."

Liable, Likely, And Apt.   See D-18, where proper use of these is explained.

Lie, Lay.   See G-34.

Like.   Colloquial when used in place of *as, as if,* or *as though*.

COLLOQUIAL: It looks *like* the Democrats will carry Virginia again.
STANDARD: It looks *as if* the Democrats will carry Virginia again.

Loan.   Formal usage prefers *lend* as a verb.

Locate.   Colloquial when used as a synonym for *settled*.

He *settled* (not *located*) in New York.

Lots, Lots Of.   An extremely popular colloquialism meaning a great number or amount. It should not be used, however, in formal writing.

COLLOQUIAL: We saw *lots of* pheasants in the field.
STANDARD: We saw *many* pheasants in the field.

Mad.   Should not be used in formal writing as a synonym for *angry*.

Math.   Colloquial for *mathematics*.

May.   See **Can.**

May Of.   Substandard for *may have*.

Mean.   Colloquial in the sense of *cruel, ill-tempered, malicious*.

Might Of.   Substandard for *might have*, as in

He *might of* lost his way.

Mighty.   A homely colloquialism for "very" or "quite."

Most.   Colloquial when used in place of the adverb *almost*.

COLLOQUIAL: They go swimming *most* every day.
STANDARD: They go swimming *almost* every day.

See **Almost.** Note, however, that *most* is Standard English as an adverb when it is not substituting for *almost;* that is, when it is part of the superlative degree of an adverb:

The venture worked out *most* successfully.

Muchly.   Substandard for *much*.

Must Of.   Substandard for *must have*.

Myself, Yourself, etc.   Although the intensive and reflexive pronouns, *myself, himself,* etc. (see page 107), are frequently heard in conversation in place of the personal pronouns as one of the elements of compound subjects and objects, this use is still rare in formal writing.

INFORMAL: Margaret and *myself* have decided to go on a vacation.

FORMAL: Margaret and *I* have decided to go on a vacation.

INFORMAL: No one resented the accusation more than *himself*.

FORMAL: No one resented the accusation more than *he*.

Nice.   An inexact, vague adjective.

He is a nice (decent? polite? pleasant?) boy.

Nohow.   Dialect word for anyhow.

He can't vote *nohow* since he isn't registered.

No Place.   Substandard for *nowhere*.

Nowhere Near.   Colloquial for *not nearly*.

The carpenters are *not nearly* (not *nowhere near*) finished.

Nowheres.   Dialectal for *nowhere*.

Number, Amount.   See **Amount.**

Off Of.   Colloquial for *off*.

COLLOQUIAL: They eat *off of* Spode plates every day of their lives.

One Another.   See **Each Other.**

Onto.   Should not be used when a simple *on* or *to* will serve.

He jumped *on* (not *onto*) his horse.

Ought.   See **Had Ought.**

Outside Of.   Colloquial when used as a synonym for *except*.

Everyone enjoyed the party *except* (not *ouside of*) Bill.

469

Party.   When used to mean a person, it should be restricted to legal documents. Used thus it is slang:

> A *party* told me last week that the price was going up.

Note, however, that among lawyers the "party of the first part" and similar expressions fulfill a necessary and valid function.

Per.   A commercial expression: "We receive three hundred applications *per* year." Standard English: "We receive three hundred applications *a* (or *each*) year."

Per is a standard Latin construction: *per diem*, etc.

Per Cent, Percent.   In formal writing or speaking, *per cent* or *percent* is used only after numbers. *Percent* has become the more common spelling.

> The interest rate on the mortgage is 6 *percent*.

Otherwise, percentage is used.

> A high *percentage* of the population was infected by the disease.

The use of the symbol % is restricted to technical or statistical reports.

Piece.   Dialectal for distance.

> Centerville is a short *piece* from here.

Plan On.   Colloquial for "plan to."

COLLOQUIAL: I *plan on* going at three o'clock.
STANDARD: I *plan to* go at three o'clock.

Plenty.   Colloquial as an adverb.

> He was *very* (not *plenty*) tired.

470

Posted. An increasingly popular substitute for *informed*, but it is still restricted to conversational and informal usage.

Pretty. Well established in colloquial English as the modifier of an adjective, although it should not be overused.

He was *pretty* tired when he reached the shore.

Principal, Principle. See D-18.

Prof. Slang in spoken English.

Proved, Proven. These forms are now used interchangeably by the majority of educated speakers and writers.

Providing, Provided. These two forms are interchangeable in modern usage when used as verbals.

Put In. Restricted to conversational and informal usage as a synonym for *spend* (time and effort).

Put Up With. Colloquial synonym for *endure*.

Quite. Labeled by most dictionaries as colloquial when used for *very* or *to a considerable degree*, *quite* nevertheless seems to have established itself in formal usage.

CORRECT: The exhibition is *quite* impressive.

Real. Colloquial or dialectal when used in place of the adverb *really* or *very*:

COLLOQUIAL: She plays the piano *real* well.

STANDARD: She plays the piano *really* well.

STANDARD: She plays the piano *very* well.

Rear, Raise. Traditionally speaking, one *raises* animals and plants, but *rears* children. This distinction is rapidly fading in contemporary usage, although the safer course in formal writing is to maintain the distinction.

Reason Is Because. Colloquial; standard English substitutes *reason is that*.

COLLOQUIAL: The *reason* I missed class last Tuesday *is because* my grandmother had to go to the dentist.

471

STANDARD: The reason I missed class last Tuesday is *that* my grandmother had to go to the dentist.

Reckon.   Dialectal or colloquial for *think* or *suppose*.

DIALECTAL: I *reckon* I can paint your house next week.
STANDARD: I *think* I can paint your house next week.

Refer, Allude.   See **Allude**.
Respectfully, Respectively.   See D-18.
Reverend.   Colloquial when applied without initials or first name to surname of a clergyman.

COLLOQUIAL: *Rev.* Potter will preach next Sunday morning.

STANDARD: *The Reverend* Richard Salmon Potter will preach next Sunday morning.

STANDARD: Rev. Dr. R. S. Potter will preach next Sunday morning.

Right.   Archaic and dialectal when used as an adverb meaning *very* or in place of another intensive.

DIALECTAL: We were *right* glad to get home safely through the flood.

STANDARD: We were *very* glad to get home safely through the flood.

Note, however, that this use which is now out of acceptance is historically correct, and may be found in Shakespeare and the King James Bible.

"God shall help her, and that *right* early."—PSLAMS 46:5

Rise, Raise.   See G-34.
Run.   As in "run the government," a well-established idiom.
Same, Said.   Appropriate only in legal documents as a substitute for *this* or *that*.

Seldom Ever. The correct idiom is *seldom if ever,* or simply *seldom.*

Should Of. Substandard for *should have.*

Sit, Set. See G-34.

Slow. May be used as an adverb in certain constructions.

CORRECT: Drive *slow.*

CORRECT: The train moved *slower* and *slower.*

CORRECT: He *slowly* removed his hat.

So. There is nothing inherently wrong in the use of *so* as a coordinating conjunction or a conjunctive adverb. But be careful to avoid overusing it; substitute words like *therefore, accordingly,* etc., for the sake of variety. Do not use *so* as substitute for *so that.*

FAULTY: He deliberately missed the train *so* he would be late for the appointment.

IMPROVED: He deliberately missed the train *so that* he would be late for the appointment.

Some. Colloquial when used descriptively.

COLLOQUIAL: "*Some* date!" Clarence said in disgust.

Someplace, Somewhere. Dialectal for *somewhere.*

Sometimes, Sometime. *Sometime* may be used as an adverb or adjective. As an adverb it means "at one time or another in the future; at some not specified or definitely known time."

We can plan to go sometime tomorrow.
He will regret this sometime.

As an adjective *sometime* means "having been formerly; former."

He was her *sometime* boyfriend.

473

Sometimes is used only as an adverb meaning "at times, now and then, occasionally."

> He comes to visit his parents *sometimes*.
> *Sometimes* I feel like a motherless child.

Sort Of, Sort Of A.   See **Kind Of.**
Sure.   Colloquial when used for *surely*.

COLLOQUIAL: That answer is *sure* wrong.
STANDARD: That answer is *surely* wrong.

Sure And.   See **Try And.**
Suspicion.   Dialectal when used as a verb.

DIALECTAL: I *suspicioned* him all the time.
STANDARD: I *suspected* him all the time.

Swell.   A dated slang word of approbation.
Take.   Well established in certain idioms.

> He was *taken* in by the huckster.
> The bus ride *took* four hours.

Tasty.   Colloquial for *delicious*.

> A *tasty* covered-dish supper was served.

Teach.   See **Learn.**
Terrible, Terribly.   Should not be used in writing as an intensive.

> I was *very much* (not *terribly*) impressed.

Theirselves.   Substandard for *themselves*.
These Kind, Those Kind.   Colloquial for *these kinds* or *this kind*.

This, That.   Well established as a modifier of adjectives or adverbs.

> He went *this* far before he stopped.
> I didn't realize it would be *that* difficult.

Thisaway, Thataway.   Substandard for *this way, that way.*

SUBSTANDARD: He went *thataway!*

This Here, That There, These Here, Them There.   Substandard expressions.

Through.   Colloquial in the following constructions:

> He was *through* talking.
> He was *through* work.

Thru.   Simplified spelling, not accepted.

Too.   Colloquial for *very.*

COLLOQUIAL: He did not object *too* much.
STANDARD: He did not object *very* much.

Toward, Towards.   Either of these forms is acceptable, although *toward* is more common in American usage and *towards* more common in British.

Transpire.   Although sanctioned by some dictionaries in the sense of "to happen, to occur," there is still a prejudice against this usage in some influential quarters.

QUESTIONABLE: What *transpired* at the meeting?
STANDARD: What *happened* at the meeting?

Try And, Sure And.   Though well established in conversation and informal writing, *try to* and *sure to* should be used in formal writing.

INFORMAL: Just *try and* do it!
FORMAL: *Try* to visualize the havoc that resulted.

475

INFORMAL: Be *sure and* let me know.

FORMAL: You should be *sure* to consult your dictionary when in doubt.

Uninterested.   See **Disinterested.**

Used To Could.   Dialectal and substandard for *used to be able to.*

SUBSTANDARD: Clarence *used to could* chin himself forty times.

Very.   Do not, in formal English, follow *very* immediately by a participle which has not yet been accepted as an adjective. It is preferable to insert another word, such as *much* or *greatly.* Instead of writing, "George was *very* excited about his new position," it is preferable, in formal English, to write, "George was *very much* excited about his new position."

Wait On.   Colloquial for *wait for.*

We *waited for* (not *waited on*) the train for two hours.

Want.   Must never be allowed to take a clause object.

SUBSTANDARD: I *want* that you should buy a good used car.

CORRECT: I want you to buy a good used car.

Ways.   Colloquial for *way.*

The Fish and Wildlife Commission still has a long *ways* to go in securing acceptance of proper conservation practices. (*Way* is preferred.)

Where.   Colloquial when used in place of *that.*

COLLOQUIAL: I see in the morning paper *where* the city has raised taxes again.

STANDARD: I see in the morning paper *that* the city has raised taxes again.

Where At. A redundancy.

Where did he build his house? (not "build his house *at?*")

While. Should not be used indiscriminately for *although, and,* or *but.*

INEXACT: *While* I saw his point, I could not agree with him.
EXACT: *Although* I saw his point, I could not agree with him.

Would Of. Substandard for *would have.*

Index

Index

Numbers in **boldface** refer to important discussions of the subject. *Italics* are used for affixes, words, and phrases, and to indicate practice exercises (*ex. 5–7*).

For full definitions of terms, consult the "Glossary of Grammatical Terms" on pages 430–452 and the "Glossary of Usage" on pages 453–477.

480

SP   Spelling

P   Punctuation

GLOS

Proofreading Symbols

¶	**Start new paragraph**	=/	**Insert hyphen**
no ¶	**Paragraph break unnecessary**	∧	**Insert**
ˆ/	**Insert comma**	ℯ	**Delete**
;/	**Insert semicolon**	∼	**Transpose**
:/	**Insert colon**	#	**Separate: leave a space**
⹂/	**Insert quotation marks**	⸮	**Do you mean this?**
⨀	**Insert period**		**or, Is this correct?**
?/	**Insert question mark**	≡	**Capitalize**
!/	**Insert exclamation point**	lc	**Lower case**
—/	**Insert dash**	sp	**Spell out**
( )	**Insert parentheses**	stet	**Leave as is**
[ ]	**Insert brackets**	Rom.	**Do not italicize**
ˇ	**Insert apostrophe**	⌒	**Close up**